STUDIES IN EARLY MODERN CULTURAL,
POLITICAL AND SOCIAL HISTORY

Volume 22

SOCIAL RELATIONS AND URBAN SPACE
NORWICH, 1600–1700

Studies in Early Modern Cultural, Political and Social History

ISSN: 1476–9107

Series editors

Previously published titles in the series
are listed at the back of this volume

SOCIAL RELATIONS AND URBAN SPACE

NORWICH, 1600–1700

Fiona Williamson

THE BOYDELL PRESS

First published 2014
The Boydell Press, Woodbridge

ISBN 978-1-84383-945-3

The Boydell Press is an imprint of Boydell & Brewer Ltd
PO Box 9, Woodbridge, Suffolk IP12 3DF, UK
and of Boydell & Brewer Inc.
668 Mt Hope Avenue, Rochester, NY 14620–2731, USA
website: www.boydellandbrewer.com

A catalogue record for this title is available from the British Library

The publisher has no responsibility for the continued existence or accuracy of URLs for external or third-party internet websites referred to in this book, and does not guarantee that any content on such websites is, or will remain, accurate or appropriate.

This publication is printed on acid-free paper

Contents

Illustrations

Abbreviations and Notes

Abbreviations

British Library	BL
Calendar of State Papers, Domestic Series	CSPD
Early English Books Online	EEBO
Her Majesty's Stationary Office	HMSO
Historical Journal	HJ
Historical Manuscripts Commission	HMC
History Workshop Journal	HWJ
Journal of British Studies	JBS
King's Lynn Borough Archives	KL
National Archives	NA
Norfolk County Quarter Sessions	NCQS
Norfolk Genealogy	NG
Norfolk Heritage Centre	NHC
Norfolk Record Office	NRO
Norfolk Record Society	NRS
Norwich City Records	NCR
Oxford English Dictionary	OED
State Papers	SP
Suffolk Records Society	SRS
Transactions of the Royal Historical Society	TRHS

Notes

All original sources are from the Norfolk Record Office (NRO) unless otherwise stated.

All primary printed texts are from Early English Books Online (EEBO) unless otherwise stated.

Dates have been kept to original format when citing from primary documents.

Preface

This book is a study of a city from the perspective of its inhabitants. The premise is that the built environment and the populace shared an intimate relationship; cities were not homogenous or passive entities but multifaceted palimpsests created by the processes of people's lived experiences. Inhabitants' culture and ideals shaped city space and lent meaning to urban places. In return, those places lent human interchanges depth and quality. Thus conceived a city had many possible faces, or cognitive maps, by which it could be imagined. This book seeks to recover some of these maps. Every inhabitant had a unique perspective of city space which depended on their lifestyle and personal circumstances. This means that recovering individuals' cognitive maps is a near impossible task, but we can seek to recover something of the shared perspectives of communities and networks by exploring the ways that people spoke about or used their city in the surviving records. In so doing, this close study will reveal something of urban inhabitants' ways of seeing, negotiating and conceptualising their environment, people's relationship with urban space, and with each other. The city is Norwich, a place that experienced many of the tumultuous events of the seventeenth century at first hand, and whose administration and people left ample records to chart its vicissitudes.

This book grew from doctoral research and has been a long time in seeing the light of day. Much of this research was undertaken at the excellent facilities of the Norfolk Record Office whose records cover city, county and church in great depth, shining a light onto the lives of many centuries of inhabitants. In researching and writing this book, I have benefitted from the help of many people and organisations. First and foremost, the endlessly knowledgeable and patient staff at the Norfolk Record Office (NRO), followed by, in no particular order, the staff at Norwich's Millennium Library and Shirehall Research Centre, the National Archives and British Library, and the library of the University of East Anglia (UEA). Involvement with the research communities of these organisations, the NRO and UEA in particular, has provided inspiration and many friendships. I owe special thanks to Andy Wood and Silvia Evangelisti, the former for supervising my PhD thesis from start to finish, and the latter for reading draft sections of this book and providing valuable suggestions for improvement. Thanks also go to Isla

Fay whose detailed PhD study illuminated the role of Norwich's corporation in promoting its image as a healthful city, and Carole Rawcliffe and Elizabeth Rutledge at the UEA for interesting discussions on the city's history. I have also been generously assisted by Funds for Women Graduates and the Marc Fitch Fund in 2008 and 2009 respectively, without whom it would have been very difficult to finish my research. Finally, I would like to extend thanks to my family (especially Pearl Crossfield and Dora Hudson) and friends for nurturing my passion for history and for being there throughout the journey.

Introduction

We link together our various perceptual spaces whose contents vary from person to person and from time to time ... parts of one spatio-temporal order...[1]

I

This is a book about a city and its inhabitants. Cities have long captured the human imagination with writers and philosophers waxing lyrical on the triumph of urbanity over rural backwardness, framing cities as the embodiment of civilisation, symbols of a perfect cosmic order, even as the earthly manifestation of godliness and purity.[2] Medieval and early-modern writers did not uniformly praise cities however; like God and the Devil, cities had their nemesis. In phrases redolent of a fire-and-brimstone preacher, Thomas Dekker described cities as dangerous, corrupting places full of sin, as wanton and lewd as the female sex; tropes that were common to early-modern readers and playgoers.[3]

Urban inhabitants were thus exposed to contradictory intellectual traditions that muddled with their own, often just as ambiguous, micro experiences of city life. Every urban street, every building or open space had been shaped for purpose by countless generations of users who, in the process of living urban space, had inscribed meaning onto each and every part. This process, which can be referred to as the dynamic creation of space, had a reciprocal effect on urban inhabitants. Spaces and places imbued with specific socio-cultural meanings acted to shape the human exchanges subsequently enacted within those places, often without people's conscious realisation.

[1] D. Hawkins, 'The Language of Nature', cited in *Mental Maps*, 2nd edn, ed. Peter Gould and Rodney White (London, 1986), p. 1.
[2] On changing concepts of the city in medieval Europe, see Chiara Frugoni, *A Distant City: Images of Urban Experience in the Medieval World* (Princeton, 1991), pp. 106–17.
[3] By way of example, see: Thomas Dekker, *The Seven deadly Sinnes of London* (1606). Dekker's 'induction' alludes to the destruction of the biblical cities Sodom and Gomorrah, and tells of how Jerusalem and Antwerp fell to corruption. Finally, he writes on 'wanton' London, 'attir'de like a Bride ... but there is much harlot in thine eyes'.

In turn, those human exchanges shaped urban development and the values attributed to places and spaces: a continuous cycle of cause and effect.[4] As Martha Howell writes 'the city ... was a spatial being – not just a creation in space but a creation *of* space'.[5]

The concept of 'city' was informed therefore by a series of available public images, and the mental pictures of the cityscape shared by groups of inhabitants. Central to this text is the existence of concomitant spatial identities within the overall public image of the urban landscape: the communicentric city.[6] These identities were fashioned from cognitive maps: the foundation of how inhabitants' conceptualised and navigated their city. These maps were essentially subjective, changing according to the personal circumstances of the beholder but it is possible, by exploring the ways in which people used and spoke about city spaces and places, to detect the presence of cognitive maps shared by individuals with common interests.

Cities are conceptualised in this book as a palimpsest of shifting, overlapping and competing cognitive maps and landscapes. This paradigm is informed by the principles of the spatial turn in history as set out by a current generation of social historians who have drawn from the social sciences to explore the relationship between people and place. The range of collective cognitive maps available to inhabitants guides the chapter themes. Starting with Norwich's public image, it moves on to explore the alternative cognitive maps informed by inhabitants' spatial experiences and social networks. By focussing on the regional city of Norwich during the seventeenth century, this book will offer a close lens into the social relationships that shaped city life and will also serve as a useful counterpoise in a field that has largely focussed on urban space in London.

The spatial turn of social history draws from almost a century of social science research devoted to understanding the interrelationship between place and people. The remainder of this section will concentrate on those pertaining to the urban environment. Urban modelling for example – which paid particular attention to people's relationship to place – became popular in the early-twentieth century. Ernest Burgess, a geographer interested in cities and

---

4 Michael Camille warns about applying the term 'space' to past societies because it is an abstract concept, which we understand in relation to modern sociological, geographic and philosophical theory. He proposes using instead 'spaces' or 'place', an approach I hope to adopt here. See Michael Camille, 'Signs of the City: Place, Power, and Public Fantasy in Medieval Paris', *Medieval Practices of Space*, ed. Barbara A. Hanawalt and Michal Kobialka (Minnesota, 2000), pp. 1–36, 9.

5 Martha C. Howell, 'The Spaces of Late Medieval Urbanity', *Shaping Urban Identity in Late Medieval Europe*, ed. Marc Boone and Peter Stabel (Leuven/Apeldoorn, 2000), pp. 3–24, 3 (my inflection).

6 For more on these terms see Richard L. Kagan, 'Urbs and Civitas in Sixteenth- and Seventeenth-Century Spain', *Envisioning the City: Six Studies in Urban Cartography*, ed. David Buisseret (Chicago, 1998), pp. 75–105, 77.

social topography, made 1920s Chicago the focus of a study that deconstructed the city, and its inhabitants, into zones, that included a business district and 'good' and 'bad' neighbourhoods. The model was subsequently criticised for failing to pay due attention to the human element, fuelling perceptions of socio-spatial stereotypes with respect to class, race, wealth and crime.[7] The problem was not so much that scholars denied different urban areas existed, more the impossibility of rationalising complex human lives and working patterns to fit a structured model. Despite this criticism, zonal theory exerted a profound influence on academic studies for years to come, arguably holding back more creative ways of understanding urban space by obstructing academic discourse and preventing effective strategic governmental urban planning.

Zonal modelling also influenced scholars seeking to explain historic urban development. In 1960, for example, the sociologist Gideon Sjoberg starkly categorised urban settlement patterns in his top-down model of a pre-industrial city. His model was based on a series of concentric zones, radiating outward from an important central hub to a marginalised periphery. The most important civic and religious buildings occupied the central zone where the rich directed city life via an arterial transport network linking centre with periphery and periphery in turn with the wider region. The city's margins were the corporeal and ideological inverse of the illustrious city centre, the houses were meaner and the inhabitants poorer.[8] As a means of describing pre-modern cities the model was inherently flawed but it was to be several years before it was challenged publically by historians, partly because of a disconnect between the fields of urban geography and urban history. One of the scholars to raise a hand was James Vance, who critiqued the organisational paradigm that Sjoberg used to equate social class with a city to periphery model. Occupational zoning, Vance argued, was important in understanding pre-modern urban landscapes and topographies, but cities had multiple foci, centred on craft quarters with their own shops, workplaces, gilds, and social hierarchies, rather than one central hub.[9] Vance's assessment advanced discussion in the field but, in the same way that Sjoberg had focussed on social class as a determinant of urban organisation, so too the preoccupation with employment obscured the full development of Vance's theorisation. Nonetheless, the basic idea of multiple urban centres, or zones, that Vance proposed marked a shift in thinking about the pre-modern city.

Running in parallel with developments in urban theory in the social sciences, urban history found a new impetus in the late 1950s and 1960s, largely inspired by the work of W. G. Hoskins. Hoskins argued that cities were

---

[7] For more on the Chicago School of Sociology's approach, see Elaine Lewinnek, 'Mapping Chicago, Imagining Metropolises: Reconsidering the Zonal Model of Urban Growth', *Journal of Urban History* 36:2 (2010), 197–225.

[8] G. Sjoberg, *The Pre-Industrial City: Past and Present* (New York, 1960).

[9] James Vance, 'Land Assignment in Pre-Capitalist, Capitalist and Post-Capitalist Cities', *Economic Geography* 47 (1971), 101–20, 105.

not one-dimensional but the sum of many years of expansion and modifica-
tion that could be exposed in a systematic analysis of cultural and environmental change.[10] M. R. G. Conzen and M. W. Beresford pioneered research
that overturned assumptions of medieval town planning, revealing it to have
been far more advanced than had once been thought: sponsorship from episcopal and royal investors had, in many cases, systematically developed settlements on sophisticated grids, burgages and plots.[11] In the same decade the
inspirational work of Harold Dyos and the establishment of the Centre for
Urban and Regional Studies at the University of Birmingham proved critical
to improving the fortunes of British urban history. Providing the foundations
for what was to become the *Urban History Journal*, the Dyos School stimulated interest in, and provided direction for, new urban research.

By the 1980s and 1990s interdisciplinary research was having a substantial
influence on the field of urban history. The introduction of new technologies, for example, including the geographic information system (GIS) moved
urban archaeology forward in leaps and bounds and, testament to the growing popularity of urban studies, several specialist debating forums and study
centres opened.[12] In terms of published urban historiography, studies by T. R.
Slater and Keith Lilley concentrated on uncovering 'the spatial development
of medieval cities' with a series of case studies aimed at better understanding
the origins of town planning. Lilley in particular took advantage of archaeological science to analyse medieval town plans in greater depth.[13] F. J. Fisher
and Peter Clark provided groundbreaking new research on the social and
cultural development of towns and cities in the early-modern period, and Asa
Briggs, Brian Robson, Ray Pahl and David Reeder did the same for the Victorian era.[14] Today, as Clark argues, urban history is largely inter-disciplinary
and its practitioners are disinclined to view cities through the lens of one-dimensional models as, he points out, we now understand that 'the complex
spaces of the city – physical, social, meta-physical; built-up grey, open-space
green, and sometimes water-front blue – are constantly contested and recon-
figured through an array of economic, political, and other processes'.[15]

---

10 W. G. Hoskins, *The Making of the English Landscape* (London, 1955).
11 M. R. G. Conzen, 'Alnwick, Northumberland: A Study in Town-Plan Analysis', *Institute of British Geographers* 27 (1962), 859–864; M. R. G. Conzen, 'The Plan Analysis
of an English City Centre', *Proceedings of the IGU Symposium in Urban Geography*, ed. K.
Norborg (Lund, 1960), pp. 383–414.
12 For example the Pre-Modern Towns Group, British Urban History Group, the Centre
for Urban History, or the European Association for Urban History (established 1989).
13 T. R. Slater, 'Ideal and Reality in English Episcopal Medieval Town Planning', *Transactions of the Institute of British Geographers* 12:2 (1987), 191–203 and Keith D. Lilley, 'Mapping the Medieval City: Plan analysis and Urban History', *Urban History* 27:1 (2000),
5–30, 6.
14 Peter Clark, *European Cities and Towns, 400–2000* (Oxford, 2009), p. 9.
15 Clark, *European Cities*, p. 10.

Social historians have also contributed to the discussion by appropriating methodologies and strategies from the social sciences that have enriched our understanding of the past. One of the biggest influences has been Henri Lefebvre's seminal 1974 text, *The Production of Space*. Building on traditions of Kantian philosophy, Lefebvre reconciled the idea of mental space (the abstract philosophical concept) with real space (the social and physical spaces in which we all live).[16] The importance of this approach is in understanding that all spaces were – and are – socially constructed, a perspective that has redefined ways of reading sources and comprehending the construction of human and spatial identities. The sociologist and philosopher Pierre Bourdieu similarly proposed the concept of 'habitus' – a term he adapted from the work of Norbert Elias – that is how meanings attached to physical spaces are fashioned through socio-spatial interactions. Both Lefebvre and Bourdieu argued that as all urban spaces and places claimed identities that were created by the processes of human exchange, it follows that the origin of these identities must – to some degree – be traceable in the study of a given society. Bourdieu, for example, theorised that social exchanges enacted within physical settings (as all are), reflected the traditions, customs and memories unique to that culture and society, ultimately creating a 'tangible, classifying system' by which we can trace the relationship between society, culture, space and place.[17]

The applications of this theoretical framework are immense.[18] Social anthropologist Shirley Ardener, for example, explored how culturally constructed notions of space and place have affected gender relations in different cultures. The tendency to label spaces and places as public or private, for example, a practice that has evolved through centuries of socio-spatial interaction, has had profound and enduring consequences for the position of women in many countries. Nevertheless Ardener, and fellow social anthropologist Doreen

[16] Henri Lefebvre, *The Production of Space*, trans. Donald Nicholson-Smith (Oxford, 1991), esp. pp. 1–9, 16–18, 68–168.

[17] P. Bourdieu, *Outline of a Theory of Practice* (Cambridge, 1977), p. 72. See also M. De Certeau, *The Practice of Everyday Life*, trans. Steven Randall (Berkeley, 1984) and J. Epstein, 'Spatial Practices/Democratic Vistas', *Social History* 24 (1999), 294–309.

[18] A selection of texts that have applied spatial methods in different fields include: Liz Bondi, 'Gender and Geography: Crossing Boundaries', *Progress in Human Geography* 17:2 (1993), 241–246; W. K. D. Davies and D. T. Herbert, eds, *Communities within Cities: An Urban Social Geography* (London, 1993); D. Pellow, ed., *Setting Boundaries: The Anthropology of Spatial and Social Organization* (London, 1996); A. Mandanipour, G. Cars and J. Allen, eds, *Social Exclusion in European Cities: Processes, Experiences and Responses* (London, 1998); L. Holloway and P. Hubbard, eds, *People and Place: The Extraordinary Geographies of Everyday Life* (London, 2001); G. Valentine, *Social Geographies: Space and Society* (Harlow, 2001); Wendy Ellen Everett and Axel Goodbody, eds, *Revisiting Space: Space And Place in European Cinema* (Bern, 2005); Jaimey Fisher, and Barbara Caroline Mennel, eds, *Spatial Turns: Space, Place, and Mobility in German Literary and Visual Culture* (Amsterdam and New York, 2010); Matthew Carmona, Tim Heath, Taner Oc and Steve Tiesdell, eds, *Public Places-Urban Spaces: The Dimensions of Urban Design* (Oxford & Burlington, MA, 2012).

Massey, have rightly pointed out how dominant cultural constructions of space are not always fixed or one dimensional: regional, personal and circumstantial variances all act to shape and contest spatial meanings in subtle ways. In this respect, Ardener and Massey conceptualise space as a fluid and dynamic framework for understanding human and environmental interaction.[19]

In the field of history, the idea that space and society are connected would not be considered new to architectural historians. The way in which domestic spaces were laid out, argued architectural historian Frank Brown during the 1980s, 'are plainly not a simple function of plan arrangement; they stem from a complex amalgam of social and cultural influences'. Brown posits an elusive yet influential relationship between society and space, explaining that 'the internal configuration of the house should be a matter of more than formal interest ... it should yield information which can enrich our understanding of society, and perhaps of social processes too'.[20] Brown's forthright claim is not unique. Other architectural historians, including John Bold and Matthew Johnson, have postulated that the changing style of domestic interiors from the late medieval to the early-modern period, that encompassed a shift from open halls to private rooms, reflected a redefinition of attitudes towards privacy and changing socio-cultural priorities.[21] The style of built structures – as one representation of socially and culturally produced space – should thus tell us much about the inhabitants of that place.[22]

With such a background, where places are seen as the 'reflection of society and its values' and 'a medium through which society and different kinds of knowledge can be created and reproduced', social and cultural historians have a range of spatial methodologies at their disposal to re-read the past.[23] Now fully 'arrived' on the history conference circuit, the spatial-turn was recently identified as one of four key issues in the 'future of social history.'[24] Nonetheless, social histories adopting the spatial turn outside of the field of gender studies or literature are still relatively scarce. This is partly because connections between human social interaction and the environment are not always

[19] S. Ardener, 'Ground Rules and Social Maps for Women', *Women and Space: Ground Rules and Social Maps*, ed. Shirley Ardener (Oxford, 1993), pp. 11, 34; Doreen Massey, *Space, Place and Gender* (Cambridge, 1994), pp. 122, 178.

[20] F. E. Brown, 'Continuity and Change in the Urban House: Developments in Domestic Space Organisation in Seventeenth Century London', *Comparative Studies in Society and History* 28:3 (1986), 558–90.

[21] John Bold, 'Privacy and the Plan', *English Architecture: Public and Private*, ed. J. Bold and E. Chaney (London, 1993), pp. 107–19; M. Johnson, *Housing Culture: Traditional Architecture in an English Landscape* (London, 1993), pp. 1–2, 28.

[22] For more, see J. Rendell, Barbara Penner and Ian Borden, eds, *Gender Space Architecture: An Interdisciplinary Introduction* (London, 2000).

[23] C. P. Graves, 'Social Space in the English Medieval Parish Church', *Economy and Society* 18:3 (1989), 297–322, 297.

[24] R. Kingston, 'Mind Over Matter? History and the Spatial Turn', *Cultural and Social History* 7:1 (2010), 111–121, 111.

obvious and the interdisciplinary path not always a popular one. Indeed, the 'spatial question' has often been buried under the ubiquity of environment: the 'passive backdrop' is, as the term suggests, an unquantifiable concept.

It is for this reason that historians interested in cognising the relationship between people and place have focussed on spaces that have a corporeal focus and defined academic boundaries, for instance, domestic or public space. Thus it has been that gender historians have led the way in exploring exactly what public and private meant to historic actors and how these dual concepts affected their day-to-day lives. The discussion has helped mature the notion of public and private, from the influential model of the 'separate spheres' that defined our understanding of women's (and men's) roles and relationships for much of the twentieth century, into a far more dynamic concept.[25] Critical analysis of the concept of 'separate spheres' was championed during the late 1970s and 1980s by feminist scholars and historians who argued that a model built on a dichotomy was too inflexible to represent people's multifarious experiences, and too much based on ideals of masculinity and femininity as espoused from pen and pulpit.[26] From the 1990s historians influenced by the spatial turn of social history have re-examined and built on these significant arguments. Using concepts from Bourdieu and Lefebvre, amongst others, historians have re-read sources with an eye to exploring how far practical necessities, like moving between public and private space, mitigated or consolidated the effect of gender ideals on people's lives.

Using coroner's inquests from London between 1275 and 1341 for example, Barbara Hanawalt found that women were more likely to die from accidental causes in the home or garden (50 per cent) than men, who were more likely to die in work-related incidents at shops and workplaces; only 20 per cent died at home.[27] Hanawalt was led to conclude that 'medieval men consciously strove through a variety of mechanisms to keep women within women's space ... the best way to control them was to enclose them'.[28] A similar approach to evaluating women's movements in and around public spaces was adopted by Laura Gowing for early-modern London, Amanda Flather for early-modern Essex and Pam Perkins for late eighteenth-century Edinburgh, although their conclusions have not always been consistent with those of

---

[25] Leonore Davidoff and Catherine Hall, *Family Fortunes: Men and Women of the English Middle Class, 1780–1850* (London, 1987).

[26] For an introduction to the debate over separate spheres, see J. Wallach-Scott, 'Gender: A Useful Category of Historical Analysis', *American Historical Review* 91:5 (1986), 1053–75 or A. Vickery, 'Golden Age to Separate Spheres? A Review of the Categories and Chronology of English Women's History', *Historical Journal* 36:2 (1993), 383–414.

[27] Barbara A. Hanawalt, 'At the Margins of Women's Space in Medieval Europe', *'Of Good and Ill Repute': Gender and Social Control in Medieval England*, ed. Barbara Hanawalt (Oxford, 1998), pp. 70–87, 81.

[28] Ibid., p. 83.

Hanawalt.[29] Gowing, for example, whilst broadly adhering to the notions of gendered space as proposed by Hanawalt, suggested that women had more freedom to move about public space, especially in the city. Like Hanawalt however, she argued that when women moved out of domestic space they had to do so with caution and preferably in company because of persistent preconceptions of the appropriateness of some public places for women, though she adds that many of the 'tensions of femininity in public space were reworked' by the 1640s.[30]

Addressing traditional concepts of masculine or feminine space in early-modern Essex, Amanda Flather has suggested that there was a gap between the prescription and practice of gender: real life was far more fluid and circumstantial than the binary model of public and private allows and, as a framework to describe the early-modern experience of gender, the model of separate spheres is limited.[31] Flather's study of space and place in Essex honed in on women's presence at sites that have been categorised by scholars as 'masculine spaces', as a way of comprehending how contemporaries internalised gendered norms and practised them on a daily basis, arguing that although gender ideals were pervasive, their impact on everyday lives was subtler than has perhaps been assumed. Adopting a similar approach, Robert Shoemaker has proposed one of the most radical re-readings of gendered space in his investigation of people's movements in and around the streets of early-modern London. Intending to uncover how far men and women adopted the gendered spheres of interaction and exchange dictated by prescriptive literature, his findings 'flew in the face of prevailing expectations ... that a woman's place was in the home'. Women, poor and middling sort women especially, went where practicality demanded and actually roamed more widely around early-modern London than their male counterparts.[32]

That historians are only now weighing people's practical experiences of spaces and places against ideologies proscribing appropriate gendered spaces shows, as Vanessa Harding posits, just how far the idea of separate spheres has dominated historical scholarship. Harding draws attention to the value system that has, from time out of mind, placed more importance on the public, rather than the private sphere, not only in our perception of what was

---

[29] Laura Gowing, '"The Freedom of the Streets": Women and Social Space, 1560–1640', *Londinopolis: Essays in the Cultural and Social History of Early-Modern London*, ed. Paul Griffiths and Mark Jenner (Manchester, 2000), pp. 130–51; Amanda Flather, *Gender and Space in Early-Modern England* (Woodbridge, 2007): Pam Perkins, 'Exploring Edinburgh: Urban Tourism in Late Eighteenth-Century Britain', *City Limits: Perspectives on the Historical European City*, ed. Glenn Clark, Judith Owens and Greg T. Smith (Montreal, 2010), pp. 187–204.

[30] Hanawalt, 'At the Margins', p. 84 and Gowing, '"The Freedom of the Streets"', p. 147.

[31] Flather, *Gender and Space*, esp. 110–20.

[32] Robert Shoemaker, 'Gendered Spaces: Patterns of Mobility and Perceptions of London's Geography, 1660–1750', *Imagining Early Modern London: Perceptions and Portrayals of the City from Stow to Strype, 1598–1720*, ed. J. F. Merritt (Cambridge, 2001), pp. 144–65, 163.

considered of consequence in the past, but during the actual practice of re-covering history in today's society. The overemphasis on the public sphere in modern scholarship has obscured the complex interdependence of public and private spaces; the 'urban public' was, Harding argues, 'physically shaped by the private spaces that surrounded and confined it'.[33] As David Rollison has also noted, the desire to place complex interconnected and mutable abstrac-tions into categories has created 'an impression of settled space … obscur-ing one of the most dynamic forces of change in the early-modern world'.[34] Binary conceptualisations of public and private spaces have a place in an early-modern world that perceived the world in terms of opposites – urban and rural, God and the Devil, master and servant – and placed great store on symbolism, but contemporaries' sensitivities were infinitely more multifac-eted and circumstantial; the spatial meanings and labels attached to places were malleable, overlapping and even contradictory.

Like Harding, Michael McKeon has proposed that scholars have coloured our understanding of the past with modern sets of assumptions. Referring in particular to the seventeenth and eighteenth centuries, a period most associ-ated with literature on the public sphere, McKeon posits that the separation of public and private space is a modern abstraction that people contemporary to the time did not share, contrived through the human propensity to label and categorise during the process of academic study. He proposes instead that contemporaries had a range of multi-dimensional spatial typologies at their disposal, none of which were exclusive. Spaces – especially public and private ones – had conceptual, literary, imaginative, political and physical meanings that overlapped at any one time and therefore it is almost impossible to fix spatial meanings with our modern labels.[35]

Gowing's work has also demonstrated the problem of defining spaces by drawing attention to the presence of liminal space in early-modern hous-ing; that is points at which public and private collided.[36] Lena Cowen Or-lin and Alexander Cowen addressed the same concerns, arguing that public space bled into private spaces in domestic properties, through noise, open windows, shop fronts and shared back yards. Cowen Orlin explains how, in London, this situation was exacerbated by the pressure of a rapidly increas-ing urban population, where overcrowding created a surveillance culture in

---

33 Vanessa Harding, 'Space, Property and Propriety in Urban England', *Journal of Interdis-ciplinary History* 32:4 (2002), 549–69, 549.

34 D. Rollison, 'Exploding England: the Dialectics of Mobility and Settlement in Early Modern England', *Social History* 24:1 (1999), 1–16, 4.

35 M. McKeon, *The Secret History of Domesticity: Public, Private and the Division of Knowl-edge* (Baltimore, 2005), esp. 194–205 for city streets and nightwalking.

36 Gowing, '"The Freedom of the Streets"', pp. 134–7. See also Fiona Williamson, 'Space and the City: Gender Identities in the Seventeenth Century', *Cultural and Social History Journal* 9:2 (2012), 169–85.

which private lives were public property, a theme to which Gowing also turns during her examination of defamatory speeches in early-modern London.[37]

Paul Griffiths took up the notion of multiple concepts of space in his study of nightwalking, defined as the practice of walking after dark, usually in connection with crime or prostitution. Focussing on perceptions of city streets, Griffiths explains how roads and alleys that were considered safe places during the day adopted a different persona as dusk fell, the encroaching dark creating hidden corners and inviting crime. The change directly impacted on how men and women found on those same streets at night were perceived,[38] bringing to mind Jane Rendell's claim that 'as men and women traverse space, their positions ... vary according to personal, social and cultural desires'.[39]

These are all themes to which this book turns. Chapter Four in particular asks whether it is appropriate to conceptualise the city in terms of male or female places and considers what public and private (in the gendered sense) meant to seventeenth-century people. It does this by drawing on the work of Flather, Shoemaker, Hanawalt and others who have used court records and reports to investigate where urban men and women spent their time. Crucially, however, this chapter aligns these findings with Gowing and Cowen's suggestions that we should not simply consider where women moved, but their reception in places historians have considered to be masculine preserves. It will consider the possibility of masculine or feminine spaces in seventeenth-century Norwich and argue that although there was some correlation of gender with certain urban spaces, such distinctions should be treated with caution.

Gender historians have not been the only scholars to explore urban space. During the 1980s and 1990s, many studies of early-modern cities considered the link between urban space and political power, as it was expressed during symbolic public events, including civic processions and celebrations. Building on the work of historians such as Robert Tittler, who demonstrated how urban corporations fashioned their own identities through ceremonies, rituals and regalia,[40] scholars like Michael Berlin, James Knowles, Sheila Lindenbaum and Mary A. Blackstone have shown how, using performative imagery, customary rituals and civic symbolism, urban corporations actively

---

[37] L. Cowen Orlin, *Locating Privacy in Tudor London* (Oxford, 2008), esp. Ch. 4; Alexander Cowen, 'Gossip and Street Culture in Early Modern Venice', *Journal of Early Modern History* 12 (2008), 313–333; Gowing, '"The Freedom of the Streets"', pp. 136–7.

[38] P. Griffiths, 'Meanings of Nightwalking in Early Modern England', *Seventeenth-Century* 13:2 (1998), 212–38.

[39] J. Rendell, *The Pursuit of Pleasure: Gender, Space and Architecture in Regency London* (London, 2002), p. 4.

[40] See in particular Robert Tittler, *Architecture and Power: the Town Hall and the English Urban Community, c. 1500–1640* (Oxford, 1991) and *The Face of the City: Civic Portraiture and Civic Identity in Early Modern England* (Manchester, 2008).

appropriated spatial tactics to bolster their authority and foster a civic identity.[41] The same could be said for urban government's practice of public punishment. By situating the tools of punishment, like the stocks or the cage, in
a market square, or by hanging criminal's mutilated body parts on city walls
and at gates, urban governments combined visual cues with features of the
landscape to their best effect.[42]

Public punishment was one way of managing people's actions in public
space but urban governments had many other methods at their disposal. In
seventeenth-century Norwich, the corporation expended a great deal of time
and money on trying to perfect their public image. They sought to do this by
issuing by-laws to improve public health and investing in cleaning and dredg-
ing programmes for the streets and the river, but they also targeted people by
attempting to curtail the freedoms of poorer inhabitants or migrants to roam
freely within the city walls. The corporation maintained strict laws for settlement and worked to eject people who could not prove they had a right to
residence, especially the poor. By removing unwanted people from the streets,
the problem of poverty was less apparent to the public eye.[43] The success
of this strategy is considered in Chapter Two, which takes the perspective
that the corporation were engaged in an unwinnable battle to manage public
space effectively. The ideal of public space held by the urban governing class
was fundamentally at odds with the reality of the urban poor, turning the
streets into a contested space.

The corporation did have some measure of success in managing their
public appearance to outsiders, however. As Peter Clark explains, urban
governments invested heavily in projecting an ideal public image to a wider
audience.[44] One way of doing this was by commissioning a map. Pre-modern
maps, as Richard Helgerson emphasised during the mid-1980s, propelled
a particular image into the public sphere, one which the commissioner or
engraver wished to become synonymous with the object of study,[45] a process

---

[41] Michael Berlin, 'Civic Ceremony in Early-Modern London', *Urban History* 13 (1986),
15–27; J. Knowles, 'The Spectacle of the Realm: Civic Consciousness, Rhetoric and Ritual
in Early Modern London', *Theatre and Government Under the Early Stuarts*, ed. J. R. Mulryne
and M. Shewring (1993); S. Lindenbaum, 'Ceremony and Oligarchy: the London Midsummer Watch', *City and Spectacle in Medieval Europe*, ed. B. Hanawalt and K. Reyerson
(Minneapolis, 1994); Mary A. Blackstone, 'Walking the City Limits: The Performance of
Authority and Identity in Mary Tudor's Norwich', *City Limits*, ed. Clark et al, pp. 106–38.
[42] P. Griffiths, 'Bodies and Souls in Sixteenth- and Seventeenth-Century England: Punishing Petty Crime, 1540–1700', *Penal Practice and Culture, 1500–1900: Punishing the English*, ed. S. Devereaux and P. Griffiths (London, 2004), pp. 85–120 and P. Griffiths, *Lost
Londons: Change, Crime and Control in the Capital City, 1550–1660* (Cambridge, 2008).
[43] For more on this see Paul Griffiths, 'Inhabitants', *Norwich since 1550*, ed. Carole Rawcliffe and Richard Wilson (London, 2004), pp. 63–89.
[44] Clark, *European Cities*, p. 85, 186–7.
[45] Richard Helgerson, for example, discusses the connection between map-making and
royal power in 'The Land Speaks: Cartography, Chorography, and Subversion in Renaissance England', *Representations* 16 (1986), 50–85.

that Christian Jacob has gone some way to explain in his interdisciplinary exploration of how a map's viewer decoded its spatial messages.[46] Helgerson, Jacob and others have described maps as social constructions, which exert a profound influence on the way that place is understood and were therefore an important governmental tool in a world that placed great value on visual communication.[47]

Norwich was the first regional city in England to commission its own map. This prospect, attributed to William Cuningham in 1558, glorified the city and conveys much about the aspirations of the civic elite on the local and national stage. Throughout the seventeenth century, Norwich's governing class continued to commission or sponsor prospects or maps that venerated their city, often elegantly decorated with the emblems of Norwich's economic and political success, including guild insignias and royal arms. The production of stylised, symbolic cityscapes dominated the European cartographic tradition for most of this period and, looking at such beautiful imagery, one could almost forget the realities of city living.

Nevertheless it should not be assumed that the map-making process was entirely top-down. Daniel Lord Smail argues, based on his study of late-medieval Marseille, that a surprising number of people had access to the process of map-making and the finished product, including administrative officials and public notaries. In Norwich, the city that informs this book, maps were hung in the public rooms of the Guildhall. The point that Lord Smail makes however is not simply that many people viewed maps passively, but that a channel existed whereby a number of complimentary and competing spatial vocabularies informed by the general public filtered into the practice of cartography through the medium of the public officials.[48] In my first chapter, on the theme of maps and ways of conceptualising the city, I argue that ordinary people's contribution to cartography was to offer alternative ways of seeing, thereby limiting a map's ability to dominate public knowledge of a place or to project the sole perspective of the commissioner. Inhabitants had a range of competing mental maps at their disposal to inform their personal perspectives of their city, some individual and some drawn from common consciousness: cartographic imagery was only one of these. The existence of competing 'maps' limited the impact of actual cartography. The final section of this first chapter thus explores the alternative shared frameworks by which ordinary people conceptualised their city. Across all the possible social perimeters, one

[46] Cristian Jacob, *The Sovereign Map: Theoretical Approaches in Cartography throughout History*, trans. Tom Conley and Edward H. Dahl (Chicago, 2006).
[47] J. B. Harley, 'Silences and Secrecy: The Hidden Agenda of Cartography in Early-Modern Europe', *Imago Mundi* 40 (1988), 57–76: J. B. Harley, ed., *The New Nature of Maps: Essay in the History of Cartography* (Baltimore and London, 2002); David Buisseret, ed., *Monarchs, Ministers and Maps: The Emergence of Cartography as a Tool of Government in Early-Modern Europe* (Chicago, 1992).
[48] Daniel Lord Smail, *Imaginary Cartographies: Possession and Identity in Late Medieval Marseille* (New York, 1999).

common strategy emerges as a device in inhabitants' verbal recollections of city space: the parish, a symbol of neighbourhood and of belonging, and a way of ordering space.

The parish provided focus for inhabitants' mental maps because it was such an important space in people's lives. Even the strangers – in Norwich commonly immigrants from the Low Countries or France – saw their city in terms of the parish: it defined how poor relief and local rates were ordered and they also attended their parish church. The strangers had a range of alternative mental maps at their disposal however, broadly based on membership of a foreign congregation and the exclusive social network this brought with it. Chapter Three considers how far the strangers' unique perspective offers a different way of seeing Norwich. By addressing the possibilities of competing maps, Chapters One, Two and Three collectively propose that no one social group had ultimate control over the labelling, ordering or managing of spaces or spatial perceptions. The creation of social space was a process generated by competing interests.

In much the same way, Chapter Five conceptualises political spaces as linked to networks, bottom-up influences, and localised customs, rather than government buildings and the political elite. The spatial dimensions of political power have recently been addressed by an important collection of essays compiled by Beat Kümin. This inspired volume goes further than drawing parallels between symbolism and space to explore the idea that 'political forms and practice are always located'.[49] Woven through the essays is a basic concept of spatial management; the ability to control, manipulate, or appropriate spatial meaning as an avenue to power, although, as many of the contributions highlight, political power was not always made manifest in formal spaces of government, neither was politics the realm of an elite. As Clark points out in the same volume, political spaces were created in clubs, societies, and guilds, their existence tied to a concept and a social network that latterly became connected to a non-political place.[50] This is a theme to which subsequent edited collections have been drawn, in particular, Caroline Goodson, Anne E. Lester and Carol Symes' *Cities, Texts and Social Networks* and David Warren Sabean and Malina Stefanovska's, *Space and Self in Early Modern European Cultures*. Both texts elucidate on the variety of places that could be considered to have manifest political identities, from hospitals and prisons, to theatrical spaces and coffee shops.[51]

---

[49] Mike Crang, 'Spaces in Theory, Spaces in History and Spatial Historiographies', *Political Space in Pre-industrial Europe*, ed. Beat Kümin (Aldershot, 2009), pp. 249–66, 249.

[50] Peter Clark, 'Politics, Clubs and Social Spaces in Pre-Industrial Europe', *Political Space*, ed. Kümin, pp. 81–117, 82.

[51] See in particular, Sethina Watson, 'City as Charter: Charity and the Lordship of English Towns, 1170–1250', and Anne E. Lester, 'Crafting a Charitable Landscape: Urban Topographies in Charters and Testaments from Medieval Champagne', *Cities, Texts and Social Networks 400–1500*, ed. Caroline Goodson, Anne E. Lester and Carol Symes (Farnham, 2010), pp. 235–62, 279–302; and Déborah Blocker, 'Theatrical Identities and

The final chapter in this book conceives of political spaces as Clark, Kümin, and others have conceptualised them, as connected to a social groups and networks as well as to sites more obviously connected to politics and government. During the seventeenth century, many urban places were commonly acknowledged as sites of popular politics and political engagement. These sets of assumptions had developed from time out of mind, becoming part of contemporaries' shared understanding of their environment. Some alehouses, for example, were recognised by ordinary people and urban governments as places for covert political activities, a fact addressed by legislation aimed at suppressing the same by generations of monarchs and urban officials. But the association of drinking houses with popular politics was entirely cultural; there was nothing in the bricks and mortar of the premises that precluded a political agenda. Drinking houses were only as politicised as the customers that drank in them, and customers were only as political as the circumstances dictated. Moreover, drinking houses were not universally recognised as hotbeds of sedition or venues for political partisanship: these associations were often specific to particular establishments because of their patrons and owners, even if a generic link between drinking houses and popular politics continued to inform legislative practice across the period.

That certain places were understood to have political meaning can be revealed through the early-modern concept of inversion. In Norwich, for example, the open space outside the city's central Guildhall (home to the mayor's court and council chamber) was used as the starting point of grand civic processions, the setting for official announcements, and other civic ceremonies. However it was also occupied for popular demonstrations when circumstances demanded. The usurpation of a place more commonly associated with civic ceremony by ordinary, angry protestors carried far more symbolic weight than a location chosen at random as it directly violated civic space which, over time, created a new spatial memory. The landscape of popular politics was, therefore, based on real urban spaces, but linked to a complex mix of localised events and commonly held assumptions with regard to symbolic meaning. By conceptualising popular politics as a separate framework or mental map through which to understand the cityscape, the seventeenth-century city emerges as a place of multiple identities and landscapes.

The idea that a wide range of forces shaped multiple urban identities is a theme taken up across all the chapters in this book, building on the claim of Marc Boone and Peter Stabel that a city was unlikely to have had unified collective identity. Rather, a city was a collection of places and spaces, used by different actors, at different times, and for different purposes, ultimately

Political Allegories: Fashioning Subjects through Drama in the Household of Cardinal Richelieu (1635–1643)' and David S. Shields, 'The Eccentric Centre: Selfhood and Sociability at the Heart of England's Culture of Enlightenment Print', *Space and Self in Early Modern European Cultures*, ed. David Warren Sabean and Malina Stefanovska (Toronto, 2012), pp. 98–111, 112–33.

expressed as a series of competing mental maps or identities.[52] Urban inhabitants' networks and identities crossed and re-crossed the city's streets, neighbourhoods, and parishes, bearing little or no relation to physical space, though at the same time intimately connected with it. Chapter Three addresses the idea of identities in more depth, and considers how these identities were linked to communities, with a close lens on the impact of immigration on city life. It considers how far strangers (overseas migrants) were a marginalised community and to what extent their separate lives became inscribed into the landscape. Immigration had always been a part of Norwich life but the two 'refuges' of the late sixteenth and late seventeenth centuries had a major impact on the city's population levels and economy. Separated by religion, culture, and law, many of the new immigrants lived in specific areas of the city and worshipped (as was stipulated by law) at their own churches. Nevertheless, it would be wrong to see these people as a ghettoised community and their mental maps of Norwich likely shared many crossovers with those of native-born inhabitants, especially those based on family, kinship, and church. This chapter therefore explores the idea of networks, exclusion and belonging and argues that the strangers, although often spoken of as a separate community in contemporary rhetoric, were part of an international network that surpassed the city's physical borders and cultural divides.

This book aims to reveal some of the mental maps that the inhabitants of Norwich had at their disposal from a study of the spaces and places in which they lived, worked and worshipped, and from the way they spoke about the places around them. It argues that it is possible to think of Norwich as a city of many spatial identities that reflected the diverse and colourful characteristics of city dwellers; as Richard Dennis states, cities functioned as *communities of difference*.[53]

II

Norwich was one of the most important regional centres of seventeenth-century England. In 1683, Thomas Baskerville was to describe Norwich as 'a great city ... full of people', Celia Fiennes likewise considered it 'a rich, thriving industrious place' driven by 'very great' markets and fairs; a city where, as

---

52 The phrase 'mental maps' was popularised by the book of the same name compiled by Peter Gould and Rodney White, eds, *Mental Maps*, 2nd edn (London, 1986).
53 R. Dennis, 'Urban Modernity, Networks and Places', *History in Focus* 13 (2008). Historians interested in urban space have recently begun to consider the sensory experiences of city living. Soundscapes, touch, vision, and smell have all been investigated by academics interested in opening up the subjective and emotional side of urban history. See, for example, D. Garrioch, 'Sounds of the City: the Soundscape of Early-Modern Towns', *Urban History* 30:1 (2003), 5–25; Alexander Cowen and Jill Steward, eds, *The City and the Senses: Urban Culture Since 1500* (Aldershot, 2007); Riitta Laitinen and Thomas Cohen, eds, *Cultural History of Early-Modern European Streets* (Leiden, 2009).

Daniel Defoe would note in 1723, employment was so high that even children of three or four could 'earn their own bread'.[54] Such descriptions were not simply narrative largesse. Seventeenth-century Norwich may not have achieved the growth rates of London or Bristol in the same period but it was steadily blossoming, with a population that rose from thirteen thousand souls in 1600 to twenty thousand in the 1620s, largely as a result of immigration.[55] The attraction of the city was its reputation as a prosperous, industrialising economy and there were few other comparable towns nearby to absorb the urban draw. By the close of the century, the city's inhabitants numbered 28,881,[56] a figure that reflected how migration had levelled out during less propitious decades.[57]

Norwich's success was due in part to its location. Situated on a good river network, it linked important trade routes between London, Colchester, Ipswich, northeast England and the continent, via Yarmouth and King's Lynn's medieval Hanseatic ports. Ships from Newcastle had brought coal and wood to the Norfolk coast since the fifteenth century, if not before.[58] Conveyed on barges downriver into the city's docks, coal provided the versatile high-energy fuel essential to developing small-scale commercial and industrial enterprises, and was increasingly the fuel of choice for domestic residents.[59]

It is by water that Norwich receives all its provisions in grain, and all its coal, of which the consumption is considerable; for its dyes and the preparation of cloths

---

[54] Penelope Corfield, 'A Provincial Capital in the Late Seventeenth-Century: the Case of Norwich', *The Early Modern Town*, ed. Peter Clark (New York, 1976), p. 233 and Richard Wilson, 'Introduction', *Norwich*, ed. Rawcliffe and Wilson, pp. xxi-xxix, xxi.

[55] John Pound, *Tudor and Stuart Norwich* (Chichester, 1988), p. 28.

[56] NRO, Miscellaneous Collection, MC 453, Loose papers, A Parochial List of the Number of Houses and Inhabitants within the City of Norwich, 1693 and 1752. By 1752, the population had risen to 36,169.

[57] Severe bouts of plague in 1625–6, 1631 and 1637–8 and a poor economy in the 1620s, 1630s, and 1640s curtailed population growth. During the 1670s, the population increased at a rate equalling that of the first two decades of the century: Corfield, 'A Provincial Capital', pp. 233–73, esp. 234–40. Corfield drew her estimates from tax records and mortality bills, whilst carefully highlighting the strengths and weaknesses of each source. Her analysis remains the leading authority on Norwich's population levels today.

[58] NCR, 21f, 76, from a selection of John Kirkpatrick's notes relating to the river. See also King's Lynn Borough Archives (KL), King's Lynn's Hall Books, 1431–50, KL/C/7/3, fols 110r, 126v, 169v; entries relating to the import of coals into the town.

[59] Norwich's probate records from 1600–1700 show how urban householders tended to use coal as their main fuel supply, with only occasional supplements of wood. Domestic fuel consumption was high throughout the period. Likewise, the corporation's accounts reveal how coal was used to heat civic buildings and institutions. See for example, the Boy's and Girl's Hospital Accounts, NCR, 25f, 1620–52; Books of Proceedings of City Committees: Bridewell, 1585, NCR 19c; St Peter Mancroft Overseer's Accounts, PD 26/102–103, 1600; and the Diocese of Norwich Probate Inventories, DN/INV/3-68b, 1587–1700.

... All the manufactures themselves are taken the twenty miles to Yarmouth, and through that port ... exported to all parts of Europe.[60]

Coal was important for other reasons too. Its ready availability facilitated the exponential number of brewers (for which the city became famous) and aided in the production of Norwich's other fundamental commodity: cloth.[61] The production and trade of cloth were the building blocks of Norwich's prosperity although the path to success had not been an easy one. A series of trade depressions – ostensibly created by foreign competition but exacerbated by a lack of viable local alternatives to fall back on – had characterised the mid-sixteenth century economy and created high levels of unemployment. Repeated outbreaks of influenza, the sweating sickness and plague had exacerbated social problems brought on by poverty, and it is no surprise that the year 1549 saw one of the region's largest popular revolts, immortalised as Kett's Rebellion.[62] But as the 1500s waned, an improving national economy, a raft of protective legislation and local government initiatives – including a grant of settlement to skilled foreign cloth workers in the 1560s – had given Norwich's economy an edge.

The improved situation lasted until the 1620s when, like a mirror image of the national situation, Norwich underwent a series of economic depressions that affected trade into the 1650s, although Penelope Corfield has argued that the disruptions to overseas markets – especially during the 1640s and 1650s – actually had a positive impact on the city's economy as cloth merchants and producers were forced to invest in domestic, rather than foreign trade.[63] The dividends of this shift in market supply became evident during the 1660s as the national demand for worsted, wool and linen (Norwich's core manufactures) reached a new high, stimulated by demand for Norwich 'stuffs', a light mixture of wool and silk produced in the 'New Draperies' ... 'either for wearing, or ornaments; to adorn houses with Hangings, Carpets, or Curtaines, of innumerable sorts, colours [and] varieties' enjoyed by the emerging middling fashion market.[64]

Stimulated by this activity, Norwich also developed a thriving retail trade. Like most towns and cities, Norwich's first retail outlets started as workshops from which craftspeople sold their products directly to the public and many of the more successful commercial businesses established their premises along

---

60 François de La Rochefoucauld, *A Frenchman's Year in Suffolk: French Impressions of Suffolk Life in 1784*, ed. Norman Scarfe (Woodbridge, 1988), pp. 205–6.

61 Provisioning was a major growth area in Norwich during the seventeenth century. It was stimulated by the growing population and the inability to be self-sufficient in the ever more crowded urban centre. Inhabitants relied instead on street hucksters and hawkers for cooked food, and alehouses and inns for light ales, beers, wine and meals.

62 Norwich's inhabitants suffered from the sweating sickness in 1506, 1551 and 1558, the flu in 1556, and the plague in 1563, 1578–9, 1582–3, 1588, and 1591.

63 Corfield, 'A Provincial Capital', pp. 246–7.

64 John Taylor, *A Late Weary, Merry Voyage and Journey* (London, 1650), p. 18.

the main thoroughfares in and around the central marketplaces. Skilled cord-wainers and goldsmiths, for example, lived and worked on the western side of the marketplace at St Peter Mancroft in St Giles' parish. The retail hub extended eastwards and southwards from the market along Great Cockey Lane which, by 1700, had been reinvented as Gentleman's Walk and London Street (the latter named in tribute to the noise and traffic).[65] Local retailers sought to stock the latest in fashionable and exotic items like tobacco, sugar, tea, coffee, cocoa and confectionary along with new book titles, at the be-hest of local gentry who had discovered the newest styles and products whilst attending the London Seasons.[66] The expanding material culture of Nor-wich's middling sorts is evident from the increasing diversity of items listed in probate inventories. By the seventeenth century it was not uncommon to find books, table linen, elegant tableware, playing tables, looking glasses, and flower pots in the homes of middling yeomen, shopkeepers and merchants.[67] Chocolate cups, coffee dishes and 'cherry ware', for example, were to be found in the home of one Norwich worsted weaver who had died in 1718.[68]

Seventeenth-century Norwich was fast becoming the 'administrative, social and shopping centre of ... Norfolk and north Suffolk'.[69] The annual migration of the county gentry into Norwich during the sessions and assize circuits inspired a regular season of entertainments, the next best thing lo-cally to the fashionable London season. Norwich boasted many diversions for those who could afford them: coffee houses, one of the earliest provincial libraries, concerts, clubs and theatrical productions were held regularly at venues that included the Red Lion Inn and St Andrew's Hall.[70] Visitors were led to comment that Norwich had a cultured air, 'in this mixture, the inhab-itants participate nothing of the rusticalness of the one, but altogether of the urbanity and civility of the other'.[71]

[65] John Kirkpatrick, *The Streets and Lanes of Norwich* (Norwich, 1889), p. 44.

[66] Ursula Priestly and Alayne Fenner, *Shops and Shopkeepers of Norwich, 1660–1730* (Norwich, 1985), pp. 4, 9.

[67] See for example DN/INV/3, the inventory of William Dunham of Norwich, who had owned playing tables and books at his death in 1587; or William Brown who had owned eight books at his death in 1595, DN/INV/12/87. In 1646, vintner Alexander Hobb's house had contained soft furnishings, damask table linen, playing tables, a looking glass and silverware, DN/INV/47b/2; and baker Richard Stevenson had owned four pictures in addition to his collection of books, DN/INV/47b/40.

[68] DN/INV/74a/20, probate inventory of Elisha De Hague, 13 January 1718. De Hague's stated occupation was worsted weaver, but the De Hague family were better known as merchants.

[69] Richard Wilson, 'The Textile Industry', *Norwich*, ed. Rawcliffe and Wilson, p. 221.

[70] Angela Dain, 'An Enlightened and Polite Society', *Norwich*, ed. Rawcliffe and Wilson, p. 194.

[71] Thomas Fuller, *The history of the worthies of England who for parts and learning have been eminent in the several counties: together with an historical narrative of the native commodities and rarities in each county* (London, 1662), p. 274.

Trade and industry also helped shape the city's topography. Access to essential resources like flowing water dictated where people settled, and necessity developed into occupational and social networks. Fishing, fish smoking, and boat construction were not unsurprisingly based on the banks of the River Wensum. The land around the southernmost section of the river within the city walls, at what is now King Street and Ber Street in the parishes of St Julian, St Ethelred and St Peter Southgate, was where heavy goods, like coal, was docked and shifted from boats and barges. It was here too that we find the city's lime-burning kilns and light industry, where the costs of transporting staple fuels and materials arriving by river or from nearby quarries could be kept to a minimum and also far enough away from the city centre to avoid too many complaints about noise and pollution.[72] Lime and flint were both sourced locally and quarried inside and outside the city boundaries. These quarries did much to shape the landscape, and provided some disruption to an otherwise relatively flat marshland to the south and east.[73] As the river wound northwards from the industrial south, past the cathedral and into the city centre, the industries on its banks were more and more likely to be linked to the city's staple trade: cloth working. It was here, close to St John Maddermarket, that the medieval Shearing Cross had stood (later giving the area the name Charing Cross), and where the worsted shearers and fullers pounded, whitened and cut cloth.[74]

The weaving industry expanded outwards across the city into the less developed northern *Ultra Aquam* (over-the-water) to encroach upon available space in Conesford and Colegate, or like the less salubrious trades of skinning and tanning, to keep apart from the main hustle and bustle of the city centre.[75] Tanning was essential but time-consuming and unpleasant work, involving the scouring of flesh and hair from animal skins with urine or lime, pounding the skin, and then treating it with alum or tannum (derived from tree bark) to preserve the hide. The finished leather was taken back across the river into the parish of St Giles where it was turned into footwear, armour, bags and riding equipment, which were then sold in the local and regional markets.[76]

---

[72] Coal was being imported into Norwich from Newcastle as early as 1422. See NCR Case 21f/76, Manuscripts of the Antiquary John Kirkpatrick: River. I am grateful to Isla Fay for this reference.

[73] Brian Ayers, *Norwich, A Fine City* (Stroud, 1994), p. 126.

[74] Kirkpatrick, *Streets and Lanes*, p. 55.

[75] These patterns had been long established, see Serena Kelly, 'The Economic Topography and Structure of Norwich, c. 1300', *Men of Property: An Analysis of the Norwich Enrolled Deeds, 1285–1311*, ed. Ursula Priestly (Norwich, 1983), pp. 13–39, esp. 34–5. Kelly identified the leather and textile workers as the largest occupational groups in medieval Norwich who, for practical purposes, tended to live in the central Wymer wards nearest the river. Shoemakers and cordwainers tended toward St Andrew and St Peter Mancroft, and drapers St Giles and St Peter Mancroft.

[76] Ayers, *Norwich*, pp. 92–4. Ayers' points out that five bridges were built in Norwich during the medieval period; the highest number in any English city at that time. The

The negative side of economic and industrial success came in the form of pollution and the unequal distribution of newly acquired wealth. Despite his generally glowing reports of Norwich, for example, Thomas Baskerville was moved to speak of how the dye works had fouled the river, which John Evelyn also described in 1671 as muddy, polluted and 'without any extent'.[77] The dyers, tanners, skinners, slaughterers and parchment-makers all took advantage of the river, not just to facilitate their trade, but as the cheapest and easiest way to remove their waste. The jakes, also known as houses of office to contemporaries, drained into the river from bankside properties and clusters of privies could also be found on the river near the Children's Hospital and at Badding's - known colloquially as Three Privy Lane - just off Fye Bridge Quay.[78] Despite the best efforts of the authorities to clean and dredge (or fye as it was known locally) the river, the problem of industrial and domestic waste was not easily solved.

Like most British towns and cities at this time, the pattern of wealth was incredibly uneven, and many of the migrants who had flocked to Norwich for work found themselves victims of the failure of wages to rise in line with inflation, unable to secure regular employment or unable to move out of low-paid, unskilled jobs. The records of the rate collection of 1633–4 – an extraordinary tax established to provide corn for the impoverished following the plague of 1630 – for example, demonstrates how the recipients of relief outweighed the number of ratepayers in many parishes. St James, St Paul, St John Sepulchre, St Michael at Thorn, All Saints, and St Julian, for instance, all had numbers of poor claimants that far outnumbered the proportion of contributors,[79] and St Margaret, St Lawrence, St Peter Southgate, St Martin, and St Peter Parmentergate had near unsustainable levels of poverty.[80] Many of these poor people lived in buildings that were badly constructed and overcrowded, often sub-divided to allow several families to share one building.[81] In 1570, a survey of the poor had revealed that multiple tenancies were the norm, including one shocking case where eleven separate families – totalling thirty-four residents – lived under just one roof.[82] Like many other towns

---

bridges were necessary as the production, finishing and sale of the cloth and leather were conducted on opposing sides of the river.

[77] Margaret Pelling, 'Health and Sanitation to 1750', *Norwich*, ed. Rawcliffe and Wilson, p. 123; Guy de Bédoyère, ed., *The Diary of John Evelyn* (Woodbridge, 2004), p. 87.

[78] Pelling, 'Health and Sanitation', p. 136–7.

[79] Walter Rye, *The Norwich Rate Book: From Easter 1633 to Easter 1634* (London, 1903), pp. 12–13, 16–17, 18–19, 21–2, 78–80, 81–2.

[80] Ibid., pp. 10–11, 13–14, 42–3, 43–4, 67–8.

[81] Pound, *Norwich*, p. 26.

[82] John Pound, ed., *The Norwich Census of the Poor, 1570: Norfolk Record Society 40* (Norwich, 1971), pp. 12–15. Christopher Barringer notes how Edward Pye, a city councillor, let four houses in Colgate to thirty people and three in 'Fyebridgegate' to fourteen people, and Alderman Thomas Parker let four houses to a total of thirty-nine people: Christopher Barringer, 'The Changing Face of Norwich', *Norwich*, ed. Rawcliffe and Wilson, pp. 1–34, 7.

and cities in England, Norwich's urban development had grown up around medieval burgages: a small parcel of land on which a one-storey house was built around an internal courtyard. To save on space and money, many of these buildings had been developed upwards or outwards into yards during the early-modern period. The result was less light and fresh air, overcrowding, problems with drainage, and a lack of privacy. By 1671, the situation had not changed. Norwich's hearth tax returns reveal how the poorer sorts numbered sixty-two per cent of the population and, although the poor lived all over the city, some parishes, including those mentioned above, had an overwhelming proportion of poor to rich.[83]

Not unsurprisingly, epidemics hit the most overcrowded areas the hardest. During the 1625–6 plague, for example, Paul Slack has shown that some of the worst affected parishes included the aforementioned St Margaret, St Lawrence, St James, All Saints, and St Peter Parmentergate.[84] Later that century, the 1665–6 plague plotted a similar path through the city. All Saints, St Michael at Thorn, St Peter Parmentergate, and St Lawrence accrued some of the highest number of deaths from the disease.[85] Epidemics also created problems around the importation, production and cost of food; the corporation had to declare emergency measures to feed the population during each major outbreak. In 1602 for example 'the infection caused such a scarcity in the city, that wheat was sold for 10s. a bushel; rye for 6, and barley for 5'; during the terrible 1625–6 plague, Norwich's sheriff was forced to use funds put aside for civic events to provide the poor with such basic necessities as food and fuel, and in 1630–1, corn licences were introduced to protect the price and quantity of corn sold at local markets, and the poor were allowed to buy corn at a special rate.[86]

The problems were especially acute during the 1620s because local crises were more often than not linked with additional local and national taxes. When news reached the city during the plague-ridden summer of 1626 that King Charles had ordered the collection of a Forced Loan for example, Norwich's citizens, already shouldering additional responsibility for their poor and infected, were understandably dismayed. By September, the Crown had stepped up its financial demands, this time to pay for two new ships of war in renewed hostilities against the Spanish. Norwich's mayor and aldermen were

[83] Corfield, 'A Provincial Capital', p. 235. The ratio of rich to poor had been established from time out of mind. In 1525 for example, John Pound explains how twenty-nine men controlled forty per cent of Norwich's taxable wealth, fifty-two men were 'wealthy', and two hundred and four men comfortably middling: in all fourteen per cent of the total population. Pound, *Tudor and Stuart Norwich*, pp. 31, 39.

[84] Paul Slack, *The Impact of Plague in Tudor and Stuart England* (London, 1985), p. 136.

[85] D. T. Jones, *Aspects of the Social Geography of Early-Modern Norwich: Applications of Computer Techniques I* (University of East Anglia Ph.D Thesis, unpub., 2003), Fig. 9.9.

[86] Francis Blomefield, *An Essay towards a Topographical History of the County of Norfolk, III: The History of the City and County of Norwich, I* (1806), pp. 376–7. John Pound, 'Government to 1660', *Norwich*, ed. Rawcliffe and Wilson, pp. 35–62, 55; Rye, *Rate Book*, p. 3.

forced to plead humbly for an exemption on grounds of poverty, arguing that the combination of plague in 1625–6, the Forced Loan levied between 1626 and 1627, and the contemporaneously high poor rate, had brought them 'to their knees'. The mayor, Basingbourne Throckmorton, petitioned the Crown to the effect that 'although in the time of their prosperity they had been called upon to bear a tenth or twelfth part of such charges, they were then so distressed as to be unable to maintain their poor'. The Crown was largely unsympathetic and responded by issuing two writs of *quo warrento* against Throckmorton and the corporation. Throckmorton only narrowly escaped charges when the case was tried in 1629.[87]

The relationship between the corporation and the Crown was placed under particular stress during the summer of 1627. The Crown's military campaigns against France had seen many of Norwich's young men impressed into service, and around two hundred soldiers (including Irishmen) had been billeted to Norwich, hosted by the city inns and taverns.[88] These strangers and foreigners could not have arrived in Norwich at a worse time, as the city was already reeling from rumours of an impending papist invasion.[89] News of the Duke of Buckingham's failed campaign to the Îlle de Rhé had reached Norwich just as the final collections for the unpopular Forced Loan to finance continued campaigns were underway, and the Crown's policy to make war on France whilst already at war with Spain was deeply unpopular.[90] Much criticism centred on the Forced Loan's legality and the balance between English liberties and absolute monarchy. The contentious issue had been given a local focus by the involvement of Norfolk man Sir John Corbet. Corbet was one of the infamous five knights imprisoned and tried for refusing to pay the

---

[87] Mayor and others of Norwich to the Council, 1 September 1626: J. Bruce, ed., *CSPD, Charles I: 1625–6* (1858), p. 418. The Norfolk antiquarian Francis Blomefield also noted that 'Two *ships* of war being demanded and refused, there were soon after two *writs* of *quo warranto* brought against the mayor'. The mayor was tried without charge in 1629 'having proved that [the corporation] used nor usurped any privileges but what their charters produced authorised them to do', Blomefield, *Topographical History III:I*, p. 374. The affair can also be explored in correspondence between the city and the Privy Council: NCR 1624–34, 6 Aug 1625, fol. 63r; Deputy Lieutenant of Norfolk to the Privy Council, NA, SP 16/24, fol. 44, 6 Ap. 1626 and 1 September 1626; and NA, SP 16/52, fol. 3, 30 January 1626–7.

[88] Series of Antiquarian Notes, MS 453, fol. 6v. For billeting in Norwich see Blomefield, *Topographical History III:I*, pp. 373–5.

[89] Rumours of an impending papist invasion had reached East Anglia by 1625. John Rous, the Suffolk clergyman and diarist, heard news that a Spanish Catholic fleet would land at Harwich and at Ipswich. The reports were taken so seriously that soldiers were garrisoned at Langer Point (Felixstowe) to repel a potential attack. See M. A. Everett Green, ed., *The Diary of John Rouse, 1625–42* (London, 1856), pp. 2, 5, 8.

[90] Thomas Cogswell, 'The Politics of Propaganda: Charles I and the People in the 1620s', *JBS* 29:3 (1990), 187–215, 187.

Loan, and a close friend to many in Norwich's corporation.[91] Perhaps not unsurprisingly, the region's Forced Loan returns were some of the lowest in the country.[92]

The plea of poverty from the corporation became a familiar one as the century progressed. In 1635, for example, in response to a 1634 order for Ship Money, the mayor and aldermen wrote to the Privy Council of

> ...the myserable desolate and distressed Condition of this Citty, by severall late Inundations of waters, the grievous Contagion of the plague, the dep[ar]ting of gentleme[n] fro[m] the Cittye, who did help to beare o[u]r Charges, and releive the poore ... our Tradesmen in stuffs & stockings susteyning great losses by deceased & decayed Londoners by the late Contagion of the plague theare, the maynteyning of fatherlesse Children and wyddowes, and impoverished handicraftsmenne to o[u]r unsupportable Charge, for want of Tradesmene to sytt them on worke.[93]

Thirty years later the plea was heard again, this time from Norwich's Town Clerk Thomas Corie whose impassioned letter to Whitehall revealed the city's desperate need for financial aid in the face of the plague. Corie wrote that 'wee [the corporation] are in greater feare of the poore then the plague, all our monie beinge gone, and not a penny yet come in from the countie. God help us.'[94]

As we have seen, the city's rapport with the Crown during the seventeenth century was often strained when it came to extraordinary financial demands. Whilst taxation was an obvious cause for friction, the relationship between Crown and corporation was far more complex, and tensions often stemmed from assumptions about the appropriate reach of the Crown's authority. The issue was rooted in Norwich's development as a city. Norwich had received a charter of incorporation in 1404. The charter had replaced the medieval system of bailiffs with a council, a mayor, two sheriffs and twenty-four aldermen, had conferred special privileges and powers to the city's governors – including a degree of autonomy from the Crown to manage local affairs – and raised the city's status nationally.[95] Over the intervening years, a combination of law, tradition and convention dictated who held the corporation's official posts. Women were of course denied this privilege, as were strangers and foreigners,

---

91 The Case of the Five Knights was heard before the King's Bench between 15 and 28 November 1627. For information see S. R. Gardiner, *Constitutional Documents of the Puritan Revolution 1625–60*, 3rd edn (Oxford, 1906), pp. 57–64.

92 The Forced Loan returns for Norfolk can be found at NA E401/1913, 1914 and 2443. For information see Richard Cust, *The Forced Loan and English Politics, 1626–1628* (Oxford, 1987).

93 Petition written to the Privy Council by the Norwich Corporation, NA, SP, 16/535/158, c. 1635.

94 Robert Hill, ed., *The Correspondence of Thomas Corie* (Norwich, 1956), p. 20.

95 Norwich was one of only thirteen English cities to have received a charter of incorporation before 1540: Robert Tittler, *The Reformation and the Towns in England: Politics and Political Culture, c. 1540–1640* (Oxford, 1998), p. 88.

and the vast majority (seventy to seventy-five per cent) of men who did not hold the freedom of the city. Of the freemen themselves, only a few gained the top positions within the twenty-four and it is quite obvious how many of these men were connected by kinship networks or guild membership.[96] They were men like Thomas Hyrne, an ironmonger who had held the office of mayor, county sheriff, burgess-in-parliament, and been knighted in 1609.[97] Hyrne was the son of Clement Hyrne, who had been mayor himself in 1593. Likewise, Hyrne's contemporary – the merchant John Pettus – was also a mayor's son, a sheriff in 1598, burgess-in-parliament in 1601, and mayor in 1608. On his death in 1614 Pettus, by now a knight, bequeathed his Norfolk and Suffolk estates to his extended family, and left a substantial bequest to the poor of Norwich. The year Pettus died, his brother Thomas became mayor. Even the two seventeenth-century 'revolutions' could not dint the ascendancy of certain local families. Brothers Thomas and Robert Cooke for example, were both aldermen for Berstreet ward, and mayors in 1689 and 1693 respectively. Between them they owned extensive property in the parish of St Peter's Parmentergate, which they endowed as alms-houses, and they also founded an institution for poor women known as Cooke's Hospital. Their family had been aldermen and mayors of the city since the fifteenth century.[98]

With only a few minor changes, the civic structure that had been created during the fifteenth century endured until 1835.[99] This incredible longevity can be attributed to the fierce pride with which the charter was guarded from Crown interference, but also the fact that the freemen were descended from a long line of men who historically 'strove for local autonomy from external controls, challenged seigneurial claims, and petitioned for incorporation [and] had the most to protect or to gain' from maintaining the status quo.[100] The charter was thus more than a simple judicial and administrative device; it was the foundation stone and symbol of Norwich's identity and independence. The corporation men jealously guarded their privileges from the

---

[96] J. T. Evans suggests that between 1601 and 1625 only six per cent of council men achieved a higher office: J. T. Evans, *Seventeenth-Century Norwich, Politics, Religion and Government 1620–1690* (Oxford, 1979), pp. 39–42. Pound suggests a reason for this low percentage; that prospective aldermen were singled out from the start of their council careers on the basis of family background and connections: John Pound, 'Government to 1660', *Norwich*, ed. Rawcliffe and Wilson, p. 37.

[97] B. Cozens-Hardy and E. A. Kent, *The Mayors of Norwich 1403–1835* (Norwich, 1938), p. 68.

[98] Ibid., pp. 69, 102–3.

[99] Electoral procedures were ratified in 1415 and an additional charter granted by Henry VI in 1452 confirmed the governmental structure of 'the twenty-four' that would have been familiar to seventeenth-century inhabitants. See R. Frost, 'The Urban Elite', *Medieval Norwich*, ed. Carole Rawcliffe and Richard Wilson (London 2004), pp. 235–53, 237. Transcribed highlights of the charters are included in W. Hudson and J. C. Tingay, *The Records of the City of Norwich* I &II (Norwich, 1906).

[100] Tittler, *Architecture and Power*, p. 99.

Crown, though within the council chamber there was some degree of debate over how, and to what extent, the system should work.

One of the keenest issues of the early seventeenth century was how far the convention that a man should serve several terms at each level of the corporation hierarchy before seeking a higher office should be enforced. Starting in the 1590s, there had been a trend for younger, less experienced men to overstep their seniors to become mayor (Clement Hyrne had been one of these men). In 1619, some of the aldermen wrote to James I complaining of how this tendency led to contested elections. The king responded with predictable concern, 'commanding them [the aldermen] to choose the senior alderman for their mayor year by year, to avoid all contentions for the future in their elections, in like manner as was observed in the city of London: and as their charters were interpreted'.[101] Norwich's charter however specified that any changes to its constitution had to be passed by the full assembly of councilmen and it was here that the dispute really took shape. Encountering fierce opposition, it took nearly a year – and magisterial intervention – for the King's order to be fleshed out into a formal proposal and put to the vote. The foot dragging over this affair revealed deep political divisions amongst Norwich's freemen and, because the underlying issues of traditional rights and privileges, convention and innovation had not been resolved to the satisfaction of many in 1619, they were to re-surface time and again over the course of the century.

Religion, that had arguably been a part of corporation politics since time out of mind, also became more a more overt part of corporation politics during the 1630s and 1640s. Seventeenth-century Norwich was a renowned non-conformist stronghold and many of the city's officials came from families with a reputation for godliness.[102] Aldermen had a fair degree of influence on religious appointments within their wards, and in some parishes paid for non-conformist lectureships out of corporation money.[103] The control of lectureships created problems between the corporation and the church, especially when the bishop incumbent lacked sympathy with the leading political faction's religious demands. Samuel Harsnett, Bishop of Norwich from 1619–29 and a proponent of the Arminian style of worship, for example, tried to supress the lectureships. Harsnett failed, but created much ill feeling and division in the process. His actions led to a small group of godly aldermen, ostensibly representing the corporation but lacking their official consent (a fact that in itself revealed the extent of division within the twenty-four), presenting a petition to parliament in 1624 that lambasted Harsnett's religious

---

101 Blomefield, *Topographical History*, III:I, p. 368.

102 P. Collinson, *The Elizabethan Puritan Movement* (London, 1967), pp. 172, 174, 176, 188.

103 Evans, *Seventeenth-Century Norwich*, p. 85. The city chamberlain's accounts reveal payments given to lecturers, including two posts in St Andrew's parish in the 1620s and 1630s: NCR Case 18a, 1603–24, and 1625–48.

direction, his leadership and supposed inclinations towards 'popery'.[104] The accession of the more tolerant bishop Richard Corbet in 1632 enabled the Puritan aldermen to extend their reach into the parishes, and they made the contentious decision to employ the radical non-conformist lecturer, William Bridge.

Bridge preached sermons on a corporation salary at St George's church in Tombland every Friday, much to the dismay of the city's religious conservatives who pressurised a reluctant Corbet into suspending Bridge in 1634.[105] The suspension prompted the godly aldermen Thomas Shipdham, Thomas Cory, Augustine Skottowe and John Toly (the same men who had instigated Bridge's initial appointment) to petition parliament for the minister's reinstatement. The remainder of the twenty-four did not support the petition however, and the godly aldermen's actions attracted strong criticism from both the corporation and the general public. The grocer Benjamin Granderge, for example, was arrested in his shop for saying publically 'that there was a great deale of dissembling & knavery amongst [the godly aldermen]'.[106] Likewise Francis Gurney and Humphrey Rowe stood accused of verbally abusing the aldermen, the former having shouted 'A turd in yor teeth, I will teach you better manners' at Shipdham in the street.[107]

In 1635, the staunch Laudian Matthew Wren replaced Corbet. Wren's attitude toward Puritanism deepened conflict within the corporate body through his fanatical pursuit of Archbishop Laud's policy of religious conformity, upsetting Puritans and religious moderates alike by his inability to compromise. Angered by the non-conformity he uncovered during the 1636 visitation of Norwich,[108] Wren suspended the practice of lay patronage to support lectureships and excommunicated William Bridge. Bridge fled to Holland as seven more non-conforming ministers were expelled from their posts.[109] Wren then turned his attention to the observation and direction of services, extraordinary ministerial preaching, and the placing and railing in of the communion table in parish churches.[110] In response, the godly mayor Thomas Baker and several aldermen penned two separate petitions to parliament complaining of what they deemed to be Wren's heavy-handed approach.[111] Whilst the

---

104 M. A. Green, ed., *CSPD, James I, 1623–25* (London, 1859), p. 246.

105 P. King, 'Bishop Wren and the Suppression of the Norwich Lecturers', *Historical Journal* 6:2 (1968), 237–238.

106 NCR 16a/20, fol. 27v, 25 October 1634.

107 NCR 16a/20, fol. 88v, January 1635.

108 The Visitation Articles for Norwich Diocese are reprinted in Kenneth Fincham, *Visitation Articles and Injunctions of the Early Stuart Church, 1625–42*, Vol. II (Woodbridge, 1998), pp. 145–50.

109 Bridge spent the next six years in Rotterdam. For more on Bridge's life see King, 'Bishop Wren', pp. 237–54.

110 Fincham, *Visitation Articles*, II, pp. 131–2, 145, 150.

111 NCR 16a/20, 1634–46, fol. 120v, 15 August 1636. The two petitions were used against Wren during his impeachment and imprisonment in 1641. See Nicholas W. S. Cranfield,

aldermen had much sympathy from fellow Puritans across the county (indeed, Wren had been denounced publically by the acerbic pen of William Prynne writing as Matthew White in 1636[112]) local support for the aldermen was less forthcoming. Nine other members of Norwich's twenty-four responded to the petitions with a separate letter to the Commons arguing that Wren could not be persecuted for simply performing the tasks required of him as a representative of the Church and the Crown.[113]

Wren was transferred to Ely after a mere three years in Norwich but, though short-lived, his incumbency had left a lasting impression on the relationship between the aldermen, the cathedral clergy, and many parish ministers.[114] There is even some suggestion, though likely exaggerated, that Wren's ministrations had encouraged some inhabitants to leave Norwich.[115] The godly aldermen refused to accept the reforms that Wren had imposed and petitioned the Long Parliament of 1640 to the effect that his dogmatism had irrevocably harmed religious practices in the diocese.[116] Wren's legacy however was not what he would have wished. Far from strengthening conformism in Norwich, adversity had only served to strengthen the Puritan's hand and, claiming the side of the opposition in the debate over the seniority in government principle – the issue that had been so divisive in 1619 – many Puritans were elected into top civic positions by their peers. Then, in 1641, the death of serving mayor Thomas Carver allowed the Puritan Adrian Parmenter to assume the post.[117]

By 1642, national events were leading the direction of local politics. With the arrest of Captain Moses Treswell, whilst he was in Norwich to muster military support for the Crown, the assembly declared in favour of parliament in the civil war. All known Catholics were placed under house arrest, the Irish refugees who had arrived the previous year were expelled, and many men (especially the poorer sorts) were pressed into military service for the parliamentary cause.[118] Later that year, the activities of the Eastern Association Committee – investigating cases of tax evasion – had led to prominent

'Wren, Matthew (1585–1667)', Oxford Dictionary of National Biography, Oxford University Press, 2004; online edn, October 2008 [http://www.oxforddnb.com/view/article/30021, accessed 7 January 2013] Matthew Wren (1585–1667): doi:10.1093/ref:odnb/30021.

[112] Prynne is generally judged to have written Newes from Ipswich (1636) under the pseudonym Matthew White: Joad Raymond, Pamphlets and Pamphleteering in Early Modern Britain (Cambridge, 2006), p. 190.

[113] Evans, Seventeenth-Century Norwich, pp. 90–1.

[114] Andrew Hopper, 'The Civil Wars', Norwich, ed. Rawcliffe and Wilson, p. 91.

[115] W. D. Macray, ed., The History of the Rebellion and Civil Wars in England begun in the year 1641 by Edward, Earl of Clarendon, Vol. I (Oxford, 1888), p. 272.

[116] Petition of the Citizens of Norwich against Bishop Wren: Assembly Book of Proceedings, 1613–42, NCR 16d/5, fol. 366r, 30 November 1640.

[117] T. Hawes, An Index to Norwich City Officers, 1453–1835 (Norwich, 1989), pp. xxiv-xxv.

[118] Mayor's Court Book, 1634–46, NCR 16a, fol. 349v; Assembly Book of Proceedings, 1642–68, NCR 16d/6, fols 2r-v, 4v.

members of Norfolk and Norwich society having weapons or horses confiscated in lieu of payment.[119] Their investigations also unearthed a number of
Crown sympathisers, findings that unfortunately coincided with a rash of stories about Cavaliers looting Norfolk villages and an influx of news books from
London that told bloody tales of Catholic plots, Irish traitors, and Cavalier
treachery.[120] Norwich's parliamentarian aldermen reacted strongly, purging
the corporation of all men suspected of royalist sympathies.

Supported by parliament, Norwich's corporation Puritans now had the ascendancy. Appointing top corporation officials to administer sequestrations,
the Bishop's Palace was appraised and its 'Goods, both library and Household
stuff ... appointed to be exposed to publick sale'. Joseph Hall, then Bishop of
Norwich, recounted with horror the actions of Sheriff Thomas Toft and Alderman Matthew Lindsey who, 'attended with many Zealous followers, came
into my Chappel to look for Superstitious pictures, and Reliques of Idolatry,
and sent for me, to let me know they found those Windows full of Images,
which were very offensive and must be demolished ... it was no other than
Tragical to relate the Carriage of that furious Sacriledge'.[121] Hall was summoned to appear before the mayor's court, charged with ordaining ministers
contrary to the covenant and, stunned by the order, declared 'when [had]
they ever heard of a Bishop of Norwich appearing before a Mayor'.[122]

The cathedral was not the only religious building in Norwich to become
a victim of iconoclastic fervour. In 1644, the corporation had appointed a
committee led by civic officials, including Toft and Lindsey who, along with
Samuel Puckle, Livewell Sherwood and John Greenwood, had visited Norwich's parishes to 'take the names of all such persons as can give any information ... of scandalous ministers' and to 'take notice of such scandalous
pictures, crucifixes, and images, as are yet remaining in the same churches,
and demolish, or cause them to be demolished'.[123] Toft, Lindsay and Greenwood ordered paintings taken from the churches and cathedral to be burned,
including artwork from St Swithin's church that was first paraded through the
city streets in a mockery of a religious procession before it went up in flames.[124]
Surviving churchwarden accounts reveal how at least eight churches had to
employ glasiers to repair windows and workman to remove 'idolatrous images

119 Evans, *Seventeenth-Century Norwich*, p. 125.
120 Anon, *Foure Wonderfull, Bloudy and Dangerous Plots Discovered: From Norwich* (London, 1642) cited in Hopper, *Civil Wars*, pp. 94, 499.
121 Joseph Hall, *Hard Measure* (London, 1689), pp. 15–16. Published in 1689, the text
had been written in 1647.
122 Hall, *Hard Measure*, p. 15. For more on iconoclasm in eastern England during this period, see J. Walter, 'Popular Iconoclasm and the Politics of the Parish in Eastern England,
1640–42', *The Historical Journal* 47:2 (2004), 261–90.
123 Blomefield, *Topographical History*, III:I, pp. 389–90. See also Trevor Cooper, ed., *The
Journal of William Dowsing: Iconoclasm in East Anglia during the English Civil War* (Woodbridge, 2001), pp. 119–20.
124 Cooper, *Journal of William Dowsing*, p. 121.

and popish trash', take down communion rails and level the chancels after the committee had finished its work.[125]

The already tense situation reached new heights at Christmas 1645. On Christmas Eve, mayor Matthew Peckover, a man who also played a leading role on the sequestrations committee, ordered all businesses to open as normal on Christmas Day and all special services to be cancelled. Many people closed their shops as normal in defiance of the order and the anonymous *Vox Populi, or the Voice of the People*, published shortly afterwards, attacked the twenty-four, accusing them of attempting to establish a Presbyterian ministry in the city.[126]

Over the next two years problems began to spiral out of control. In 1647, Norwich was revisited by the plague, and hard on its heels was a great flood that devastated the low-lying central wards. That winter's unusually severe storms must have appeared to the inhabitants as portents of disaster. In the midst of deep snows, a group of apprentices presented a petition to mayor John Utting, entreating the reinstatement of Christmas Day celebrations that, officially at least, were banned.[127] The appeal of observing a traditional festivity in the midst of a long and demoralizing winter had much popular support, but was furiously rejected by the corporation Puritans. The incident set into motion a string of events that were to culminate in the most dramatic, yet short-lived, riot in Norwich that century: the Great Blow.[128] The circumstances of the riot will be discussed in detail in the final chapter, suffice to say here that the incident provided the excuse for corporation parliamentarians to purge anyone suspected of harbouring royalist sympathies from the council (despite the fact that the riot was not ostensibly a royalist uprising).

The civil war period also had dramatic repercussions for the local economy. Prices of basic goods reached at an all time high, and many staple goods were simply unavailable. The city's records reveal how supplies of coal were disrupted between 1643 and 1645, with a total absence of the all-important fuel source during the 1644 siege of Newcastle.[129] Prices skyrocketed. In 1635, the corporation had been able to purchase a chaldron of coal for fifteen shillings to heat the city's hospitals; by 1643, one chaldron of coal was worth fifty

---

[125] Ibid., pp. 367–9.

[126] Anon, *Vox Populi, or the Voice of the People* (London, 1646). See also the response to *Vox Populi*: BL, Thomason E.358[4], Anon, *An Hue-and-Cry after Vox Populi, or an Answer to Vox Diaboli and Vox Norwici* (London, 1646). For information see D. Zaret, *Origins of Democratic Culture: Printing, Petitions, and the Public Sphere in Early-Modern England* (Princeton, 2000), p. 238.

[127] Blomefield, *Topographical History*, III:I, p. 393.

[128] The main sources of information about the riot are Depositions relating to the Great Blow, NCR12 C (1) 1648, and a pamphlet published shortly after the event, BL, Thomason Tracts E438(6), Anon, *A true relation of the late great Mutinie* (London, 1648).

[129] Many of the city's institutions relied on coal as their main source of fuel. The accounts of the Boy's Hospital, for example, show a total lack of coal purchased during 1644–5: NCR 25f fols 40r-46r.

shillings.[130] Brewers, long dependent on coal as their fuel source and who provided most ordinary people with their staple beverage, were forced to depend on less efficient furze and wood for energy. An excise tax, which had been imposed on staple goods including meat and beer since 1643, compounded the problem. The fuel shortage and the tax proved catastrophic for the city's poorest inhabitants, and of course, the local butchers and brewers. Resistance to the excise tax had erupted in November 1646 when many inhabitants, encouraged by the irate butchers and brewers, took to the streets in protest. The economic situation only gradually improved over the course of the 1650s.

Although the corporation had remained steadfastly loyal to parliament throughout the Protectorate, after Charles II was restored to the throne they were quick to demonstrate their loyalty to the new monarch. The final parliamentarian mayor of the Protectorate years, the staunch Independent William Davy, was ejected in early 1661 along with his fellow pro-parliamentarian aldermen Robert Allen, John Andrews, Thomas Ashwell and William Rye, in accordance with the King's wishes that the corporation 'restore such as had been removed' and 'proceed to new elections of others in their places ... as in your discretion you shall think most fit for our service', referring of course to the vacant positions left by the ejected officers.[131] Charles' letter to the corporation followed the issue of the 'Act for the Well Governing and Regulating of the Corporations' which ensured 'that the succession in such corporations may be most probably perpetuated in the hands of persons well affected to His Majesty and the established Government',[132] and granted Charles emergency powers to intervene in local affairs directly from December 1661 until 1663.[133] Notwithstanding the fact that this was exactly the type of intervention the corporation had always traditionally resisted, the remaining aldermen were keen to please, writing back to the King, telling him how 'their spirits were much cheered by the princely regard set forth in his letter', and confirming that the 'five aldermen unduly elected were put out, the only one living of the five removed for loyalty was restored, and four faithful subjects put in'.[134] The corporation also extended their newfound compliance to religious matters: in the November of that year the assembly agreed to bring to an end the lectureship of the non-conformist Thomas Allen.[135]

---

[130] Prewar figures are from the accounts of the Boy's Hospital for 1634–35, NCR 25f, fols 22r-25r. Blomefield noted the increase in coal prices to fifty shillings a chaldron in 1643. Blomefield, *Topographical History*, III:I, p. 385.

[131] M. A. Everett Green, *CSPD, Charles II, 1660–1* (London, 1860), p. 481. King Charles at Whitehall to the City of Norwich, 21 January 1661.

[132] Charles II, 1661: An Act for the well Governing and Regulating of Corporations: John Raithby, ed., *Statutes of the Realm 1628–80* (1819), pp. 321–3.

[133] The act's implementation rested on the individual efforts of local commissioners and little, if any, evidence remains of their visits. Evans, *Seventeenth-Century Norwich*, p. 238.

[134] Mayor and Aldermen of Norwich to the King, 25 February 1661: Green, *CSPD, Charles II, 1660–1*, p. 515.

[135] Assembly Book of Proceedings, 1642–68, NCR 16d/6, fol. 223r, 6 November 1661.

The corporation proved less willing to submit to Charles' demands when these involved making changes to the city's charter of incorporation however. After it became clear that Charles wished to substantially remodel its terms, including scaling back many liberties established from time out of mind, negotiations between the Crown and the corporation broke down. In May 1661 the aldermen had sent a strongly worded petition to Charles explaining that as everyone disaffected towards the King had already been purged from office, there was no need to alter the corporation's rights to nominate candidates in either aldermanic or council elections.[136] After a series of protracted and sometimes tense negotiations, the corporation were happy to welcome a relatively unscathed charter back to the city in 1663.[137]

In 1671 Charles II and Queen Catherine made a progress to Norwich. It had been almost a century since the last royal visit and Norwich's inhabitants welcomed the King with all the pomp and circumstance they could muster.[138] Town clerk Thomas Corie described how

> at the bounds of the city liberties, [the king] was met by the Mayor, Sheriffs and Aldermen ... the Bishop, and the Dean and Chapter ... and likewise the Lord Henry Howard with his coaches. His Majesty was ... so conducted through the Militia of the City, ranked on both sides the streets, to the Duke's Palace, the passages being thronged with incredible numbers of people. About two hours after, the Queen also arrived, attended by several ladies of the chiefest quality of her court ... And at eight in the evening, both their Majesties, together with the whole court, which was very numerous, were treated with a magnificent supper, in a very large room, beautifully illuminated with wax Flambeaux. The next day, having visited the Cathedral and Bishop's Palace, and being everywhere attended with the loud acclamations of the people, their Majesties were treated by the City with a glorious Banquet at the New Hall; and before the King parted from the City, he conferred the honour of Knighthood upon the famous Physician, Dr. Thomas Brown.[139]

Corie's description painted a picture of a city united in celebration of the Crown but the following year, after Charles' Declaration of Indulgence suspended penal laws against Catholics and Dissenters and licensed their private worship, the corporation – who were by majority Anglican – reviled the Declaration publically, criticising the King's use of his prerogative in ecclesiastical matters. They demanded the reinstatement of the laws against Dissenters and summoned all known Dissenters to take a public oath of allegiance to

[136] M. A. Everett Green, *CSPD, Charles II, 1661–2* (London, 1861), p. 608. Petition from the Mayor and Aldermen of Norwich to the King, May 1661. The original petition does not survive.

[137] Evans, *Seventeenth-Century Norwich*, p. 242–3. Evans suggests that the freemen's rights to nominate candidates after 1663 were better than they had been for the previous forty years.

[138] Elizabeth I had progressed to Norwich in 1578.

[139] Dawson Turner, ed., *Narrative of the Visit of His Majesty King Charles II to Norwich in the September of the Year 1671* (Yarmouth, 1846), pp. 8–9.

the Anglican Church.[140] Bowing under public pressure, including that from Norwich, Charles revoked the Declaration in March 1673. From 1674 he began to withdraw public support for Dissenting congregations, seeking instead favour with High Church Anglicans. In Norwich, as elsewhere, the change in direction led to resistance amongst those who had been offered a brief glimmer of religious toleration. Town clerk Corie wrote to then Secretary of State, Sir Joseph Williamson, describing the winter riots the revocation had inspired

> by reason of the meetings of very great numbers of people at two conventicles of the Presbiterians and Independents in places called the Granaries of this City; the first wer on Sunday the sixth instant; and wer convicted ... before Mr Maior and two other Justices of the peace, but now warrant issued for the levying of the penalties (the said Justices hopeing they would forbeare anie further meetings publically). But not withstandinge this tender and prudent forbearance, upon Sunday last the 13th instant, ther wer twoe other meetinges of the said parties, both in the fore-noone, and the after-noone, in greater numbers than at the first meeting; and the said John Faucet disturbinge the meetinge of the Presbiterians in the after-noone, was violently assaulted, beaten and troden on by severall rude persons, and in great danger of his lyffe, being pursued into the streets by some hundreds of people who cryed out fall on, knocke the rogue on the head...[141]

Corie blamed the Presbyterians for the disturbances. In his opinion they were 'valuing themselves much upon his Majestyes ... promise (as they say) of Liberty of Meeting' and had, since the Declaration's inception, assumed their right to assemble.[142] The corporation by necessity supressed the riots but it seems there was much sympathy for the rioter's aims, if not their methods, amongst Norwich's citizens. This proclivity deepened over the next two to three years as a steady flow of Dissenters gained important civic positions, a number which included the conventicler Robert Cooke, who became sheriff in 1674, and John Levington who became a councilman in 1675. The ascendancy of Dissenters in high office ensured that the suppression of dissenting meetings and conventicles gained little momentum.[143] By the late 1670s however, all this had changed.

The close relationship between city, county, and state politics was never more apparent than during times of crisis. As Crown and parliament dealt with the escalation of the events commonly referred to as the Exclusion Crisis, Robert Paston, Viscount Yarmouth, Lord Lieutenant for Norfolk, and a fervent Tory and Anglican, resolved to overturn the political rise of Whigs and Dissenters in Norwich. A friend of the King, a firm believer in the royal prerogative, and a passionate defender of the Anglican faith, Paston became

---

140 Assembly Book of Proceedings, 1668–1707, NCR 16d/8, fol. 36v, 3 May 1673.
141 Hill, *Correspondence of Thomas Corie*, p. 36.
142 Ibid., p. 37.
143 Evans, *Seventeenth-Century Norwich*, p. 250.

the figurehead for Norwich's Anglican-Tory faction. When the death of Norwich MP Christopher Jay forced a local by-election in late 1677, Paston seized the opportunity to promote his own son, William, as a candidate. The predominantly Whig aldermen, led by Mayor John Richer – a man as equally devoted to the non-conformist cause as Paston was to the Anglican – countered with the nomination of his own candidate, the moderate Anglican Augustine Briggs.[144] An intensive five-month campaign period ensued during which time the corporation Whigs were aided by the influential ex-MP for Norfolk Lord Townshend of Raynham Hall and John Hobart of Blickling. Just before Christmas 1677, John Doughty – Paston's agent in Norwich – updated his employer about the activities of the 'Raynham and Blickling Caball' as he called them, telling Paston how the 'strange stratagems and tricks' the 'Caball' employed to manipulate the voters had backfired. 'My Lord Towneshend sent his Secretary Phillipps to Norwich this week' Doughty wrote, 'to blow the coals, who is as much railed at as can be wished, a true reward for his industry. The Mayor has been very false and base as well as one of his brethren who was very little suspected as well as sufficiently obliged to the contrary. The common people are in a rage against them both for it.' Doughty was also pleased to report that 'there are a great many honest persons who are extra-ordinarily active and honest to your concern'.[145]

This was probably no exaggeration as, despite resistance from within the top ranks of the corporation, many of Norwich's ordinary inhabitants and citizens had pledged to support Paston. That Paston had popular support was evident in November 1677 when he and his son visited Norwich to be 'met and conducted by such a number of citizens, not to name the gentry' and accompanied by 'great shouts and acclamations that were given at the three great places of the city'.[146] Robert Paston asserted that opposition was limited to a minority 'who infect a party with anti-monarchical principles',[147] writing to his wife of his fervent belief that 'his son will come in nobly' at the forthcoming election.[148] The corporation's obvious underhand tactics (including the admission of an additional three-hundred freemen to swing the vote in favour of Briggs in January 1678) did little to win them public support. William Paston was elected with 2,163 votes, his opponent gaining only 672.

---

[144] Briggs refused to stand against Paston, so on the day of the election the Presbyterian alderman Mark Cockey stood in his place. Evans, *Seventeenth-Century Norwich*, p. 258.

[145] John Doughty to William Paston, 21 December 1677: Historical Manuscripts Commission (hereafter HMC), *Sixth Report of the Historical Manuscripts Commission* (London, 1877), p. 384.

[146] John Hildeyard to Lady Yarmouth, 28 November 1677: HMC, *Sixth Report*.

[147] Paston further added 'I am in quest of them all, and shall, as far as his Majesty commands, be ever ready to serve and obey him'. Lord Yarmouth to Secretary Williamson, 8 February 1677: F. H. Blackburne Daniell, ed., *CSPD, Charles II 1677–8* (London, 1911), p. 634.

[148] Lord Yarmouth to his wife, 28 November 1677: HMC, *Sixth Report*, p. 384.

Support for the Whigs in Norwich did not end with the election, if anything, their loss led to local rivalries becoming even more embittered and entrenched. Immediately after the city election Sir John Hobart had written to William Windham at Felbrigg expressing his belief that 'before I left [th] e Countrey what I am since more confirmed in, That [th]e battle must be fought over againe'.[149] Likewise, Robert Paston did not become complacent after the election but devoted himself instead to finding ways of removing Whiggish or Dissenting aldermen from civic office. In a telling letter to Secretary Williamson, Paston wrote

> I beseech you to inform his Majesty with all speed that the Mayor and most of the Aldermen at Norwich are actually out of their employment by not subscribing according to the Act for regulating corporations. This put an opportunity into my hands to make that city the loyalest in England. I only desire a speedy order from you to communicate to the freemen to proceed to a new election, which will weed out 10 or 12 notorious ill-affected men to the Government and confirm the honest ones, and make such a supply as will be highly for his Majesty's service and an excellent example to this country.[150]

Paston's investigation into corporation legalities instigated a protracted argument between the Privy Council and Mayor Richer, which came to be known as the case of the 'New Elected Aldermen', the result of which was that fifteen aldermen found themselves eligible for re-election. Mayor Richer won few county allies during the battle, even 'the Duke of Norfolk swears he will undo the Mayor of Norwich; and truly if by letter from the King, or otherwise as law shall appoint, he were turned out of his mayoralty, it would be for the safety of the King and country, for he is the impudentest fanatic in the world'.[151]

Paston might have been fooled into thinking that he had won, but the subsequent election did not result in his sought after Tory majority. The two major wards of Wymer and Mancroft were unmistakably Anglican and pro-Tory strongholds, yet Conesford and Over-The-Water returned Whigs and non-conformists in this, and other, elections across the period.[152] On arriving in the city in August 1681, Norwich cathedral's new dean, Humphrey Prideaux, quickly noted 'the two factions, Whigs and Tories', observing that of the two 'the former are the more numerous, but the latter carry all

[149] Family and Estate Papers of the Ketton-Cremer Family of Felbrigg Hall, WKC 7/6/17. Sir John Hobart to Sir William Windham, 1 March 1678.
[150] Lord Yarmouth to Secretary Williamson, 15 March 1678: Blackburne Daniell, *CSPD*, 1678, p. 34.
[151] Lord Yarmouth to his wife, 21 January 1677: HMC, *Sixth Report*, p. 385.
[152] Mark Knights, 'London Petitions and Parliamentary Politics in 1679', *Parliamentary History* 12:1 (1993), 29–46, 41–2 and Mark Knights, 'London's "Monster" Petition of 1680', *Historical Journal* 36:1 (1993), 39–67, 61–3. For more on the political landscape of Norwich see Mark Knights, *Representation and Misrepresentation in Britain: Partisanship and Political Culture* (Oxford, 2006).

before them as consisteing of the governeing part of the town, and both con-
tend for their way with the utmost violence'.[153] Prideaux's comments draw
attention to the ascendancy of the Anglican-Tory faction that cannot be
entirely attributed to Paston's efforts, but also those of the Crown. Issuing
strict guidelines to control the Whig press, Charles' actions signalled a shift
in Crown sentiment from Whig to Tory. Determined to make changes to
Norwich's charter that would allow him to intervene in corporation appointments (which he had failed to do in 1663), he instructed the corporation to
surrender their charter for review. The order encountered fierce resistance
from inhabitants of all political persuasions because, as we have already seen,
the document symbolised all that the urban dwellers held dear: the city's
ancient rights and liberties. At least nine hundred people signed a petition
against the surrender, and those people who had organised the petition and
collected the signatures were arrested.[154] Nevertheless, the magistrates had
great trouble in finding anybody willing to testify because

> no person appeared to make good a charge against any member of this Court to be
> an encourager or abetter of the petition ... as Captain Helwys promised this day
> to make good his charge of last Saturday against several persons of this Court but
> did not, nor any of the persons examined the last Saturday in Court affirm that
> any of the Aldermen did encourage the promotion of the petition, but absolutely
> denied the same.[155]

The inhabitants' unwillingness to bow to Crown pressure did not stop the
King from achieving his goal and a new charter was issued in April 1683, one
that effectively granted Charles control over corporation appointments. Robert Paston's goal of unseating the Whigs had been realised, but he never lived
to see the fruits of his labour, dying shortly before the charter was released in
the midst of Tory infighting over the election of his son, William, to the office
of city recorder.[156]

The Whigs had effectively been removed from positions of authority and –
with the exception of a contested mayoral election in 1686 – it appeared that
the Tories had gained the upper hand.[157] It was not to last. Between 1687 and

[153] E. M. Thompson, ed., *Letters of Humphrey Prideaux to John Ellis, 1674–1722* XV
(1875), p. 90.

[154] W. Rye, ed., *Depositions Taken Before the Mayor and Aldermen of Norwich 1549–1567
& Extracts from the Court Books of the City of Norwich 1666–1668* (Norwich, 1905), p. 167,
28 June 1682.

[155] Rye, *Depositions*, p. 167, 5 July 1682.

[156] Evans, *Seventeenth-Century Norwich*, p. 262. Paston died on 8 March 1683, one month
before the charter was released to Norwich and his son became city recorder. See Norwich
Assembly Minute Books 1668–1707, NCR 16d/8, fol. 106v, 1 April 1684.

[157] John Wrench, a Whig alderman who had lost his place in the 1678 corporation purge,
had popular support in 1686. In a bold and calculated move to fix the election, Wrench
was put forward as a mayoral nominee alongside the unpopular Robert Bendish, with the
intention that there would be no choice but to elect Wrench. The plan backfired when

1688 the Crown led the country's corporations through some seismic political shifts. James II, in an about turn from his brother's pro-Tory stance, began to court the country's Whigs by packing parliament, regulating corporation membership and, dedicated to promoting Catholic interests, by preparing the way to a repeal of the Test Acts. All officers of parliamentary corporations were requested to answer three questions in support of the promulgation of the Declaration of Indulgence and the planned Test Act repeal.[158] Then, on 30 March 1688, James ordered Norwich's corporation to remove ten aldermen and nineteen councilmen to change the balance of power within the Tory majority civic government, and Whig John Wrench – who had been ousted from power during the reshuffles earlier in the decade – was elected as the city's next mayor.[159]

By the summer of 1688 the tide of public opinion had turned against James' pro-Whig agenda. Rumours of an impending Dutch invasion fleet forced James to seek support from the spurned Tories and, in a surprisingly see-through volte-face, James abolished the ecclesiastical commission, ordered the pre-1683 corporation charters to be resurrected nationwide, and issued orders to muster county militias and urban trained bands to deal with the Dutch threat. On the latter point, Norfolk was spectacularly lax, contemporary reports suggesting that Norfolk's recruitment figures were some of the lowest in the country.[160] Norwich received James' writ to restore the city's charter on the twenty-ninth of October 1688.[161]

On 1 December 1688, the openly Catholic Duke of Norfolk was welcomed warmly by Norwich's inhabitants as he rode into the city to declare for a free parliament following the collapse of James' government,[162] but only a week later Norwich's Catholic population, who had enjoyed a brief moment of freedom after James' Declaration of Indulgence in 1687, were forced into hiding as Norwich's inhabitants rioted, burned Catholic houses and pulled down the recently erected Catholic chapel (notoriously located in the city granaries, the scene of the 1674 Presbyterian riots).[163] The troubles continued for a whole month. On the fifteenth the mayor ordered 'that all housekeepers do keep in their servants and children so that they do not join with the tumult that disturb the peace of the City ... And that such persons as

the Privy Council ordered the selection of new candidates. Wrench resigned his position as alderman in protest. Evans, Seventeenth-Century Norwich, p. 310.

[158] The King's right to dispense with the Test Act was affirmed in the Court of King's Bench by the case of Arthur Godden v. Sir Edward Hales in 1686.

[159] Order of King James to the Norwich corporation from the Earl of Sunderland, 30 March 1688: Norwich Assembly Minute Books 1668–1707, NCR, 16d/8, fol. 139r-v. See also notes in MS 453, entry 30 March 1688.

[160] Steve Pincus, 1688: The First Modern Revolution (Yale, 2009), pp. 230–1.

[161] Rye, Depositions, p. 186, 15 December 1688.

[162] B. Cozens-Hardy, ed., Norfolk Lieutenancy Journal, 1676–1701 (Norwich, 1961), pp. 94–5.

[163] Evans, Seventeenth-Century Norwich, p. 316 and MS 453, 7 December 1688.

shall hereafter meet in a tumultuous manner as heretofore hath been done shall be apprehended and proceeded against with the utmost severity of law'.[164] On the twenty-second, one Jaspar Butler was indicted at the Sessions for 'entering the house of Edward Tompson and opening the doors and letting in the rabble', as was Robert Hargate for 'committing several riots'.[165] Robert Paston's work to fill the corporation with Tory men loyal to the King was all but forgotten.

William and Mary were crowned in April 1689 and the change of monarch had profound consequences on Norwich's politics. Many of the city's Tories were sympathetic to the Jacobite cause and inhabitants from all walks of life had strong views on the issue.[166] In March 1689, for example, Edmond Nockalls was arrested for uttering seditious words against Phillip Stebbing, an Anglican and radical Tory who had been mayor in 1687,[167] and the House of Commons heard how Catholics had purportedly set fire to a house.[168] That September, Robert Poynter was arrested for spreading rumours of an imminent Jacobite invasion against the 'imposters' William and Mary, adding that 'he would rather be under [th]e power of the Devill than under [th]e Presbeterian Government'.[169] Two months later, John Scrimpson was arrested for announcing that King William was the 'sone of a whore by God' during a drunken alehouse toasting session.[170] In 1693, magistrates drew up a list of all 'disaffected troublemakers' known in the city, and concluded that at least 'the eighth part of this city is ill-affected to [th]e government'.[171] As Mark Knights suggests, from 1689 until 1714, 'politics in Norwich was hard fought between two parties ideologically opposed about the nature of the Revolution settlement in church and state'.[172]

The 1630s, 1640s and the 1680s stand out as decades of particular instability in Norwich's social, economic, political and religious history. The city's problems were frequently representative of those taking place at a national level but reconstructed through sets of concerns particular to local inhabitants. Norwich's story thus provides an important window into seventeenth-century urban life, culture, society, and politics outside of London. Certainly, Norwich's 'vibrant, exuberant, partisan and sometimes violent' political scene vividly reveals the impact of the century's social and political

---

164 Rye, *Depositions*, p. 186, 15 December 1688.

165 Ibid., p. 186, 22 December 1688.

166 Mark Knights, 'Politics, 1660–1835', *Norwich*, ed. Rawcliffe and Wilson, pp. 167–92, 171.

167 Norwich City Quarter Sessions Interrogations and Depositions, NCR, 12a-b, The information of John Mard and Phillip Barthe against Edmond Nockalls, 5 March 1689.

168 Pincus, *1688*, p. 266.

169 NCR 12a-b, The information of William Symonds of St Gyles, Grocer, 12 September 1689.

170 NCR 12b/1, The information of Zachariah Mulyew, 4 November 1689.

171 Knights, 'Politics', p. 171.

172 Ibid., p. 172.

upheavals at first hand, and provides an intimate insight into the formulation and reception of the debates that helped shape English politics, culture and mentalities across the century.[173]

III

The sources that inform this book are the records left by the urban corporation and people of Norwich. They include the city's numerous administrative records and accounts, correspondence with the Crown and Privy Council, and maps, but also the rich and well-preserved records of the city's secular and religious courts, in the form of the city and county sessions, mayoral court and the court of the Norwich Diocese.[174] The appeal of Norwich's religious and secular records lies in the fact that they survive for the whole period in almost continuous succession.[175] With the notable exceptions of Susan Amussen, Paul Griffiths, and Robert Tittler, few early-modern social historians have explicitly published on Norwich's seventeenth century records, or placed the church records in context with their secular counterparts, usually choosing to approach one or the other.[176] This monograph however explores civic and religious sources in conjunction in the hope of presenting a balanced and wide-ranging study. Church court records, for example, contain cases of a moral and religious nature, such as defamation, and they preference deponents from the middling sorts – and to an extent, women – whereas secular court records encompass a wider social spectrum and range of issues. Though largely representing the views of the city's governing class (these were the people responsible for making and keeping the records), enough remains of poorer to middling inhabitants' voices in court depositions to gain some insight into these people's lives. Placing religious and secular court records together, alongside non-criminal records, such as the civic records of the city corporation, builds a rounded impression of city life and a way of mitigating the formulaic method of recording evidence though quantitative analysis.

From the court records, the depositions have been particularly rewarding, for they contain something of the original voices and speeches of Norwich's

---

[173] Ibid., p. 168.

[174] For information on the workings of the court, see A. Tarver, *Church Court Records: An Introduction for Family and Local Historians* (Chichester, 1995) or D. Spaeth, *The Church in an Age of Danger: Parsons and Parishioners, 1660–1740* (Cambridge, 2000).

[175] The mayor's court and county quarter sessions records survive almost in entirety for the whole of the seventeenth century, and the church courts are complete with the exception of the civil war period. Piecemeal entries survive for the latter between 1641 and 1647, but between 1647 and 1661 the courts were suspended. The city sessions are fragmentary.

[176] See, for example, P. Griffiths, 'Masterless Young People in Norwich, 1560–1645', *The Experience of Authority in Early Modern England*, ed. P. Griffiths, A. Fox, and S. Hindle (Basingstoke, 1996), pp. 146–187; S. Amussen, *An Ordered Society: Gender and Class in Early Modern England* (Oxford, 1988); Tittler, *The Face of the City*.

inhabitants who gave detailed eyewitness accounts of life in the city's streets, markets, drinking houses, shops, and homes. Frozen in time, the depositions offer a close lens into inhabitants' lives as they shouted, cursed, argued, traded, shopped, worked, drank, entertained and relaxed. Studying these everyday and perhaps seemingly unimportant events does more than just provide a picture of early-modern life: their study illustrates the innumerable avenues that created and informed urban inhabitants' identities, communities and networks. As James C. Scott argued, it is the everyday stories and encounters that impart the potential of human agency in constructing, navigating, and informing life experiences, whether in the negotiation of power relations as Scott intended, or in the shaping of locational identities.[177]

Thus the statements of witnesses and compurgators offer a way in to how contemporaries thought about the places and people around them. The depositions of witnesses in defamation cases or eyewitness accounts of crimes, for example, are rich in details and colloquialisms. Whilst much of the detail, such as a wordy description of where a defamatory speech took place rather than simply giving a street name, appears anachronistic at first, these colloquial and regionally specific descriptive devices are imperative to understanding how early-modern people framed their immediate environment. References to place frequently followed a formulaic pattern, suggesting a shared understanding and specific localised knowledge known only to local inhabitants. Phrases such as 'upon the open ground in the parish of'; 'under the leades of the Guildhall'; at the 'office' of Richard Grix' brewery; 'a cockey adjoining the backside of Dr How's house';[178] or at the 'Shepperds Bing' are valid only within the frame of reference of that particular parish, or city, and allow a valuable insight into contemporary perceptual signifiers. Used with caution, these records are an inimitable resource about urban dwellers and their relationship with the places they inhabited.

---

[177] James C. Scott, *Weapons of the Weak: Everyday Forms of Peasant Resistance* (New Haven, 1985), p. 29.
[178] DN/DEP/45/48b, fol. 79v, 17 September 1640. Loveday v. Fuller; DN/DEP 47/51, fol. 43, September 1664. Harding v. Wade; NCR, Case 6a/2, no. 23, 20 November 1694; NCR, Case 6a/3, no. 11, 3 May 1710, and NCR, Case 6a/4, no. 12, 21 March 1712.

1

The City and the Parish

... The images by which cities were represented ... while these images were by no means fully accurate reflections of how urban life was carried on ... played crucial roles in establishing urban identity.[1]

Seventeenth-century people were familiar with the convention of communicating ideas through visual symbolism. Images were regularly used in place of words in a society where many people were illiterate or poorly educated: in shop signs in the streets, in woodcuts illustrating pamphlets or ballads, in pictures painted across the walls of alehouses. Even for the reading public, a symbol or a picture could convey far more than a few words. Monarchs had long capitalised on the premise that promoting the correct image in art was a form of self-propaganda.[2] Take Van Dyke's series of portraits of Charles I during the 1630s for example. Picturing Charles on horseback in *Charles I with M. de S. Antoine* or the *Equestrian Painting of Charles I*, for instance, the artist expressed with classical styling the centuries of socio-political thought that fed into the ideal of divine right kingship. Such paintings communicated messages to both the educated and uneducated eye, from recognised classical artistic conventions and allusions, to a simple message of power and authority. In just the same way, maps could be appropriated as a propaganda device.

Early maps were commonly presented in the form of a prospect or profile. Elaborately decorated, urban prospects had become fashionable in Europe, especially Italy, during the 1470s.[3] They were created using a combination of surveying techniques, artistic skill and observation; then engraved and reproduced in the ever-increasing diversity of printed materials that included geographies, travel writing, didactic texts, local histories, *emblemata* and

---

1 Martha C. Howell, 'The Spaces of Late Medieval Urbanity', *Shaping Urban Identity in Late Medieval Europe*, ed. Marc Boone and Peter Stabel (Leuven/Apeldoorn, 2000), pp. 3–24, 3.
2 For a good introduction to the topic, see Kevin Sharpe, *Selling the Tudor Monarchy: Authority and Image in Sixteenth Century England* (Yale, 2009); Louis Montrose, *The Subject of Elizabeth: Authority, Gender, and Representation* (Chicago, 2006); or Roy Strong, *The Cult of Elizabeth: Elizabethan Portraiture and Pageantry* (Berkeley, 1977).
3 Peter Barber, *The Map Book* (London, 2005), p. 86.

cosmographia. Print expanded the possibilities for budding cartographers to explore the science and many urban maps were replicated in this format.[4] The armchair voyeur no longer had to rely on tales of far-flung cities but could indulge his passion as if he himself were arriving at the city gates.

During the late sixteenth and seventeenth centuries, corporation governments increasingly recognised the value of maps as tools to be manipulated for the purposes of propaganda. An expensive luxury though they may have been, maps were nonetheless understood as a creative device that enabled mapmakers and commissioners to project an image, or a message of their own choosing. This type of self-promotion was nothing new; corporation officials had commonly used symbolic conventions in civic ceremonies and dress to advertise their wealth and authority.[5] Maps played an important part in the process of propagandising 'a form of political discourse concerned with the acquisition and maintenance of power' by advertising territorial boundaries, natural resources, and architectural achievements in a way that traditional methods of self-aggrandisement failed to do.[6] By commissioning and creating a map, urban governors became involved in manufacturing the place that map represented, imbuing it with their own values, preferred identity and history to an audience.[7] Indeed, to control the image of the city was to help control the city itself, as the process of 'shaping spatial form' grounded, as well as communicated, governmental authority.[8] The following section explores how Norwich was represented over the late sixteenth and seventeenth centuries in cartography, keeping in mind the underlying contemporary significance of imagery and symbolism, to explore how far maps were in fact

[4] Thomas Frangenberg, 'Chorographies of Florence: The Use of City Views and City Plans in the Sixteenth Century', *Imago Mundi* 46 (1994), 41–64, 42.

[5] For more on this see R. Tittler, *Architecture and Power: the Town Hall and the English Urban Community, c. 1500–1640* (Oxford, 1991) or 'Civic Portraiture and Political Culture: English Provincial Towns, c.1560–1640', *Journal of British Studies* 37 (1998), 306–29.

[6] J. Brian Harley, 'Silences and Secrecy: The Hidden Agenda of Cartography in Early-Modern Europe', *Imago Mundi* 40 (1988), 57–76, 57. See also James Ferguson and Akhil Gupta, 'Spatializing States: Toward an Ethnography of Neoliberal Governmentality', *American Ethnologist* 29:4 (2002), 981–1002, 981 and Richard Helgerson, 'The Land Speaks: Cartography, Chorography, and Subversion in Renaissance England', *Representations* 16 (1986), 50–85, 71–5. Helgerson suggests that towards the end of the sixteenth and the beginning of the seventeenth centuries, maps increasingly represented loyalty to a *place* or *land*, rather than to a specific monarch. He connects this cartographic change to wider ideological shifts about monarchy and the rise of national identity.

[7] Catherine Delano Smith, 'Cartographic Signs on European Maps and Their Explanation Before 1700', *Imago Mundi* 37 (1985), 9–29, 11 and Frangenberg, 'Chorographies of Florence', esp. 44.

[8] Michael Biggs, 'Putting the State on the Map: Cartography, Territory, and State Formation', *Comparative Studies in Society and History* 41:2 (1999), 374–405, 376; Daniel Lord Smail, *Imaginary Cartographies: Possession and Identity in Medieval Marseille* (Ithaca: Cornell University Press, 1999), p. xii.

projections of the mental map of the commissioner(s) who appropriated the power of cartography for their own ends.

The timeframe for the following discussion extends before and beyond the seventeenth century with good reason. The first map to be discussed, for instance, will be the Cuningham Prospect, published in 1559. Although published before the seventeenth century, it had a great influence on the direction of Norwich cartography for generations: the prospect forming the baseline for all subsequent maps produced of the city until 1696. The representation of Norwich as conveyed in this prospect was the most enduring image of the city that the public of England and Europe would have seen. Moving into the early years of the eighteenth century, the style and content of maps created then could arguably be considered to represent something of the ideas and aspirations of those people who lived through the final years of the previous century.

Cartography and the Imagined City

By the mid-sixteenth century, the corporation of Norwich had been involved in the creation of some of the earliest urban maps to be commissioned in England. In 1541, for example, the painter Thomas Boswell had been paid 6s 8d to correct a map detailing places of sanctuary within the city's boundaries. This bird's eye view, known today simply as the Sanctuary Map, is the first surviving example of Norwich's involvement in cartographic ventures.[9] Interest in cartography accelerated over the next few decades and by 1571 the corporation were employing a salaried surveyor, in the form of citizen John Goodwin. The appointment led to great things for Goodwin, as his work caught the eye of Elizabeth I who subsequently appointed him as her special surveyor.[10] By the 1580s, two maps were a permanent feature of Norwich's council chamber and the office of chief surveyor to the city continued into and throughout the seventeenth century.[11]

The man commonly credited with the creation of Norwich's first prospect – and the earliest surviving prospect of an English regional city – was William Cuningham.[12] Cuningham was a Cambridge educated physician, who

[9] Christopher Barringer, 'The Changing Face of Norwich', *Norwich Since 1550*, ed. Carole Rawcliffe and Richard Wilson (London, 2004), pp. 1–34, 3.

[10] Isla Fay, *Health and Disease in Medieval and Tudor Norwich* (University of East Anglia Ph.D Thesis, unpub., 2007), p. 7.

[11] Chamberlains' Account Book, NCR 18a, 1580–9, fol. 125. Peter Eden suggests that working opportunities for the early-modern surveyor were piecemeal. Their 'bread and butter' were estate surveys, so to be appointed to survey a city by a corporation or great magnate was the ideal situation: Peter Eden, 'Land Surveyors in Norfolk, 1550–1850', *Norfolk Archaeology* 35 (1970), 474–81, 474.

[12] The practice of cartography in England lagged behind that of Europe, where it was already an established field. For a comprehensive introduction to English urban cartography,

had learned the science of triangulation and longitudinal calculation during his travels in Europe. From around 1556 he had become involved with the London printer John Daye, with whom he collaborated on a number of projects including astronomical almanacs. Cuningham lived in Norwich until 1563 when he moved to London, probably to pursue a career in medicine.[13] Cuningham apparently drew up his prospect of Norwich between 1556 and 1558. The corporation did not sponsor the survey officially but were likely appraised, or even involved in its production, as Cuningham would have required the backing and support of influential citizens to complete his project. Certainly, the timing of such a venture could not have been more propitious for the corporation, coinciding as it did with the recent renegotiation of the city's geographic jurisdiction, and the accession of Queen Elizabeth to the throne. The prospect was the perfect vehicle for advertising the city's most positive features.

After the survey had been completed, John Bettes was commissioned to make the engraving and the prospect was duly published in Cuningham's most famous work, entitled *The Cosmographicall Glasse*, in 1559. Ostensibly a compendium of geography and scientific methodology, Cuningham used the Norwich survey as the basis for his *Table of the Sun's Meridian Altitude above the Horizon*, wherein he 'calculated for every degree in the *zodiac*, respecting the elevation of the *pole-artic* at *Norwich* ... and the sun's declination', also determining 'such eclipses of the moon as shall happen from the year 1560 till 1605'.[14] The prospect printed in the *Glasse* incorporated 'curious wooden *cuts* ... particularly one of the author in his doctor's habit', depicted as explaining his complex trigonometric calculations to an apprentice, and tells us that geography 'delivereth us from greate and continuall travailes'.[15] Cuningham's not so hidden agenda behind this apparent self-promotion as a doctor of great scientific learning, was an appeal to the interests of the notable patron of arts and sciences, Robert Dudley, to whom the book was dedicated. Indeed, it has been suggested that Dudley may well have funded the project.[16]

The work of surveying Norwich for this prospect had begun during the lifetime of Mary I but it was not to be published until the year after her death.

see Sarah Bendall, 'Draft Town Maps for John Speed's "Theatre of the Empire of Great Britaine'", *Imago Mundi* 54 (2002), 30–45.

[13] There is some evidence to suggest that Cuningham took up a position as a public lecturer at the Barber Surgeon's Hall, but Matthew Champion has raised questions about the lack of evidence in *The Doctor, the Printer and the Queen's Favourite: William Cuningham and the First Printed Plan of Norwich*, p. 4. Available at www.heritagecity.org/user_files/downloads/cunninghams-map-of-norwich-by-matthew-champion.pdf

[14] Francis Blomefield, *An Essay towards a Topographical History of the County of Norfolk, Vol. III: The History of the City and County of Norwich, Part I* (1806), p. 278.

[15] Ibid. Second quote cited in Jess Edwards, *Writing, Geometry and Space in Seventeenth Century England and America: Circles in the Sand* (Abingdon, 2006), p. 12.

[16] Champion, *The Doctor*, pp. 6–7. Dudley's circle of intellectuals and academics with an interest in astrology, surveying and mathematics included John Stow and John Dee.

The finished prospect reflected the change of monarch – Elizabeth's coat of arms can be found in the top left corner – and the publication of the *Glasse* honoured the new queen with its dedication to her favourite, Dudley. The prospect and text also said something of Cuningham's commitment to the Elizabethan religious settlement, a fact that likely suited Norwich's interests. The connection between the *Glasse* and Protestantism ran deep. Cuningham's printer, John Daye, was a Londoner with a reputation as a fervent Protestant who had been imprisoned by the former Catholic queen for printing Protestant literature in 1554. Daye was also patronised by Robert Dudley, as well as Elizabeth's Secretary of State, William Cecil. It is through the latter connection that Daye became the printer for the infamous Book of Martyrs either during, or shortly after, the publication of the *Glasse*. It is entirely possible that the profits made from the *Glasse*, which 'was then in such great repute, that *Day* … obtained a royal license for him and his assigns solely to print it',[17] went towards the enormous costs involved in publishing the Book of Martyrs.

It has been suggested that the prospect itself may well contain hints about England's change of religious direction, as well as the corporation's influence. At the time of the survey, a substantial flint wall had circumnavigated the cathedral precinct but it is not to be found on the map.[18] Built prior to the Reformation, it has been suggested that the decision to omit the wall from the prospect may have been deliberate 'civic propaganda to illustrate the desegregation of church lands and their integration with those of the city'.[19] Indeed, the building of the wall in the late eleventh century cut the Saxon marketplace of Tombland in half and had been a constant source of tension between the city and the cathedral for years after. The omission of the structure from the prospect may have been a mistake but, equally, it may have been a deliberate choice designed to satisfy intended viewers. The same argument may also apply to the choice of churches that were depicted in detail, which were by no means all the churches that existed in Norwich at that time. These included the vehemently Protestant St Peter Parmentergate, 'St Johns at the gates' (probably St John Sepulchre), and St Stephen. Curiously however Cuningham also included three churches – St Botolph, St Martin-on-the-Hill and St Leonard – the former having been demolished some years before the survey, and the latter two in private hands since the Reformation.[20] It is possi-

17 Blomefield, *Topographical History*, III:I, p. 279.

18 Harley, 'Silences and Secrecy'. Harley argues that political messages were conveyed as much by what was included on maps, as by what was left out.

19 Melissa Gaudoin, *The Green Spaces and Culture of Late Medieval Norwich: Municipal, Ecclesiastical and Medical* (University of East Anglia MA Thesis, unpub., 2007), pp. 17–18.

20 St Botolph at Fye Bridge had been sold off into private ownership in the early sixteenth century and demolished, probably during the 1540s. St Martin-on-the-Hill was more commonly know as St Martin-at-Bail (at the Bailey) or St Martin at the Castle Gate. It stood in an area of open ground that, by the seventeenth century, went by the name of Skouldsgreene. This St Martin should not be confused with the any of the three

ble to infer from this, as some historians have, that Cuningham's loyalties lay with pleasing the monarch of the day, given that the majority of the survey had been completed under a Catholic monarch. However another argument has been put forward, one that perhaps better explains Cuningham's rather erratic approach to religious buildings. Christopher Barringer has noted the absence of several important features of the landscape, including the busy trading thoroughfare known as Pottergate, and perhaps most surprisingly, the omission of the city's Guildhall, a fact that could not have pleased the corporation. Barringer puts this down to imprecision, as too does David Lobel who has questioned Cuningham's tendency to overplay the city's green spaces.[21] Matthew Champion offers the convincing explanation that the survey may actually have been carried out far earlier than 1556, which explains why the old churches were included on the prospect. Based on the inclusion of several aspects of the city's defences – such as one of the towers of the gate-house at Bishop's Bridge and sections of the defensive walls – that had actually been destroyed during Kett's Rebellion of 1549, Champion argues that the survey must have been finished at least a decade earlier, if not before.[22] This line of reasoning begs the questions as to how far Cuningham was actually responsible for the survey. Exactly why Cuningham, a man who knew Norwich well, would knowingly print such discrepancies is hard to ascertain, but it is quite possible that the man credited with such a significant achievement in England's cartographic history had simply reworked earlier surveys, such as those commissioned by Henry VIII in the 1530s, rather than completing a new survey.[23] The attribution of the prospect to Cuningham results largely from its insertion in the *Glasse* and from the presence of the figure in the doctor's habit on the picture, always assumed to have been Cuningham.

The prospect has been misleading in more ways than one. It also led to propagating one of the most famous urban myths about Norwich that became ingrained into popular consciousness for many years to come. Norwich is shown from the west, as though the viewer were arriving on the road from London. In real life, Norwich had been surrounded by small settlements, including the villages of Heigham and Pockthorpe, which had been brought

other churches of St Martin in Norwich: at Palace, at the Gates, and at Oak. Cuningham's situation of the church causes some confusion, but it can be identified as between St Peter Parmentergate and St John Timberhill. Its situation is noted in Carole Rawcliffe and Richard Wilson, eds, *Medieval Norwich* (London, 2004), p. 59. It was probably demolished around 1564 after it had been sold by the Crown: Francis Blomefield, *An Essay Towards the Topographical History of the County of Norfolk IV: The History of the City and County of Norwich II* (London, 1806), pp. 120–2. St Leonard had been a priory before the Reformation and had passed to the Howard family, eventually becoming the family's city home, Surrey House. Champion, *The Doctor*, p. 14.

21 Barringer, 'Changing Face', pp. 6–7 and M. D. Lobel, 'The Value of Early Maps as Evidence for the Topography of English Towns', *Imago Mundi* 22 (1968), 50–61, 52.

22 Champion, *The Doctor*, pp. 14–15.

23 Ibid., p. 16.

under the city's jurisdiction in the charter of 1556. However, the prospect so attractively illustrating the *Glasse* was of a walled city fronted by rolling fields. There is some effort at depicting Pockthorpe at the outer northeastern edge of the walls, but Heigham does not appear in the west. It is likely that this was deliberate, rather than a mistake. It was typical for early-modern prospects to present cities as islands in a sea of green, a convention that symbolised the cityscape as a unique cultural space, distinct from the barren emptiness of the countryside. This image of the bounded city signified an exclusive and urbane civilisation; the countryside by contrast was bucolic, parochial and backward. The city thus conceived protected urbanites from the cultural and actual threat of outsiders, concomitant with the notion of inclusion and exclusion that operated throughout early-modern society. In this instance the concept was ratified in the perfect image of a walled city. Such theories aside however, put simply, having depicted Norwich from the west, Heigham would have obscured the view.

Within the city's walls, our surveyor (or series of surveyors as the evidence may well suggest) also adopted a familiar device of elevating the city's image by exaggerating the truth and re-imagining the more negative features of the landscape.[24] From the very first glance Norwich is established as an ideal place to live: the magnificent walled fortifications are bordered by well-tended fields and woodland and windmills catch the breeze on the rolling hills to the northeast. Just inside the walls archers practise their skills in an open field, healthy-looking livestock graze, and fishermen dot the river. The well-appointed houses and buildings of the central and western areas overlook wide thoroughfares and the northern, eastern and southern peripheries are given over to trees, orchards, fields and pasture. Suspended above this idyllic scene sits Mercury, the classical god of financial gain, commerce and travel, keeping watch over the city from the clouds. It is here that we might also see something of Cuningham's personal influence in the prospect's 1559 incarnation. Norwich's situation 'downe ... a litel swellynge or arerynge of erthe passynge the pleyne grounde and nought rechynge to highnesse of an hille' fitted perfectly classical theories espousing how good air and environment were conducive to vigorous good health.[25] As a doctor, Cuningham would have been very familiar with the Hippocratic and Galenic theories of balanced bodily humours, for which the right environment was key.[26] For the corporation too, public health was a priority. There was much interest in propagating the idea that Norwich was a healthy city, as it reflected directly on their civic management. Nothing is as like to ward away visitors and investment than

[24] Harley, 'Silences and Secrecy', pp. 66–7.

[25] From John Trevisa, *On the Properties of Things: John Trevisa's Translation of Bartholomaeus Anglicus' De Proprietatibus Rerum*, II (Oxford, 1975), pp. 717–18, quoted in Gaudoin, *Green Spaces*, pp. 11–12.

[26] For a concise explanation of humourism, see Carole Rawcliffe, *Leprosy in Medieval England* (Woodbridge, 2006), pp. 65–72.

a reputation for poor public health. Given that the prospect's production overlapped with one of the city's most severe influenza epidemics, healthful propaganda would have been a potent weapon in restoring people's faith in the city.[27]

The Cuningham Prospect presents Norwich as a city rich in fertile plains, orchards, and healthy green spaces. The reality however was that much of city was built on marshy, low-lying land, especially adjacent to the river that ran directly through the city centre. Inhabitants suffered at regular intervals when the river burst its banks during heavy rains or snows, and many of the riverside parishes were particularly affected by the plague.[28] The boggy ground also shortened the lifespan of many buildings. The most famous example was the Duke of Norfolk's Palace, substantially renovated during the seventeenth century, but prone to subsidence. The contemporary antiquarian John Kirkpatrick wrote about the palace's structural problems caused by poor drainage, 'its great fault was sinking in the cellars too deep that the water annoyed them much'.[29] Daniel Defoe too, writing with characteristic wit, noted how the 'Duke of Norfolk's house was formerly well kept, and the gardens preserved for the pleasure and diversion of the citizens, but since feeling too sensibly the sinking circumstances of that once glorious family'.[30] Visiting Norwich in 1696, Celia Fiennes had also seen how the decaying palace cast a grim shadow over the city centre, and John Evelyn described the place as 'an old wretched building, & that part of it, newly built of brick, is very ill understood; so as I was of the opinion, it had ben much better to have demolish'd all'.[31] It seems his comments were taken to heart, as after a quarrel with the corporation in 1711, the Duke of Norfolk ordered that the house be pulled down.[32]

[27] Norwich's 1559 influenza epidemic took the lives of rich and poor alike, including ten aldermen. Fay, *Health and Disease*, p. 11.

[28] The connection between poverty and disease was more explicit, but of those parishes that suffered the most during the plagues of 1579, 1603, 1625–6 and 1665–6, most were by the river. These included St Margaret, St Lawrence, St Peter Parmentergate, St Michael Coslany, St James, St Peter Southgate, St Ethelred and St Julian: P. Slack, *The Impact of Plague in Tudor and Stuart England* (London, 1985), pp. 39, 136 and Jones, *Social Geography*, Fig. 9.6. The exceptions were All Saints and St Giles.

[29] John Kirkpatrick, quoted in Leonard G. Bolingbroke, 'St John Maddermarket, Norwich: its Streets, Lanes, and Ancient Houses, and their Old-time Associations', *Norfolk Archaeology* XX (1921), 215–39, 218–19.

[30] D. Defoe, *A Tour through the whole island of Great Britain* (London, 1971), pp. 86–7.

[31] C. Morris, ed., *The Illustrated Journeys of Celia Fiennes, 1685-c.1712* (London, 1995), p.137; E. S. De Beer, *The Diary of John Evelyn* (Oxford, 1959), p. 562.

[32] Bolingbroke, 'St John Maddermarket', 219. Parts of the house were sold to the corporation and were turned into a workhouse during the eighteenth century.

Evelyn had noticed other urban problems too. In 1671 he told how 'most of the Church-yards (though most of them large enough) were filled up with earth, or rather the congestion of dead bodys on[e] upon another, for want of Earth &c to the very top of the Walls, & many above'.[33] Likewise, Daniel Defoe was surprised to discover that many of the 'public edifices ... chiefly the castle [were] ancient and decayed, and now for many years past made use of for a gaol'.[34] Even the city walls – a symbol of civic pride – suffered under a barrage of masonry theft and general atrophy. Evelyn and his contemporary Thomas Baskerville also wrote of how the river was 'very narrow' and 'muddy', 'fouled by the effluent of dyeworks' and tanning, the air thick with the fumes of the staple domestic and industrial fuel, sea-coal.[35] The Cuningham Prospect avoided any of these realities, just as it avoided illustrating the city's five leper hospitals, including only two of the buildings and referring to neither as hospitals, and the site of the Great Hospital on Bishopgate was presented as an area of open ground.[36] Indeed, the prospect pointedly avoids any association between the city, bad air, and poor health.

The prospect connected Norwich with a healthy reputation for at least a century. Between 1559 and 1696, all fourteen of the maps and prospects produced of the city were based on the Cuningham Prospect.[37] It was copied widely across Europe, finding its way into printed geographies and educational texts, for example, George Braun and Franz Hogenberg's major cartographic project *Civitates Orbis Terrarum* published in 1581 in Cologne. Braun and Hogenberg's reproduction of the prospect demonstrates just how far the idea of Norwich as a healthy idyll had taken root. A poem attributed to Daniel Rogers decorates the reverse of the 1581 prospect, comparing Norwich, London, York and Bristol, 'Far-famed for commerce each of them; their trade beyond compare ... The land round each is fertile; and each city richly glows, Adorned in cultured opulence which civic zeal bestows'.[38]

In similar manner, Daniel Meisner's reproduction of the Cuningham Prospect also reflected the connection made between the city and good health. Norwich comprised one of the 830 urban engravings contained within the emblem book *Politischen Schatz-Kastleins* or *Thesaurus Philo-Politicus* published in Frankfurt-am-Main in 1631. The book was compiled between 1623 and 1631 with Meisner writing the poetry for the first edition and the engravings

---

[33] De Beer, *John Evelyn*, p. 563.
[34] Defoe, *A Tour*, pp. 86–7. The house remained empty throughout most of this period, but the gardens were finally converted into pleasure gardens during the eighteenth century.
[35] Margret Pelling, 'Health and Sanitation to 1750', *Norwich*, ed. Rawcliffe and Wilson, pp. 117–38, 123.
[36] Brian Ayers, *Norwich: A Fine City* (Stroud, 2003), p. 140.
[37] Raymond Frostick, *The Printed Plans of Norwich, 1558–1840* (Norwich, 2002), p. xi.
[38] Frostick, *Printed Plans*, p. 5. The poem had been written to commemorate Elizabeth I's 1578 progress to Norwich.

created in copper at the workshop of Eberhard Kieser.[39] The engraving of Norwich is a very basic copy of the Cuningham Prospect, only recognisable because of the civic arms in the top right-hand corner and the distinctive presence of the walls and river. Emblem books normally comprised some combination of picture and didactic tale and this was no exception, the title above the prospect reading *Remedia Ad Sanitatum Creata Sunt* (remedies were created to preserve health). In the foreground the engraver has added a bay tree that shades the dead, or dying, body of a salamander. A raven perches in the branches and peers down at the salamander's body. Many contemporaries would have instantly recognised the symbolism, the former beast representing poison and the latter putrefaction and death.[40] Under the map, a section of Latin text taken from Arnold Freitag's 1579 *Mythologica Ethica* connected Norwich with a moralistic tale incorporating elements of medical thought and practice.[41] The text reads that the raven has killed the venomous salamander and has been poisoned in the process. The raven then eats the life-giving bay leaves that restore him to full health.[42] The association of Norwich with this symbolic tale concerning life, death and the application of medical knowledge cannot simply have been a coincidence; we know through other contemporary sources that Norwich's reputation for health had spread far and wide.[43]

There was a notable absence of new prospects of Norwich until the end of the seventeenth century, by which time two-dimensional street plans were gaining in popularity alongside the traditional prospect. Thomas Cleer was the first surveyor to produce one of these more functional plans of Norwich and also the first surveyor to move away from the now iconic image that had so typified Cuningham, Meisner, Braun and Hogenberg's prospects. Dedicating his plan to the mayor, aldermen and citizens of Norwich and Henry, Duke of Norfolk in 1696, Cleer pointedly avoided artistic additions, such as people

[39] Meisner died only two years into the project. Ibid., pp. 13–15.

[40] The image of the salamander was used to represent the pope in an anti-pope tract written in Nuremberg in 1527 by Andreas Osiander and Hans Sachs.

[41] Frostick, *Printed Plans*, p. 15. Freitag's *Mythologia Ethica* was an adaptation and translation into Latin of the first emblem book in Dutch, illustrated with the famous Aesop-series of Marcus Gheeraerts: Edewaert de Dene's *De Warachtige Fabulen der Dieren* (Bruges, 1567). Freitag was a humanist, physician and professor at the University of Helmstadt.

[42] Ibid., p. 14. The translation offered by Frostick reads 'When the raven is poisoned because it killed the chameleon, it needs the medicine from the bay tree which expels the poison from him.'

[43] John Harrington and Thomas Tusser both alluded to Norwich's reputation as a healthful city, though neither author agreed that the city deserved the epithet. For Harrington see T. Park, ed., *Nugae Antiquae II* (London, 1804), p. 170, quoted in John Pound, *Tudor and Stuart Norwich* (Chichester, 1988), p. 67. Tusser's short stay in the city had resulted in an illness. Recalling the experience, he wrote how he had fled 'From Norwich air, in great despair, Away to fly, or else to die, To seek more health, to seek more wealth, Then was I glad': Thomas Tusser, *Five Hundreth Points of Good Husbandry* (London, 1573), p. 323.

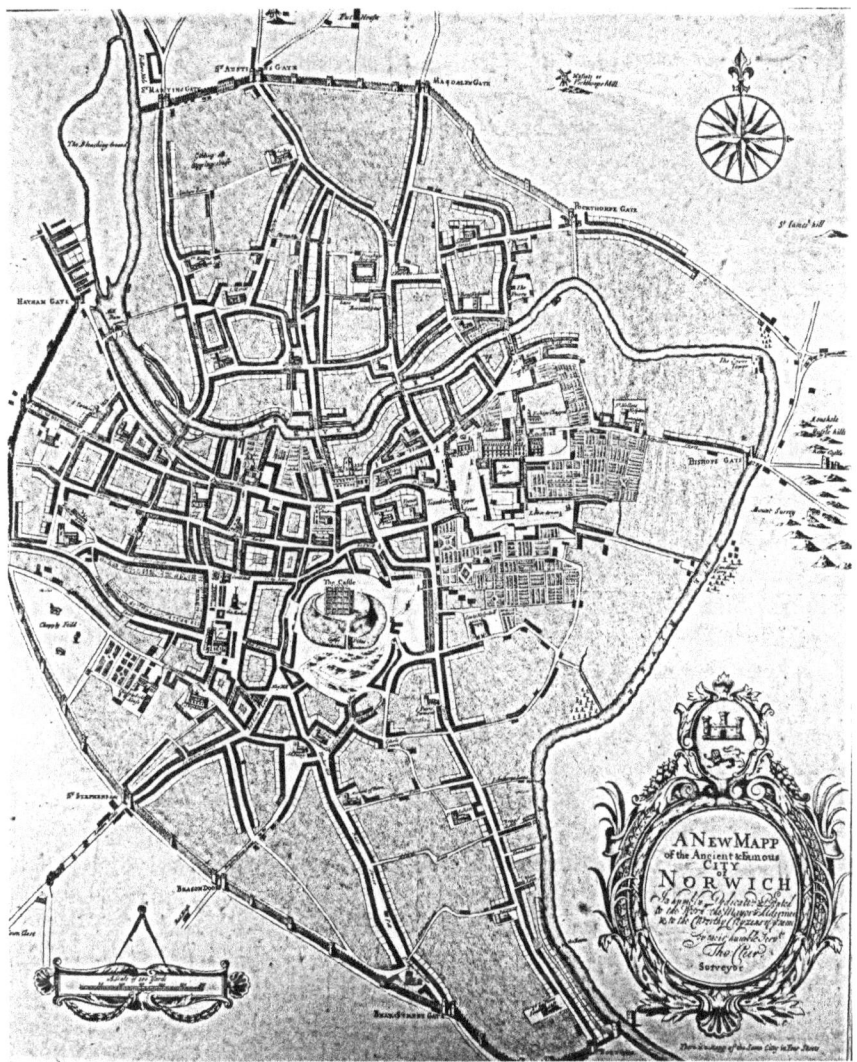

1 A New Map of Norwich by Thomas Cleer, 1696.

and animals, favouring instead a practical, to scale drawing.[44] Gone too was any acknowledgement of Norwich's reputation as a healthful city. Cleer's maps are now very famous, but the 'new mapp' of Norwich proved to be very unpopular with his contemporaries. Local booksellers George Rose and Mr Olliver acted as Cleer's distribution agents, but after two years a lack of sales had forced them to cancel their order. Originally printed on four sheets for 18d, Cleer perhaps hoped that by reproducing the plan as a smaller, cheaper,

[44]   Norfolk Heritage Centre (hereafter NHC): A new mapp of the ancient and famous city of Norwich by Tho. Cleer, 1696.

single sheet version it would be easier to sell, but even then only managed to sell three copies.[45] Quite why the map was so unpopular is hard to tell, but perhaps the rather plain design was unappealing to enthusiasts more used to the elaborate prospect style. This disinterest is very revealing, suggesting that contemporaries viewed urban cartography in much the same way as a piece of art – as a talking piece, wall hanging or collector's item – rather than as a finding aid. Certainly whilst Cleer's plan prioritised precision over imagination, the result was that the plan possessed none of the charm, symbolism, or artistic allure of its predecessors. That Cleer's map did not sell showed just how important it was for a map to contain more than simple geographic detail; ownership of a map was an expression of the possessor's culture, education and knowledge of the wider world and the simple, if cartographically superior, plan fell short of the mark.[46]

Subsequent cartographers made sure not to repeat the same mistake and the map engraved by John Hoyle in 1710 is a good example. An almost exact copy of Cleer's 1696 plan, Hoyle's map was sold at only 2d for a single sheet. Substantially smaller and cheaper than the 18d map produced by Cleer fourteen years earlier, it was perhaps hoped that the price difference would make up for the lack of originality. However it was to be eighteen years before the map really achieved any recognition and this because of a major innovation in marketing strategy. In 1728 Hoyle's plan was reproduced as the illustrative companion for new history of Norwich. This project was backed the renowned bookseller, printer, publisher and Whig William Chase, the man behind the publication of one of the county's first regional news, the *Norwich Mercury*.[47] With the regular publication of regional news, mass marketing had become a real possibility. Thomas Kirkpatrick's rather beautiful prospect of Norwich from the northeast, for example, was advertised in four issues of the *Norwich Gazette* (the *Mercury's* Tory rival), as well as in the *London Journal*.[48] The *Mercury* and *Gazette* also featured bastardised versions of Kirkpatrick's prospect as their masthead between the 1720s and 1740s, the perfect way of illustrating a local newspaper with a picture of the city itself.[49]

Over the course of the eighteenth century it became clear that cartography had moved a long way from allegoric tales and classical allusions. Whilst still prioritising artistic talent and attractiveness, the new prospects and plans were more accurate and contained simpler messages more instantly gratifying to a wide audience, a shift that most likely represented the increasing

[45] Frostick, *Printed Plans*, pp. 21–2.

[46] Cleer's lack of success with his plan of Norwich did not affect his career path: he was appointed surveyor to the Crown in 1705.

[47] For more on Chase and the *Norwich Mercury* see David Stoker, 'Prosperity and Success in the Eighteenth-Century Book Trade: The Firm of William Chase & Co.', *Publishing History* 30 (1991), 1–58.

[48] Frostick, *Printed Plans*, p. 29.

[49] Stoker, 'Prosperity and Success', 34–5. The *Gazette* ran the illustrated title header between 1725 and 1744 and the *Mercury* between 1726 and 1740.

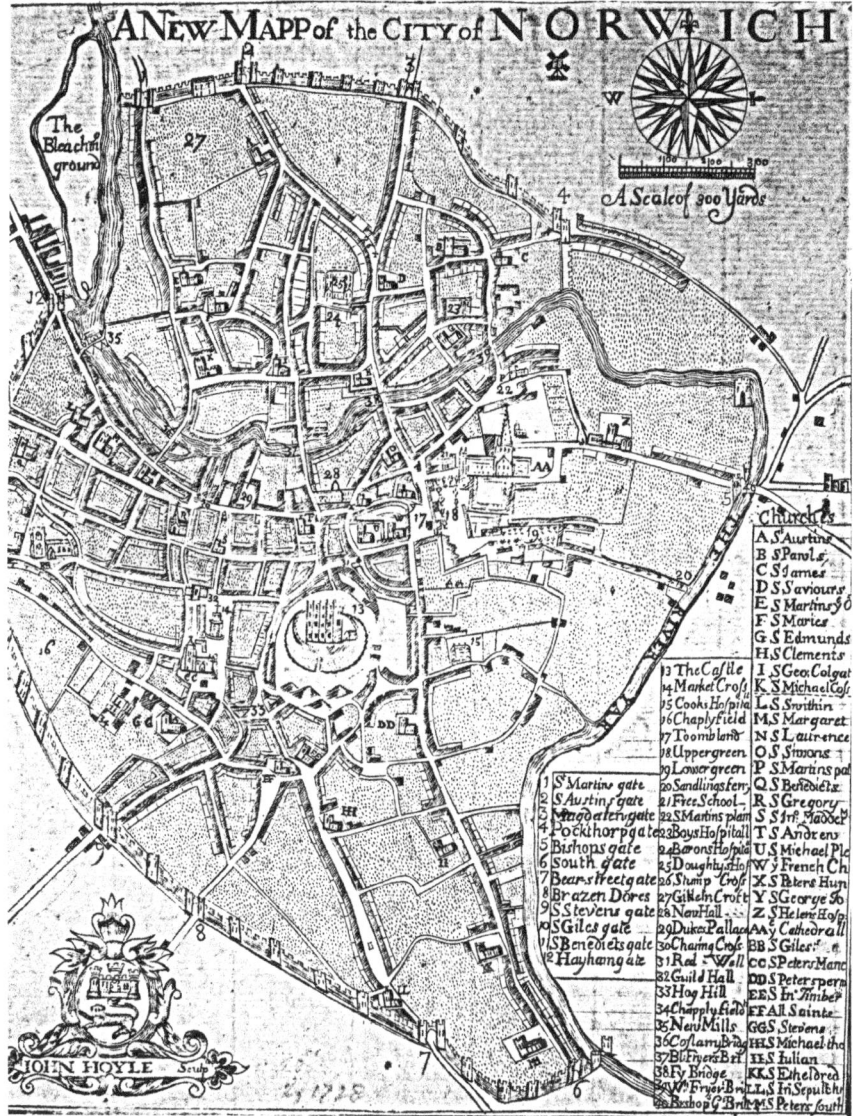

2 Plan of Norwich by John Hoyle, 1728.

availability of cheap printed material designed for a mass market. The message conveyed by most of these maps was easy to understand. James Corbridge's 1727 Norwich map is a good example. Commissioned in 1724 by the serving mayor, John Croshold, it was dedicated to the third Baron Townsend, Lord Lieutenant for Norfolk and had helped launch Corbridge's career as a surveyor.[50] The map is a bird's eye plan but with many of the key buildings highlighted in elevation. Around the central plan are individual vignettes

50 Barringer, 'Changing Face', pp. 14–15.

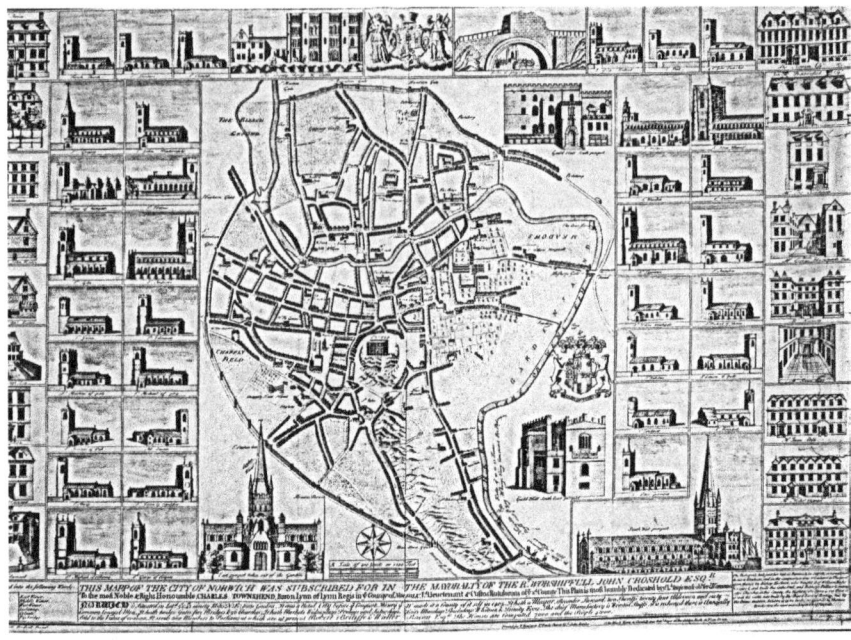

3 Map of the city of Norwich by J. Corbridge, 1747.

illustrating some of the elevations in detail, a number that include the houses of Norwich's great and good, civic buildings and churches.[51] It is likely that the choice of which house or building to include was based on subscriptions to the map from private citizens, corporate bodies and vestries.[52] Corbridge's map communicated a clear message: these are the people and the places central to the life of the city. Cartography, civic position, wealth, religiosity, masculinity and citizenship were bound together in this one iconic image.

Following Corbridge's exemplar, Francis Blomefield's 1746 plan achieved a level of civic propaganda not seen since Cuningham's prospect almost two centuries before. Blomefield was a Cambridge-educated rector with a keen interest in writing the history of Norwich and Norfolk. He was not employed by the corporation to publish his map, but it no doubt served their interests. The map was probably produced between 1741 and 1745 as an illustrative appendage to his several volume topographical and chronological history of Norfolk and Norwich, printed in Norwich and issued separately to subscribers

---

[51] Among the private properties engraved onto the map were those belonging to Mr George Hainsworth, councillor; Captain John Reeves; Mr Miles Brathwayte; Mr Robert Gamble, constable and guardian of the poor; Mr Charles Harwood, gentleman; Mr Thomas Newton, alderman, sheriff and mayor; Mr John Bedingfield; Mr Thomas Churchman, alderman; Mr Samuel Fremolt, sheriff; Mr Nicholas Vipont, gentleman and guardian of the poor; Mr James Cobb, constable; and Mr Thomas Beavors, councillor and auditor.
[52] Eden, 'Land Surveyors in Norfolk', 481.

from 1746.[53] The plan itself was dedicated to the Bishop of Norwich, Thomas Gooch and like Corbridge's before it put important civic and religious buildings in elevation, the scale of the work demonstrated by the two-hundred and two places referenced in the key. Surrounding the plan with engravings of local and historic note, including guild seals, ceremonial treasures, and coins that had been produced at Norwich's mint since the Anglo-Saxon period, the map is an exemplar of civic pride. Blomefield also made sure to include the city's swan marks and paid tribute to Norwich's long-standing connection with St George, whose post-reformation celebrations had become incontrovertibly linked with the Company (previously guild) of St George, its annual processions, and the Lord Mayor's inauguration.[54] A rector since 1729, it is no surprise that pre- and post-reformation religious buildings also found a central place in Blomefield's creation.[55] Noting disused or demolished churches, friaries and anchorages alongside Independent, Quaker and Presbyterian Meeting Houses, and a Jewish synagogue and school, Blomefield's map has provided generations of observers with a unique visual account of the city's colourful and relatively tolerant relationship with religion. With his formidable knowledge of local history, Blomefield created a map rich in detail and evidence. Nevertheless, in the way of each map produced since the Cuningham Prospect, it had an agenda. Presenting the city from a single perspective, one that glorified the city's governing elite, details of the lived city played second fiddle to the buildings and objects associated with Norwich's governmental and religious history. Indeed, the propensity to promote a single image and civic identity had not been dulled with advances in the science of cartography. Blomefield's map, for all that it was far more accurate than the Cuningham Prospect, still had civic propaganda at its heart.

It is clear from the examples above that mapmaking was an art form and a science that the corporation actively encouraged. A carefully constructed map was a useful tool in promoting only the aspects of Norwich they wanted the outside world to see. But this raises the question: who was the intended audience? As we have seen, printed maps had a limited audience, especially during the sixteenth century. The Cuningham Prospect was widely circulated across Europe but would only have been seen by an educated elite who could afford to purchase *cosmographia*, or who had access to a library. Likewise, Meisner or Braun and Hogenberg's reproductions had a limited audience. Cleer's 1696 Norwich map was a resounding failure in terms of sales.

Nevertheless, many of Norwich's inhabitants may have seen a map of their city. As mentioned earlier, the corporation had two great maps in their public chambers at the Guildhall from the late sixteenth century that could have

---

[53] David Stoker, 'Blomefield's History of Norfolk', *Factotum: Newsletter of the XVIII Century STC*, XXVI (1988), 17–22.

[54] For more on swan marks, see Register of Swan Marks, MC2712/1, 1649-c.1900.

[55] Blomefield included, for example, the seals of the Convent of the White Friars, Grey Friars, Friars Preachers, and the Mark of the Dean and Chapter of Norwich.

been seen by a wide range of people.[56] The Guildhall was home to the city's law courts and, until 1625, the sheriff's office. Public hearings and trials would have brought ordinary inhabitants in numbers as witnesses and onlookers. The Guildhall was also the focus of the city's cloth trade and any number of merchants (local, visiting, and strangers) may have bought wools and yarns here.[57] The annual elections would have seen Norwich's freemen gathering in the cloth hall to vote and a large number of civic events were held here for the mayor and citizens.[58] Thus it might be reasonably concluded that the audience for city maps would have been far wider than that of the great *mappamundi* that graced the formal rooms of royal houses or state buildings. Many of the city's inhabitants would have been privy to the image of Norwich as a healthy, rich, devout and attractive city. As we move into the early eighteenth century this was ever more so as city maps became smaller, cheaper, more easily duplicated, and more likely to be replicated for a mass audience.

The significance of the audience is in the power that maps held. Mapmaking was not simply a process of explaining geography during the early-modern period. It was a way of communicating territorial boundaries and expressing power: that of a state to its neighbouring territories, of a city to other cities, or of a government to its people. Maps were therefore an integral part of the formation of knowledge about the world and the individual's place within it.[59] The wider the audience the more the myth of governmental omnipotence could be promoted by this unique style of imagery that suspended a particular value system in time and space.[60]

This was certainly the case in Norwich where mapmakers helped to facilitate a fabricated, yet pervasive image of the city as healthful, prosperous, and powerful, constructing and articulating Norwich's identity. Mapmaking was an expensive business and thus new maps were commissioned and designed with the city's governing class and landowners in mind (if not directly sponsored by the same). It would not be too great a leap to presume that the end result reflected the principles and the values of the same class, a microcosm of their world. The maps of Norwich discussed above were as much a mental map or constructed city as any of the other perspectives yet to be explored in the remainder of this book.

---

[56] Chamberlains' Account Book, NCR 18a, 1580–9, fol. 125. The late seventeenth-century Guildhall was also home to a silver mace, an embroidered 'cap of maintenance', a ceremonial sword and scabbard, plate, an assortment of paintings of Norwich's great and good, and a Turkish carpet. W. Rye, ed., *Depositions Taken Before the Mayor and Aldermen of Norwich 1549–1567 & Extracts from the Court Books of the City of Norwich 1666–1668* (Norwich, 1905), p. 104.

[57] Blomefield, *Topographical History*, IV:II, p. 232.

[58] J. T. Evans, *Seventeenth Century Norwich: Politics, Religion and Government 1620–1690* (Oxford, 1979), p. 32.

[59] P. Carroll, 'Articulating Theories of States and State Formation', *Journal of Historical Sociology* 22:4 (2009), 553–603, 585.

[60] Biggs, 'Putting the State on the Map', p. 375.

Parish Identities

The corporation may have had vested interests in producing an idealised, static image of Norwich but it is unlikely that the ordinary inhabitants of seventeenth-century Norwich would have conceptualised the streets and places around them in the same way. This was still a time long before maps became ubiquitous or cheap (Cleer's 1696 map is a good example of the failure of maps to be widely produced) and although many people might have seen the great maps hanging in the Guildhall, most people's frame of reference would have related to the immediate area in which they lived, the places connected to their work, their family, or their social life. They would have had a broad sense of their city but would have been on far more intimate terms with their neighbourhood. This is quite clear from the fact that witnesses in court records referred to the 'house of ... in the parish of' as their way of expressing where an event had taken place, with the assumption that listeners would have immediately understood this reference to person and parish without any further details. In this way, inhabitants' mental maps of Norwich would have been exclusive to the Parish, fragmentary and variable, shifting as people moved through their life cycle. Nevertheless, it is possible to establish a few commonalities of experience that would have found root in many people's mental maps of the city.

The parish was the spiritual, social and cultural focus of most people's lives whether they lived in the city or in a tiny rural village. It provided far more than religious education and guidance. The parish was the foundation of people's lives from their birth until their death and despite immigration and population movement, the sense of belonging to a parish brought benefits in the form of stability, kinship and support in times of need and was the bulwark of moral and social order.[61] The parish was a physical entity as well as an abstract one. Even in a city like Norwich where it might be expected that parish boundaries would become blurred, parish limits were zealously guarded and the ancient customs that bound people to their parish in rural areas were just as rigidly enforced in the city. Parish limits often grew up around physical features of the landscape. In Norwich it is quite clear that their limits were not always man-made. Watercourses – the river, streams and the larger cockeys – offered the clearest framework into which many parishes were fixed and major roads (often developed because of the position of watercourses) frequently edged parish limits. The Great Cockey, for example, created the

---

[61] For more on the processes and conventions of parish belonging and exclusion, see S. Hindle, 'Hierarchy and Community in the Elizabethan Parish: The Swallowfield Articles of 1596', *Historical Journal* 42:3 (1999), 835–51; S. Hindle, 'The Political Culture of the Middling Sort in English Rural Communities, c. 1550–1700', *The Politics of the Excluded, c. 1500–1850*, ed. T. Harris (Basingstoke, 2001) or S. Hindle, 'Destitution, Liminality and Belonging: The Church Porch and the Politics of Settlement in English Rural Communities, c.1590–1660', *The Self-contained Village? The Social History of Rural Communities, 1250–1900*, ed. C. Dyer (Hatfield, 2006), pp. 46–71.

eastern boundary for St Andrew, St Peter Mancroft and St Stephen leading due south from the River Wensum.[62] The river itself marked at least one edge of twenty-four of the city's thirty-four parishes, no parish crossing the water.

Once established, the territory that belonged to a parish was reinforced by customs, traditions, and ceremonies ensuring that everyone, especially the younger members of a community, committed parish limits to memory, particularly where obvious geographic markers were absent. One of the most important of these practices was rogation. Rogation, or 'beating the bounds', originated with the Catholic celebration of Ascension, but unlike many other rituals did not die out with the dissolution. 'Beating the bounds' was far more than a spiritual affair. It educated parishioners as to their duties and responsibilities in a way that was not easily forgotten and inscribed a mental map of the parish into people's minds. Youngsters were walked around their parish's boundaries by their elders and betters, stopping at key points which the child was instructed to commit to memory (occasionally reinforced by a punishment to make sure he or she did not easily forget), usually in a procession specifically organised to reflect that parish's social order. The perambulation was a striking form of visual theatre designed to bind parish boundaries into the common memory of its inhabitants.[63] Social events were also centred around the parish, often around alehouses, where feasting and celebrations were held. People got together to celebrate births and weddings, as well as public holidays, all of which were given a parish focus by the church. For the poor residents, the parish formed the administrative centre for the collection and distribution of poor relief, including money, food, clothes, or fuel, and it was the parish community who rallied during times of particular hardship.[64]

Norwich had an unusually high number of parishes (commented on by contemporary travellers such as Daniel Defoe and Celia Fiennes) yet still they existed quite perceptibly as individual communities. Each parish was a division and microcosm of the city's overall administrative apparatus and church, responsible for the collection and distribution of relief, welfare, and moral policing within their area. To complete this task every parish had its own officers: two churchwardens, one surveyor for the poor, two overseers and at least one constable.[65] Residents had a moral duty to support this

[62] Pelling, 'Health and Sanitation', pp. 126–7.

[63] Barry Reay, ed., *Popular Culture in Seventeenth Century England* (Worcester, 1985), pp. 7–8.

[64] P. Griffiths, J. Landers, M. Pelling and R. Tyson, 'Population and Disease, Estrangement and Belonging, 1540–1700', *The Cambridge Urban History of Britain, Vol. 2*, ed. P. Clark (Cambridge, 2000), pp. 195–234, 228. See also J. Barry, 'The Parish in Civic Life: Bristol and its Churches, 1640–1750', *Parish, Church and People: Local Studies in Lay Religion 1350–1750*, ed. S. J. Wright (London, 1998), pp. 152–78 and N. Alldridge, 'Loyalty and Identity in Chester Parishes, 1540–1640', *Parish, Church and People*, ed. Wright, pp. 84–124.

[65] Mark Goldie, 'The Unacknowledged Republic: Officeholding in Early Modern England', *The Politics of the Excluded, c. 1500–1850* (Basingstoke, 2001), pp. 153–94, 162.

system where possible, perhaps by looking out for their neighbours, or reporting misdeeds. That inhabitants identified closely with their parish can
easily be recognised in the rhetoric devices they employed when discussing
their surroundings.

At court, the location of a crime or immoral act was central to its investigation. Thus the investigating officers of any court – whether secular or religious – would always ensure that details regarding the crime's location were
recorded. Witnesses' depositions are therefore excellent sources for exploring
how people conceptualised space and place, from the manner in which they
articulated their response when questioned about location, verbalising their
frame of geographic reference. It is possible to detect many commonalities
across the depositions. When asked where a crime or immoral act took place,
witnesses very rarely used street names. The most common response was that
the crime had taken place in a certain parish. Where evidence was more specific, respondents referred to the 'house' or 'shop' of a given person, usually
taken to mean a business premises, domestic residence or alehouse, or some
combination of the same. However, a description of the house and parish
were far more common than a street name. Thus it was in 1640 that Jacob
Fisher 'being at the house of John Prior in the p[ar]ish of St John Maddermarket' overheard an argument between Helen Prior and Thomasina Melchor;
Francis Heyward 'at the doore of Elizabeth Seaman in St Stephens p[ar]ish'
witnessed Jane Mylles call Seaman a whore in 1669; and single woman Elizabeth Wring 'at the house of Henry Dodgeson in St Saviours parish' saw
Thomas Dawson call Dodgeson a rogue in 1674.[66] Many of Norwich's parishes were quite small, covering only a few streets and lanes in some cases, but
others – St Peter Mancroft, St Peter Parmentergate, or St Stephen, for example – were far larger. To give a parish as the scene of a crime in these cases was
thus rather non-specific. But the frequency with which the parish was used
as a geographic descriptor says much about its significance in inhabitants'
mental map of their city. So it was in 1607 that John Barnes of Norwich,
weaver, overheard Albert Ansten 'in the parish of St Clements of Norwich at
Hardyes dore ... that Mr Thomas Claxton had the use of the bodye of Amyes
wife as often as his owne' in 1608 and Thomas Francis had heard Barnaby
Leighton say that Elizabeth Browne had been 'whipt at the post for a whore
... w[i]th[i]n the parish of St Michaell' in 1618.[67] The parish emerges as the
most common rhetoric frame for describing the location of incidents.

It is also significant that when people discussed gossip and reputation it was
often done within the localised frame of reference of the parish. In 1608, for
example, John Skott had declared Mr Thull's wife 'w[i]th childe by an honest

66 DN/DEP/45/48b, fol. 62v, 15 October 1640. Prior v. Melchor; DN/DEP/48/52, fol.
107r, February 1669. Seaman v. Mylles; DN/DEP/49/53, fol. xx, March 1674. Dodgeson
v. Dawson.
67 DN/DEP/33/36a, fol. 834r, 24 June 1607. Amyes v. Ansten; DN/DEP/37/40, fol. 389v,
27 July 1618. Browne v. Leighton.

man of the parishe', to which Elizabeth Dynsdale had replied, 'Ay marry that is by her husband is not he an honest man of the parishe?'[68] Similarly, there was a common rumour abounding in St Peter Mancroft that Anne Inman was of 'lewd life ... and hath suffered her body to be knowne in scandalous adultery' in 1640, and in 1662 John Cooke had the parishioners of St Augustine to 'take notice of ... Francis Dye [for] she was a whore'.[69]

This kind of information was put to use in court, where great value was placed on localised knowledge. The most reliable compurgators and witnesses were judged to be people of good standing who hailed from the same parish as the participants of a suit or criminal case and could thus be relied upon to offer first-hand knowledge of an individual's character and supposed crimes. This was certainly the case in 1664 when the personal animosity between two families living in St Saviour's parish – Frogg and Austin – developed into a mutual suing session at the Diocesan Court. At least thirty of their friends, relatives, and neighbours, the majority from St Saviour, became involved as witnesses and compurgators as their protracted suit ran on into its second year.[70] Likewise, when the cantankerous Mary Kettle of St Martin at Palace was sued for defamatory speeches against her neighbours in 1682, it was her fellow parishioners who provided evidence against her. Kettle had accused George Wannington of the same parish of having had a bastard child and running away to Holland to avoid responsibility for the same, and Elizabeth Kinderley, also of the same parish, of having murdered her own bastard child with help from her midwife. Susanna White, Wannington, Kinderley, and Elizabeth Trill – all of St Martin's parish – each provided statements in the series of suits that ensued.[71] That same year, William Kempe was called upon to give evidence against Frances Gothan, key witness in a defamation case against Nathanial Russell, his master. Kempe, who lived in the same parish, provided information that brought into question Gothan's reliability as a witness, stating that he 'dependeth wholly upon him [his master] & ... is of noe credit or estimac[i]on & soe is looked upon' in that parish.[72] Furthermore, his knowledge of parish history allowed him to remember how 'about 8 or 9 years ago [Gothan] was questioned for feloniouslie taken away of some goods & ... found guilty'.[73] As the examples above demonstrate, local knowledge was

68 DN/DEP/34/36b, fol. 50r, 1608. Thull v. Skott.
69 DN/DEP/45/48b, fol. 104r, 1640. Inman v. Meen; DN/DEP/46/50, fol. 27r, 6 April 1662. Dye v. Cooke.
70 A selection of entries related to this case includes DN/DEP/47/51, fols 12r-14v, 55v, 209r-14v, November 1664-August 1665.
71 DN/DEP/51/55, fols 234r-237v, 18–20 October 1682. George Wannington v. Mary Kettle; Elizabeth Kinderley v. Mary Kettle; Maria Wannington v. Mary Kettle.
72 For more here on individual estimations of credit and self-worth in church court records, see A. Shepard, 'The Worth of Married Women in the English Church Courts, c. 1550–1730', *Married Women and the Law in Premodern Northwest Europe*, ed. C. Beattie and M. F. Stevens (Woodbridge, 2013), pp. 191–211.
73 DN/DEP/51/55, fol. 209r, 12 February 1682. Gothan v. Russell.

frequently framed in relation to the parish, and individuals' reputations were made or broken because of parish specific memories.

When witnesses gave information about their own selves, it was again the parish that was given to mark their identity. People always gave their place of residence as their parish, not their street, their business, or their street address, although on occasion further context might be given. Thus it was that Stephen Barker, worsted weaver, Edmund Lockwood, labourer, and Robert Fidimont, weaver, who had witnessed Matthew Norgett call their minister Mr Lowe a 'contentious' and 'wrangling preist' in 1608, all gave their place of abode as St Benedict's parish, and John Rawley, Toby Perkett, and Benjamin Granderge all stated that they lived in the parish of St Andrew when they were asked to give evidence at the October 1635 visitation about Thomas Ingram, 'a woleman in the said p[ar]ish'.[74] At no point did the examiners in the above case seem interested in uncovering the exact house or street of the deponents, despite the fact that St Andrew was one of the larger parishes in the city with around five or six hundred parishioners.[75]

At first glance, it might be argued that the geographical borders apparent in these cases – all drawn from the Diocesan Court – simply reflected the preoccupation of that court with the parish as an administrative and spiritual territory of the church. On further examination this argument does not stand up however, as the sense of identification with a particular parish is obvious in the secular records as well.[76] In 1684, for example, constables who 'went to execute a warr[an]t to Apprehend Mary Goodale, Ann Leasey, Thomas Deereing and Edmund Preston' described their location as 'the p[ar]ish of St James in Pockthorpe', no more and no less specific. Likewise, in 1689 Mary Meeke, described as the wife of Joseph Meeke of St Paul's parish, 'saith that she went to Mr Winkes house of St Saviour p[ar]ish … to see her husband' only to find him gambling in a card game.[77]

The parish was only one of the many available frameworks inhabitants had to conceptualise the urban landscape around them, but it was a significant one. A potent symbolic division linked to the church calendar and customary practices, parish boundaries and responsibilities were well known to inhabitants. Poor relief was gathered and distributed on a parish-to-parish basis, local officers, such as churchwardens and constables, had the parish as the basis of their jurisdiction, and the parish community existed as the nub of support and information networks. The linguistic convention of referring to a parish as a place of residence or to describe where an event took place offers

[74] DN/DEP/34/36b fol. 55r, 1608. Lowe v. Norgett; DN/DEP/42/47a fol. 501v. Ingram v. Greenwood, 1635.

[75] The nearest population estimates for St Andrews are 436 in 1569 and 663 in 1671: Jones, *Social Geography*, Fig. 3.26a.

[76] Norwich's City Sessions, Mayor's Court, and Norfolk's Quarter Sessions reveal a similar use of language when speaking about place. The linguistic device was not specific to the church courts.

[77] NCR, Case 12/a-b, 5 December 1684 and NCR, Case 12/b1, 9 January 1689.

evidence as to the importance of the parish in inhabitants' eyes, suggesting that one of contemporaries' most pervasive mental maps of the city related to their own parish. The conceptualisation of the parish was inherently linked to identity and a sense of belonging to a community. It is evident that the parish was understood as a distinct place, one that in turn defined the individual. In this way, an individual's frame of reference was based as much on subjective visual and mental cues, symbolic rituals, common experience and memory, as the reality of available tools of reference, such as maps, in a pre-modern, still largely visual culture.[78]

All cities functioned as 'civic communities' with regulatory, representative and legal powers shared unequally between a corporation elite and voting citizenry.[79] The civic community was an essential component of urban identity. In seventeenth-century Norwich, as elsewhere, the city corporation went to great lengths to advertise a powerful, time-honoured, and prosperous civic image to the nation. Nevertheless, there were many ways of conceptualising a city, many of which contrasted sharply with the civic ideal. Across the seventeenth century, population growth fundamentally altered Norwich's social makeup. Immigrants brought with them new cultural and religious ethics, and intensified pressure on housing, resources, and the civic purse. City life became increasingly complex and riven with problems of disorder born out of social dislocation, cultural diversity and competition, and this dynamic human interaction constantly collided with the static ideals inherent in civic imagery. Relatively few urban inhabitants left enduring traces on the urban fabric, but *collectively* urban dwellers created new urban maps and cityscapes based around their shared interests and identities.

[78] For a comprehensive introduction to this topic, albeit for an earlier period, see Lord Smail, *Imaginary Cartographies*.
[79] Christopher R. Friedrichs, *The Early-Modern City, 1450–1750* (Harlow, 1995), pp. 44–58.

2

Claiming Public Space:
Competing Perceptions

At Norwich fine, for me and myne, a Citie trim.
Where straungers well may seeme to dwell,
That pytch and pay, or keepe their day,
But who that want shall find it scant so good for him.[1]

The previous chapter considered two competing visualisations of one city. On the one hand was a stylised prospect laden with symbolic meaning and representing the interests of a relatively small social group, on the other was a city as it was lived and negotiated by its inhabitants. In the former, the city is conceptualised from above as one entity and the eye is drawn to landmarks, such as the walls, castle and cathedral, as ways of deciphering the landscape and, in the latter, the city is the sum of its parts, conceptualised from the bottom-up as parishes, neighbourhoods and people. Inhabitants thought about the city around them in terms relating to their immediate lives and these can be identified by the use of common linguistic tropes in the records of people's words and voices. Understanding these two different perspectives is one way of unpacking contemporaries' understanding of their urban landscape but they were by no means the only frames of reference available. Every individual had their own unique way of referencing, seeing and negotiating the city around them. The city that governed the lives of the poor, for example, was not the remote, static, and romantic affair portrayed in its maps, but a gritty reality. Indeed, if the poor had had the opportunity to view any of the artistic cartographic portrayals of their city, they might have been surprised that the sanitised bird's eye view they were seeing was the same place that they inhabited. This chapter explores the tensions that were produced when different social groups attempted to use or claim public space, especially the efforts of the corporation to more effectively manage the streets and open areas. Problems occurred when different agendas collided, and conflict often arose over the question of who had the dominant claim to a certain place, especially when one group tried to enforce boundaries to restrict the freedoms of another, in this case the corporation (as representatives of the better sort

[1] Thomas Tusser, *Five Hundreth Points of Good Husbandry* (London, 1573), p. 322.

of inhabitants) and the impoverished or unsettled. Beginning with a discussion of some of the city's most obvious corporeal boundaries – the city walls and parishes – the chapter moves on to consider the ways in which the government of Norwich sought to restrict and control the freedoms of ordinary people and the poorer sorts in public places. The second section explores the ways in which ordinary people claimed back the streets and public places, revealing that, no matter how hard the corporation tried, the streets and lanes would always be contested places. Finally, the last section considers how some public places attracted a reputation over time, often without inhabitants' conscious realisation.

Managing the Streets

On the contemporary maps discussed in the previous chapter, Norwich was commonly portrayed as a walled island in a sea of green.[2] Its medieval walls were the flint boundary that¡ delimited settlement, their scale and magnitude rivalling those of London. Built between 1297 and 1334, the walls were an expression of the city's status and wealth, though the building project was in fact only completed because of the generosity of a single individual, Robert Spink.[3] By the seventeenth century Norwich's walls were rarely employed for defence, but as a boundary marker they held both a practical and symbolic function.[4] The walls were 'architectural manifestations of municipal virtue, an emblem of ... civitas, or community of citizens banded together ... for mutual benefit',[5] a classical ideal that equated urbanity with civility and perfection, quite distinct from the supposed earthiness and primitivism of rural hinterlands.[6]

The city walls represented many things to many people. For the city's governors, some of whose interests were bound up in territory, the walls grounded urban ideals in flint and mortar, providing them with the means to more easily monitor and regulate the movements of inhabitants and strangers.[7] For

---

[2] The copies of Cuningham's prospect become increasingly more homogenous. In, for example, Meisner (1631), Walton (1668) or Coronelli (1706), only the shape of the walls and the surrounding countryside distinguish Norwich from other contemporary cities.

[3] Brian Ayers, 'The Urban Landscape', Medieval Norwich, ed. Carole Rawcliffe and Richard Wilson (London, 2004), pp. 1–28, 23.

[4] Kathryn L. Reyerson, 'Medieval Walled Space: Urban Development vs. Defence', City Walls: The Urban Enceinte in Global Perspective, ed. J. D. Tracy (Cambridge, 2000), pp. 88–116, 88.

[5] Richard L. Kagan, 'A World without Walls: City and Town in Colonial Spanish America', City Walls, ed. Tracy, pp. 117–152, 117.

[6] Chiara Frugoni, A Distant City: Images of Urban Experience in the Medieval World (Princeton, 1991), p. 29–32. See also Sylvia Thrupp, 'The City as the Idea of Social Order', The Historian and the City, ed. O. Handlin and J. Burchard (Cambridge, MA, 1966), p. 124.

[7] For more on settlement, community boundaries and belonging, see B. Waddell, 'Neighbours and Strangers: The Locality in Later Stuart Economic Culture', Locating Agency: Space, Power and Popular Politics, ed. F. Williamson (Newcastle, 2010), pp. 103–32; Keith

some inhabitants, the right to settlement within the walls afforded a sense of belonging and protection. When times were hard, settled inhabitants had the right to claim poor relief or hospital treatment, and when the city was threatened the gates could be closed against would-be assailants. For some the walls offered a more immediate solution. The walls, which included some forty towers in addition to the twelve gates, were almost impossible to maintain adequately as the cost of materials for repairs, which included sand, lime, bricks, and stone, were astronomical.[8] By the seventeenth century, time (in combination with a constant onslaught of theft by inhabitants) had left ample opportunities for the walls to be appropriated by the homeless, taking shelter in the quieter nooks and crannies away from the hustle and bustle of the main roads.

But for others, the walls represented exclusion, persecution, and hardship. The homeless, the peddlers of wares, wandering tinkers, chapmen, or the migratory labouring poor were often treated like criminals. With no ties to a permanent residence they were excluded from a system that privileged householders over the itinerant. The peripatetic – even those plying a trade – were considered deviant, threatening, and even dangerous. For these visible, yet so often invisible, poor, the walls marked the physical barrier to belonging to a parish community. Fears of a vagrant, criminalised subculture prompted the corporation to devise new methods of tackling the problem and the city walls were integral to these strategies.[9]

One means was to prevent impoverished migrants from entering, or remaining in, the city. To this end, travellers were stopped at the city's gates on orders from the mayor and aldermen to 'lette no man inne but in the presence of the wetchemen. And porters shall lye upon the gates and ... euery porter shall haue a horne to giue knowledge to the wetchemen to come to the porter to se the lettyng of euery person'.[10] If poor migrants escaped

---

Snell, *Parish and Belonging: Community, Identity, and Welfare in England and Wales, 1700–1950* (Cambridge, 2006), esp. Ch. 3; S. Hindle, *On the Parish?: The Micro-Politics of Poor Relief in Rural England, c.1550–1750* (Oxford, 2004), esp. Ch. 5; M. Berlin, 'Reordering Rituals: Ceremony and the Parish, 1520–1640', *Londinopolis: Essays in the Cultural and Social History of Early Modern London*, ed. Paul Griffiths and Mark Jenner (Manchester, 2000), pp. 47–66; S. Hindle, 'Hierarchy and Community in the Elizabethan Parish: The Swallowfield Articles of 1596', *Historical Journal* 42:3 (1999), 835–851; A. Mandanipour, G. Cars and J. Allen, eds., *Social Exclusion in European Cities: Processes, Experiences and Responses* (London, 1998), esp. pp. 75–6 or K. Wrightson, 'The Politics of the Parish in Early Modern England', *The Experience of Authority in Early-Modern England*, ed. Paul Griffiths, Adam Fox and Steve Hindle (Basingstoke, 1996), pp. 10–46.

8   Ayers, 'The Urban Landscape', p. 23.

9   'Rogue literature' sensationalised criminality during the Elizabethan and early Jacobean period. Examples include: Thomas Harman, *A Caveat For Common Cursitors* (1566); Robert Greene, *A Notable Discovery of Cozenage* (1591) and *The Black Book's Messenger* (1592); or Thomas Dekker, *Lanthorne and Candle-Light* (1608).

10   Order of the Convocation of Aldermen, 28 March 1523, reprinted in W. Hudson and J. C. Tingay, *The Records of the City of Norwich*, Vol. II (Norwich, 1910), p. 160.

detection – something that happened frequently judging by the records – it fell to ward constables to deal with them. This they achieved by the policy of moving people on, in this case out of the city altogether. Such was the fate of the two Irish women found wandering the streets in 1632, who were escorted out of Norwich on pain of punishment if they returned.[11] Many of these strangers and foreigners who were thus ejected were presented with passes by which the bearer was expected to return to his or her place of origin. The idea underpinning such measures was practical more than it was xenophobic. Parishes had a duty of care for their own and were expected to provide relief to their underemployed poor. During times of particular hardship, Norwich's ratepayers found it hard to support their poor residents and therefore, like most urban governors at this time, the corporation adopted a policy of moving on non-residents to deal with the escalating numbers of poor claimants, beggars, or people 'living at their own hand'.[12] Thus it was that the unfortunate Richard Paule and his family, originally from King's Lynn, were ordered out of the city and told not to return 'upon payne of beinge punished as vagrants'; John Tonge 'A seller of Almanacks [was] taken vagrant … [and] ordered forthwith to depart, and not to returne', and the cook Jeremy Fletnor, arriving in Norwich seeking work, was told to depart on pain of punishment as a vagrant.[13] The pass worked by instructing the constables of each town or city to escort the bearer to their destination. So, William Wormewell and his wife who, sent by the mayor of King's Lynn with a pass to Newington but stopping instead in Norwich, were quickly moved on to Newington with another pass, this time from the mayor of Norwich.[14] Or Thomas Jones, who had been taken vagrant in 1649 and whipped according to the law, was then issued with a pass that did 'charge and Command you [the constable] to passe and Convey the said P[ar]ty from Constable to Constable the next and Rediest way to Buckham in the County of Sury who upon his Examination saith that was the place of his Last abode & that there his Wife dwell … & there to be sete to worke…'.[15] The pass was a one-way ticket, but after the holder had been escorted outside the city limits it was not always easy to keep track of their movements and many people returned. One example is that of Leonard Foxe, alien, who had been sent with 'Robert Stevenson gaoler to be placed in a boate and so conveighed from this cytie into the parties beyond the seas'

11   W. L. Sachse, ed., *Minutes of the Norwich Court of Mayoralty, 1632–1635* (Norwich, 1967), p. 43.

12   For more on vagrancy and living 'at their own hand', that is, without a master or governor in the Norwich context, see P. Griffiths, 'Masterless Young People in Norwich, 1560–1645', *Experience of Authority*, ed. P. Griffiths, et al., pp. 146–186. For London, see P. Griffiths, *Lost Londons: Change, Crime and Control in the Capital City, 1550–1660* (Cambridge, 2008), esp. Ch. 8.

13   Sachse, ed., *Minutes, 1632–1635*, pp. 119, 108.

14   Ibid., pp. 71, 77.

15   Three vagrant passes for Norfolk, PD 100/129, 1649.

in October 1579. Despite having been sent abroad, Foxe was discovered in Norwich again the following spring.[16]

Passes were issued for other reasons too. It was not uncommon for apprentices to run away from their master for a variety of reasons, cruelty only one of many. Norwich's corporation were keen to prevent this from happening, not simply because an apprenticeship was contracted by law but because it might prevent yet another individual from falling into poverty. Furthermore, young people were expected to live within a household (of a parent, relative, or employer) because this provided supervision and stability in a society governed by patriarchal ideals.[17] So in 1633, when Richard Bircham, apprenticed to Thomas Jagges of Edgefield was found instead in Norwich, he was punished at the post and sent back to Jagges by 'passe', presumably to suffer further punishment at his master's hands.[18] Likewise, when the locksmith's apprentice Joseph Hemblinge ran away to Norwich he was punished as a common vagrant and sent back to his master by pass, as was young Thomas Bensley, returned from Norwich by pass to the mason Thomas Biggott.[19]

Restrictions placed on people entering the city, or on settlement within the city's walls, did not apply to the wealthy. Those people who could afford to pay taxes, buy land, build property, or bring in trade were welcomed, and the city went to some trouble to ensure that anyone attempting to settle for the long term had the ability to contribute to society. Clear terms and conditions were imposed on entry and period of stay on the basis of certain qualifications – usually financial – that acted to exclude unsuitable candidates. In 1633, for instance, the mayor's court had decreed that 'a strict Inquiry be made of such persons as are newly come to this City that they may be Certified to the Aldermen of every ward to the end that the takers of them may be proceeded withall by Rates'.[20] Thus it was that the Londoners Rowland Reynolds and his wife, lodging with Widow Harrison of St Stephen in 1633, were ordered to contribute to the poor rate of that parish or else leave the city.[21] Under the same set of rules cordwainer Ambrose Rose and the London man John Griffen were charged six pence a week each to stay in Norwich, and John Wiseman twelve pence a week.[22] The steep rates and terms of immediate payment were a serious disincentive to many. Wiseman, for example, had been given only forty-eight hours to come up with his twelve pence, or suffer being removed from the city on pain of vagrancy. The strict rules reflected a

16   Hudson and Tingey, *Records*, II, p. 188.
17   Griffiths' chapter on masterless young people in Norwich is especially pertinent here, see Griffiths, 'Masterless Young People', esp. pp. 148–9.
18   Sachse, *Minutes, 1632–1635*, p. 71.
19   Ibid., pp. 164, 193. Between 1632 and 1635, twenty-four apprentices appeared in court for running away from their master, see: Sachse, *Minutes, 1632–1635*.
20   Ibid., p. 92.
21   Ibid., p. 71.
22   Ibid., pp. 20, 41.

general concern that migrants be able to support themselves financially and not become a burden on the city. Better still, wealthier migrants could help provide for the growing numbers of urban poor as their money went into the civic purse.

Poor inhabitants born within the city's parishes were a different matter; they could not be forced out of the city and they had the right to claim relief from the parish of their birth in the form of fuel, food, clothes, or money. Each parish had a responsibility to look after their own poor but in many cases they were assisted by the corporation or by charities. The corporation's answer to the problem of poverty was based extensively on a series of late sixteenth-century innovations. Responding to a perceived increase in the numbers of poor people within the city's walls, the corporation commissioned a survey in 1570 that identified 2,359 poor people living in the city.[23] The greatest achievement of this survey was to transform poor relief into a far more structured, controlled and documented system, but many of the measures also acted to marginalise the poor further, including restricting their freedom of movement, in a 'project of legibility and simplification'.[24]

Subsequent plagues in 1583–6 and 1590–3, in combination with a general population increase, only served to intensify the levels of poverty in the city. Indeed, at peak points of poverty during the seventeenth century, the poorer sorts numbered the biggest proportion of Norwich's inhabitants, with those in need of relief climbing to unmanageable proportions.[25] All Saints was one such example: in 1633 the number of claimants exceeded contributors by eight, as was the case in St Paul where forty-nine people made regular claims from only thirty-one contributors.[26] Some of the larger, wealthier parishes were expected to share their rates with their poorer neighbours when circumstances obliged them. In 1689, St Peter Mancroft (probably the wealthiest

[23]   For more on the 1570 survey, see J. Pound, ed., The Norwich Census of the Poor 1570, Norfolk Record Society 40 (Norwich, 1971); M. Pelling, 'Healing the Sick Poor: Social Policy and Disability in Norwich, 1550–1640', The Common Lot: Sickness, Medical Occupations and the Urban Poor in Early Modern England, ed. M. Pelling (Harlow, 1998), pp. 79–102; P. Slack, Poverty and Policy in Tudor and Stuart England (Harlow, 1998); or P. Griffiths, 'Bodies and Souls in Norwich: Punishing Petty Crime, 1540–1700', Penal Practice and Culture, 1500–1900: Punishing the English, ed. S. Devereaux and P. Griffiths (Basingstoke, 2004), pp. 85–121. For more on the subject of pre-modern information gathering see Edward Higgs, The Information State in England: The Central Collection of Information on Citizens Since 1500 (Basingstoke and New York, 2004).

[24]   James C. Scott, Seeing Like A State: How Certain Schemes to Improve the Human Condition Have Failed (New Haven, 1998), p. 9.

[25]   Fumerton suggests that the impoverished numbered around twenty per cent of the population but other sources suggest that this figure should be higher. See Penelope Corfield, 'A Provincial Capital in the Late Seventeenth-Century: the Case of Norwich', The Early Modern Town, ed. Peter Clark (New York, 1976), pp. 233–72, 235, compared to Patricia Fumerton, Unsettled: The Culture of Mobility and the Working Poor in Early Modern England (Chicago, 2006), p. 6.

[26]   W. Rye, ed., The Norwich Rate Book, 1633–1634 (Norwich, 1903), pp. 21, 78.

of Norwich's parishes) and St George Tombland both made contributions to the poor of St Augustine's parish. Their better-off parishioners also made payments in kind, including making gifts of bread and coal.[27] In some cases, wealthy benefactors left bequests in their wills to provide for the poor of their own, and other, parishes. In 1694, for example, Edward Warnes' bequest established the Warnes Charity for the poor of St Peter Parmentergate, which provided 'every year in Coals Cloths & ... in money' for the needy parishioners.[28] Likewise, a prominent Norfolk family were able to provide a legacy for the poor people of St Andrew's parish in Norwich from a combination of contributions raised by the churchwardens at Elveden, Thetford and their own personal funds. The charity, known as the Suckling Jay Charity after its founder, donated bread and money to the poor at St Andrew for over one hundred and fifty years.[29]

As in 1570, the seventeenth-century corporation had found that poverty was a particular problem for women and children, especially widows.[30] In St John Maddermarket, for example, all seven claimants were widows; in St John Sepulchre, a parish known for its 'greate neede', twenty-seven poor people including fifteen widows relied on only eight rate payers; and in St Martin's at Palace, women represented fourteen of the eighteen claimants, of whom thirteen were widowed.[31] Even in St Andrew, a relatively affluent parish, where a listed fifty-eight ratepayers had the responsibility of only ten poor people, six of these ten were women and at least two of these were registered as widows.[32] Many widowed women were helped when specific circumstances conspired to aggravate their need, rather than all year round, such as the Widow Whales who was given four shillings to support her child during the 'tym of hir sicknes' in 1623; or Widow Huddle who was allocated two shillings and six pence to help her with costs when she was ill that same year.[33] Others however relied on poor relief for more regular periods, such as the Widdow Elveine who received relief for fifty weeks during 1623, or the Widdow Bets who, that same year, received twelve shillings over thirty-six weeks.[34] These women were thought deserving of relief. Those inhabitants who became impoverished because of the death of a spouse, sickness, or general misfortune outside of their control, were generally considered so.[35] In 1626, for example, the overseers of the same parish gave money toward the 'surgery and phisicke' of the infected poor during that decade's great plague

27 St Augustine Overseer's Accounts, PD 185/41, 1689–1713.
28 Warnes Charity Accounts, PD 162/80, 1712–1804.
29 Suckling Jay Legacy Book, PD 165/114, 1691–1856.
30 Pound, *Census of the Poor*.
31 Rye, *Rate Book*, pp. 16, 48, 58.
32 Ibid., p. 49.
33 St Andrew Overseer's Accounts, MC 992/1, fol. 1r, 1623–1713.
34 Ibid.
35 See R. Jütte, *Poverty and Deviance in Early Modern Europe* (Cambridge, 1994), p. 159 for an overview of the definitions of deserving and undeserving.

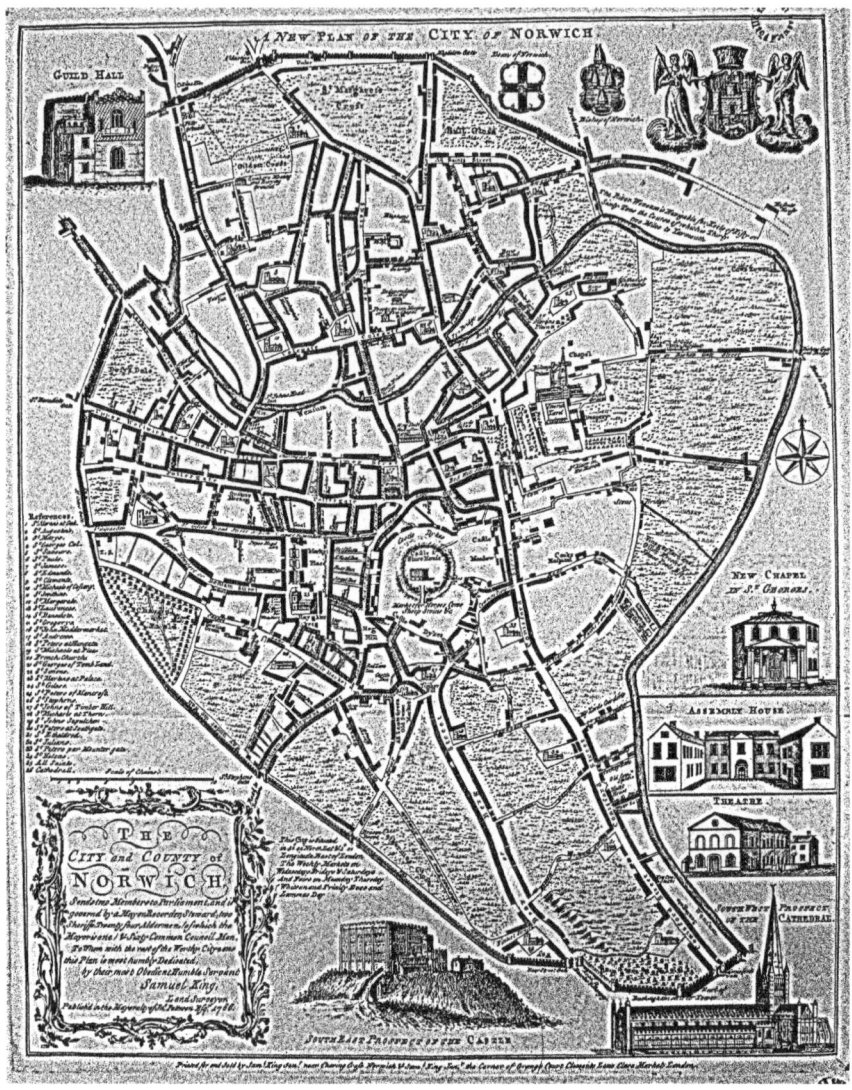

4 The city and county of Norwich by Samuel King, 1766 (Chapter 1).

outbreak, and distributed clothing to the parish's poor children.[36] Poverty for many inhabitants was not unchanging, but followed their life cycle and specific circumstances.

The fate of the deserving poor and the disturbing ratio of poor to rich were of tremendous concern to Norwich's corporation. Local organisations, such as the Wardens of the English weavers, or the Wardens of the Strangers, were

---

[36] St Andrew Overseer's Accounts, MC 992/1, fol. 4r.

taxed to help meet shortfalls in individual contributions.[37] Aldermen also left substantial gifts and endowments to the poor of their wards and of the city, like the former mayor Thomas Pettus who left the sum of twenty pounds in his will for 'the setting on work of poor orphans and children' in 1614, or Robert Bacon who, at his death in 1649, left two hundred and fifty pounds towards the training of young girls in 'spinning, knitting and dressing of wool under the tuition of some aged discreet religious women'.[38] But even these commendable efforts could not solve the problem for everyone. Complaints came thick and fast from 'dyverse of the citizens [who] felte themselves agreeved that the cittie was so replenysshed w[i]t[h] greate nombres ... whoe for the most parte wente dayely abroade from dore to dore counterfeattinge a kinde of worke but indeede [worked] verie little or none at all'.[39] For the 'crewes' of wandering poor who were resident within the city but condemned to a life of 'contynuall beggynge' the situation was very different.

The corporation could not move on a beggar who could prove he or she was born in the city, thus they had to work on strategies to punish, contain, or help poor beggars. Many of these strategies worked on the principle of establishing whether a poor individual was deserving or undeserving of relief; registering the former whilst punishing the latter. This judgement was normally based on a variety of subjective and objective facts and perceptions about that individual's religiosity, morality, honour, and road to poverty.[40] If a beggar was considered to have genuine need – perhaps he or she had a debilitating illness or no family to live with – they might be granted a begging licence for a specific period. If this licence was abused however – perhaps an individual claimed a licence after they had already claimed poor relief – punishments could be severe, although there was some leniency granted on a case-by-case basis. The punishment for begging set out by a statute of the assembly in 1571 was a whipping of six stripes, to be issued if a person was found begging 'in the stretes, at the sermon, or at anie mans dore' after a 'generall warning gyven'.[41] Thus it was that when Margaret Crabbe was found begging without licence after a prior warning she was whipped at the post in 1632,[42] but when John Bridges was discovered 'begging haveinge collection allowed him' in 1668 he was arrested and warned that he would be put to the lash if he offended again.[43]

To have a family or place to stay yet be found begging on the streets was probably the most serious abuse of the system as it was then conceived. To

---

[37] Ibid., fol. 1v.

[38] B. Cozens-Hardy and E. A. Kent, *The Mayors of Norwich, 1403–1835* (Norwich, 1938), pp. 72–84.

[39] The Orders for the Poor 1571, reprinted in Hudson and Tingey, *Records*, II, p. 345.

[40] For contemporary definitions of the deserving and undeserving poor see William Harrison, *Description of England* (1577), esp. Ch. 1.

[41] Hudson and Tingey, *Records*, II, p. 347.

[42] Sachse, *Minutes, 1632–1635*, p. 36.

[43] NCR 16a/24, fol. 76r, 17 June 1668.

choose to live 'at one's own hand' intentionally was to evade the patriarchal paradigm that governed society, thus it comes as no surprise that vagrancy was one of the most common 'crimes' to appear in the local courts of law. Between 1632 and 1635, for example, there were one hundred and thirty-one separate prosecutions specifically for the crime of vagrancy. Of this number, seventy-seven cases involved men, thirty-three related to women, and the remaining twenty-one were family groups. In addition to these cases, a further forty-one people were prosecuted for 'living idly', that is to be able-bodied and wilfully unemployed.[44] Thus it was that young Thomas Clay 'taken wandringe in this City' was ordered back to his mother's house and from there to be 'sett ... on work' and Dorothy Sadlington was punished for 'living idely' before being sent to her father's house in 1632.[45] Sadlington repeatedly appeared in the mayor's court records over the 1630s for begging, living idly, and vagrancy. Quite why she kept leaving her father's house to beg on the streets remains a mystery; we can only assume that the streets offered a better alternative to what awaited her at home.[46]

One of the reasons that vagrancy was considered so offensive was because it existed in the public eye. Thus it was that emergency measures were enacted to deal with vagrants at times when the city expected important visitors. During the assizes circuits, for example, many county dignitaries flocked to the city and remained for a time, enjoying the delights of the Norwich season.[47] During these weeks the corporation employed additional watchmen to patrol the city centre, Guildhall and marketplace, with the specific duty of suppressing begging; the sheriff granted constables additional capacities to deal with disorderly behaviour by issuing them with extraordinary warrants; and the watch were empowered to restrain beggars for the duration of the assizes.[48] From 1634, the corporation went even further by requesting parish overseers to warn their poor inhabitants – not just beggars – to stay inside during the assizes season. Without specific records, it is hard to gauge the success of this policy but, as the corporation were prepared to offer compensation for loss of earnings as a result, perhaps some were persuaded.[49] Over the course of the 1630s, the corporation reinforced and broadened existing legislation that excluded the poor from public space, reaffirming publically a view that the poor ought to stay out of sight not only on special occasions, but all the time. In 1636, for example, the poor were ordered to 'goe not abroad wanderinge & if they doe after warning that they be punished openly as Rogues'.[50] Nevertheless, ideal and reality rarely bonded. In 1678, for

---

44 Figures compiled from Sachse, Minutes, 1632–1635.
45 Ibid., pp. 19, 35.
46 Ibid., pp. 19, 28, 46, 88, 104, 156, 164. Sadlington's case is also mentioned in Griffiths, 'Masterless Young People', p. 162.
47 Corfield, 'A Provincial Capital', pp. 254–6.
48 Sachse, Minutes, 1632–1635, pp. 57–8.
49 Ibid., p. 159.
50 Ibid., p. 234.

example, the town clerk described how 'horrid crowds' and multitudes of the poor had roamed the streets and pestered 'the corners of the house' where King Charles was staying during his Norwich progress,[51] and in just one week ending 30 December 1687, nine people 'taken vagrant were whipped and passed to their homes'.[52] Keeping the poor from public places was evidently an unending battle.

The corporation also employed other strategies to deal with the public problem of the poor. Norwich, like Colchester, Exeter, Wisbech, Cambridge, and London, issued badges to its poor, a practice that had been introduced as a way of making the administration of relief more effective and to distinguish from the deserving and undeserving poor, an assessment made by overseers based on whether – in their opinion – a person's poverty-stricken situation was genuine, wilful or circumstantial. The badges were part of a wider move to regulate and manage the problem of poverty by categorising those who received relief. In their own words, 'the Aldermen of every warde shall confer w[i]th every inhabitaunte therewhat he will quietly be content to gyfe to the relief of the poor weekly and make a boke therof and certifie the same, and that money to be gevyn and distributed weekly to suche poore people as be blynde, lame, sicke and bedred'.[53] Badges were also given out to distinguish beggars who had been licensed by the corporation which, in theory at least, enabled a constable to carry out his job more efficiently, making a decision on a person at a glance.[54] The corporation expended a lot of civic money on making these badges. In one year alone, the goldsmith Nicholas Isbourne was paid sixteen shillings and eight pence (more than was given to a pauper for a year's relief) from the civic 'hamper' for just twenty-five badges.[55]

There is precious little evidence of poor people's own feelings about this highly visible classification of their need to the public. Some historians, including Steve Hindle, have argued that some poor people may have considered the wearing of a badge as a token of empowerment.[56] The series of pictures created by Marcellus Laroon, for example, presented the deserving poor as industrious and cheerful, in stark contrast to the ill-mannered and

51 Robert Hill, ed., *The Correspondence of Thomas Corie* (Norwich, 1956), p. 35.
52 W. Rye, ed., *Depositions Taken Before the Mayor and Aldermen of Norwich 1549–1567 & Extracts from the Court Books of the City of Norwich 1666–1668* (Norwich, 1905), p. 183.
53 Norwich Assembly Order, 9 August 1557, reprinted in Hudson and Tingey, *Records*, II, pp. 132–3.
54 Ibid., p. 133.
55 Norwich Clavor's Books, NCR 18d, 1550–1601, 57r.
56 See Steve Hindle's comprehensive article on the subject: 'Civility, Honesty and the Identification of the Deserving Poor in Seventeenth Century England', *Identity and Agency in England, 1500–1800*, ed. H. French and J. Barry (Basingstoke, 2004), pp. 38–59, and esp. pp. 8, 10, 13.

dirty wilfully idle.[57] In such associative symbolism, the appellation of the label 'deserving' demonstrated a level of individual religiosity and morality, and the method of giving of alms or relief supported this perception, performed as it often was after attendance at a church service as a testimony to good behaviour.[58]

Equally, the attainment of a badge might represent the culmination of a long fight to gain the help a person needed to survive. Petitions written on behalf of the poor explained at length how the person in question had been a victim of circumstances beyond their control. Henry Goldman, for example, petitioned for relief in 1636 on the basis that his father's premature death had left him in charge of his younger brothers and sisters as well as his own children, increasing his burden to the point where he was simply unable to cope.[59] He took care to explain, very humbly, that his father had been an honest man who had worked every day until he died. Similarly, Richard Laste's petition explained how he had made his living as a cobbler until he had fallen sick and he now needed help to support his family until such time as he recovered. Laste was given a licence to collect relief from his parish for six weeks 'in respect of his long tyme sycknes'.[60] Likewise, Katherine Lyne, a lame, sick widow was given six weeks' relief, and John Presson, a worsted weaver, was granted relief for three months 'in respect of his poverty' because his son 'by some misschaunce brake one of his legges' and thus he needed unexpected money for his son's 'care and cures'.[61] These people, and the many others like them, went to great pains to iterate through the pen of the scribe that their stricken circumstances were no fault of their own, and their petitions were couched in very meek and unassuming language, as befitting their subservient position as a supplicant for relief.

Though some may have been proud of the badge as the visible recognition of their deserving status, it is unlikely that everyone welcomed them. Some people, perhaps the Richard Lastes or John Pressons of Norwich who, under normal circumstances, supported themselves may have been embarrassed for their neighbours and fellow parishioners to know the situation to which they had fallen. As Steve Hindle has demonstrated, many parish authorities elsewhere knew full well how unpopular badging could be and tried to avoid the practice.[62] In Norwich, the very fact that the corporation had to reiterate to every parish overseer that the poor be forced to wear badges on their right

---

57 Marcellus Laroon, *The Cryes of the City of London* (c.1710). For discussion, see S. Shesgreen, ed., *The Criers and Hawkers of London: Engravings and Drawings by Marcellus Laroon* (Aldershot, 1990).

58 Hindle, 'Civility', p. 26.

59 Norfolk County Quarter Sessions (hereafter NCQS), C/S3/31 12 Charles, 1636–7, loose sheet entitled 'The Petition of Henry Goldman'.

60 Assembly Minute Book, NCR 16c/5, 1585–1613, fol. 106.

61 Ibid., fols 115, 175.

62 Hindle, 'Civility', p. 26.

shoulder, and would be punished if they refused, suggests that many poor people did indeed do just that.[63]

In the late sixteenth century, the corporation of Norwich had also taken the lead in modernising the Elizabethan system of relief as it groaned under the weight of the perceived escalating number of poor people. The city's pioneering reforms had included opening one of the country's first reformative institutions in 1585. Known contemporaneously as the Bridewell, or the House of Correction, its purpose was moral reformation. It was in many respects the precursor of the workhouse but, arguably, the line between reformative punishment, incarceration, and care for the poor was blurred. A term in the Bridewell was considered a stopgap where poor vagrants could be fed, housed, instructed in prayer and set on work to improve their moral and physical wellbeing, often before being placed in, or ordered to find, work, or simply because there was nowhere else for them to go. Margaret Utting, for example, was an elderly ex-prostitute suffering from syphilis. The authorities were concerned by her dubious morality so, instead of sending her to a hospital or poor house, as the deserving poor would have been, they sent her to the Bridewell, there to remain until her death.[64] The deserving poor were the sick, children, the elderly, less able or the mentally ill – those who had quite clearly not influenced their destiny by immoral actions.

The Bridewell was not intended to be a prison and was operated quite separately from the city's gaol. Nevertheless, a term at the Bridewell was frequently used as threat by the mayor's court as a punishment for wilful idleness. People did not choose to go to the Bridewell, they were ordered there. Equally, the inclusion of two whipping posts, a pair of stocks, and a chair for punishing disagreeable inmates on the premises, strongly suggested that moral reformation was not expected through prayer alone.[65] In the autumn of 1632, for example, the unfortunate runaway apprentice Ann Goose was charged with vagrancy and sent by pass to her master in South Wooton. When she was found wandering the city streets two weeks later, she was ordered to the Bridewell. Nicholas Wilson too, found 'liveinge idely' in the streets was threatened with the Bridewell if he did not find a job within the week; Pleasance Moore, a masterless woman, was committed to the Bridewell until she could be found a place as a maidservant, and in 1668 Elizabeth Brewster was ordered to find herself a job within fourteen days. If she failed, she was to be sent to the Bridewell.[66]

For many then, the Bridewell was little better than a prison. Indeed, just like the prison system, the mayor's court set the period of incarceration, usually days or weeks, but occasionally months at a time, and occupants might find themselves rubbing shoulders with people accused of petty crime. Reflecting

63 Guardians of the Poor Minute Book, NCR 20e, fol. 14v, 1712–14.
64 Assembly Minute Book, NCR 16c/5, 1585–1613, fols 143, 182.
65 Griffiths, 'Bodies and Souls', p. 107.
66 Sachse, *Minutes, 1632–1635*, pp. 101, 119; NCR 16a/24, 1666–77, fol. 83v.

the connection between poverty and criminality, in July 1632 Barbara Bloy was whipped at the post for 'ill rule and michery' before she entered a short reformatory spell at the Bridewell.[67] Three months later she had clearly reverted to her old ways, because she was whipped at the post again and ordered to the Bridewell to be 'sett on worke'.[68] The following year, Thomas Campe was sent to the Bridewell for violence against the watch, John Key for defying the corporation by refusing to reveal the name of the mother of a bastard child he had taken in, John Clarke for threatening to kill his wife, and Jane Crowne for running an unlicensed alehouse.[69] That contemporaries saw the Bridewell as a place of punishment, not of care, is also revealed in William Kyffyn's complaint to the mayor's court in 1630 that Henry Church had called him a knave, a rascal, and a 'Bridewell byrd'.[70] Certainly, the fact that the magistracy used the name of the Bridewell to threaten people into finding work says much about how the institution was used.

In the first half of the century, the corporation had ordered that every ward should have a special beadle appointed to the task of 'avoyding of rogues and other idle persons' and to give 'nedie people' without work, but able to work, employment.[71] This distinction between the wilfully idle and criminals on the one hand, and the deserving poor on the other, influenced contemporary responses to poverty, but the reality was that it was not always easy to place people in such black and white categories. The Bridewell especially blurred the distinction between poverty and crime, and even the deserving and undeserving. The contrast of the provision of beds, food, fuel, clothes, prayers and work, next to the practice of hard labour and whipping, was stark, reflective of how poverty was viewed as both a moral failing and a sad circumstantial reality for the many who could no longer help themselves.[72] Margaret Utting, the elderly syphilitic ex-prostitute is a case in point. Her criminal background meant that she required supervision, moral guidance and correction, in addition to care, and the Bridewell was one of the few institutions to combine all these elements, despite the emphasis on correction. Utting is a classic example of the blurred boundaries of crime and poverty and, in providing for the 'remainder of her life', the corporation reveal their understanding of this conundrum.[73]

The connection made between poverty and criminality is also evident in the similarity of punishment used for correcting vagrancy and general disorder. These punishments were always administered publically, reflecting the emphasis placed on symbolism in the exercise of corporation authority. One of Norwich's pillories, for example, would have been found at the east end of

---

67 Sachse, *Minutes, 1632–1635*, pp. 27, 31, 33.
68 Ibid., pp. 22, 23, 37.
69 Sachse, *Minutes, 1632–1635*, pp. 92, 93, 98, 123.
70 W. L. Sachse, ed., *Minutes of the Norwich Court of Mayoralty 1630–1631* (Norwich, 1942), p. 118.
71 Assembly Minute Book, NCR 16c/5, 1585–1613, fols 156r, 175v.
72 Griffiths, 'Bodies and Souls', p. 107.
73 Assembly Minute Book, NCR 16c/5, 1585–1613, fols 143, 182.

the Guildhall overlooking the central marketplace. The pillory was symbolic of community values, ancient traditions, and order. Originally built next to an ancient common well in 1404, the structure was redesigned many times. In 1453, Alderman Thomas Alleyn paid to erect 'a house under [the pillory] for to buy and sell corn in, and Thomas Veyle then rebuilt, painted, and adorned the common well-house'. In 1550 'part of the house was turned into a cage, with stocks therein; the whole was sixsquare, each side nine feet long, and was now paved with the stone pulled down and brought from Chapel-field steeple; [and] in 1679, the well was new railed in'.[74] Then, in 1685, the aldermen ordered that the 'pillory ... be repaired and set upon the Cross in the market'.[75] The pillory's location in the busiest section of the city, its positioning near the mayor's court patronised by various of the city's great and good, and the structure's mounting extravagance over the years, had ensured its place in urban inhabitants' collective memory as well as playing a role in their everyday panorama. As Griffiths also points out, the pillory's situation was especially redolent of civic authority, at first at the Guildhall then later in a place more commonly associated with official proclamations and civic announcements.[76] Both positions ensured a visibility akin to or in excess of that associated with the original crime, as Rebecca Franke discovered when she was sent to the pillory as punishment for violently abusing the sheriff's officers in public in 1628, as too did Mary Clay for 'skowldinge with her neighbours and raylinge [th]e magistrates' publically in 1670.[77]

Whipping was one of the more common punishments, used for a variety of crimes from vagrancy to slander. Thus in 1603 Anthony Fothergill, tapster at The Castle alehouse, was threatened with a whipping and banishment for his drunken rant against a constable; in 1615, Thomas Sayer was actually whipped at the post 'for abusynge Mr Maiors officers and the watch in Mr Maiors presence'; likewise Thomas Allyard for threatening Alderman Cocke and addressing him in 'vile and incivill tearmes' in 1619, and in 1635 Francis Gurney was whipped at the post for drunkenly abusing Alderman Cory.[78] The corporation paid for their own 'whipper' out of the civic chest.[79] The whipper also doubled as a collector for the poor prisoners held in the city gaol, assisted by a prisoner whom the corporation had set on work.[80]

The pillory and the post were not the only forms of public punishment available in Norwich. Unruly and disorderly inhabitants might find

---

[74] Francis Blomefield, *An Essay towards a Topographical History of the County of Norfolk, IV: The History of the City and County of Norwich, II* (1806), p. 235.

[75] Rye, *Depositions*, p. 177, 22 July 1685.

[76] Griffiths, 'Bodies and Souls', p. 234.

[77] NCR 16a/16 fol. 200r, 18 July 1628 and NCR 16a/24, fol. 144v, 20 July 1670.

[78] NCR 16a/14, fol. 63r, 28 November 1603; NCR 16a/15, fol. 15r, 1615; NCR 16a/15, fol. 240r 1619 and NCR 16a/20, fol. 57v, 1635.

[79] Clavor's Books, 1550–1610, NCR 18d, fol. 100r. Barnaby the 'whipper' was paid two shillings and sixpence for whipping vagabonds and twenty pence for 'converting offenders'.

[80] Hudson and Tingey, *Records*, II, p. 196.

themselves condemned to periods of time in the stocks. In 1616, for example, Edward Stephenson and his wife Amy were sent to the stocks for 'abusinge of Thomas Levy the constable of St Stephens … causing an outrage in the same p[ar]ish and for drinking at the Angel contrary to the lawe'; in 1635 Robert Bunsdale was punished 'six howers for drunkenness … fower howers for drinkeing & one hower … for swearinge' at the Cock in St Giles; and in 1685 John Oakes was 'set in the stocks at the end of this hall for an hour' for 'letting two infamous wenches out of the stocks'.[81]

Each ward had its own set of stocks so miscreants would be on show where their neighbours, friends, and family were most likely to see them. So in 1603, the stranger John Mortere faced his peers from Conisford stocks after he had shouted drunken comments at his ward's alderman Roger Gaywoode, as did Edward Cocket for exactly the same crime against Gaywoode six years later.[82] In 1687 Henry King, one of South Conisford's own watchmen, was set in the stocks for an hour at lunchtime 'for the great offence he has committed in setting one of the King's soldiers in the stocks, knowing him to be a soldier and having not misdemeaned himself other than by being late out of his quarters'.[83]

The expediency of community-located stocks also meant criminals could be punished symbolically near the scene of their indiscretion, a concept that would likely satisfy a victim who could witness at first-hand the perpetrator's penance. In 1630, for example, Humfrey Smyth, who had sworn 'fower oths in the parish', was fined: the money intended for the civic coffer. But this was not the last we hear of Smyth. He then attacked a constable who had tried to stop him beating his wife publically and on another occasion had verbally abused his ward alderman 'and in the presence of [forty] people turned down his hose & did his busyness'. Smyth's punishment was to be 'sett in the stockes accordinge to the lawe' in front of all those whom he had offended.[84] Crimes committed in public places were particularly heinous as they infringed upon commonly held values of good neighbourliness. A public punishment therefore restored public order.

Ducking was also used sporadically throughout the seventeenth century. There were two ducking stools known to have been operational in Norwich: one at Jack's Pit, where Jone Mason had been ducked for 'skolding and other misbehavyour' in 1572, and the other next to the pillory at Fye Bridge.[85] Jack's Pit was described as 'a large piece of water', the source for the Great Cockey, a parochial boundary and stream flowing from the junction of All

---

81 Sachse, *Minutes, 1632–1635*, p. 28; Rye, *Depositions*, p. 177.

82 NCR 16a/14, fol. 64r, 30 January 1603 and fol. 299r, July 1609.

83 Rye, *Depositions*, p. 182.

84 Sachse, *Minutes, 1630–1631*, p. 86.

85 Hudson and Tingey, *Records*, II, p. 185; John Kirkpatrick, *The Streets and Lanes of Norwich* (Norwich, 1889), p. 13.

Saints Green and Surrey Street into the river Wensum.[86] Fye Bridge was the main thoroughfare linking northern and southern Norwich across the Wensum, and the location of a stone market cross called 'Stump Cross' until the latter was demolished in 1644.[87] These sites afforded high footfall and visibility, the former adjacent to the swine market and the latter the city's fish market.[88] It was the Fye Bridge stool where Margaret Crookbill – having narrowly escaped the cage in 1628 for calling Merable Church a witch – was threatened with a ducking if any more complaints were made against her,[89] and the unfortunate Mary Clay was 'dipped ther thrice over her head' in 1670.[90] Contrary to popular belief though, the practice of ducking was not common in Norwich.

Norwich's mayor's court routinely prosecuted small-scale crimes like vagrancy, scolding, living idly, ill rule, begging without licence, and general disorder. After 1660, however, its records reveal a general decline of criminal business and the court's activities related ever more often to the day-to-day administration of the city. By way of example, between 1632 and 1635 one hundred and fifty-one men and women were cleared off Norwich's streets for the crime of vagrancy or living idly, but in 1668 there were only five confirmed cases of vagrancy. Certainly this was not the result of a drop in the numbers of the poor. The same records show that poverty had remained a central concern of the courts, their weekly business overshadowed by the needs of the many poor children and elderly people cared for at the city's three main hospitals. Two years later, the town clerk was moved to write that 'poverty invades us dayly like an armed man', a fact that the heath tax records also confirm.[91] One possible explanation is that the punishment of poverty as a crime was no longer central to the business of the mayor's court: indeed this is also reflected in the decline of other criminal incidents that had previously featured with regularity in that court's records, seditious speech being one such example. By the end of the seventeenth century the court had most definitely passed from being an all-round criminal prosecution and administrative body to one that focused on issues of urban management and development, administration, and the care of the poor; duties that included the confirmation of civic appointments, the collection of taxes, hospital administration, the management of relief for the poor, sick, and infected, the cleaning of the rivers and streets, the regulation of weights, measures and the sale of beer, and the confirmation of corporation-sponsored scholarships

---

[86] Margaret Pelling, 'Health and Sanitation to 1750', *Norwich Since 1550*, ed. Rawcliffe and Wilson (London, 2004), pp. 117–37, 126–7, 134.

[87] Kirkpatrick, *Streets and Lanes*, p. 83.

[88] In 1608, Mayor Sir John Pettus had ordered that new fish stalls be erected in the marketplace: Anon, *A compleat history of the famous city of Norwich: From the Earliest Account, to this Present Year 1728* (1728), p. 37.

[89] NCR 16a/16, fol. 207v, 17 August 1628.

[90] NCR 16a/24, fol. 144v, 20 July 1670.

[91] Hill, *Thomas Corie*, p. 30.

and patents.[92] During one week in April 1668, for example, the court issued orders to the aldermen 'to bind out such poore children as are in their wardes … or in the Boys or Girls Hospitals' and ordered that their expenditure be reimbursed by the overseers; that Edward Bell be allocated fifteen shillings for 'the taking in of Mary Gostlinge a poore childe'; that 'Barton the Cannoneer shall have tenne pounds of powder for the fiering of the brasse guns upon the 23rd day'; and that fifty shillings be paid toward the repair of the city's walls.[93]

It is possible that the lack of criminal cases represented a disinclination on the part of the corporation to punish poverty as a crime. The court had certainly not had its jurisdiction for prosecuting petty crime removed, as the occasional case of vagrancy, or abusive speech against corporation officials, that still appeared reveals, so specific legal changes to the court's jurisdiction is not an entirely satisfactory answer. If we look again at the records for 1668, where five people were punished in the manner of poor vagrants (with whipping and/or a spell in the house of correction as their punishment), their cases reveal a shift. Catherine Myller, for example, a poor widow from St Stephen's parish, had been sent to the house of correction for ten days after she had abused her overseers and the city swordbearer. Martha Cole was likewise incarcerated for threatening to 'fyer' her neighbours' houses, and Mary Smith and John Manser for 'lewd behaviour'.[94] From this very small sample, it seems that by the latter half of the century poverty was less likely to be treated as a crime at the mayor's court for its own sake, but only when it caused, or was linked to, anti-social behaviour.

Examining the records of the city sessions – a court that routinely dealt with more serious crime – for the same period, however, we can see that around the same time as the mayor's courts were recording fewer problems with vagrants, the sessions were still reporting vagrants being whipped and sent out of the city, or sentenced to hard labour in the Bridewell. In 1667, for example, Jane Sandys was presented to the court as a vagrant and sent back to London; in 1671 William Bardwell of Easton, caught on Norwich's streets by the night watch, was ordered to be sent to the Bridewell if he did not return home, Robert Barret likewise to Bracondale; in 1673 Charles Cotterell was sent back to Wymondham; in 1681 eleven vagrants were ordered to be whipped and escorted out of town by constables, and nine vagrants were dealt with in the same manner during 1687.[95] Although cases like these were not

---

92   In 1668, for example, the corporation gave a scholarship to Francis Cruso, son of Aquila Cruso, to continue his studies at Cambridge: NCR 16a/24, 1666–77, fol. 76r. Norwich's mayoral court opened in the 1400s as a petty sessions court but its operations were gradually scaled back to educational and hospital administration; the decline in criminal proceedings is particularly apparent in the latter part of the seventeenth century. The Court ceased to operate in 1837.

93   NCR 16a/24, 1666–77, fols 68r, 69r, 69v.

94   Ibid., fols 101r, 103v, 105v.

95   Rye, *Depositions*, pp. 120, 127, 131, 162, 183.

as common as they had been in the mayoral records for the earlier part of the century, certainly vagrants were still being treated like criminals.

Paul Griffiths, who has examined extensively the records of Norwich's petty crime, noticed the decline in criminal punishments, particularly public punishments, meted out at the mayor's court but argues that care should be taken to avoid reading too much into this because the same change was not apparent in the sessions court records.[96] His findings also counter claims that the early-modern period witnessed a linear transition between a medieval culture of public punishment to private internment for crimes that included vagrancy and living idly.[97] Certainly, the introduction of the Bridewell in Norwich was new, but a decline in public punishment should not be overstated as, arguably, public and private punishments continued to operate hand-in-hand. Confinement had long been the consequence of many crimes, if limited in its scope and duration, and the practice of public penance has continued even into modern times in ways that have included public hanging and community service. We see this in the idea of punishment within the Bridewell itself, where traditional forms of public punishment, such as the stocks, continued to be used in conjunction with incarceration. Griffiths also argues that although the variety of public punishments fell, public whippings continued to be common throughout the seventeenth century.[98] Both Griffiths and Martin Ingram suggest that historians' tendency to focus on the more serious crimes, such as felony, has overshadowed the

[96] Ibid., pp. 90–1.

[97] Robert Jütte uses the term 'the great confinement' to discuss the role of reformative punishment in 'proto-penal institutions' in early-modern European cultures. Jütte follows closely the arguments of Michel Foucault, especially those found in Foucault's *Discipline and Punish: The Birth of the Prison* (London, 1977), suggesting that private confinement and institutionalisation were, for many, one stage in a process whereby the very poor lost their claim to public space. See Jütte, *Poverty and Deviance*, pp. 169–70. J. R. Ruff argues that the increasing inclination to confine criminals was a response to population growth and the inability of medieval methods to cope with growing levels of crime, rather than a cultural shift in itself. See J. R. Ruff, *Violence in Early-Modern Europe, 1500–1800* (Cambridge, 2001), pp. 5–9 for a brief review of the evolution of thought about crime in pre-modern societies, including a critique of the work of Michel Foucault and Norbert Elias.

[98] Paul Griffiths suggests there may have been a decline in public punishment in Norwich over the course of the seventeenth century based on figures collated from Norwich's mayoral court 1560–1645, 1660–1700 and quarter sessions, 1570–1700. According to these sources Griffiths discovered that although public whippings continued to be common, the last use of the cage in Norwich was in 1666; only six men were placed in the stocks after 1660, and the last woman to be ducked was in 1670. Nevertheless, the mayoral court turned away from criminal proceedings over the course of the seventeenth century, a fact that may well affect the statistics. Griffiths raises awareness of this factor by highlighting how each court favoured different punishments, warning that caution needs to be applied when undertaking any statistical analysis: Griffiths, 'Bodies and Souls', pp. 90, 107.

study of petty crime, and that this in turn has obscured a fuller reading of corrective culture.[99]

Moving the poor from parish to parish and telling them when, and how, they should been seen in public, were all expressions of a fundamental battle to claim public space. This contest was partly created by, as Vanessa Harding points out, competition over the increasingly small amounts of free space in crowded urban societies, thus the 'particularly urgent need to find ways of controlling access and allocating rights, by means of partitions and restrictions'.[100] But there was more to this particular contest than competition over common resources and places. The successful domination of public space was also about imposing a value system onto the urban landscape, one which normalised a particular way of life over and above alternatives, either with or without conscious realisation.[101]

Alternative Perceptions of Public Spaces

The corporation went to some lengths to manage the streets and public places of the city, but the reality was that this was a near impossible task. Poor vagrants acted out of necessity, not wilful disobedience, and the system of policing the streets was simply not fit for purpose. The continual erosion of the corporation's authority by ordinary people, criminals, or the poor, for example, when walking the streets advertised alternative perceptions of public places, many of which were simply unacceptable to the dominant world view of the ratepayers, householders, and civic elite. By claiming streets and open places, mobs forced businesses to close and prevented thoroughfares from being accessed by pedestrians and traffic, criminals made certain areas taboo for honest citizens, and the poor and itinerant spoiled the perfect image of civic space. Inhabitants complained how the poor, for example, were everywhere they looked: at their doors begging for food, vomiting in the street, and lying around in every available space.[102] Norwich's *Orders for the Poor* recounted in prose that could have come straight from the pen of Thomas Harman, how the poor congregated in 'churche porshes … barnes … haye chambers, and other back corners'.[103] The city's streets, lanes, and plains were contested spaces.

[99] Griffiths, 'Bodies and Souls', pp. 85–120, 86.
[100] Vanessa Harding, 'Space, Property and Propriety in Urban England', *Journal of Interdisciplinary History* 32:4 (2002), 549–69, 549.
[101] Setha M. Low and Denise Lawrence-Zúñiga, eds, *The Anthropology of Space and Place: Locating Culture* (Oxford, 2003), p. 22. See also Mandanipour, Cars and Allen, eds, *Social Exclusion in European Cities*, pp. 75–76.
[102] The Orders for the Poor 1571, reprinted in Hudson and Tingey, *Records*, II, p. 345.
[103] Ibid. Harman wrote of how sturdy vagabonds lurked 'at the backside about backe houses, eyther in hedge rowes or some other thicket, expectyng their praye': Harman,

Nightfall in particular shifted the perimeters. Darkness affected perceptions of spaces and places because of the inability to see clearly, the gloom of poorly lit, or unlit, alleys and streets fundamentally altering the cityscape. Shadows disguised familiar landmarks and cast new shapes onto walls and roadways. The imagination played tricks on the mind, conjuring illusions of thieves and rogues hidden in shadows and dark corners. There were also mysterious, otherworldly connections that were made with the night: the realm of the prince of darkness and his children, the officers of the night.[104] The image of the nightwalker, for example, vacillated between an ordinary late-night drinker, gamer, or rake, to the n'er do well criminal and, at the most extreme, something approaching preternatural.[105] Fernandos Rojas' comedic and cautionary tale of false servants and cunny-catching bawds, for example, framed the nightwalker as a 'Hobgoblin … this phantasticall spirit; long-shanked like a Stork; in shape and proportion, like a picture in Arras, that is ill-wrought'.[106] On one count however, all agreed: the nightwalker was to be feared. The seventeenth century comedy *Madame Fickle* mocked the concept of the 'innocent nightwalker' (such an oxymoron could not have existed),[107] and George Chapman's *Everyone* uttered the term in fear of the late-night visitor whom she could not see for the darkness of the hour.[108]

The city had a night watch to patrol the streets, commonly supposed to comprise 'sober' and 'substantial' householders, but complaints in 1676 of several fires led the corporation to question the diligence of their current number, concluding that they were in fact rather 'mean' of condition.[109] It is perhaps no surprise that substantial householders – who were expected to perform the duty on rotation – did not wish to trek the city's streets between the hours of ten and five in the morning 'when the stage of the world was hung in blacke … wherein they [nightwalkers] might so safely walke muffled!'[110] The dark corners and shadowy alleyways made the perfect hiding place for rogues, thieves and cutpurses like Thomas Nabbe's pick-pocketing

---

Warning for Common Cursetors, p. 56.

[104] See Thomas Dekker, *O per se O. Or A new cryer of Lanthorne and candle-light* (London, 1616).

[105] For more on this subject, see Griffiths, 'Meanings of Nightwalking'.

[106] Fernando Rojas, *The Spanish bavvd, represented in Celestina: or, The tragicke-comedy of Calisto and Melibea* (London, 1631), p. 55. The term nightwalker might also refer to a somnambulist: Antoine Le Grand, *An entire body of philosophy according to the principles of the famous Renate Des Cartes in three books* (London, 1694), Ch. 8 and esp. p. 219 on slumber and dreaming.

[107] Thomas D'Urfey, *Madam Fickle, or, The witty false one* (London, 1677), p. 66.

[108] George Chapman, *Monsieur D'Oliue A comedie* (London, 1606).

[109] Rye, *Depositions*, p. 141.

[110] Dekker, *Lanthorne and Candle-light*, Ch. 12.

nightwalker *Mortilla*,[111] or Barnaby Rich's '*impudent, immodest, shameles, in-solent, audacious … night-walker*'.[112] As Robert Abbott had warned in 1639:

> Ye shall one day find that this darknesse breeds carlesnesse, sinful delight, feare, and doubting … In darknesse men are carelesse of their goings and doings … In darknesse sinfull delights are most welcome: when drunkards were more modest, and ashamed of the noon-day, the Apostle saith, *they that are drunke are drunke in the night:* And *Job* saith, that the Adulterer hunteth for the twilight, and flattereth himselfe, that GOD cannot pierce throw the darke cloud.[113]

Equally, some of Norwich's streets had an especially bad reputation. In 1620, for example, John Roads was found with 'certain women' in a notorious alley near New Hall.[114] This passage, which had been known as *turpis vicus* or 'the shameful street' since the 1300s, was, even by the seventeenth century, still understood locally as the place to pick up prostitutes.[115] Likewise, St Martin's Lane just north of the river was colloquially dubbed Whore's Lane after its nocturnal goings-on, and an area near the castle ditches called the Back of the Inns – literally from the string of alehouses backing onto it – was a rec-ognised trouble spot. It was at the latter that constables found John Lewys keeping company with a woman of rather dubious morals in 1620, and Anne Greenwood was caught entertaining two soldiers in 1696.[116] To fight prosti-tution was to fight a losing battle. Despite the prosecution of women like Eliz-abeth Bell, Anne Bud, or Ellen Wright – the latter going by the alias Beaten Gold – in the Bridewell, or the many attempts to shut down drinking houses that facilitated prostitution, like Thomas Garrard's alehouse where 'Gawdy Black' was to be found in 1632, it could not be erased from the streets.[117]

The reputation of these areas also rubbed off on their inhabitants and pas-sers-by. Sometimes just being in the wrong place, and crucially at the wrong time, was enough to risk a person's reputation. Respectable people were ex-pected to be at home after dusk and those people who 'sleep by day and walke

[111] Thomas Nabbes, *The Muse of New-market, or, Mirth and drollery being three farces acted before the King and court at New-market* (London, 1680), p. 35.

[112] Barnaby Rich, *The excellency of good women* (London, 1613), p. 11.

[113] Robert Abbot, *The young-mans warning peece, or, A sermon preached at the buriall of William Rogers, apothecary with an history of his sinful life and woefull death* (London, 1639), p. 42.

[114] NCR/16a/15, fol. 308v, 5 August 1620.

[115] Popularly known as 'Gropekuntelane' during the medieval period, the street was later renamed Opie Street. Despite the name change, the area's reputation lingered into the seventeenth century. The name was a generic one, used across England to signify an area of prostitution. For more on this see Richard Holt and Nigel Baker, Indecent Exposure – Sexuality, Society and the Archaeological Record', *Towards a Geography of Sexual Encoun-ter: Prostitution in English Medieval Towns*, ed. Lynne Bevan (Glasgow, 2001), pp. 201–2.

[116] NCR/16a/15, fol. 240r, 5 August 1620; DN/DEP/53/58a, 16 March 1696. Greenwood v. Colfer.

[117] Sachse, *Minutes, 1632–1635*, pp. 15, 24, 25, 159. See also NCR, 16a/b, fol. 24r, 1688, for corporation orders regarding houses of ill repute.

abroad by night' were 'suspected to live by dishonest courses'.[118] In 1639, for example, Mary Fiske's neighbour had defamed her by saying publically that she played 'the whore by moonlight'.[119] Such allegations and associations were hard to shake off once they had become lodged in people's imaginations.

Mixed Messages

The tensions over public space observable between the corporation and the impoverished, criminal underclass discussed thus far have suggested that a competitive dichotomy born out of social tensions determined the image and impressions of the city's streets. Nevertheless this would be too simple a way of describing the many-faceted aspects of public space. Many of Norwich's open areas had a very mixed social and cultural heritage that muddied inhabitants' perceptions of these places; perceptions that also changed with time.

Processions, pageants, plays, ales and music, for example, had been traditionally staged in public spaces like market squares, broad roads, greens, and fields. Such events appealed to a socially diverse audience and were organised by, or in honour of, a wide range of people or organisations. Some might have been born out of Norwich's popular customs and traditions; others were connected to the religious calendar and some, the civic year.[120] Over the course of the seventeenth century the practice of large-scale public entertainments, especially processions and pageants, had gradually declined. This subtle shift was also reflected in the increasing privatisation of public spaces and entertainments, a change that was especially apparent after the Restoration. The major markers of the civic year – the annual mayoral inauguration for example – continued to be celebrated, but Peter Clark and Paul Slack have argued that such celebrations began to place more emphasis on winning 'the custom and patronage of county society by pandering to gentry taste' rather than appealing to the masses.[121] Cultural activities were increasingly regarded as commercial opportunities for the middling merchants and shopkeepers who capitalised on the inflow of county gentry during assizes,

---

118 M. Dalton, *The Countrey Justice Conteyning the Practice of the Justice of the Peace Out of their Session* (London, 1618), p. 66.

119 DN/DEP 44/44A, fol. 102r, 2 October 1639. Fiske v. Clampe.

120 For more on Norwich's annual civic events see, Mary A. Blackstone, 'Walking the City Limits: The Performance of Authority and Identity in Mary Tudor's Norwich', *City Limits: Perspectives on the Historical European City*, ed. G. Clark, J. Owens and G. T. Smith (Montreal, 2010), pp. 106–38 and Victor Morgan, 'A Ceremonious Society: An Aspect of Institutional Power in Early Modern Norwich', *Institutional Culture in Early Modern Society*, ed. Anne Goldgar and Robert I. Frost (Leiden, 2004), pp. 133–63.

121 Peter Clark and Paul Slack, *English Towns in Transition, 1500–1700* (Oxford, 1976), p. 149.

sessions, committees, elections, and inaugurations.[122] The corporation also recognised the commercial potential and invested in improving facilities for visitors and encouraging appropriate entertainments for Norwich's seasons.[123] The practice of public entertainment became gradually more commercialised and socially restricted to those who could pay.

In the same way that the corporation endeavoured to manage the flow of people on the streets, they also tried to manage what people could view in the streets. For example, only the entertainments that they had licensed could be shown. In this way they controlled (though not always successfully) the type and duration of the performances put on for a public audience. Their motivations were partly financial – licensing was a means of raising revenue – but they were also keen to protect inhabitants from entertainments that might not be entirely respectable, or could distract them too long from work and encourage them to loiter in or around drinking houses. These aims were illuminated most clearly by the corporation's petition to Lord Arlington during Christmas 1669, a missive that asked for Crown assistance to back their recent, and rather fruitless, efforts to impose time limits on 'stage players, actors of comoedies, tragedies, pastoralls, interludes, lotteries, puppet playes, mountebanckes, and all other showes whatsoever, whoe by their frequent resorte to this city from their labors diverted the meaner sort of people in their severall manufactures, thereby occasioninge a vaine expence of their tyme and monie'.[124] This was also the case in 1616, for example, when visiting players had been asked not to play at the White Horse Inn at the Haymarket but to perform instead at a chapel near New Hall: an offer the corporation proposed to limit drunkenness and disruptions to local businesses. The players rejected the offer and the corporation were forced into a compromise whereby the players were allowed to use both venues but with time restrictions on the performances held at the inn.[125] The corporation's attitude was not unique to Norwich. It reflected a national sentiment – often inspired by godly congregations and a reforming social elite – to supress many popular forms of entertainment, especially during the 1640s, 1650s, and 1690s.[126] The change reflected a growing disinclination on the part of the richer sorts to participate in, or condone, traditional forms of entertainment that were increasingly considered vulgar.[127]

[122]   Angela Dain, 'An Enlightened and Polite Society', *Norwich Since 1550*, ed. Rawcliffe and Wilson, pp. 193–218, 194.

[123]   Corfield, 'A Provincial Capital', pp. 254–6.

[124]   Hill, *Thomas Corie*, pp. 28–9.

[125]   NCR 16a, fols 62, 70r, 30 March 1616.

[126]   The idea that political and cultural changes over the course of the fifteenth to the eighteenth centuries amounted to a 'reform of popular culture' was famously explored by Peter Burke in *Popular Culture in Early-Modern Europe* (Farnham, 1978). See also Barry Reay, *Popular Culture in Seventeenth-Century England* (London, 1988), esp. Ch. 4.

[127]   Martin Ingram, 'Ridings, Rough Music and the "Reform of Popular Culture" in Early Modern England', *Past and Present* 105 (1984), 79–113, 79.

The corporation's attitude and insistence on licensing each and every act, however small, also reflected attitudes towards strangers, foreigners and the itinerant. Wandering entertainers were only one small step away from vagrants, especially if they could not afford to pay the licence fee. The musician John Gyrlynge, for example, was not allowed to perform in Norwich on the grounds that he was 'an idle minstrel' and William Denny, a juggler by profession, was punished for vagrancy and sent by pass to Ipswich rather than being allowed to perform for Norwich's public.[128] Such prosecutions reflected how money often determined an individual's ability to move freely about public places.

Building on Clark and Slark's assertion of the changing nature of popular entertainment at this time, it can certainly be seen in Norwich that there was also a marked difference in the type and number of places utilised for entertainment. Although many shows, performances and processions continued to take place on the streets or in the marketplaces, these practices coexisted more and more often with private showings (requiring paid entry). Attendant to this was the development of dedicated public areas for the specific purpose of entertainment, usually aimed at the better sorts. Chapel Field, for example, was an area of open fields about eight acres in size on the western edge of the city and a very early example of the changing use of urban green spaces. Originally owned by the church and used for farming, the land had passed into a combination of private and civic ownership after the Reformation. In 1579 the corporation had ordered that part of Chapel Field be explicitly designated a training ground for the 'exercysyng of shotyng and for the learning to shoote in any manner of handegonnes, harquebuzes, callivers, or suche lyke', an order that merely formalised its historical use.[129] Nevertheless, by the end of that century military training was only one of the many ways the open ground was being employed. The common practice of taking morning exercise – usually only practised by those with time on their hands and without a physical, manual job – had become formalised into a special walkway, specifically for the exercise of gentlemen and ladies of leisure. It was later planted 'at the expense of Tom Templeman' with tree-lined avenues.[130] Thomas Cleer's 1696 map of Norwich reveals how Chapel Field had eventually become integrated into the formal landscaped gardens of Chapel Field House and the avenues and walks had evolved into the city's earliest pleasure garden. The whole area gradually became the heart of an entertainment district for the wealthy. Chapel Field House was the scene of grand assemblies – tickets for which could be purchased at a nearby coffee house – and the previously open

---

[128] Hudson and Tingey, *Records*, II, p. 188; NCR, 16a, fol. 525, 24 April 1624.

[129] Court of Convocation, 5 September 1579, reprinted in Hudson and Tingey, *Records*, II, p. 188.

[130] Richard Gardiner, *The History of Pudica: A Lady of Norfolk* (1754), p. 21.

space between the house and the pleasure garden was developed for a theatre and a bowling green in the early eighteenth century.[131]

Norwich was one of the first cities outside of London to have hosted pleasure gardens. The first purpose-built pleasure ground had been the pet project of Lord Henry Howard, fifth Duke of Norfolk. Opened in 1663 on the site once belonging to the Austin Friars that his family had acquired after the Reformation, it was rather unimaginatively called My Lord's Gardens.[132] Howard intended that the open ground lying on a southeastern bend of the river be converted into a 'wilderness' and formal gardens for the pursuit of walking and recreation, and a bowling green was also added in 1670.[133] Just north of My Lord's Garden the ancient site of the Grey Friars had also been acquired by the Dukes of Norfolk in 1539. The family preserved many of the Grey Friars' gardens including its 'dovecotes, ponds, waters ... orchards',[134] and they developed the southeastern edge of the priory land into another pleasure ground, known as the Spring Gardens (later Vauxhall Gardens), its formal landscaped trees clearly visible on Cleer's 1696 map of the city.[135] The Dukes of Norfolk were also responsible for one of the other major landscaping projects in the city: the Duke's Palace Gardens. In 1563, the ducal territory had been described as 'a capital messuage new built with buildings, courts, orchards, gardens, ponds and vineyards', and a fountain[136] but by the end of the seventeenth century the house had seen better days, despite a reputed thirty thousand pound refurbishment in 1681.[137] The royal visit of 1671 was the last time the house was seen at the height of its glory, although contemporaries still noted how much work had to be done to the property to ready it for the King and Queen's arrival.[138] The gardens however were well equipped with a covered bowling alley, tennis court, and playhouse.[139]

Just outside the city wall to the northeast, Mousehold Heath was also a popular though less formal recreational spot. Infamously associated with the violent events of Kett's Rebellion of 1549, the heath had a longstanding

[131] Dain, 'An Enlightened and Polite Society', p. 194. The development can be clearly seen on Samuel King's 1766 map of Norwich.

[132] Dain, 'An Enlightened and Polite Society', p. 205.

[133] Kirkpatrick, *Streets and Lanes*, p. 8.

[134] Melissa Gaudoin, *The Green Spaces and Culture of Late Medieval Norwich: Municipal, Ecclesiastical and Medical* (University of East Anglia MA Thesis, unpub., 2007), pp. 29–30.

[135] The Spring Gardens can also been seen in the foreground of Kirkpatrick's View of Norwich from the North East published in 1723.

[136] A. Carter, ed., *East Anglian Archaeology Report No. 15 – Excavations in Norwich, 1971–1978 Part I* (Norwich, 1982), p. 54.

[137] Corfield, 'A Provincial Capital', p. 255.

[138] Town clerk Thomas Corie noted that although the Duke was 'no stranger' to the city, his long absences had left his home neither 'finished or in order' at the time of the royal visit, thus was the Duke 'forced ... to post hither out of Yorkshire to prepare'. Hill, *Thomas Corie*, p. 33.

[139] John Chambers, ed., *A General History of the County of Norfolk* (1829), p. 1172. The house had been abandoned by 1711 but the gardens continued to be used.

relationship with archery and energetic sports. In the 1560s, for example, guests of the Duke of Norfolk, including the Earls of Northumberland and Huntington, Thomas Howard and Lord Willoughby, had entertained themselves here with shooting and military exercises.[140] The gently undulating hills of Mousehold afforded a fabulous prospect across the city's skyline, and the riverbanks from Cow Tower to Sandling's Ferry were popular destinations for walking parties and picnicking.[141] An area just north of Cow Tower (the southernmost section of Mousehold heath) was reserved for shooting until well into the eighteenth century, but contemporary maps and prospects reveal how this common land was increasingly being challenged by urban sprawl.[142]

The utilization of large areas of urban space for pleasure reveals how changes in social culture were making an impact on the landscape. Nevertheless few of the open green spaces so enthusiastically promoted by the likes of William Cuningham to sell Norwich's image as a healthy city during the sixteenth century were common land. All the land within the city walls was owned by private interests, the church, or by the corporation. What we see taking place during the early-modern period is the appropriation of former fields for the purposes of formal gardens or building projects, rather than farming, or grazing. By 1700, therefore, there were a range of different options available for entertainment aside from the customary bonfires, plays, music, and processions that took place in the streets, markets and inns. One of the more significant points associated with the new entertainment spaces was that, unlike the traditional popular festivities, these were socially exclusive. My Lord's Garden, for example, captured simply within its name the selectivity of the pleasure garden ethos: *public* space that was not open to a *general public*. As new fashions in popular culture fundamentally altered the face of public urban popular culture it created yet another perceptible separation between the better sorts and the poor.

Having said this, the process was piecemeal and should not be overstated. As John Pound has argued, it was really only after 1660 that changing fashions became felt in Norwich's urban landscape and even then the change was not dramatic.[143] That an area of green fields had perhaps been developed into an area of trees and avenues would not have had an immediate or significant impact on the mentalities of the city dwellers and for much of the seventeenth century, traditional and new ways of using public spaces for entertainment were bedfellows. Neither was there a lack of open space for ordinary folk to enjoy. Gildencroft, for example, was a large extent of open land north

---

[140] Blomefield, *Topographical History*, III:I, p. 280.

[141] The church had owned the heathland until the 1880s, at which point its management was taken over by the corporation.

[142] NWHCM: 1922.135.4: M, N. & S. Buck, South East Prospect of the City of Norwich, 1741.

[143] J. Pound, *Tudor and Stuart Norwich* (Chichester, 1988), p. 27.

of the Wensum that crossed the parishes of St Martin at Oak, St Clement, and St Augustine. Owned by the Great Hospital of St Giles at Bishopgate and incorporating farmland known as The Lathes, the land had been used for archery practice and jousting for time-out-of-mind. By the seventeenth century this practice had almost petered out, but the croft – especially an area near St Martin's Gate called the Folly Ground – was often still used for sports and leisure. Very different from the gentile pleasure grounds south of the river, the Folly Ground was notorious for its open-air revels that pierced the calm of long summer evenings. Local inhabitants, often weavers, would make merry at the nearby Tabor's Folly inn and sing, dance, and play games on the Folly Ground long into the night. Camping (an early and often violent form of football) and dancing were such regular events at Gildencroft that in 1671 complaints were heard by the mayor of how the grass there had been ruined by the rough festivities, and in 1682, the city marshals were ordered to arrest boys and young men playing there on the Lord's Day.[144] The Folly Grounds were the rougher alternative to the pleasure gardens of the south and east, an ideal green space where urban labourers and artisans could relax after a long day spent working in the busy, polluted city centre.

Equally, few public places were entirely exclusive. Ordinary youths, not the vagrants or the poor, but apprentices and young labourers, claimed the streets and leisure grounds in ways that caused consternation for the corporation and many inhabitants. On 31 March 1677, for example, marshals had to be sent several times to apprehend boys who were 'stripping themselves naked and running about Chapel Field', and in 1682 'boys and young fellows' were stopped from playing in Chapel Field, the churchyard at St Augustine's, and the castle dykes.[145] That young men congregating in urban open spaces was considered a social problem would not look out of place today. In seventeenth-century England, the matter of peripatetic urban youths was compounded by the widespread belief in a social system that assumed all men should have a master; that idleness was immoral; and that youths were prone to hotheaded irrationality. It was the latter idea that perhaps unfairly connected youths (especially apprentices) with riots and anti-social activities.

Norwich retained many of its open fields and orchards until well into the eighteenth century.[146] Indeed, as Daniel Defoe had noted during his visit to Norwich in 1723, 'the walls seem to be placed, as if they expected that the city would in time increase sufficiently to fill them up with buildings'.[147]

---

[144] E. A. Kent, 'The Gildencroft in Norwich', *Norfolk Archaeology* 29 (1946), 222–7; Rye, *Depositions*, p. 167.

[145] Rye, *Depositions*, pp. 144, 167.

[146] 'A New plan of the city of Norwich' published by Samuel King in 1766 clearly shows how large areas of open space could still be found within the city walls, including St. Margaret's Croft and Gildencroft in the north, the cathedral grounds in the east, Chapelfield in the west and an orchard in the south. This evidence is also supported by Blomefield's 1746 and Cleer's 1696 maps.

[147] D. Defoe, *A Tour through the Whole Island of Great Britain* (London, 1971), p. 87.

Nevertheless, the examples of Chapel Field (later Chapelfield) and My Lord's Garden reveal how the changing social culture of urban inhabitants influenced the form and use of the physical landscape around them. It would be unrealistic to suggest that the better sorts never trod the grass of Gildencroft or that ordinary folk never ventured onto the tree-lined avenues of Chapel Field, but ideas that connected public places with social class crept insidiously into inhabitants' perceptions of their city. At the same time, traditional recreational activities were in decline and the newer forms of entertainment were, more often than not, aimed at a paying audience to the exclusion of the poorest inhabitants.

The corporation of Norwich understood the benefits of managing public places. Controlling who went where, and when, was a form of social control.[148] As James C. Scott has noted, 'functions [such as] certifying, counting, reporting, registering, classifying, and identifying' were all essential activities in the process of channelling civic power through seemingly 'natural (rational and normal)' processes.[149] The corporation of Norwich did this as they surveyed the city's poor, registered them for relief, and labelled them as deserving or undeserving. Likewise, removing the poor from the public eye, or refusing them settlement within the city walls, were powerful ways of managing people's lives by determining their access to, and agency within, public places. The corporation also appropriated symbolic elements of public space to project messages, perhaps by making punishments public performances, or by influencing how and where people spent their leisure time. The corporation's schemes were not always successful, however. Removing the poor from public places was a challenge the corporation were bound to lose and the battle for Norwich's streets and open spaces was an on-going contest.[150] This was also apparent in the growing fashion for the wealthier sorts to alter the landscape with the aim of developing exclusive entertainments for their own kind, a trend that co-existed alongside traditional forms of, and places for, popular entertainment.

The practice of managing public places was not all about the maintenance of political or cultural superiority by one group over another, though it might be rather negatively interpreted in this way. The relationship between the

---

[148] It would be useful here to refer to Paul Rabinow's discussion of 'spatial-tactics', that is, the deliberate manipulation of space by a ruling power: P. Rabinow, 'Ordinance, Discipline, Regulation: Some Reflections on Urbanism', *The Anthropology of Space and Place: Locating Culture*, ed. S. M. Low and D. Lawrence-Zúñiga (Oxford, 2003).

[149] Daniel Lord Smail, *Imaginary Cartographies: Possession and Identity in Medieval Marseille* (New York, 1999), p. 31. Lord Smail refers here to Bernard S. Cohn and Nicholas B. Dirks, 'Beyond the Fringe: The Nation State, Colonialism, and the Technologies of Power', *Journal of Historical Sociology* 1:2 (1988), 224–9.

[150] Michel De Certeau argued that as rulers sought to classify, survey and order space, the weak diverted, manipulated and subverted its meanings via intentional or unintentional acts of transgression. See G. Ward, ed., *The Certeau Reader* (Oxford, 2000), p. 218.

government and public space was more often determined by the rather less coherent government tactic of responding to, rather than creating, change, or simply shifting fashions. The corporation of Norwich faced many pressures as a result of the city's steadily increasing population, resulting in more competition over land and resources, a higher crime rate, and unmanageable numbers of people who needed relief in times of hardship. These dynamics, along with cultural attitudes towards rich and poor, underpinned the corporation's attitude towards managing public spaces.

3

Separations and Intersections: The Norwich Strangers

Yes While I this describe
And in green dales
I walk beside the Yare
To take a little air
And to the city
Through thick woods do turn
How I am there regaled
By the choir of Nightingales![1]

Jan (John) Cruso, a Dutch poet and writer who had lived in seventeenth-century Norwich, penned the verse above, his words quite clearly expressing his pleasure at the verdant urban hinterlands of the Yare Valley that had become his new home. Cruso was one of the many migrants who came to East Anglia during the early-modern period and his story is revealing of how the so-called 'strangers' managed the remarkable transition of starting afresh, often as refugees, into a land that was in parts hostile and welcoming to the newcomers.[2] In leaving their home countries, many strangers found that legal discrimination made their lives problematic and they relied on their own church and congregation to provide them with the stability, familiarity and support that they could not achieve by other means. By so doing, they maintained a distinct identity and close community ties that connected them more with their homeland than with their new city. From the records pertaining to the strangers' communities – which differentiate their people at every step in language and in law – it is easy to assume that they lived sequestered lives but

---

[1] Jan Cruso, excerpt from 'Expansion on the Eighth Psalm of David, 1642' reprinted in William Woods, 'Publications connected with the Dutch Church in Norwich', *Religious Dissent in East Anglia: Historical Perspectives*, ed. N. Virgoe and T. Williamson (Norwich, 1993), pp. 29–36, 35.

[2] Immigrants in early-modern England were referred to collectively as strangers or foreigners, a homogenous label that ignored nationality and reflected contemporary attitudes towards outsiders. This chapter adopts the appellation 'strangers' to refer to the Dutch, Walloon and French communities of Norwich because of the problems of identifying nationality in the records.

this would be to ignore the ways in which social networks crossed conventional boundaries of belonging.

Cruso, for instance, had managed to maintain close links with his homeland at the same time as he settled into East Anglian life. He was the son of a cloth merchant in Flanders who had fled the country with his family during the 1570s or 1580s. Jan, as the eldest son, took over his father's Norwich-based business in the early 1600s and his brothers, Aquila and Timotheus, became a minister in the Church of England and a merchant in London respectively. Jan's son, John, went to Cambridge and became a Church of England chancellor.[3] Jan Cruso was a respected and successful member of Norwich's community of inhabitants and had fully integrated into English life but he did not do this to the detriment of his own community identity. During the civil wars, for example, Cruso captained the strangers' militia, a company who wholeheartedly supported Norwich after the corporation declared for parliament but was entirely funded and managed by private donations from the strangers' congregation. Cruso's authorship likewise spanned Dutch and English interests. His *Expansion on the Eighth Psalm of David* (from which the above lines were taken) was published in Amsterdam in 1642 and, according to William Woods, has the reputation of being the first original Norfolk poetry to have been penned in Dutch.[4] Aside from poetry, Cruso wrote works building on his experiences with the militia in Norwich and the wars in the Netherlands.[5] He also translated several texts from Dutch into English.

Inside the back cover of *Expansion*, Cruso had written an elegy to his contemporary John Elison, minister of the Dutch church in Norwich between 1603 and 1639, and an inspirational character in Cruso's early life. Elison had been born and raised in Norwich but sustained strong ties with the church in Amsterdam, visiting there in 1634 on behalf of Norwich's Dutch community.[6] His son Theophilus was educated at Gonville and Caius College Cambridge, with Cruso acting as surety for his fees. Theophilus succeeded his father as minister at Norwich in 1639.[7]

Cruso and Elison were but two of the several thousand strangers and foreigners who made Norwich their home during the late sixteenth and seventeenth centuries. Their experiences only represent those of the middling sorts but the sense of a community living at the interstices of two worlds was not unique to the better sort. This chapter explores the lives of the strangers

3 Ole Peter Grell, 'Cruso, John (fl. 1595–1655)', Oxford Dictionary of National Biography, Oxford University Press, 2004 [http://www.oxforddnb.com/view/article/6852, accessed 1 Aug 2013]

4 Woods, 'Publications', p. 35.

5 Grell, 'Cruso', ODNB. Cruso joined the militia in 1621 and published *Militarie Instructions for the Cavallrie* (1632). Although he had worked his way up the ranks in the militia, it is unlikely that he had any actual combat experience when he wrote the *Instructions*.

6 Woods, 'Publications', pp. 29, 35.

7 John Venn, ed., *Biographical History of Gonville and Caius College*, Vol. I (Cambridge, 1897), p. 270.

who lived in seventeenth-century Norwich and considers how far they were a distinct community. In line with the themes of this book, it explores the possibility of alternative landscapes relating to the social, cultural or political dynamics of that community, coterminous with but not always subject to, the urban environment. It is perhaps easier to discuss segregation than it is to discuss integration; an observation that has been at the heart of the contemporary and modern literature on the strangers. Even by using the appellation of 'stranger', the settlers are defined by their differences. Stranger communities exist in a linguistic isolation that is difficult to avoid. The contemporary civic administration marked the strangers from native inhabitants with different sets of rules and labels and it can be hard to see past restrictive laws to witness how they affected strangers' lives in practice or to gauge the impact of economic legislation on social perceptions of the strangers as inhabitants and neighbours. The Church of England and the Crown marked out religion as a point of difference by enforcing a practice of separate places for worship and congregational membership, though this process was not entirely one-sided: the strangers' church had much to gain from looking after their own. Yet immigration was a common feature of seventeenth-century life and especially so in Norwich where immigration sustained the urban population and bolstered an ailing economy. Without the strangers, Norwich's story may have been a very different one.

This conundrum characterised the strangers' relationship with the urban landscape. Strangers tended toward living in particular areas, especially north of the river Wensum, but not apart from native inhabitants. Certainly, for many strangers, especially those who were second or third generation, it would be anathema to describe them as a segregated or ghettoised community. It is simply not a precept that they themselves would have recognised. Likewise, although they worshipped at their own congregational churches, maintained at their own expense, many strangers also chose to worship alongside native inhabitants at parish churches. For as much as differences in their faith may have worked to isolate the strangers from the Church of England, their faith also provided a bridge to, and a model for, the nonconformist inhabitants of one of England's most godly cities. At the same time, stranger families were expected to provide monies for the care and education of their own, but they also contributed to local and national taxes and subsidies. This relationship was not always one-sided; on some occasions the Crown or the corporation made donations toward the strangers' sick and impoverished.

In these ways and more, the strangers moved across tangible and theoretical boundaries of exclusion and inclusion within city life. Their community's relationship with the native inhabitants, the corporation, and indeed the city itself, was a complex and multi-layered affair. Their identity as strangers coincided at points of mutual interest with native inhabitants, relating to occupation, neighbourhood, or faith, and separated at interstices based on the same factors. As Naomi Tadmor states, 'when people moved' they found 'themselves once more living in local communities, surrounded by new yet structurally similar sets of neighbours and neighbourly relation-ships'.[8] Foreign immigration and the presence of new networks amongst old pushed at the close-knit ideological boundaries of belonging that existed in seventeenth-century society: as new migrants passed through the city gates they brought with them links that transcended civic limits, subtly working to extend urban communities into an international network. With each new ar-rival (or loss) each city and each neighbourhood underwent a subtle change, opening that community to outside influences, cultures and ideas.

This chapter considers the experience of communities from the perspec-tive of the stranger migrants who lived in Norwich during the late sixteenth and seventeenth centuries. It will cross social, economic, religious and top-ographical platforms to ask how far the strangers' presence created another face of the city; one uniquely bound to the places and spaces associated with the migrant community. However it will also argue that their landscape was ever shifting and always porous, without a doubt one of the most abstract and ephemeral maps considered in this book.

The Norwich Strangers

With the exception of one or two key texts, the story of overseas migration into England's seventeenth-century regional cities had barely been chartered until the last forty years or so.[9] It was during the 1980s and 1990s that schol-ars, influenced by the previous generation of new social historians, began to take an interest in exploring the history of marginal groups and racial minor-ities. Laura Yungblut emerged as a key figure in understanding contemporary perceptions of strangers, as did Randolph Vigne and Charles Littleton who considered the integration of stranger communities in Elizabethan England.[10] Nigel Goose and Lien Luu's 2005 landmark volume of essays brought togeth-er a range of leading authors on the subject, a number that included Raingard Esser and Andrew Spicer, and the volume serves as one of the most compre-hensive publications to date in the history of English immigration.[11]

Scholars interested in the history of the strangers in Norwich have perhaps been luckier than most: the city had one of the largest immigrant populations

8 N. Tadmor, 'Friends and Neighbours in Early Modern England: Biblical Translations and Social Norms', *Love, Friendship and Faith in Europe, 1300–1800*, ed. L. Gowing, M. Hunter and M. Rubin (Basingstoke, 2005), pp. 150–76.

9 With perhaps the exception of the classic: William Cunningham, *Alien Immigrants to England* (London, 1897).

10 Laura Yungblut, *'Strangers Settled here amongst us': Policy, Perception and the Pres-ence of Aliens in Elizabethan England* (London, 1996); Randolph Vigne and Charles Lit-tleton, eds, *From Strangers to Citizens: The Integration of Stranger Communities in Britain* (Brighton, 2001).

11 Nigel Goose and Lien Luu, eds, *Immigrants in Tudor and Early Stuart England* (Brighton, 2005).

of any town or city in England outside of London during the late sixteenth and early seventeenth centuries, and the city corporation kept extensive administrative records concerning their lives.[12] Several antiquarians have studied this documentation in some depth. During the 1880s, for example, W. J. C. Moens transcribed and translated many of the original documents relating to Norwich's Dutch and Walloon settlers, as did W. Hudson and J. C. Tingay, whose interest in the city's civic documents led to the publication of many items relating to the strangers in the first decade of the twentieth century.[13] Since then, the strangers have been subject to continued, though not extensive, interest by a range of local and national scholars.[14]

Norwich was an obvious place for the strangers to settle. With a river deep and wide enough to expedite the passage of barges and small river traffic, Norwich's merchants had been conducting trade with the Low Countries since at least the fifteenth century. The city's historic relationship with the Low Countries had developed because of their close geographic proximity at a time when travel by sea was often far quicker (and cheaper) than travel by land. We see this quite clearly in 1607 when the freezing of the river Wensum revealed just what a difference river travel made to the cost of transporting goods. That year, merchants had to pay 'more than 24s. for carriage of that by land from Yarmouth to Norwich' rather than the 1s. 4d they normally paid by river.[15] The East Anglian river network facilitated the movement of people and goods between Norwich, the East Anglian ports, Holland and the Low Countries with relative ease, a journey from Ypres to Norwich taking a total

---

[12] Before the 1560s much less is known about immigrant's lives in the city. Medieval Norwich had been home to a small Jewish community who mainly resided in an area between the marketplace and the castle dykes. Their population had likely never surpassed the two hundred mark and, by the time of their expulsion in 1290, was likely no more than fifty. For more see V. D. Lipman, *The Jews of Medieval Norwich* (London, 1967). There is also evidence of a small number of French settlers, probably the result of early merchant trade between England and northern France, from as early as the 1200s: James Campbell, *Norwich*, in M. D. Lobel, ed., *Historic Towns* II (London, 1975), 1–25, 16. Early-modern Norwich was home to a very small French and Scottish population. The fifteenth-century settlers are less well known, though the connections between the city and the Low Countries had been well established by this time through trade. On September 2 1542, for example, the convocation of aldermen reported seventeen Frenchmen apprenticed to local freemen and three Scots: W. Hudson and J. C. Tingay, *The Records of the City of Norwich*, Vol. II (Norwich, 1910), pp. 170–1.

[13] W. J. C. Moens, *The Walloons and their Church at Norwich*, (London, 1887), Hudson and Tingay, *Records*, II.

[14] See for example, Douglas Rickwood, 'The Norwich Strangers, 1565–1643: a Problem of Control', *Proceedings of the Huguenot Society* 24 (1984), 119–28; Christine Vane, 'The Walloon Community in Norwich: the First One Hundred Years', *Proceedings of the Huguenot Society* 24 (1984), 129–37; Woods, 'Publications', pp. 21–9.

[15] Campbell, *Norwich*, p. 21.

of fourteen days and the section between Nieuport and Yarmouth – a distance of one hundred and forty miles – considerably less.[16]

The long-established trade and shipping network meant that Norwich was no stranger to travellers, merchants and foreign traders who, from time out of mind, had lent the city's docks and waterfront around King Street a cosmopolitan air. It was not unusual for a few of these merchants and traders to make Norwich their permanent home but the late sixteenth and seventeenth centuries saw immigration on a scale never before seen.[17]

As a new century dawned in 1600, at least one third of Norwich's population were immigrants. The story of this incredible circumstance is well documented. In 1564, seeking a solution to a downturn in the local worsted trade, then mayor Thomas Sotherton realised that an injection of new cloth-working skills and techniques might revive the flagging textile industry. Seeing an opportunity in the steadily increasing flow of Protestant refugees fleeing the Spanish Netherlands, he petitioned the Duke of Norfolk for thirty master weavers (comprising twenty-four Dutch and six French-speaking Walloons) and their families to be invited officially into Norwich to instruct the local inhabitants in their specialist weaving skills and practices. The Low Countries' weavers were renowned for their innovative and unique cloth-working techniques: the Dutch with woollen cloths and the Walloons' with caungeantry, a practice described by Ursula Priestly as the mixing of standard yarns with silks, mohair, or linen.[18] The Duke of Norfolk discussed the possibility with the minister of the Dutch congregation in London, Jan Utenhove, whom he already knew and, satisfied, agreed to bear the cost of the letters patent needed to receive the thirty weavers.[19]

The letters patent were quickly approved by the Crown. Elizabeth I and Sir William Cecil understood that the strangers could bring about positive economic benefits for the country but were not without reservations. These doubts were made abundantly clear in the wording of the letters patent which explained that the strangers' only purpose in Norwich was to make 'bays, arras, says, tapestry, mockadoes, staments, carsay, and such other outlandish

16   T. S. Wilan, *River Navigation in England, 1600–1750* (London, 1936), p. 123; Moens, *Walloons*, p. 71.

17   A few foreign merchants made huge profits in Norwich from exporting worsteds and importing luxury goods. One of the most famous was Robert Toppes (c.1405–67) who built an extensive merchant house on the banks of the river: A. Shelley, ed., *'Dragon Hall, King Street, Norwich: Excavation and Survey of a Late Medieval Merchant's Trading Complex'*, East Anglian Archaeology 112 (Norwich, 2005) 29–88.

18   U. Priestly, 'Marketing of Norwich Stuffs, c. 1660–1730', *Textile History* 22:2 (1991), 193–209.

19   Letters patent granting permission of settlement, NCR 17d, 1564; Copies of Letters Patent allowing Norwich Corporation to admit thirty Dutch families, etc., FC 29/2, 1565; the Introduction of the Strangers from the Low Countries in 1564 from the *Book of Orders for the Dutch and Walloon Strangers in Norwich* transcribed and reprinted in Hudson and Tingey, *Records*, II, pp. 332–3.

commodities as hath not bene used to be made within this our Realme of England'.[20] The Crown's attitude was borne less from xenophobia than a sense of caution and protectionism which was reflected in the stringent economic guidelines that protected the rights of native inhabitants to trade. The lessons of the London riots of 1507, inspired as much by economic distress as by racial hatred, had been learned.

The arrival of the master weavers was recognised as a positive step in reviving the local economy. Contemporary reports told of how they

> Brought a great commoditie thether … which wer not made there before, wherby they do not only set on worke their owne people but do also set on worke our own people within the citie as also a grete number nere 20 myles about the citie, to the grete relief of the porer sorte there.[21]

The Queen had also given generous praise to Norwich's stranger community on her progress to the city in 1578,[22] but their arrival did not prevent the economic depression of the 1580s and 1590s from adversely affecting local trade. Nevertheless, the strangers' range of skills offered the potential for diversifying local cloth production. The manufacture of stuffs (a combination of spun worsted and linen or silk) at Norwich's 'new draperies' and a new focus on the domestic, rather than foreign, markets ushered the whole region into an era of economic success and technological advancement: by the early seventeenth century Norwich was thriving. The range, uniqueness and quality of the stuffs being produced made Norwich cloth highly appealing.[23] The Walloons, for example, had singlehandedly introduced around forty different types of cloth, including mixtures of linens, silks, and cottons that tempted all pockets from the luxury market to the general public. Alexander Neville was one of many contemporaries who attributed the change in Norwich's weaving fortunes to 'the Invencion and Industry of the Dutch, and French Flemings which inhabite there in great numbers', as did John Taylor, the eccentric pamphleteer and poet, who described how the strangers 'inriched' Norwich with 'the making of sundry sortes of Sayes, with other Stuffs innumerable'.[24]

Though few could dispute the strangers' positive impact on the local economy, success has never been without its drawbacks. The original invitation to

---

[20] Letters patent, NCR 17d, 1564.

[21] R. H. Tawney and E. Power, eds, *Tudor Economic Documents*, Vol. I (London, 1924), p. 315.

[22] Elizabeth gave nineteen and eleven pounds to the poor of the Dutch and Walloon communities respectively: Hudson and Tingay, *Records*, II, p. 186. One of the Dutch ministers, Hermanus Modet, welcomed her with a long, humble and very religious speech and afterwards presented her with the gift of a silver-gilt cup worth fifty pounds: Moens, *Walloons*, pp. 43–4.

[23] Nigel Goose, 'Immigrants and English Economic Development', *Immigrants*, ed. Goose and Luu, pp. 136–60, 140, 142.

[24] Alexander Neville, *Norfolke Furies, and their foyle under Kett* (London, 1623), fol. 2r; John Taylor, *A Late Weary, Merry Voyage and Journey* (London, 1650), pp. 17–18.

thirty master weavers in 1564 extended to their families and servants: when all had been accounted for, there were around three hundred and thirty new arrivals. These people could have been absorbed into the local infrastructure without too much trouble had it not been for the Dutch and Walloon churches who, having helped facilitate the passage of the weavers and their families into Norwich, now appeared set on extending the invitation to people seeking refuge from religious persecution overseas. Seemingly 'thousands' of migrants poured into the city in the decades following the 1560s and the city was in many ways unprepared for the large numbers of people arriving within such a short period of time.[25]

In 1571, greatly worried by the influx of refugees, Queen Elizabeth wrote to Norwich's mayor to the effect that 'in no one city or town there should be a greater number of strangers (even of honest conversation) than might be consistent with the welfare of the natural inhabitants of the place'.[26] In response the mayor ordered a survey identifying 3,999 Dutch and Walloon settlers which, given that the total number of inhabitants only equated to around 12,000 souls, was a sizable proportion of the population.[27] The vague terms of the royal order left much to regional government's discretion but in 1574 Norwich's corporation did order the strangers' churches to cease all immigration. That they did not was probably the result of a combination of tragic events.

The year 1579 heralded catastrophe for the stranger community. Norwich suffered periodically from the plague and that year around one in five of Norwich's inhabitants died in what was one of the worst outbreaks that century. The disease struck the poorest and the immigrant populations the hardest because so many lived in close quarters in the low-lying, boggy riverside areas, which conditions allowed the disease to spread rapidly. More than 2,000 strangers died over the course of that fateful year, their lives tragically cut short.[28] It was 1584 before the mayor was again compelled to ask the Dutch church to cease the passage of new arrivals, though much doubt has been cast on the corporation's efforts in this respect.[29] That the stranger population held steady at around 4,000 souls from the 1580s to 1600 was likely the result of further epidemics in 1584–5, 1589–92 and 1597–99 and national dearth during the 1590s as much as any coherent or effective corporation policy. Indeed, had it not been for the plague in 1579, the numbers of strangers would have been far higher.[30]

---

25 Taylor, *A Late Weary, Merry Voyage*, pp. 17–18.

26 J. Southerden Burn, ed., *The History of the French, Walloon, Dutch, and other foreign refugees settled in England, etc.* (1846), p. 66.

27 Hudson and Tingay, *Records*, II, p. 184. Population figures cited in Paul Slack, *The Impact of Plague in Tudor and Stuart England* (London, 1985), p. 128.

28 Slack, *Impact of Plague*, pp. 128–9.

29 Goose, 'Immigrants', p. 18.

30 A survey undertaken just before the plague struck had numbered the strangers at c. 6,000 people. For population see P. Corfield, 'From Second City to Regional Capital', *Norwich since 1550*, ed. C. Rawcliffe and R. Wilson (London, 2004), pp. 139–67.

The last decade of the sixteenth century saw a number of international events that also affected the scale of immigration. Many of the 10,000 or so Dutch, French and Walloons who had come to England in the later sixteenth century did so to escape persecution. Many came to Norwich from the Spanish Netherlands where the increasingly savage policies of the Duke of Alva (especially after the failure of the first Dutch Revolt in 1566–7) had forced many inhabitants to leave as refugees. Escalating violence between the Dutch Republic and the Spanish Netherlands between 1572 and 1585 compounded the problem. In France, the Wars of Religion had seen extreme social and economic dislocation and violence towards Huguenots, especially after the Massacre of St Bartholomew's Day in 1572 and the final conflict, often referred to as the War of the Three Henrys in 1585.[31]

The mass migrations of the later sixteenth century are often referred to as the 'first refuge' and many of the strangers did not arrive in England with the expectation that they would stay permanently – only until the situation at home had improved and they could be reunited with their families, property and possessions. This partially explains the Dutch church's recalcitrance to comply with civic requests to cease facilitating new arrivals in Norwich and also explains why the numbers of strangers did not continue to increase. The stabilisation of the political situation in the northernmost parts of the Low Countries by the creation of the Dutch Republic in 1581 in combination with a worsening economic situation in England may have led some strangers to quit Norwich and return home.[32] On December 6 1587, for example, the mayor's court heard how the strangers, 'occupying is so farre decayed and they becoom so poore' and on November 15 1589 the court were likewise told how 'the Wallownes in this citie are growne into great powertie by reason their trades and occupacions are greatly decayed'.[33] The issue of the Edict of Nantes by Henry IV in France had a similar effect for the French Huguenots, many of whom took the chance to return home.

Contemporary figures do seem to suggest that many strangers quit the city. In 1613, another stranger survey by the corporation put the Dutch congregation (including women and children) at only 1,200 people, a substantial decline from the late sixteenth century figures. By 1629 this number had dropped again, though rather more slowly, to 999. By 1634–5 another civic count suggested that the stranger congregation numbered around 678, whereof only 103 were aliens (that is born overseas) and 575 were native born (second or third generation). The following year the city records reveal that there

---

[31] J. A. Van Houtte, *An Economic History of the Low Countries, 800–1800* (London, 1977), p. 135.

[32] Lien Luu, 'Alien Communities in Transition, 1570–1650', *Immigrants*, ed. Goose and Luu, pp. 192–210, 194, 196.

[33] Hudson and Tingay, *Records*, II, p. 195.

were 396 Walloon and 363 Dutch communicants, a figure combined that was actually slightly higher than the previous year's account had suggested.[34]

We should not be surprised by such discrepancies. Laura Yungblut has argued that the statistics collected on the stranger communities in England were unlikely to have been entirely accurate. Mistakes made by the surveyors were not unheard of and the deliberate evasion of the same by the strangers was common. The assimilation of second or third generation settlers also made it very hard to identify strangers from native inhabitants.[35] Nigel Goose has also come to the same conclusion, arguing that Norwich's 1634–5 total of 678 strangers, for example, underrepresented the real number, which he estimates to have been as high as 1,500 to 2,000.[36] Equally, it would be an assumption that if the strangers left Norwich it was to leave the country. Indeed, many migrated nationally, like the Fleming Bischof who left Norwich in 1601 to take up work in Edinburgh under the terms of settlement of foreign workers to employ skilled craftsmen.[37]

Thus although there was a decline, it is unlikely that it was as extreme as the contemporary figures suggested and it is also doubtful that the 1630s, despite a worsening religious situation for the nonconformists in England, saw anything akin to a mass exodus. What we are witnessing is assimilation, more so than emigration. In 1598 the corporation had changed civic law to allow strangers to be admitted to the freedom of the city on the same terms as native-born inhabitants; for the second or even third generation of weaving families with some money this may have seemed an attractive option. By the mid-seventeenth century assimilation appears typical of the stranger community in Norwich.

During the 1670s and 1680s a changing international situation once again ushered a new wave of migrants to Norwich. Known nationally as the 'second' refuge, the forcible conversion of the Huguenot population in France followed by the revocation of the Edict of Nantes and the declaration of the Protestant religion's illegality under the terms of the Edict of Fontainbleau resulted in one of the largest movements of people from France that century. Norwich's population rose by around 8,000 people over this twenty-year period, which Penelope Corfield argues was largely the result of foreign immigration, rather than a substantial increase in birth rate.[38] The term 'foreigner' in this context does not necessarily equate to 'stranger', simply a person not born in the city, but there are many examples to suggest that overseas migrants, especially the French Huguenots, did make up a proportion of this figure. William Cunningham explains how England was a 'natural

34 Dutch Congregation Numbers, NCR Case 10h, no. 11.
35 Yungblut, *Strangers Settled Here Among Us*, p. 14.
36 Goose, 'Immigrants', p. 19.
37 Cunningham, *Alien Immigrants*, p. 184.
38 P. Corfield, 'A Provincial Capital in the Late Seventeenth Century: The Case of Norwich', *The Early Modern Town*, ed. P. Clark (London, 1976), p. 239.

asylum' for Huguenots because of the geographic proximity of the two countries and, importantly, the religious freedoms afforded the established Dutch and Walloon churches.[39] The Crown also, reluctantly, offered incentives. In 1681, for example, Charles II had issued a proclamation to the effect that distressed refugees would be welcomed into England, and four years later, James II encouraged collections in church for their cause.[40] In Norwich, there were certain local particularities to encourage alien settlement. It was one of the few regional cities in England with a French- and Dutch-speaking church and a reputation for encouraging non-conformism. There were also economic initiatives. In a situation reminiscent of that in 1564, for example, Onias Phillipo, a leading Norwich manufacturer, employer, and freeman of Walloon descent, invited around two hundred Huguenot refugees to Norwich in 1682, some of whom were to work for Phillipo.[41]

Looking back across the whole century suggests that the reasons for immigration into Norwich were complex and that fluctuations in the numbers and nationalities of migrants were characteristic of the period. We do not have access to accurate statistics but, at any one time, it is safe to assume that a quarter to a third of the urban population comprised strangers and foreigners and that their arrival had an impact on Norwich's economy and society. Such a significant stranger population could not have failed to have had an impact on the urban landscape, real or imagined.

The Strangers' City: Topographies and Networks

Immigrants were not physically segregated in seventeenth-century Norwich. There was no clause in the letters patent granting the strangers permission to settle in 1564 that specified where they should live, and neither was there any official guidance on habitation.[42] Nevertheless, many scholars have pointed to evidence of residential patterns and a social topography unique to the strangers' communities. The great wards of Wymer (which ran along the southern edge of the river), the Ward over the Water (comprising Coslany, Colegate and Fye Bridge wards), and an area comprising mid-Wymer and Mancroft wards around the central marketplace, Guildhall and castle have all been associated with the strangers.

Such conclusions have been drawn from population surveys and taxation records. The most comprehensive evidence on strangers' residential patterns

---

[39] Cunningham, *Alien Immigrants*, pp. 226, 229–30. Cunningham proposed that some 80,000 refugees arrived in England and Ireland over the 1680s, one of the highest mass immigrations of the early-modern period.
[40] Ibid., p. 227.
[41] Corfield, 'A Provincial Town', p. 239. The number of invitations ranges in contemporary accounts from one to two hundred.
[42] Letters patent, NCR 17d, 1564.

really begins in 1572 with the corporation-sponsored population survey undertaken to comply with Elizabeth I's wishes that strangers should not exceed that which 'might be consistent with the welfare of the natural inhabitants of the place'.[43] Although rather early in the timeframe of this study, the survey provides a baseline against which later, and sparser, evidence can be compared for changes and continuities. The survey reveals that more strangers inhabited West and Middle Wymer and Colegate wards than any other, with 827, 567 and 471 stranger inhabitants respectively. Following close behind were the wards of Fyebridge, Coslany, and East Wymer with 442, 412 and 316 strangers residing in each.[44] These wards skirted the river as it dissected the city and ran to the north in an area known colloquially as *ultra acquam* or 'over-the-water'.

The settlement patterns that can be established for the late sixteenth century held fast into the seventeenth. In 1622, for example, the corporation were ordered to make a return of all the heads of stranger households. The undertaking returned three hundred and thirty-one householders[45] and, although the return excludes women and children (with the exception of widows), it is a fascinating list, not only of strangers' names and parish of residence, but of their occupation and whether they were 'borne of parents strangers', i.e. native born, or 'borne beyond the seas'.[46] The return lends depth to our understanding of how immigrants were perceived as a separate community and labelled accordingly despite, in many cases, being born in the city.

From this return it is easy to see that the cloth industry was the strangers' chief employer. In order of the most dominant trade, strangers were weavers (111), combers (82), hosiers, twisterers, tailors, dyers and saye makers; around ten were merchants (two of whom specialised in cloth) and a few could be found plying the variety of trades common to a seventeenth-century city, as schoolmasters, grocers, and bakers.[47] It is also quite clear from this material that the majority of the householders lived in the same central and northern wards that had dominated the 1572 survey, with a slight shift from Middle Wymer to Colegate. In 1622, the vast majority of stranger combers lived in Colegate, with a figure of sixty-eight of ninety-eight given trades in that area; Fye Bridge, with a much smaller stranger population, had sixteen combers and sixteen weavers; and Coslany had one of the highest concentrations of hosiers per ward, alongside twenty-four weavers and seven twisterers. The

43 Southerden Burn, *History of the French, Walloon, Dutch*, p. 66.
44 Survey of Strangers in Norwich, NCR 17d, fols 69–70.
45 Moens, *Walloons*, p. 193. The return concludes with a figure of 291 names but there are in fact 331 names listed.
46 Moens, *Walloons*, p. 189.
47 Ibid., pp. 189–93.

latter ward also had the highest number of mixed trades, with tailors, grocers, bakers, a schoolmaster, a physician, and an aqua vitae seller, amongst others.[48]

Other sources confirm the same trend. Over the course of 1624–5, for example, a lay subsidy assessment notes the parishes where the strangers lived, rather than simply the wards of the 1622 return. While the subsidy record would not account for less affluent strangers, the lists are useful in pinpointing settlement patterns in more detail than in 1622. The assessment returned the names of seventy-six subscribers in Coslany, forty-five in Colegate, thirty-seven in Fye Bridge, thirty-five in West Wymer, thirty in Middle Wymer and finally, only six in East Wymer. By parish the highest number of strangers lived in St Augustine, St George Tombland, St Mary Coslany, and St Andrew with twenty-four, twenty-one, nineteen and sixteen subsidy contributors respectively.[49] Fifty years on, the 1673 hearth tax returns confirm that these trends had continued. Though lacking the detail of the surveys and returns, Coslany, Fye Bridge, West Wymer, and Middle Wymer still retained the largest proportion of strangers respectively.[50] Likewise the forty-nine strangers who made contributions on properties containing between one and eleven hearths in the 1684 hearth tax returns predominantly, though not exclusively, lived in Wymer, Coslany, and Fye Bridge.[51]

Since the 1970s, several large-scale archaeological excavations have confirmed the strangers' presence in these areas by uncovering evidence of the immigrants' material culture. Fragments of imported North Holland slipware, cookware and ceramics were found in the remains of tenements and cess pits on Alms Lane, Calvert Street and Botolph Street in Colegate and St Benedict's Street in West Wymer, in quantities suggestive of long-term occupation by strangers, rather than imports by native inhabitants.[52] Archaeology has also connected the area extending southwards from Charing (Shearing) Cross in St John Maddermarket and the grand merchant house of Thomas Sotherton, known colloquially as Strangers Hall, to Dove Street (once associated with a small Jewish community and synagogue), Pottergate and St Andrew, the latter home to Norwich's first printer, the stranger Anthony Solempne, with the stranger communities.[53]

The strangers' churches were also located in the same area. Archbishop Matthew Parker had arranged for the large Dutch congregation to use

---

48   Ibid., pp. 189–93.
49   Ibid., pp. 184–7.
50   Ibid., pp. 187–8.
51   Ibid., pp. 187–8.
52   Norfolk Archaeology Unit finds, cited in C. King, '"Strangers in a Strange Land": Immigrants and Urban Culture in Early Modern Norwich', *The Archaeology of Post-Medieval Religion*, ed. C. King and Duncan Sayer (Woodbridge, 2011), pp. 83–106, 91. See also B. Ayers, *Norwich: A Fine City* (Stroud, 1994), p. 144.
53   Leonard G. Bolingbroke, 'St John Maddermarket, Norwich: its Streets, Lanes, and Ancient Houses, and their Old-time Associations', *Norfolk Archaeology* 20 (1921), 215–39, 230–1.

the vacant Dominican friary, known as Blackfriar's Hall, from 24 December 1565.[54] The building, on the southern bank of the Wensum in the parish of St Andrew, had come to the corporation at the dissolution and a section was already being used as a sale hall for the strangers' cloth. The French-speaking Walloons were permitted the redundant Bishop's Chapel in the grounds of the cathedral for their services, but were asked to move to St Mary-the-Less in 1637, a disused church that had been granted to the strangers during the sixteenth century as a cloth hall.[55] St Mary was centrally placed, not far from either the cathedral or Blackfriar's hall in the parish of St George Tombland. The lease of these redundant religious buildings to the strangers in an area densely populated by that community could not have been entirely coincidental.

It is quite plausible to assume from the facts and figures above that native inhabitants saw the places and spaces connected with the strangers as a manifestation of the latter's identity and an embodiment of their culture. The strangers themselves may have shared this perception. The evidence makes for a compelling argument of a social and cultural separation that was manifest in place, but this simplistic statement ignores some fundamental crossovers in the lives of strangers and native inhabitants.

Strangers' residential patterns were not exclusive to them alone and neither were they deliberate, evolving over time from largely practical origins. The strangers were predominantly weavers and it was in the area most intimately connected with the production, finishing, and sale of cloth that the strangers had made their home. Weaving had been Norwich's staple for several centuries before the first early-modern refuge and the industry was well established in the central riverside wards because access to water and proximity to the city's markets were vital to the production and sale of cloth.[56] Middle Wymer, for example, had been home to the city's worsted shearers from time out of mind, and the southern sections of Coslany, Colegate, and Fye Bridge all abutted the river, providing the flowing water necessary for cloth dyers and finishers.[57]

The strangers' topography was also determined by their time of arrival in the course of Norwich's urban development. A great fire had laid waste to the northern and central wards in 1507 and by the 1560s much of that area

54 Moens, *Walloons*, p. 23. Parker had been born in Norwich in the parish of St Saviour.
55 'The city of Norwich, chapter 27: Of the city in Queen Elizabeth's time', *An Essay towards a Topographical History of the County of Norfolk, Vol. III: The History of the City and County of Norwich, Part I* (1806), pp. 277–360. URL: http://www.british-history.ac.uk/report.aspx?compid=77997. Date accessed: 11 April 2013.
56 Norwich had produced cloth since the 1200s, specializing in worsted since at least the fourteenth century.
57 John Kirkpatrick, *The Streets and Lanes of Norwich* (Norwich, 1889), p. 55; Serena Kelly, 'The Economic Topography and Structure of Norwich, c. 1300', *Men of Property: An Analysis of the Norwich Enrolled Deeds, 1285–1311*, ed. Ursula Priestly (Norwich, 1983), pp. 13–39, esp. 34–5.

had not been rebuilt. Pressure on existing housing meant that the redevelopment of waste grounds made practical sense and the strangers can be thanked for redeveloping large sections of the wards over-the-water. The northern wards were also less densely populated than their southern counterparts and were thus more able to absorb new arrivals of any origin. The residential proclivities of the Dutch, Walloon and French congregations in Norwich related directly to considerations of practicality and occupation: they were not unique to that community but mirrored the living patterns of native inhabitants and English migrants arriving during the same period and engaged in cloth working.

We should also be careful to avoid assuming that the stranger population was in any way restricted to a small proportion of the city. The wards mentioned above in connection with the strangers encompassed twenty-two of Norwich's thirty-four parishes and, although a majority of the stranger population lived in those wards, they were not absent from the city's other wards. The 1622 return and the 1624 subsidy reveal strangers residing in the smaller wards of Berstreet, St Stephen and St Peter Mancroft. The 1673 hearth tax rated strangers in the wards of St Giles, Berstreet, and North and South Conesford.[58] The most comprehensive evidence can be drawn from the 1633–4 collection for the poor, which noted ninety-five strangers out of a total of 1,250 ratepayers and recipients.[59] Although this figure by no means represented the stranger population as a whole – only those householders (men and widows) deemed wealthy enough to contribute – it is possible to extrapolate that strangers made up approximately five to ten per cent of each ward's population. In Coslany ward, for instance, of the one hundred and five ratepayers, sixteen can be identified by their surnames as strangers; in West Wymer, of one hundred and thirty ratepayers, sixteen were strangers; and in Mid Wymer, of one hundred and thirty-nine ratepayers, eight were strangers.[60]

Finally, there are some serious problems with considering the strangers a homogenous community with a shared set of common experiences that informed their social and residential topography. The strangers were some of the most socially diverse and international inhabitants living in Norwich. Their kinship network extended across East Anglia, southern England, and over the water into France, Holland and the Low Countries. In 1565, for example, the original thirty families who had been invited to Norwich by the corporation had already experienced more of the world than many native Norwich inhabitants. Their journey had taken them from the Low Countries to Sandwich in

---

58 Moens, *Walloons*, pp. 184–93.
59 Walter Rye, the Victorian antiquarian and historian of Norwich, identified ninety-three names that belonged to strangers in the 1633–4 parish poor-rate assessment. To his figure, I have added two more based on a reading of the various lists of strangers transcribed by Moens. See Walter Rye, *The Norwich Rate Book: Easter 1633–4* (London, 1903), p. 6 and Moens, *Walloons*.
60 Rye, *Rate Book*, pp. 6, 39–54, 63–7.

Kent in 1561 and then on to London before they arrived in Norwich.[61] The majority of the Dutch and Walloon settlers in seventeenth-century Norwich hailed from the heartland of the Flemish textile industry in Flanders, Brabant and Zeeland, although over the course of the century the balance tipped more towards those hailing from French-speaking areas than Dutch, a shift that was probably located in changing continental politics.[62]

Once in England, the strangers did not remain isolated from their homeland but made frequent visits and exchanged a regular correspondence with the families they had left behind. On 31 March 1568, for example, Thomas Willemot wrote to Jan Thevele at Ypres to enquire after his Flanders' property and to chase up a debt owed to him by one Christiaan de Haze that he had not received before he had left for Norwich. The following year, Jan Willemsz wrote to his sister Lysbeth at Ypres about a quarrel in the church that had led Norwich's congregational ministers to journey to London to resolve.[63]

The church was one of the foremost channels for communication between the strangers and their overseas families and various traditions specific to the strangers' congregations helped keep these links alive. The consistories, for example, insisted that strangers wishing to marry in England receive their parent's formal approval first. This could not be done by letter but only in person.[64] The continental reforming churches also paid close attention to the performance and practice of the English congregational churches in the hope that they would adopt the same structure of regional classes and colloquies with provincial and national synods. This necessitated a constant exchange of letters and representatives to discuss church matters, especially as the English congregational churches proved reluctant to adopt the proposed systems. Their resistance to foreign intervention stemmed as much from a sense of self-government as from the fact that any move to adopt a radically different structure would antagonise the Church of England and stress their delicate relationship. The strangers had to take care that their allegiance to a foreign church was not considered to outweigh their fidelity to their adopted land. Their one concession was the adoption of regular colloquies, membership of which affirmed their integration into the continental reformed church.[65]

---

[61] Marcel Backhouse, *The Flemish and Walloon Communities at Sandwich During the Reign of Elizabeth I, 1561–1603* (Brussels, 1995), esp. pp. 17–20.

[62] Raymond Fagel, 'Immigrant Roots: The Geographical Origins of Newcomers from the Low Countries in Tudor England', *Immigrants in Tudor and Early Stuart England*, ed. Nigel Goose and Lien Luu (Brighton, 2005), pp. 41–75, 53. The patterns evident in Norwich reflected national trends where immigrants hailed from the Low Countries, comprising Dutch-speaking Zeeland, Holland and Friesland in the north, and French-speaking Flanders, Belgium, Luxembourg and parts of northern France in the south.

[63] Moens, *Walloons*, p. 224.

[64] Charles G. D. Littleton, 'The Strangers, their Churches and the Continent', *Immigrants*, ed. Goose and Luu, pp. 177–91, 178, 180.

[65] Littleton, 'The Strangers, their Churches', pp. 184–5.

The shipping routes between Norfolk and the Low Countries provided the means of sending of letters, personal goods, and items for trade. In 1567, for example, Boudewyn de Cuupere sent his nephew's 'trade tools' from Ypres to his new home in Norwich and in return asked that his nephew Franche send wood back with skipper Wulfaert Boeteman, who ran a regular passenger service between Nieuport and Yarmouth, deemed the safest route of passage between the two countries.[66] The strangers were actively encouraged to foster these networks as they helped bolster the city's trade and, on occasion, facilitated aid during times of dire need. In the late 1590s, for example, national and local dearth had led the corporation to seek the strangers' help in securing three hundred quarters of rye from Amsterdam at a good price, to alleviate the food shortage at home.[67]

Norwich's strangers certainly had a unique, but not an isolated, topography. Sharing neighbourhoods with fellow strangers was common but there were no ghettoes or segregated areas, a fact that Raingard Esser suggests contributed to the relative lack of conflict with native inhabitants as compared to London, where ghettoization led to problems of assimilation and the escalation of periodic violence.[68] Settlement in Norwich was largely determined by occupation and led to strangers and native inhabitants sharing neighbourhoods and, potentially, perceptions of space created in the process of sharing economic networks. We should not however ignore that fact that physical and social segregation are two very different sides of the same coin.

Foreign Congregations: Neighbours or Strangers?

On the accession of James I to the throne of England in 1603, Norwich's strangers sent a stirring and patriotic message to the new monarch. The king was, apparently, so moved that he penned a response in person reassuring them that he recognised their contributions to the country and that the privileges they had enjoyed under his predecessor, Elizabeth I, would continue.[69] James' response was not atypical of the reception that the strangers enjoyed in Norwich. Alexander Neville, for instance, wrote of how Norwich was 'A City seated daintily, Most faire built she is knowne, pleasing and kind to strangers all, Delightfull to her owne'.[70] Many others were to comment on the reception given to the immigrants, including the poet Michael Drayton who wrote how Norwich was a 'hospitable place to the industrious Dutch'.[71] As Nigel

---

66   Moens, *Walloons*, p. 71.
67   NCR 16A/13, fol. 93, 11 October 1596.
68   Raingard Esser, cited in Robin D. Gwynn, *Huguenot Heritage: the History and Contribution of the Huguenots in Britain* (Brighton, 2001), p. 143.
69   Moens, *Walloons*, p. 21.
70   Neville, *Norfolke furies*, fol. 4r.
71   C. Rawcliffe, 'Introduction', *Medieval Norwich*, ed. C. Rawcliffe and R. Wilson (London, 2004), p. xxii.

Goose has argued, relations between native inhabitants and strangers outside the capital were generally cordial.[72]

In Norwich, there were only a few instances where immigration inspired outright violence and these coincided with periods of economic stress, attempts to alter pre-existing legislation, or when a large number of migrants arrived within a very short period. Blomefield writes of 'great disturbances between the citizens and Dutch strangers' in 1613, for example, which took place when the Dutch 'began to attempt to exercise the ancient trades of the city, contrary to their agreement at their admission, and against the will of the Walloons, who lived peaceably, and aimed at no such thing'. According to Blomefield, the Dutch had proceeded 'without knowledge of the city or their countrymen ... to procure a charter from the King ... by which all strangers communicants of the Dutch congregation were to come in, and use the trade of making any particular stuff (cloth) by which they became a company not depending on the city'.[73] Their attempt at forming a company failed after the mayor, George Cock, made a direct appeal to the Privy Council.

The most serious incident that century was inspired by Onias Phillipo's invitation to around two hundred Huguenot weavers in 1682.[74] Fearing that the immigrant workers would accept cheaper wages and create unemployment there was a 'mutiny' where a 'mob' of Norwich inhabitants broke open one of the Huguenot's houses and a young woman was beaten so badly that she died two or three days later. A few months later another mob descended on Mr Barnham's house in St Andrew's parish – where many of the French workers were staying - and 'pulled them and their goods out of their houses, abused their persons, &c. till the trained bands were raised to appease them'.[75] The ringleaders of the mob were arrested and the immediate violence died down but fears that employing the French would undercut local wages did not disappear overnight. In 1690, for example, parliament received a petition from Norwich's French weavers complaining of harassment and the spreading of false reports about their conduct. Apparently some Norwich men had spread rumours that the French began working before finishing their apprenticeships, contrary to the law.[76]

---

[72] Nigel Goose, '"Xenophobia" in Elizabethan and Early Stuart England: An Epithet Too Far?', *Immigrants*, ed. Goose and Luu, pp. 110–35.

[73] 'The city of Norwich, chapter 28: Of the city in James I's time', *An Essay towards a Topographical History of the County of Norfolk, Vol. III: The History of the City and County of Norwich, Part I* (1806), pp. 360–71. URL: http://www.british-history.ac.uk/report.aspx-?compid=77998. Date accessed: 09 May 2012.

[74] The first influx of strangers during the 1560s had not led to riots in Norwich but there were complaints heard from local weavers, dyers, and shearmen in 1567: John Pound, 'Government to 1660', *Norwich Since 1550*, ed. Rawcliffe and Wilson, pp. 35–61, 41.

[75] Francis Blomefield, *An Essay towards a Topographical History of the County of Norfolk, Vol. III: The History of the City and County of Norwich, Part I* (1806), p. 418.

[76] Corfield, 'A Provincial Capital', p. 239.

The situation in which the strangers found themselves – welcomed by some and victimised by others – must have been at best confusing and at worst, impossible to endure. They were treated differently in law, yet were at times considered indispensable to the economy; they could be the targets of socio-economic unrest, yet could also buy their way into the freedom of the city and climb the corporation hierarchy like any other wealthy inhabitant. These ambiguities inform the remainder of this chapter, which explores the intricate and complex position of the strangers as a community within a community and considers points of intersection and difference between the strangers and the city.

Many of the strangers who came to England did so to escape religious intolerance at home, hoping for a situation where they could practise freedom of conscience. They were not disappointed. Edward VI had founded the first stranger church in England in 1550 at the site of the Austin Friars in London and regional cities followed suit, allowing strangers to redevelop disused religious buildings as their own. In Norwich, the large Dutch congregation were leased the Dominican Friary, and the Walloons the redundant Bishop's Chapel and later the church of St Mary-the-Less.[77] Many of the early arrivals wrote to their families in praise of the religious tolerance and practices that they found in Norwich. One man wrote to his wife begging that she join him quickly for 'here [in Norwich] people do not hear, as in Flanders, of iniquity and wickedness but where we could live in a Godly manner'; Gilles Navegeer wrote to his grandmother telling her of how in Norwich 'we are living in great quietness and peace and the word of God is much preached amongst us', and Claeis van den Nieuwenhuuze requested his mother and father make haste to join him in Norwich 'where the word of God is so richly preached'.[78]

For the Dutch and Walloons, the churches were the focal point of their communities. The church offered them financial, emotional and spiritual support, helped them into work, and cared for them when they were sick or too elderly to look after themselves and also operated as a channel of communication, not just for news and correspondence from overseas but as the intermediary between the stranger community and the corporation. The church's ministers and elders performed the dual role of spiritual leader and mouthpiece of the stranger community, expected to deal with all aspects of business as no city official, with the exception of the mayor, was allowed to interfere

---

[77] 'The city of Norwich, chapter 27: Of the city in Queen Elizabeth's time', *An Essay towards a Topographical History of the County of Norfolk, Vol. III: The History of the City and County of Norwich, Part I* (1806), pp. 277–360. URL: http://www.british-history.ac.uk/report.aspx?compid=77997. Date accessed: 11 April 2013.

[78] From a selection of letters written by refugee strangers to friends and relatives in Ypres, 1567, transcribed and reproduced in Moens, *Walloons*, pp. 222–3.

directly in the strangers' affairs.[79] As a result the elders arbitrated and set-tled disputes between members of the congregation and investigated alleged criminal activities before referring them, if necessary, to the appropriate civic authorities. The church was the backbone of the stranger community.

Officially, the Crown, the corporation, the Church of England and the strangers' church in Norwich believed that membership of the congregation was non-negotiable. The Crown's position stemmed from the notion of reli-gious compliance, although the strangers' churches functioned outside of the Church of England, they were expected to operate within limits proscribed by the state and the Church of England. Enforcing membership removed the strangers' largely Calvinist style of nonconformist worship from the parish churches, in theory at least, on the basis that segregation would help com-bat the dangerous rise of the sectaries (especially the Anabaptists) that be-came increasingly prevalent as the century progressed. Forcing new settlers to join the stranger congregation also offered the authorities a method of monitoring the strangers without having to intervene directly in their affairs. Church membership was made an essential condition of the strangers' stay in the country, a fact reiterated by the Privy Council at several points over the course of the century, including in 1621 and 1631.[80]

The law stipulated that the congregation take financial and moral respon-sibility for their own poor, disadvantaged, unemployed, or sick but from 1612 they were also expected to make contributions to the poor rate for the parish in which they lived. The problem of paying to both geographic and notion-al parish became a cause for much resentment over the next few years. In 1621 the issue was propelled into the spotlight when several long-standing members of the strangers' church had refused to continue to serve as elders, as was the expectation, and the congregation was forced, unusually, to seek outside of their own circle for a resolution. Appealing to the Privy Council, who in turn referred the petitioners back to the mayor and corporation, they complained that the men in question were neglecting their responsibilities. The situation was complex. Dennis Larmett, for instance, freeman of Nor-wich, a tax-payer and a stranger, 'frequented his own parish church, and paid all duties to Mr. Fulk Roberts, minister of St. Saviour's, and to that parish, yet the French congregation made him pay to their minister, and frequent their congregation, and lately elected him an elder, and he was obliged to serve, and pay'. As a result, Larmett discontinued his payments of twenty shillings per annum to St. Saviour's parish church and, despite being ordered by the council to pay, refused. Larmett was an associate of Joel Desurmeaux

[79] Raingard Esser, 'Politijcke Mannen: A Particular Institution of the Norwich Strangers' Communities', *Religious Dissent*, ed. Virgoe and Williamson, p. 21–8, 22–3.
[80] Andrew Spicer, '"A Place of refuge and sanctuary of a holy Temple": Exile Commu-nities and the Stranger Churches', *Immigrants*, ed. Goose and Luu, pp. 91–109, 92, 95. Original references: J. V. Lyle, ed., *Acts of the Privy Council 1621–3*, Vol. 38 (1932), p. 58: P. A. Penfold, ed., *Acts of the Privy Council 1630–1*, Vol. 46 (1964), p. 181.

and Samuel Camby, who 'upon some displeasure misconceived against Mr. Peter de Lawne, their minister, whom we know to be a learned, grave, and discreet preacher, not only withheld from him their usual contribution, but have withdrawn themselves from their congregation and church'. The two men were forced 'to pay to, and be members of the French church, and pay to St. Saviour's officers and minister' by order of the council.[81] The situation highlighted not only how the strangers had mixed loyalties to parish and to congregation but reveals how people manipulated the law to make their point. The agency of the men in question was limited, as they were ultimately forced to pay, but their ability to manage their allegiances and withhold money from congregation or parish was a forceful combination. The cases also demonstrate the curious position of the strangers, as valued and highly regarded members of their congregation, as inhabitants of their parish with all the responsibilities that this entailed, and as citizens and freemen of the city. None of these roles should have been at odds but the responsibilities entailed in committing to each were prohibitive.

The situation was resolved temporarily but the underlying issue continued to cause problems. Ten years later John Vanixon and Peter Vanhovan, who had been rated to pay seven and fifteen shillings respectively to the consistory of the ministers and elders of the Dutch church for the 'government of their people', failed to make reparation and were presented to the mayoral court for the offence on 15 December 1632. Still refusing to pay even when confronted with the mayor and magistrates, the two men were bound over in contempt of court and ordered to show just cause why they should not pay. The men do not appear at the civic court again (at least not for that offence) so we can assume that they made the required payment.[82] The conflict of paying twice towards the maintenance of parishioners, especially when the strangers were expected to look after their own and received little or no help from the parish chest, was an obvious bone of contention but it is curious that in the high-profile cases above, the men chose to support their parish over their congregation until pressed to do otherwise. On further investigation it seems that Joel Desurmeaux, merchant, Samuel Camby, dyer and John Vanixon Junior, hosier, were all native-born strangers and freemen. This might suggest that, having been born and raised in Norwich, they had a lack of empathy or ties with the Dutch community that had been a stanchion for their parents.[83]

The issue of membership was not simply a financial one but a broader reflection of how some native-born inhabitants may have felt estranged from the stranger community and, importantly, of freedom of conscience. In 1615, the conflict was recognised by then Bishop of Norwich John Jegon, who seized on the matter as a way of reinforcing religious conformity amongst the

---

81   Blomefield, *Topographical History*, III:I, p. 365.
82   W. L. Sachse, ed., *Minutes of the Norwich Court of Mayoralty 1632–1635* (Norwich, 1967), p. 47.
83   Moens, *Walloons*, pp. 190, 191, 193.

stranger population. Taking a dim view of those people who chose to leave the congregation, Jegon argued that 'sundry licencious persons … have thereupon taken occasion to cast off the yoke of ecclesiasticall gouvernement off these congregations, and have forthwith adjoyned themselves to the parish churches, in w[h]ich their severall habitations were'.[84] Jegon fully supported enforced membership, even for second or third generation strangers, as it kept their potentially subversive influence outside of the established church. He was not alone in his views on enforcing membership, and found much support from within the stranger community itself. In the July of that year, John Elison, 'the aforementioned' Dutch minister, and Jacques de Heem, an elder, responded to the question of whether the native-born children or grandchildren of strangers should be allowed to renounce their membership, by drawing up a formal document arguing in no uncertain terms that to allow the change would be 'repugnant', seriously detrimental to the congregation, and even offensive to the King, who had 'always opened his land for the refugee strangers'.[85] Their argument hinged on the fact that, as the second and third generation comprised the majority of their worshippers, losing them would mean the loss of financial support for their clergy and for their poor. The Bishop of London, to whom this passionate appeal had been sent, responded with an order that sat firmly on the fence, his message simply reinforcing a situation whereby strangers could join their parish church if 'they reconciled themselves unto the sayd congregations' at the same time.[86] This compromise may have placated the elders but did not offer a permanent solution as the case of Desurmeaux, Camby, Vanixon, and others like them demonstrates.

The vexatious question of belonging to congregation or to parish balanced on the issue of freedom of conscience. The church was happy to support Elison and de Heem because the elders' appeal coincided with their own aim of suppressing nonconformity, especially in the East Anglian towns and cities which were becoming known for dissenting practices. In Norwich, the successive bishops John Jegon, Richard Corbet and Matthew Wren all uncovered what they saw as a worrying trend toward Puritanism and nonconformist practices in the city's churches. As pressure mounted to reform church practice and procedure in the 1620s, Corbet had, for example, attacked the Walloon congregation for their supposed casual and impermanent style of worship, whereby people brought their own chairs to service. He argued that such practices demonstrated how the Walloon 'cares not much for a consecrated place',[87] declaring that 'any other roome in Norwiche that hath but

---

84 Letter of the Bishop of London, cited in Moens, *Walloons*, p. 86.
85 Moens, *Walloons*, p. 310.
86 Ibid., p. 87.
87 Spicer, 'Exile Communities', p. 101. It was also Corbet who was responsible for pressurising the Walloons to move from the Bishop's Chapel to the church of St Mary-the-Less over the issue of costs for repairs to the chapel. The move took place a year after Wren's succession but the battle over reparations continued: Kate Hotblack, 'The Dutch and Walloons at Norwich', *History* 6:24 (1922), 234–9, 239.

breadth and length may serve your turne as well as a chapell. Wherefore I say unto, without a miracle, *Lazare prodi foras!* Depart, and hire some other place for your irregular meetings.'[88]

As Archbishop William Laud embarked on his reforming agenda during the 1630s, Matthew Wren helped make his desires a reality in Norwich. Rooting out nonconformists at the cost of isolating the godly, he increased scrutiny of the stranger congregation. Wren feared that the strangers' different styles of worship openly mocked the established church, encouraged nonconformist practices and, in sharp contrast to the official stance taken by the Bishop of London in 1615, believed that the continued segregation of, and privileges awarded to, the stranger congregation with regard to freedom of worship acted to make the problem worse. The visitation articles of the 1630s inquired as to what liturgy was then used, how many of the strangers were native-born subjects and, of those, how many would conform to the Church of England. The strangers responded as a united body and as firmly and decisively as they had in 1615, clearly stating their legal position and rights. The response, penned as a national effort by ministers at Sandwich, Canterbury and Maidstone, set out their exclusive position exempt from the scrutiny of the Church of England as set out by Crown authority since the time of Edward VI, and reinforced by each successive monarch since. Laud was forced to back down and the strangers continued to be allowed to join both their congregational and their parish churches, so long as they continued to contribute financially to each.[89]

Laud's hard-line policy was not universally popular in a city with a large godly population but this is not to say that he lacked support from all quarters. Religion in Norwich, especially during the first half of the century, was characterised by its fractiousness. In 1635, for example, Thomas Allen, rector of St Edmund, was accused of allowing strangers to creep into the church after dark 'who would neyther kneele at any prayers nor stand up at Creed but sitt...upon their tayles all the tyme'.[90] Allen was deprived of his living in 1636 (only two years since he had been granted the same) for failing to appear at the visitation.[91] The situation became unbearable for a small minority who in a poignant reversal of the situation in the late-sixteenth century removed from Norwich to the Low Countries, especially Rotterdam and Amsterdam where they were welcomed as religious refugees.

In civic life, the strangers were also discriminated against; deliberately excluded from aspects of civic life by draconian laws and regulations. Rigorous trading regulations, for example, restricted what strangers could sell and

88 NA, SP 16/400/45 quoted in Andrew Spicer, 'Exile Communities', p. 101.

89 M. J. Power, 'London and the Control of the Crisis of the 1590s', *History*, 70 (1985), 371–85, 385.

90 NRO, DN/DEP/42/47A. Unmarked folio, statements against Thomas Allen, 1635.

91 M. Reynolds, *Godly Reformers and their Opponents in Early Modern England: Religion in Norwich c. 1560–1643* (Woodbridge, 2005), p. 218.

when, including some rather arbitrary laws such as one that stipulated that no stranger baker or dyer was allowed to purchase corn or wood respectively at the market before one o'clock in the afternoon; that no dyer could burn charcoal, only sea coal; and that no stranger be allowed to buy butter or cheese with intent to resell it. They were also barred from walking the streets or leaving the city on a Sunday, upon pain of a five- to ten-shilling fine.[92] The latter impractical law led to some difficult situations, such as that on 22 February 1670, when Abraham Castle attempted to wriggle out of his conviction for the same by denying that he was a member of the Walloon congregation.[93] These laws should not be automatically viewed as top-down measures imposed on a powerless community however, as there were some points on which the strangers were complicit. The benefits of enforced church membership to the congregation have already been mentioned and it is worth noting that the law restricting strangers' movements on a Sunday, for example, originated in a request by Salomon Smyth, minister of the Dutch church during the 1580s, that the mayor help him tackle the problem of drink and absences from church in his community. It was Smyth who conceived the rule that no stranger who made or sold aqua vitae could allow anyone to drink in his house during the time of divine service and that no strangers could visit a drinking house, walk the streets or go 'abroad' until after four in the afternoon on a Sunday; the mayor only passed the words into law.[94] Thus, similar to the issue of congregational membership, the strangers – or at least the church elders – were involved in the processes that worked to preserve a fundamental divide between the strangers' community and Norwich's native inhabitants.

In helping to safeguard this division, the strangers were complicit in a system that categorised and labelled them as outsiders. This process essentially restricted many strangers' options, as the law managed immigration by connecting rights with labels. The basic legal labels under which strangers were categorised were: alien enemy; alien friend; denizen or natural-born subject. Alien friends were those who were born abroad but had taken an oath of allegiance to the English Crown. The Crown protected them, but they could not own, inherit or bequeath real property, hold a political office or vote, or become a freeman with the right to trade, own a shop, or take on an apprentice. Denizens were aliens who had purchased a letter patent granting them this status from the Crown but this still did not allow them to inherit property, which was the privilege only of the natural-born subject.[95]

[92] Walter Rye, 'The Dutch Congregation in Norwich', *Norfolk Archaeology* 16 (1907), 320–7, 321–3.

[93] W. Rye, ed., *Depositions Taken Before the Mayor and Aldermen of Norwich 1549–1567 & Extracts from the Court Books of the City of Norwich 1666–1668* (Norwich, 1905), p. 125.

[94] Moens, *Walloons*, p. 81.

[95] Nigel Goose, 'Natural Born Versus Stranger-Born Subjects', *Immigrants*, ed. Goose and Luu, pp. 57–75, 59–60.

These rules made labels part of what it meant to be a stranger in seven-teenth-century Norwich and took away something of strangers' individuality at the same time as it measured their worth. The horizontal layering evident in the categories of alien, denizen, or native-born can be seen in the subsi-dy return of 1622, for example, which distinguished between those people 'borne of parents strangers' or 'borne beyond the seas',[96] but the corporation also made regular use of common tropes which marked vertical distinctions between the strangers as homogenous French, Dutch or Walloon groupings. The mayor's court, for example, made a record of each week's certificate of christenings and burials for the city. On 6 October 1632 for example, John Goodwyn presented a certificate for twelve baptisms 'whereof Two French Doch none'; on 2 November 1633 Nathanial Crotch reported the baptism of 'Twelve wherof one Duch, one French, Buried Nyne whereof two Strangers'; and on 19 April 1634 there had been seventeen baptisms 'whereof one French' and 'Nyne English' were buried.[97] That the certificate made nation-ality a priority, over and above other possible forms of differentiation, say name or gender, is a telling example of how the strangers inhabited a unique linguistic and social space.[98]

The same sets of linguistic conventions can be seen across the raft of civic administration. In 1630, for example, the mayor's court saw to it that the stranger congregation provided for a French woman who 'lately came from Kent' at their 'own charge'[99] and, when individuals were presented at court for minor crimes, strangers were identified as aliens, Dutch, or French, even though the designation bore no relation to the case. So in 1603 'John Mor-tere stranger' was 'sett in the stockes for drunkenness and abusinge of Mr Gaynard Alderman', and in 1609 when 'John De Weaver Dutchman' was presented 'for using threatening & disgraceful speeches against Mr Ellison' (quite possibly John Elison, minister of the Dutch church), he was bound over for his good behaviour.[100] The nationality of travelling performers was also noted when they applied for the licence to play in a city drinking house, like John Angligrove, for example, a Dutchman who brought a monkey, bear, and performing dog to the Red Lion in 1686.[101]

That such distinctions were made regularly in the daily business of the city reveals much about contemporary attitudes towards belonging. The use of common rhetoric devices identified the strangers as different from the Eng-lish, marking them as the 'other'. Labelling is a powerful form of social demar-cation and its constant usage worked to reinforce socio-cultural stereotypes

[96] Moens, *Walloons*, p. 189.
[97] Sachse, *Minutes, 1632–1635*, pp. 105, 137.
[98] W. L. Sachse, ed., *Minutes of the Norwich Court of Mayoralty 1630–1631* (Norwich, 1942), p. 80.
[99] Sachse, *Minutes, 1632–1635*, p. 34.
[100] NCR 16a/14, fol. 64r, Jan uary 30 1603; NCR 16a/14, fol. 307r, 1609.
[101] W. Rye, *Depositions*, p. 180.

in the wider world, not just within the legal and administrative system. In seventeenth-century Norwich, such a practice would have subconsciously set the stranger community apart.

On the other side of the coin, the strangers were in a unique position, able to be a part of both congregation and parish and, where religion was concerned, there were many points of intersection between native and foreign inhabitants. Ironically, the high-profile loss of nonconformist ministers, like William Bridge to the Low Countries during the 1630s, actually led to a strengthening of links between the stranger congregation in Norwich and their counterparts in Holland.[102] Many strangers empathised with Norwich's godly and may well have found common ground against the enemy as represented by Archbishop Laud and the almost universally hated Matthew Wren. It has certainly been argued in the case of London that the city's godly and nonconformist inhabitants welcomed the strangers, many looking to the strangers' churches and practices for reforming inspiration.[103] If this were the case in the capital, then it would not be too far a stretch of the imagination to assume this would have been the case in the godly cities of East Anglia.

An appeal to Protestant solidarity was also of national interest as a weapon against the threat of Catholic Spain and France. Across the seventeenth century, the Stuart monarchy found itself embroiled in continental struggles, most notably the wars with Spain in 1625–30, France in 1627–9, and the Thirty Years War between 1618 and 1648. At home, too, fear of Catholic plots were never far from people's minds and events such as the Gunpowder Plot of 1605, the marriage of Charles I to Henrietta Maria in 1625, the ascendancy of Archbishop Laud and the centrality of the Arminian faith to the Stuart church during the 1630s and 1640s did nothing to allay contemporary concerns about the spread of popery. After the Restoration, the domestic politics of the period commonly known as the Exclusion Crisis and the oppression of French Huguenots by Louis XIV (leading to the second refuge) did little to quieten the supposed threat of Catholicism at home and abroad. Despite the economic competition between the Dutch and English that oscillated over the course of the century, leading on occasion to skirmishes, resentment, and outright war in 1652, 1665, and 1672, the Dutch remained natural allies of the English in matters of faith. It is for these reasons, amongst others, that the Dutch, the Huguenots and the English managed to coexist in

---

[102] P. King, 'Bishop Wren and the Suppression of the Norwich Lecturers', *HJ* 6:2 (1968), 237–8. Bridge returned to English preaching in 1642 and was granted a living in Great Yarmouth. Bridge and Allen were evicted at the Restoration: Sachse, *Minutes, 1632–1635*, p. 176; J. T. Evans, *Seventeenth Century Norwich: Politics, Religion and Government 1620–1690* (Oxford, 1979), p. 195; King, 'Bishop Wren', 237–54.
[103] S. Brigden, *London and the Reformation* (Oxford, 1989), pp. 628–39; P. Collinson, 'Elizabethan Puritans and the Foreign Reformed Churches in London', reprinted in P. Collinson, *Godly People: Essays on English Protestantism and Puritanism* (London, 1983), pp. 257–72.

relative peace in England's towns and cities, and why the godly English put aside other would-be differences to seek common ground in religion.

In Norwich, this common ground can also be explored in the context of social geography. The churches of St Peter Hungate and St George Tombland were pivotal in Norwich's early nonconformist movement and it is striking that their location placed them at the heart of the weaving district and very close to the strangers' churches at New Hall (Blackfriar's Hall) and St Mary-the-Less. The nonconformist ministers William Bridge and Thomas Allen were linked to both churches, as were the pre-war Puritan aldermen Robert Craske, John Toly, Augustine Scottowe and Thomas Atkin, key figures in a county-wide group of the rich and powerful who pooled resources to purchase church impropriations and advowsons to fill parishes with their own godly preaching ministry.

The same district, just northeast of the market and castle in Wymer ward and at Colegate, continued to be the focus for Norwich's nonconformists during the civil war period and after the Restoration. Allen, on his return from New England in 1651, held a position at St George Tombland, and later became a pastor for the Independent congregation in 1657.[104] The history of the Independent's Meeting House can be traced back to 1644 when a temporary base was erected in Colegate, thereafter moving to St George Tombland during the Commonwealth. After the Restoration, the congregation moved to the West Granary at the New Hall – sharing their residency with both the strangers and the corporation – until 1685 when they adopted the site of an old brewery in the parish of St Edmund: Thomas Allen's pre-1636 territory.[105] Their first permanent meeting place was on Colegate and was constructed between 1688 and 1693. The Quaker's story in Norwich can also be connected to the strangers, as it was Onias Phillipo who sold them land in Colegate for the building of their first permanent Meeting House from 1676.[106] Likewise, Norwich's Presbyterians leased the East Granary at St Andrew's Hall from the corporation after the Declaration of Indulgence until 1688 when a more permanent building of red brick and gables was constructed in Colegate.[107]

The Compton Census of 1676 confirms the presence of known nonconformists in parishes already linked to the strangers. Proportionate to the size of the population, St Clement's parish in southern Fye-Bridge had the highest percentage of nonconformists in Norwich. The parish was located in Colegate, near the Presbyterian and Independent Meeting Houses and just a few

---

[104] King, 'Bishop Wren', 237–8.
[105] The ancient nave at New Hall was regularly used by the corporation for the celebration of annual civic events; in this way the strangers and the nonconformists shared a venue closely connected with the corporation's identity.
[106] From Society of Friends (SF), Norwich Monthly Meeting Minute Book 1671–90 transcribed by Margaret Gripper Ray and reproduced at www.nationalarchives.gov.uk/a2a/records.aspx?cat=153-sf_1&cid=0#0
[107] C. Stell, 'Nonconformist Chapels in East Anglia', Religious Dissent, ed. Virgoe and Williamson, pp. 11–20, 13.

hundred yards away from Alms Lane and Calvert Street. The small parish of St Simon and St Jude faced St Clement over the river and had the next most significant nonconformist population; it is perhaps no coincidence that this parish abutted St Peter Hungate and, like St Clement, was home to many inhabitants engaged in the weaving industry. With the exception of three parishes in the south of the city (St Stephen, St Michael at Thorn and St Peter Southgate), the nonconformist areas were largely those running the length of the river and associated with the weavers and the strangers.[108]

The intersections between the lives of the native and foreign-born inhabitants also extended to administrative and judicial business. Congregational self-government, for example, was a notional concept that did not always work in practice. The influx of strangers at the end of the sixteenth century had stretched the abilities of the congregational ministers to manage their own affairs to breaking point. Realising that their customary forms of self-regulation were no longer appropriate, the congregation worked with the civic authorities to introduce a series of new appointments, the 'hommes politiques' or 'politicjke mannen'. These annually elected officials represented their community and acted as official intermediaries between the strangers, the corporation and the magistracy. Proportionate to their numbers, there were eight serving Dutchmen and four Walloons elected each year and their duties (as clarified in the 1571 Book of Orders for the Strangers) crossed civil, political and ecclesiastic affairs including, for example, the guardianship of orphans and the settlement of disputes (the most frequent being between a master and apprentice or trade rules and regulations), the execution and testation of wills, and immoral behaviour including Sabbath breaking and drunkenness. The politic men operated in conjunction with the ministers and between them they settled a great number of the community's problems internally without needing help from the corporation.[109] Nevertheless, many cases still had to be brought before the mayor and judiciary because the politic men lacked the authority to deal with them, such as that occurring on 6 March 1585 when the 'politique men' presented three aliens (two male, one female) as 'leawd persons' and asked for them to be banished from the city, on punishment of a whipping if they returned.[110]

Strangers also became part of the corporation and the city by purchasing their freedom. Despite the strict regulations governing strangers' rights to trade, money was a great leveller. One early, high-profile freeman was Anthony de Solempne, the bookseller and printer, who had arrived in Norwich from Brabant in 1567 with his wife and sons. He was printing as early as 1568

---

[108] A. Whiteman, ed., *The Compton Census of 1696: A Critical Edition* (Oxford, 1986), pp. 217–18. Analysis of the Compton Census figures can be found in Jones, *Social Geography*, Fig. 11.12.

[109] Ibid., pp. 24–5.

[110] Hudson and Tingay, *Records*, II, p. 193.

at the sign of the White Dove in St John Maddermarket and by 1570 had purchased his freedom at the large sum of forty shillings, hardly surprising as the 1581 lay subsidy reveals him to have been one of the wealthiest strangers in Norwich at that time.[111] Solempne was not the only stranger in the book trade to have purchased his freedom. Leonard Delyson of St Peter Mancroft, for example, had become a freeman in 1550 and it is likely that the printer Anthony Rabat did the same some time before 1567.[112]

There were many other strangers who gained the freedom and contributed to civic life during the seventeenth century. The most well-known include the Cruso family, who passed their freedom from father to son, starting with the previously mentioned Jan Cruso, merchant and hosier of St Peter Mancroft during the 1620s and 1630s, then his son Aquila, his grandson John, and great-grandson, also named Aquila.[113] The Phillipo family were also wealthy merchants and freemen of the city. Descending from French Huguenots, the seventeenth-century male line of that family all gained the freedom through a variety of apprenticeships to master weavers, bakers, glovers, and soap boilers.[114] Ely (or Elie) Phillipo was of the first generation to be native-born, and earned his living as a baker in Colgate ward. His eldest son Onias, whom we have already met, became a merchant employer and his younger son Elisha became a soap boiler by trade, living first in St Peter Hungate and then in St Saviour's parish. As third-generation wealthy freemen they were heavily involved in civic life. Elisha had been a collector for the rate on two occasions before purchasing himself an exemption from future civic offices for the princely sum of £100 in 1672, but he did not decline the position of High Sheriff of Norfolk when it was offered in 1675.[115] He was buried in the chancel of St Saviour's church with his wife Isabel in 1678, a sign of their high status and patronage.[116] Church sponsorship was just as common for wealthy immigrant families as it was for native inhabitants. The De Hague family, for example, who had arrived in Norwich during the sixteenth century, sponsored the church at St Augustine, where the grocer John De Hague,

111   Anthony Solempne, MC 2577/2/7; Moens, *Walloons*, pp. 72, 166; D. Stoker, 'The Norwich Book Trades Before 1800', *Transactions of the Cambridge Bibliographical Society*, VIII (1981), 79–125, entry under 'Solempne'.

112   Stoker, 'The Norwich Book Trades', 79–125, entries under 'Delyson' and 'Rabat'.

113   The latter Crusos are listed in P. Millican, ed., *The Register of the Freemen of Norwich 1548–1713* (Norwich, 1934), p. 88: John Cruso, Son of Aquila, 24 December 1672, Aquila Cruso, son of John, 19 August 1710, both hosiers; Rye, *Rate Book*, p. 32.

114   Millican, *Register of the Freemen*, pp. 4, 69, 122, 181, 237.

115   Blomefield, *Topographical History*, IV:II, pp. 446 and *Topographical History*, III:I, p. 415; T. Hawes, *An Index to Norwich City Officers 1453–1835* (Norwich, 1989), p. 121. Elisha Phillipo was rated for the poor for St Saviour's parish in 1634 and had been rated at eight hearths in the Lady Day 1666 hearth tax assessment for the same: Rye, *Rate book*, p. 77 and P. Seaman, ed., *Norfolk and Norwich Hearth Tax Assessment: Lady Day 1666*, NG XX (Norwich, 1988), p. 72.

116   Extract from the will of Elisha Phillipo, FC 29/28, 1678; Blomefield, *Topographical History*, IV:II, p. 446.

son of John, who had gained his freedom through an apprenticeship in 1692, was buried in 1723.[117] The family have been remembered because of their descendant Elisha De Hague who became town clerk and was responsible for introducing Norwich to gas lighting during the eighteenth century. There is also a road named after him.

For the wealthy strangers, there was an obvious route to becoming an important member of the civic community, and for those strangers who were not free there were other options, albeit less high-profile ones. In the same way that the better sort of strangers were expected to give to the parish chest, wealthier strangers were also expected to make reparations to the state, including the payment of special subsidies and voluntary contributions. From 1672, for example, the Crown raised a subsidy from the chief inhabitants of all the major cities to finance the Third Dutch War.[118] In Norwich, eleven strangers volunteered sums ranging from two shillings and sixpence to ten pounds to help finance the English fleet, including the sum of one pound from the widow Abigall Mackerall.[119]

The strangers also made important contributions to England's defence by supporting Norwich's militia, perhaps by joining the Company of Dutchmen, contributing arms and armour, or both. In 1595, for example, the Dutch and Walloons contributed 138 of the 780 separate items of weaponry and armour collected from Norwich's inhabitants, including muskets, calivers and corselets, and in 1618 the corporation compiled a list of all those people then registered in the Company of Dutchmen considered 'sufficient to find armor'.[120] Two years later an almost identical list was produced, along with the 'Rolle of the Wallons Companie' on 18 September 1620. The Walloons were led by Captain Joel Desurmeaux, the same man who was later to be involved in the dispute of parish versus congregational taxes and interestingly, his comrade in the dispute, Samuel Camby, was Desurmeaux's bearer.[121] The list of the Company of Dutch produced in 1621 revealed ninety-five members under the captainship of Jacques van Berten and Lieutenant Marcus Baelde, two sergeants and an 'Auncient Baror', with a company of twenty-seven corselet and sixty-three musket.[122]

Despite their obvious contribution to national defence, there were some who viewed arming strangers with suspicion. In 1631, the Lord Lieutenant

---

[117] Millican, *Register of the Freemen*, p. 80; Blomefield, *Topographical History*, IV:II, p. 476. His father John had died in Norwich in 1687: Will of John De Hague, ANW, will register, 1687–8, fol. 97, 1687.

[118] 'Charles II, 1672: An Act for raising the Summe of Twelve hundred thirty eight thousand seaven hundred, and fifty Pounds for supply of his Majesties extraordinary occasions', J. Raithby, *Statutes of the Realm, 1628–80*, Vol. 5 (1819), pp. 752–82.

[119] Moens, *Walloons*, p. 187.

[120] Musters List of Dutch Soliders, NCR 13a/17, fol. 76, 1 March 1595; Muster list of Dutch soldiers of Norwich, NCR 13a/20, 24 September 1618.

[121] Rolle of the Wallons Companie, COL 5/5/3, 18 September 1620.

[122] Moens, *Walloons*, p. 225.

of Norfolk proposed that the various companies of strangers nationwide be brought under the control of the English companies in their wards, an action that never took place. This was because of strong objections from the strangers' companies themselves who resented the tone of the proposal and did not wish the management of their companies to leave their own hands.[123] In 1640, worried about the escalation of violence nationally, the loyalties of the 'Aliens and Strangers' and 'the danger of homebred mischiefes', Sydrake Jorey wrote to the Earl of Northumberland, then Lord Chief General of the King's forces, to advise him that in places 'namely Ipswich, Yarmouth, and Norwich (where the French, Walloons, & Dutch, are as many; if not more, then the natives: and exercise Millitarie discipline once every fortnight) that if occasion should happen: they may easily become a great Incombrance to the native subject, or at least be ayding and assisting to any forraigne Invad[e]r'.[124] Such sentiments did not stop the Norwich strangers from marching to Cambridge to join the Parliamentarian army stationed under the Earl of Manchester in 1644; perhaps Jorey had been right to doubt the loyalty of Norwich strangers to the Crown. Nevertheless, in 1644, the strangers represented Norwich in as great a number as the native inhabitants when 'in repect of the eminent danger of the approach of the enemy ... it is agreed that Captaine Rawley & his Company & the Company of the Dutch & French in this Citty shalbe the two Companyes that shall goe out'.[125] Outside of the militia companies, William Woods has suggested that the stranger community in Norwich actually maintained a fairly low profile during the civil wars because, although their faith may have allied them with the Parliamentarian cause, they owed much to the favour of the Crown.[126] The strangers may have had many boundaries set to limit their involvement in civic life but this certainly did not stop many from overcoming them.

The Norwich that the strangers knew was, in many respects, based on their experiences as immigrants and outsiders. It is certainly possible that these experiences coloured their perceptions of Norwich and that the spatial propinquity of their lives, based as it was on shared social, occupational, and religious networks, lent them a particular way of seeing city space. Nevertheless, this conclusion conceals the complexity of the strangers' connections with the numerous networks and communities in and outside of Norwich. Although the strangers' social topography was shaped to some degree by their propensity to work in professions and trades related to the cloth industry and by membership of the central Wymer churches, their networks also extended across the city, county and region. Equally, wealth, status, occupation,

123 Ibid., pp. 82–3.
124 NA, SP 16a/470/92, c. October 1640.
125 Company of Strangers in Parliament's Army, NCR 16a/20, fol. 417r, 26 March 1644.
126 Woods, 'Publications', p. 34.

religious affiliations and personal networks worked to shape individual experience of urban life.

The propensity to view the strangers as a homogenous community stems in large part from the written records which were constructed in a language that conceptualised the strangers as the 'other', and has been emulated by antiquarians and historians ever since. The process worked in both directions and there were some benefits to the strangers maintaining some measure of exclusivity. Thus exclusion, where it existed, was not something always done to the congregation as the passive recipients of the xenophobic policies of local and national government. The strangers fought hard to retain their own identity and preserve their congregation from attrition, and in so doing they preserved their financial and spiritual autonomy, a rare privilege in the early-modern world. They could be considered a community within a community but social perception, rather than physical segregation, worked to keep its boundaries alive.

4

Gendering the Streets:
Men, Women, and Public Space

Previous chapters have considered the transformative effect of personal circumstances, networks and interests on perceptions and experiences of the
city. This chapter considers how far gender may have coloured perceptions
of urban space in Norwich. In particular, it asks the question – was the city a
different place for men and for women? There has been a great deal of literature that has addressed the notion of 'gendered' space.[1] A popular focus of
this recent work has been to compare the lived experiences of city men and
women with dominant socio-cultural narratives concerning gender roles and
appropriate spheres of movement. Much of this recent work builds on the sophisticated critiques of the 'separate spheres' model that emerged during the
1980s and 1990s, which argued that concepts of 'public' and 'private' space
were more fluid and infinitely more complex than had once been thought.[2]
As Laura Gowing has explained, there are many 'problematic elisions of
meaning in the model of separate spheres ... One of these is the confusion

---

[1] See for example, Lin Foxhall and Gabriele Neher, eds, *Gender and the City before Mo-
dernity* (London, 2012); Ritta Laitinen and Thomas V. Cohen, eds, *Cultural History of
Early-Modern Streets* (Leiden, 2008); Clare Brant and Susan Whyman, eds., *Walking the
Streets of Eighteenth Century London: John Gay's Trivia* (Oxford, 2007); A. Flather, *Gender
and Space in Early Modern England* (Woodbridge, 2007); R. Shoemaker, 'Gendered Spaces:
Patterns of Mobility and Perceptions of London's Geography, 1660–1750', *Imagining Early
Modern London: Perceptions and Portrayals of the City from Stow to Strype, 1598–1720*, ed. J.
F. Merritt (Cambridge, 2001), pp. 144–65; B. A. Hanawalt and M. Kobialka, eds., *Medieval
Practices of Space* (Minnesota, 2000); L. Gowing, '"The Freedom of the Streets": Women
and Social Space, 1560–1640', *Londinopolis: Essays in the Cultural and Social History of Ear-
ly Modern London*, ed. P. Griffiths and M. Jenner (Manchester, 2000), pp. 130–51.
[2] Formative critiques of the separate spheres model include: A. Vickery, 'Golden Age to
Separate Spheres? A Review of the Categories and Chronology of English Women's History', *Historical Journal* 36:2 (1993), 383–414; Catherine Hall, *White, Male and Middle Class:
Explorations in Feminism and History* (Cambridge, 1992); J. Wallach-Scott, 'Gender: A
Useful Category of Historical Analysis', *American Historical Review* 91:5 (1986), 1053–75;
and Joan Kelly-Godal, 'The Social Relation of the Sexes: Methodological Implications of
Women's History', *Signs: Journal of Women in Culture and Society* 1 (1976), 809–33.

between public or private *issues* and *events* and public and private spaces.'[3] Michael McKeon also proposes that

> In 'traditional' cultures, the differential relationship between public and private modes of experience is conceived as a distinction that does not admit of separation. In 'modernity' the public and the private are separated out from each other, a condition that both sustains the sense of traditional distinction and, axiomatically, reconstitutes the public and private as categories that are susceptible to separation.[4]

Most recently, the influence of interdisciplinary studies and the 'spatial turn' of social historians' methodological approaches has led to further explorations of the relationship between people, place, and ideology.[5] This chapter builds from this, by exploring the reception of women in Norwich's public areas, especially its streets, markets, and alehouses. Specifically, it aims to question the elision of masculine identity with public or semi-public places, by arguing – in line with McKeon's claim above – that for contemporaries, distinctions between 'public' or 'private' space were blurred, thus it is hard to equate gender-specific labels to places and spaces. Indeed, the tendency of academic dialogues to frame gender within a dichotomous model has obscured the manifold ways in which early-modern people internalised, expressed and generated normative gendered codes and negotiated the various concepts of public and private that were available. As Alexander Cowen argues, 'to the eyes of local observers, the boundaries between public and domestic space were real, but hardly sharp and not always significant'.[6] The following discussion focuses on a different array of public places and ideas for comparison: the juncture between domestic and public places and people's interactions between the two, the streets, markets, and finally, the semi-public space of drinking houses. By exploring where men and women were most likely to spend their time and, more importantly, by analysing how men and women were treated, spoken about, or to, in these places, we can gain a better understanding of how far these places might have been considered appropriate for either sex.

[3] Gowing, '"The Freedom of the Streets"', p. 133.
[4] M. McKeon, *The Secret History of Domesticity: Public, Private and the Division of Knowledge* (Baltimore, 2005), p. xix.
[5] Kingston argues that the 'spatial-turn' is not a passing phenomenon but one that will continue to influence social historians for the foreseeable future: R. Kingston, 'Mind Over Matter? History and the Spatial Turn', *Cultural and Social History* 7:1 (2010), 111–21, 111.
[6] Alexander Cowen, 'Gossip and Street Culture in Early Modern Venice', *Journal of Early Modern History* 12 (2008), 313–33, 319.

Blurred Boundaries

Seventeenth-century Norwich was internationally renowned and acclaimed for its open spaces. Orchards, gardens and fields broke up the monotony of houses and industrial activity in the outlying parishes and the several markets provided open plains in the concentration of houses in the city centre. Few people waxed lyrical about the lattice of streets and lanes that facilitated the essential flow of people, animals and information around the city. Norwich's main roads resembled the spokes of a wheel. One paved avenue linked each gatehouse with the central market, cathedral and Norman castle: the focal points of the city centre. Some of these roads traced the natural features of the original landscape (long since lost under the effluence of the city) and, like Great Cockey Lane for example, the roads' names reflected this connection. Crisscrossing the principal thoroughfares were a series of smaller residential streets and a maze of back alleys and narrow lanes: the veins that transported life around the houses, shops, churches, inns and alehouses. The streets acted as bridges between all the composite parts of city life.[7] But urban streets were not simply conduits: they were *lived* spaces.

People worked, socialised, communicated, and on occasion, lived, on the city's streets. Signs, arches, and overhangs forced commercial and private properties into the public domain. Doors, windows and shop fronts opened directly onto the streets through which people moved continually across the liminal thresholds of private and public property. The close proximity of domestic interiors and the streets – most ordinary houses lacked hallways or had shops/workshops as their front room – meant that boundaries between public and private space were hard to draw.[8] Thin walls, shutters instead of glass windows, and a lack of soft furnishings to dull noise must have only forced the affairs of domestic interiors even more forcefully into the streets. In this way neighbours overhead private goings-on and private words became public defamations. This was certainly the case in 1600 when Randolph Godwin, 'in his owne shoppe being ... next doore and but a wall being between his howse and Susan Goodwards howse' when he clearly overheard Thomas Blosse say that 'Ann Rowse was as arrant a whore as any and ... had had two base children'. Likewise, Robert Hastings overheard Ester Warren in the next shop gossiping about a neighbour rumoured to be pregnant in 1698,[9] and Mary Mannings heard her neighbour Robert Wright call her 'a damned lying

---

7   R. Laitinen and T. Cohen, 'Cultural History of Early Modern Streets: An Introduction', *Journal of Early Modern History* 12 (2008), 195–204, 195–6.

8   Norwich's large population of ordinary labourers and artisans – especially weavers – lived in two- or three-roomed houses built around a communal yard. Most of these houses opened directly onto the street at the front, and the yard at the back. For more on Norwich housing see U. Priestly and P. Corfield, 'Rooms and Room Use in Norwich Housing 1580–1730', *Post Medieval Archaeology* 16 (1982), 93–123.

9   DN/DEP/31/34, fol. 38r, 20 July 1600. Anne Rowse v. Thomas Blosse, and DN/DEP/53/58a, section xi, 27 October 1698. Ann Horne v. Ester Warren.

whore' whilst she was serving in her family shop, even though Wright was in his own shop on the opposite side of the street. Wright's accusation had stemmed from that fact that he had overheard Mannings boasting about the quality of her tobacco.[10]

These were not isolated cases but examples of the daily happenstance of private lives that continually threatened to spill out onto the streets. Thus it was in 1634 that the private conversation of neighbours Elizabeth Ridout and Elizabeth Shipdham at Deborah Redman's shop (the front room of Redman's house) became a public defamation punished in the Diocesan Court. The two women had been gossiping about the paternity of a child who lived in their parish, and the accused man sued them for it after he found out.[11] In 1684 there was an incident where Anna Spill, who had been walking outside Thomas Whitehead's door in St Stephen's parish one Saturday night, witnessed Whitehead lean out of one of his windows and cry out abusive words to Elizabeth Armes who was on the other side of the street and, in 1695, when John Nailes called his servant Roberta Benn a whore in his front room, Benn immediately went out into the street to ask passers-by to act as witnesses for her in court, the assumption being that anyone walking by would have heard Nailes' words.[12] From such examples we could perhaps argue, as one scholar has claimed, that the transition of private to public space was gauged by earshot.[13]

As we have seen, domestic disputes often crossed household boundaries into public places and it has been suggested that doorways, thresholds, and windows were a liminal space – a place of interchange, a grey area, neither public nor private. In London, Laura Gowing found that women were more often connected with this liminal place than were men. She argues that there was a practical reason behind this; thresholds and doorways were places that women sat to work, spinsters for example, to take advantage of the natural light whilst perhaps keeping an eye on children playing in the street. Gowing found that this physical association often led to a high frequency of defamatory words being spoken against women in this location, these connections leading to an assumption that the doorway could be considered a symbolically gendered place.[14] With regard to defamation, the Norwich evidence suggests otherwise however. In 1602, for example, John Chapman and John Shackle

10 DN/DEP/53/58A, section xi, 11 November 1699. Mary Mannings v. Robert Wright.
11 DN/DEP/42/47a, fol. 502v, January 1635. Nathanial Stallworth v. Deborah Redman. For similar incidents, see DN/DEP/32/35, fol. 6v, 1602. Rose v. Pettewe; DN/DEP/38/43, fol. 147r, 6 May 1629. Woodgate v. Skurlett; DN/DEP/53/58a, section xvi, 12 November 1697. Rant v. Wick; DN/DEP/53/58a, section xi, 9 March 1697. Elizabeth Ward v. Samuel Swift; or DN/DEP/53/58a, section x, 30 July 1700. Ringstead v. Hall.
12 DN/DEP/51/55, fol. 71r, 5 August 1684. Elizabeth Armes v. Thomas Whitehead; DN/DEP/53/58a, section xvi, July 1695. Roberta Benn v. John Nailes.
13 S. Ardener, ed., *Women and Space: Ground Rules and Social Maps* (Oxford, 1981), p. 12.
14 Gowing "'The Freedom of the Streets'", p. 137.

had argued in the doorway of Chapman's house, Chapman calling Shackle a bastard, and in 1607 John Barnes had been at Hardy's door when he had heard Albert Ansten declare that Thomas Claxton was having an affair with Amyes' wife.[15] From the vantage point of her own front door, Katherine Brotherhood had observed William and Anne Austin walking along the street when Mary Frogg, who was standing at her own gate at the time, had shouted to the nearest passer-by to 'bid him stare and see a whore and a rogue come by together'.[16] On another occasion Brotherhood had witnessed Mary Frogg and Anne Austin shouting at one other from the safety of their own doorways.[17] Likewise, Elizabeth Harris, 'standing at the gate of [Mary Frogg's] howse being the signe of the Golden Dog ... observed ... William Austin to follow ... Mary Frogg comeing to her owne howse and heard him say ... thou arte a whore ... with an intention to defame'.[18] The same year, John Morston was 'sitting in company with ... Katherine Goodwin att her dore' from which vantage point they could watch an argument unfold in the street,[19] and Francis Hayward had stood at Elizabeth Seaman's door in St Stephen in 1668 and watched whilst Seaman and Jane Mylles argued with one another in the street.[20] Likewise, when Alice Clapham and Elizabeth Steele were 'att hot words' in the street in 1684, they drew a small audience. Sara Woods and her husband had watched from their doorway, and their neighbour, Robert Cooke, 'sitting att his doore between John Claphams doore and John Steeles doore' heard the whole dispute.[21] Three years later, Thomas Davy had stood in his own doorway to tell his neighbour, Margaret Burrell, that she was a 'whore, bitch and a jade', and William Lawrence had been standing at his own doorway when he had heard Mary Sayer at James Wilkinson's door calling Wilkinson a 'Rascall', a 'curr', and a 'grey lock't Rogue'.[22] The correlation of defamation and doorways is significant certainly but – in the evidence from Norwich's ecclesiastical courts at least – it was not specific to women.

If we look at the depositions from secular courts, the connection with domestic doorways and the female sex is even less apparent; Norwich's mayoral court records, for example, reveal how domestic thresholds were often appropriated by men as a way of asserting their autonomy as householders. In 1628, for example, constable Thomas Greenfield was sent to arrest Lewis Sharfe. When Sharfe discovered the constable on his doorstep he barred his doorway

---

15   DN/DEP/32/35, fol. 834r, 23 June 1607. Amyes v. Albert Ansten.
16   DN/DEP/47/51, fol. 12b, 18 December 1664. Austin v. Frogg.
17   DN/DEP/47/51, fol. 12r, 26 September 1664. Office v. Austin. An office cause was a case presented by the court, rather than an individual: as opposed to an instance cause.
18   DN/DEP/47/51, fol. 136r, 4 November 1664. Frogg v. Austin.
19   DN/DEP/32/35, fol. 233v, January 1602. Shackle v. Chapman, and DN/DEP/47/51, fol. 135r, 4 November 1664. Frogg v. Austin.
20   DN/DEP/48/52, fol. 109r, 26 February 1668. Elizabeth Seaman v. Jane Mylles.
21   DN/DEP/51/55, fol. 122r, 1683. Elizabeth Steele v. Alice Clapham.
22   DN/DEP/52/56&57, fol. 4v, 1688. Margaret Burrell v. Thomas Davy, and fol. 5r, 1687. James Wilkinson v. Mariam Samuel.

to him, exclaiming loudly 'I will not goe … come into the howse [i]f you dare'.[23] Greenfield was forced to leave without making the arrest. Sharfe's words and actions had tangibly curtailed Greenfield's civic authority during the symbolic act of barring the way. This was not an isolated case. Hugh Page had also evaded arrest by shutting his front door in constable Hugh Jacques' face and refusing to leave his own house.[24] On another occasion Jacques – this time in pursuit of one William Jary – went 'to the howse of Mr Homberston and did there in the Bruehowse speake w[i]th … Jary who utterly refused to goe … And the said constable fearing to lay hold of … Jary hee being alone … went out to call ayde And then one Mary a servant of the said Mr Homberston shutt the gate against him'.[25] Likewise, when constable Richard Lawson attempted to arrest Thomas Costerden, he was prevented from so doing by having the door slammed in his face. When a different constable was sent to make a second attempt to arrest Costerden a few days later, Costerden shut the constable's foot in the door and barred his entry.[26] The physical act of barring a door may have only temporarily obstructed the course of the law, but the symbolism is striking. By denying civic representatives access to domestic property, ordinary people resisted the incursion of public life into their homes, in a way that was often lacking in the personal disputes we saw earlier. These men, and the many others like them, manipulated the household boundary as a tool of personal agency. The door could shut out the street if necessary.

This was particularly evident in the case of William Burlington. Burlington was a worsted weaver from Norwich who in 1698 had managed to evade a conviction for the murder of John Hall despite a number of witnesses. Burlington had been visiting the widow Mary Pedley at her 'mansion' in St Peter Mancroft when Hall and some companions had broken into the house. Hall insulted Burlington before fleeing to the garret hotly pursued by a furious Burlington with a carbine. Burlington shot Hall through the left eye, killing him instantly. The verdict was recorded as self-defence although clearly Burlington was chasing after the escaping criminal, not being attacked. The case aptly illustrates how the interpretation of an act that would probably not have been acceptable in public, fundamentally changed when committed in private.[27]

As we have already seen, the boundaries of domestic property were both permeable and impermeable. Voices travelled freely through the doors and windows of private homes into the streets for anyone to hear yet, when it suited, physical access to the same place could be restricted. This complexity, this crossing and re-crossing of boundaries and merging of public and private, was also evident in contemporaries' attitudes towards public and private affairs.

23 NCR 16a/16, fol. 219r, November 1628.
24 NCR 16a/16, fol. 223r, 17 December 1628.
25 NCR 16a/16, fol. 229r, 4 February 1628.
26 NCR 16a/20 1634–1646 fol. 86r, December 1635.
27 NCR Case 6a/2, fol. 46, 25 March 1698.

Neighbours also interfered in private affairs, such as domestic disputes, when they saw fit, as did the law. Indeed, the rule of thumb in neighbourhoods was that this kind of close monitoring was not only socially acceptable but a neighbourly duty. It was common for inhabitants to keep a close eye on their neighbours' comings and goings. Communities tended to be close and neighbours were expected to help one another out in times of need, or look out for one another's property or personal wellbeing as part of their moral duty as a good neighbour. However there were negative and positive aspects to this close relationship. People who wanted their affairs to stay hidden often found it hard to keep them so. In 1600, for instance, Olive Barrowes and John Chettleburgh's illicit affair had been made public after their eavesdropping neighbour – having long been suspicious that something had been going on but lacking the proof to prove it – had realised that the pair were together in their 'naked bed' and called the constables to catch them in the act. Likewise, it was Ann Leasey's neighbours who called the night watch to Leasey's home in 1684 after they had been waiting for the right moment to prove she was having an affair. The watch caught Edward Preston naked, trying to hide in Leasey's bed.[28]

Public scrutiny was an integral and, crucially, an accepted part of maintaining harmony in communities. Indeed, the household was the very foundation of community, thus a healthy household equalled a healthy community. In 1680, therefore, Andrew Faireman's neighbours rallied to help him win a defamation case. Faireman was the victim of a malicious gossip who had contrived to ruin his reputation because of a personal grudge. The gossip, John Metcalfe, with the help of some 'poor' and debt-ridden low-life characters, had spread rumours around their parish that Faireman was having an affair with the married Anne Bately. Faireman's friends were outraged on his behalf and, knowing that the rumours could not possibly be true, determined to spy on him to prove the gossip false. One evening, a group of Faireman's neighbours made a hole in his bedchamber shutters and settled in for a night of spying into the room. Seeing nothing out of the ordinary, the group acted as Fairman's compurgators at the church court declaring that he 'hath carried himself soberly and civillie amongst his neighbours & was never ... suspected of anie such crime ... with anie woman'.[29] In a rather different set of circumstances, Hannah Robinson's neighbours had acted as her main witnesses in a suit that she had filed in the church court against her own husband, John, in 1696. The court heard how Hannah was the victim of domestic abuse, whereby John Robinson regularly beat and kicked Hannah so hard that she cried out. John was a cruel husband and a cruel master and his neighbours had hoped to put an end to his unseemly behaviour which was gradually

---

[28] DN/DEP/31/34, fol. 11v, 10 May 1600. John Chettleburgh v. William Camplyn, and NCR 12a-b/1 1684–1689. The information of John Bensley, William Jell and John Barnham, 5 December 1684.

[29] DN/DEP/51/55, fol. 349r, 26 January 1680. Faireman v. Metcalfe.

undermining their community's peace of mind. On one occasion, for example, 'Mrs Cooke the next neighbour hearing [Hannah] came to the window & asked [their servant Roberta Mallows] what doe you stand there & see your mistress cract on the head' to which Mallows had replied that Robinson had threatened he 'would cut her throat' if she opened the door to cry for help.[30] Regardless of John's caution it was still obvious to his neighbours as to what was taking place indoors. Both these cases serve as useful reminder that intruding into domestic space could be done with good reason.[31]

As McKeon has pointed out, scholars tend to make an artificial division between public and private spaces that were not really there during lived experiences, or at least, not at all times. Dividing lines between street and home were real, symbolic, and recognised but they were also continually penetrated and circumvented. On one occasion the erection of a boundary might suit a person hoping to evade arrest, but on another occasion that boundary might be pulled down to help another. Boundaries that moved with individual events and circumstances could perhaps not be considered real boundaries at all.

Men and Women on the Streets

That public and private spaces were fluidly integrated can perhaps also be seen in some contemporaries' reactions to the phenomenon. Those writers and moralists who devoted any time to the quandary regarded the lack of boundaries with some dismay. Conduct book writers for example, found it hard to reconcile strict, and often spatially and ideologically static, ideas about women's proper place and behaviour when the conventions of community living and practical realities continually challenged them. William Gouge, for example, dealt with the problem by urging women to carry their domestic, or private, persona out into the streets by assuming a 'mild and amiable countenance', being 'sparing in speech' when in public, and not journeying 'abroad without their husbands consent'.[32] This expectation created a paradox. Gouge, and others like him, expected women to appropriate a submissive attitude outside the home, but very many women had working roles that required quite the opposite. Female street hawkers, market traders and shop and alehouse keepers had to be assertive and confident in order to run their businesses effectively. At the lower end of the social scale, female prostitutes and petty criminals needed to be pushy and even aggressive to survive. The streets could be hostile, dangerous places for women who were too

---

30 DN/DEP/53/58a, section xvi, 28 January 1696. Robinson v. Robinson.
31 See Gowing, '"Freedom of the Streets"', p. 134 and Cowen, 'Gossip and Street Culture', 328.
32 William Gouge, *Of Domesticall Duties* (1622), ed. Greg Fox (2006), pp. 197, 199, 203.

timid.[33] This paradox raises a series of important problems. We know that the idea of women as submissive, delicate creatures as espoused in contemporary prescriptive literature does not represent the reality of seventeenth-century women, but gender ideals still had much persuasive power. This suggests some interesting questions about how women dealt with the contradiction in their day-to-day lives. If women had to be assertive in many public situations, for example, did this put their reputation at risk?[34] If so, did this mean that the streets were inherently masculine places that advantaged men over women?

Robert Davis – writing about gendered spaces in early-modern Venice – argues that this was indeed the case. Women were not excluded from the streets per se but men had freedoms in public places in a way that women did not. Men stood on street corners in male groups, loitered around markets and public squares, and dominated drinking houses. The presence of groups of men in public places created an atmosphere that worked to exclude women, or a feminine culture. Women were forced thus into moving from place to place more often, rather than loitering at a place – perhaps an alehouse – where their reputation might be brought into question.[35] Robert Shoemaker's survey of women's movements in and around early-modern London demonstrated that women of middling status did indeed move around the city more than men of the same social class. Middling men often tended to stay in one place because they were tied to a business premises during the day and evening, whereas women of the same status visited friends or went to the market. Poorer women had a similar range of movement to their male counterparts: both sexes were actively engaged in looking for work and taking what opportunities arose wherever they may have been. The exception was the richer sorts. Shoemaker found that wealthier men tended to travel extensively around and outside of the city to pursue business and pleasure but women of the same rank were more likely to stay closer to home for extended periods. Yet the conclusions Shoemaker drew from his study were remarkably different from those of Davis. Davis argued that men loitering in public places in Venice – for social or business purposes – demonstrated a more concrete claim over urban space than women's ephemeral and passing occupation of space. Shoemaker, on the other hand, argued that rather than men having the dominant claim to space in London, women actually experienced more freedoms.[36] Nevertheless, if we accept that women did indeed range widely around cities – which up to a point must have been a practical necessity – this still does not answer the question of whether women in public were less

---

[33] Gowing, "'Freedom of the Streets'", pp. 130–1: M. Wiesner, *Women and Gender in Early Modern Europe* (Cambridge, 2000), p. 103.

[34] Laura Gowing argues that women had to be more aware of damaging their reputations in public places: "'Freedom of the Streets'", pp. 138–40.

[35] Robert C. Davis, 'The Geography of Gender in the Renaissance', *Gender and Society in Renaissance Italy*, ed. Judith Brown and Robert C. Davis (London, 1995), pp. 19–38.

[36] Shoemaker, 'Gendered Spaces', p. 163.

acceptable than men in public, and thus whether there was something about public space that was inherently more 'masculine'.

We can approach these thorny issues using Norwich's records in a variety of ways, not least by exploring general attitudes toward men and women in the city's streets. As many scholars have shown, defamation cases are a useful point of entry into early-modern ways of thinking about gender and gender-appropriate behaviour.[37] If we also consider the *location* where defamatory words were spoken, then we can build a picture of how attitudes towards gender might be affected by internalised meanings affixed to public spaces. Were, for example, women more likely to be defamed when they were in public places than men? If so, we might conclude that women's reputations were less secure in public places than were those of men, thus men's claim to being in public was more developed than that of women.

A total of one hundred and twenty-nine defamation suits were filed at Norwich's Diocesan Court for parishes located within the city walls between 1600 and 1700. In almost every case, the court clerk had recorded the place where the defamatory words were spoken. This information was considered vital to the case. To file for defamation three legal points had to be proved. The first related to a person's good character before the defamatory words were spoken, the second, to the loss of that reputation after the defamatory words had been spoken, and the third, to the circumstances under which the words were spoken.[38] Location was integral to this final point, as the words had to be spoken in public hearing. This did not necessarily mean that defamatory words had to be spoken outside of private property, but words uttered in shops, alehouses, streets and other public places were considered the most injurious.

William Tracie, for example, had defamed Anne Fuller in 1640. In the presence of Etheldreda and Thomas Perrie, Tracie had called Fuller a whore and 'a base whore' in the streets of St Stephen's parish.[39] The same year, Gregory Meen publically alleged Anne Inman was a 'strumpetly jade' in the parish of St Peter Mancroft, and George Nelson had accused Frances Sherwood of acting the 'whore and a drunken whore' on Timberhill.[40] Sara Portland was another woman whose reputation was challenged in the street. In 1684 Portland, Mary Moore and Sara Browne were in the streets of St Peter Parment-

---

[37] See for example Laura Gowing, *Domestic Dangers: Women, Words and Sex in Early-Modern London* (Oxford, 1999); E. Foyster, *Manhood in Early-Modern England: Honour, Sex, and Marriage* (London, 1999); F. Dabhoiwala, 'The Construction of Honour, Reputation, and Status in Late Seventeenth- and Early Eighteenth-Century England', *TRHS* 6 (1996), 201–13; S. Amussen, *An Ordered Society: Gender and Class in Early Modern England* (Oxford, 1988); or M. Ingram, *Church Courts, Sex and Marriage in England 1570–1640* (Cambridge, 1987).

[38] A. Tarver, *Church Court Records: An Introduction for Family and Local Historians* (Chichester, 1995), p. 113.

[39] DN/DEP/45/48b, fol. 98r, 27 October 1640. Anne Fuller v. William Tracie.

[40] DN/DEP/45/48b, fol. 112v, 5 February 1640. Frances Sherwood v. George Nelson.

ergate, when Moore and Portland began quarrelling. Moore accused Portland of having married on Whitsun Sunday and being 'brought to bed' a week and three days before Candlemas, inferring that she had been pregnant and given birth before she had wed.[41] These cases were typical of those brought to the church court in Norwich during the seventeenth century, many of which targeted women. Of those one hundred and twenty-nine cases where the location of the defamatory words was recorded, eighteen victims were male and forty were female. The evidence appears conclusive.

Nonetheless, if we hark back to Shoemaker's argument, then the high number of cases of women defaming each other in public streets, yards, and alleys, as opposed to at home, may simply reflect the fact that more women were abroad during the day than men of the same social status; indeed, his study highlighted the prominence of middling sort women on the streets, exactly the type of women who predominated in church court cases.[42] We might also consider the number of cases as a percentage of the whole number of men and women at court. Urban women outnumbered urban men in bringing defamation suits to the church at a figure of seventy-five to fifty-one respectively. While there may be a number of conclusions drawn about this fact and the importance of female reputation more broadly, it does suggest that the percentage difference for defamatory words uttered on the street against men or women was not as great as first imagined. It is also worth asking the question as to whether the defamatory words spoken in any of the Norwich defamation cases reflected a specific anxiety with women on the streets.

The language that early-modern people used to defame one another reflected commonly held ideals about appropriate behaviour and personal morality. These ideals were just that: standards that were not always achievable in real life. But despite acknowledging human fallibility, there were certain acts that were never acceptable under any circumstances: adultery, fornication, and illegitimacy. Contemporaries were well aware that personal honour could be lost more quickly than it could be gained, and were thus keen to fight to hold onto it at any cost. So in 1618, when goodwife Elizabeth Browne was accused in front of several men by Barnaby Leighton in the streets of St Michael's parish of having been whipped at the post and 'taken in a cart' for 'playing the whore … w[i]th some other man besides her husband', she sued him for defamation.[43] Likewise, when Nicholas Weston announced in front of several witnesses outside the sign of the Castle on Timberhill that Richard Cubbit's adult daughter was illegitimate, or in 1690 when Robert Money

---

41 DN/DEP/51/55, fol. 124r, 16 August 1684. Sara Portland v. Mary Moore.

42 The majority of defamation suits filed in the diocese of Norwich involved people of middling status. Studies of defamation suits in other areas reveal the same social composition. See, for example, Gowing, *Domestic Dangers*; Ingram, *Church Courts*; or R. Houlbrooke, *Church Courts and the People during the English Reformation 1520–1570* (Oxford, 1979).

43 DN/DEP/37/40, fol. 389v, 27 July 1618. Elizabeth Browne v. Barnaby Leighton.

told Mr Lawes he was a 'whoreing rogue' in the street outside a blacksmith's shop, the individuals accused decided that repairing a damaged reputation was worth the expenditure of a court case.[44]

In Norwich, as elsewhere, common insults against women were 'whore', 'quean', 'jade', or 'bitch'.[45] Women were accused of making men cuckolds, of having sex outside of marriage, drunkenness, or occasionally minor criminal behaviour. Defamatory words aimed at men included 'rogue', 'whoremaster', 'knave', 'jack', 'jackanapes', or some combination of the above. The term rogue had multiple meanings, implying anything from sexual immorality to criminal behaviour, idleness, vagrancy, sexual licentiousness, and even a servant.[46] Thomas Harman's 'rogue' was a bawdy wandering criminal who

> …will picke and steale as the upright men, and hath their women and meetings at places appoynted, and nothing to them inferiour in all kind of knauery There be of these Roges Curtales, wearing short lokes, that will change their apparell as occasion serueth, and their end is eyther hanging, which they call Tr[i]ming in their language, or dye miserably of the pockes… Yet before he skyppeth out of his couche and departeth from his darling (if he like her well) he will appoynte her where to meete shortly after, with a warning to worke warely for some chetes, that their meeting might be the merier.[47]

Harman makes the sexual connotations of the term 'rogue' explicit, a connection that was frequently made in defamation cases when the word was employed to describe a man who had committed adultery, or fathered an illegitimate child. So, in 1633 for example, John Pye wished that his neighbour had been hanged for his frequent affairs, saying 'he had bin a burnt arste roague these seven yeares'; in 1682 Phillipe Starre told Edward Watson he was 'a rotten Pocky Rogue' and three years later William Barker had shouted 'you are a rogue … & you fuck't Robin Ellis his wife' at Jeremiah Clifton.[48] The

---

44 DN/DEP/38/43, fol. 476r, 10 January 1629. Richard Cubitt v. Nicholas Weston, and DN/DEP/52/56&57, unmarked folios, 6 October 1690. Mr Lawes v. Robert Money. For more on the legal processes and costs, see Tarver, *Church Court Records*.

45 For York and London see L. Gowing, 'Gender and the Language of Insult in Early Modern London', *HWJ* 35 (1993), 1–21; Ingram, *Church Courts*; or J. A. Sharpe, *Defamation and Sexual Slander in Early Modern England: the Church Courts at York*, Borthwick Papers, 58 (York, 1980).

46 The OED entry under rogue states 'one belonging to a class of idle vagrants or vagabonds'. The etymological context includes: 'The sturdie roag vnworthie of an almes', *Bullinger's Decades* (1592) p. 129; 'Wildly to wander. Withouten pasport or good warrantye, For feare least we like rogues should be reputed,' E. Spenser, M. *Hubberd* (1591) p. 187 ; 'And was't thou faine…To houell thee with Swine and Rogues forlorne, In short, and musty straw?,' W. Shakespeare, *Lear* IV, vii. 39 (1605).

47 T. Harman, 'A Caueat or Warning for Common Cursetors 1573', *Nash's Lenten Stuff*, ed. C. Hindley (London, 1871), pp. 9–10.

48 DN/DEP/41/46, fol. 302v, December 1633. Coe v. Pye; DN/DEP/51/55, fol. 229r, 20 September 1682. Watson v. Starre; and DN/DEP/51/55, fol. 21r, July 1685. Clifton v. Barker.

term 'knave' also had a sexual component. Derived from the medieval term for a servant, it was often adopted as an insult implying lowly status, but it was also used in conjunction with an allegation of sexual dishonesty. In 1635, for example, Robert Fuller had called George Cooper a 'lyeing pockie nosed knave' whose nose was eaten 'w[i]th the French pox and kannie run'.[49]

As the above examples demonstrate, defamatory words that appeared in church court depositions reflected a general concern for sexual honesty and morality, regardless of the recipient's gender. There was however one important gendered difference. Insulting words about men were more likely to have been couched in possessive terminology. Men were the masters of whores, or kept whores; women *were* the whores. Actions were instigated and performed *by* men, but *to* women. Only occasionally were there were exceptions to this rule. In 1690, for example, Jane Colman had referred to Thomas Cook as 'Mother Pococks Rogue' and when Cook approached Colman in the street, she told him 'he was a cuckoldy rogue' to his face.[50] Though both men and women were expected to behave in a chaste and moral manner, public insults reflected the idea that men were women's masters.[51]

When sexual reputation was not in question however, differences in the tone of insulting words towards men or women were less acute. Words uttered against drunken men and women in Norwich's streets, for example, contained none of the gender bias of defamatory words alleging sexual misconduct. In 1600, when Richard Carlton was walking home from supper along the streets of St Andrew's parish, Henry Bloye stopped him saying 'Carleton, I know thou well Inoughe, thou art a drunken Rascall', and in 1632 Mary Murman uttered similar words against Elizabeth Dey in the streets of St Peter Parmentergate.[52] Likewise, Robert Loveday was accused simply of being a drunk by Elizabeth Fuller on the green at All Saints in 1640, as was Frances Sherwood when George Nelson stopped her on Timberhill the same year.[53]

The gender of the speaker is also significant. In Norwich, men were more likely to utter defamatory comments (in any location) than women, at a figure

---

[49] DN/DEP/42/47A, fol. 207r, July 1635. Fuller v. Cooper.

[50] DN/DEP/52/56&57, unmarked folios, 31 July 1690. Thomas Cook v. Jane Colman.

[51] The sexualized language of defamatory speech – especially toward women – has led some scholars to claim that sexual morality was the cornerstone of female honour. See Ingram, *Church Courts* or L. Gowing, 'Women, Status and the Popular Culture of Dishonour', *TRHS* 6 (1996), 225–34. Subsequently, this claim has been modified by, for example, B. Capp, *When Gossips Meet: Women, Family and Neighbourhood in Early Modern England* (Oxford, 2003); B. Capp, 'The Double Standard Revisited: Plebeian Women and Male Sexual Reputation in Early Modern England', *Past and Present* 162 (1999), 70–100; or G. Walker, 'Expanding the Boundaries of Female Honour in Early Modern England', *TRHS* 6:6 (1996), 235–45.

[52] DN/DEP/31/34, fol. 31v, 23 June 1600. Richard Carlton v. Henry Bloye, and DN/DEP/40/45, fol. 68r, 3 July 1632. Elizabeth Dey v. Mary Murman.

[53] DN/DEP/48b, fol. 78r, 17 September 1640. Robert Loveday v. Elizabeth Fuller and DN/DEP/48b, fol. 113v 5 February 1640. Frances Nelson v. George Nelson.

of eighty-four to forty respectively. In the streets, men were also most likely to utter abusive words, at a figure of thirty-four men to twenty-one women. Of those cases of abusive words uttered in the streets, thirteen men defamed other men; twenty-five men defamed women; six women defamed men, and seventeen women defamed other women.

The figures clearly show that men were more aggressively attacking the reputations of others – especially women – in public. Nevertheless, none of the words or terms contained within the defamatory speeches implied that a woman simply *being* in the streets was the cause of the defamation. Public space was the adjuvant rather than the instigating factor of defamation suits: it added meaning to insulting words and provided the forum for those words to be uttered. However we should not draw the obvious conclusion that men defamed women in public places because of an underlying assumption that women's reputations were more vulnerable in public places. A contrast with the figures for defamatory speeches uttered in domestic or semi-public places, for example drinking houses, shops and churches, shows some interesting results:

Men defaming men in domestic or semi-public places	18
Men defaming women in domestic or semi-public places	20
Women defaming men in domestic or semi-public places	7
Women defaming women in domestic or semi-public places	10

These figures suggest we should not be too fast to jump to conclusions about how men felt about women's presence in public places. Men were quick to defame women whether in public, *or* in private. This perhaps suggests more about how men perceived themselves as regulators of women's behaviour in general, than any overt concern about women being in the streets. Men and women were as likely to be defamed (by any gender) in domestic, or in semi-public places, at a figure of twenty-five to thirty respectively: a number that includes cases that took place in churches, alehouses, a coffee-shop, and even a bowling alley. The spatial context here is about variety: only men were slandered at the coffee house or the bowling alley. This may well suggest more diversity in places for masculine sociability, though the number of cases here (only two over a period of one hundred years) is really too small a sample to draw any firm conclusions from. The most interesting figure here is that for women insulting other women, which was much higher in public than in private. Given the communality and focus of female labour and sociability in and around the home this figure is perhaps surprising, and we might be forgiven for assuming that if women spent more time in and around the home than men, women would be more likely to be defamed in this location. As this was not the case, the high number of insults may confirm what many scholars have argued – that it was less socially acceptable for women to be out in the streets. Nevertheless, the same figure may also confirm what Shoemaker suggests was the case in London, that middling women were simply more often on the streets than men.

*

Moving away from church court depositions that were by their nature overly preoccupied with morality, coroner's inquests are also a valuable source of information about people's movements about the city. Inquests documented where a body was found, the circumstances leading to the death, and usually included some small biographical detail about that person's life.[54] Like court depositions, inquests offer a narrow but tantalising glimpse into inhabitants' everyday activities: the places they went to and the reasons why. The inquests that survive in Norwich cover a period of thirty-one years, and reveal that men were more likely than women to have died in a variety of different places, though there was no particular correlation between gender and any specific place.

The most commonly investigated deaths were at the Common Gaol located in the castle, predominantly, though not exclusively, affecting men. Conditions in the Gaol were poor, and for those who could not afford a room, it was communal living in the dank ground floor of the keep. Most of the men held here were poor debtors and could not afford to purchase food to supplement their meagre diet of bread and water, or purchase additional fuel for heat and warmth.[55] As a consequence disease was rife. A high proportion of inmates never saw the outside world again, not because of the length of their sentence, but because they died of illness before they were released. Between 1669 and 1700 forty-eight men died from illnesses directly related to their living conditions and malnutrition, including fevers, sickness, dropsy, jaundice and scurvy. Only two female deaths in the Common Gaol required a coroner's report during this period. Both of these women had been poor debtors, the first the sixty-nine-year-old widow Mary White in 1694, and the second the married Elizabeth Ward aged fifty, three years later.[56]

Death by drowning was the second most common cause of death investigated by Norwich's coroner. Between 1669 and 1700, twenty-five people died in accidents on the River Wensum.[57] Twelve were children, nine were men, and four were women. Two women and three young girls drowned at the staithe (wharf), and a further two women and four girls suffered accidental falls into the river. Of these four women, two had been washing clothes when they had drowned and the other two had simply been walking along the river's banks or staithe when they had lost their balance and fallen in. One of the unfortunate women who had been washing clothes was the eighty-year-old Margaret Wilkinson who, leaning over the side of a boat to rinse

---

[54] Coroner's inquests have been used by several historians interested in gendered space see, for example, B. A. Hanawalt, 'Of Good and Ill Repute': Gender and Social Control in Medieval England (Oxford, 1998), pp. 76–83, esp. 76–7.

[55] Norwich's prisons – the Bridewell and the Common Gaol – were supplied with sea coal and charcoal during the winter months. For records of supply at the Bridewell see Books of Proceedings of City Committees: Bridewell, 1585–1686, NCR 19c.

[56] Coroner's Reports, NCR Case 6a/2, fol. 20, 8 July 1694 and fol. 45, 31 May 1697.

[57] NCR Case 6a/1–2, 1669–99. This figure does not include those people who committed suicide by jumping into the river.

some laundry, had overbalanced and toppled in.[58] The other was forty-year-old Temperance House, servant to Mrs Alice Powell of Heigham. House had been leaning over Powell's staithe washing dishcloths when the wooden bar of the staithe broke and she tumbled into the river.[59] Two of the men had drowned in work-related accidents: John Wharton had been angling on the river near Whitlingham Staithe when he had died, and John Wilkinson had suffered a fall at the New Mills.[60] The two other men had drowned when they were bathing. The remainder were accidental falls from a bank or staithe.

The third most commonly investigated demise was accidental death, often related to occupational hazards. Two men had died during their employment at an alehouse, including the sixty-six-year-old James Wilkinson who fell down a flight of cellar stairs onto the axe he was carrying.[61] Thomas Norfer died when his heavily laden turnip cart overturned on the road into Norwich; Robert Bettes was crushed after the well he had been digging collapsed in on him; and John Kempe, at only eighteen years old, was killed when the cart he was driving collided with a gatepost.[62] Another three men died in public places, including the unfortunate John Wilkinson, a worsted weaver, who had been walking just outside the city walls in the winter of 1694 when, it being very dark and freezing cold, he stumbled into some marshland and perished from exposure.[63] Three more men died in domestic incidents, and five men died at home after an illness. Finally, there were ten male suicides: seven bodies were found inside homes, like that of Samuel Dey who hanged himself in his room in St Peter Parmentergate, or John Inman who hanged himself at his father's house in the spring of 1690; two male bodies were found in their lodgings at inns, including that of William Rayner who had stabbed himself in the heart at The White Horse; and one young apprentice who hanged himself in his master's weaving shop.[64]

With the exception of the two women who had drowned washing clothes in the river, the coroner did not investigate any further work-related accidents involving women between 1669 and 1700. Only one woman died in an accident on Norwich's streets. This was the twenty-one-year-old Elizabeth Clarke, who had been riding on horseback past the Maid's Head Inn in the company of her father John when her horse was rushed down by a wagon. Elizabeth was crushed and died almost instantly.[65] The remaining female deaths included six domestic suicides, together with the rather tragic case

58 NCR Case 6a/1, fol. 2, 16 March 1670.
59 NCR Case 6a/1, fol. 9, 10 December 1685.
60 NCR Case 6a/1, fol. 6, 17 August 1673 and fol. 10, 25 August 1692.
61 NCR Case 6a/1, fol. 20, 1 October 1688.
62 NCR Case 6a/1, fol. 22, 27 October 1688; fol. 26, 13 February 1689; and fol. 43, 21 December 1689.
63 NCR Case 6a/2, fol. 18, 1–2, 16 June 1694.
64 NCR Case 6a/1, fol. 16, 28 May 1688; NCR Case 6a/1, fol. 53, 31 May 1690; NCR Case 6a/1, fol. 6, 4 May 1692; and NCR Case 6a/1, fol. 22, 2 October 1694.
65 NCR Case 6a/2, fol. 40, 23 July 1696.

of a fifteen-year-old girl who had killed herself by consuming 'ratinbane' or 'astnicke' (ratsbane or arsenic).[66]

To summarise, the sample of one hundred and fifteen investigated deaths between 1669 and 1700 does not necessarily suggest that men were more active in public than women – rather, it suggests that men were more likely to be performing manual jobs that brought them into dangerous situations more often than women; that and the preponderance of men as prison debtors. The sample reveals perhaps more about working patterns and practicalities than gendered places. Men's investigated deaths in domestic settings were more often than not related to their occupation, or suicides. Women's household deaths were predominantly suicides. More men died in public places than women, but more male deaths were investigated overall. With the exception of the two women who drowned whilst washing out clothes at the river, no other women died as an unequivocal result of their work. This was certainly not because women were less active in the urban workforce, but because of the difference in male and female work. The men in this set of inquests died as a result of their very physical labours – digging a well, chopping wood with an axe, or driving a heavily laden cart – these were not occupations that urban women would likely have engaged in.[67] The anonymous misogynistic woodcut entitled *The Severall Places where you may hear News* depicts gossiping women at work and at leisure in a nameless cityscape. Women are shown collecting water at a conduit, taking the waters at a bathhouse, working and buying goods at a bake house, serving and drinking in an alehouse, and washing clothes.[68] The image, though aimed at satirising the 'gossiping' woman, is a useful, if somewhat stereotypical, reminder of women's public commercial interactions.

The main conclusion to be drawn from this sample of inquests concerns variety. From these records alone, men appeared to be engaged in a wider variety of pursuits (both within and without the home), and within a wider timeframe, than did women. Of the few cases of accidental death on the city's streets or open places, all those bar one that occurred at night concerned men, like John Wilkinson, the worsted weaver mentioned above, who died of exposure; the fifty-three-year-old Robert Dixon who fell into the river because it was such a dark night; or Charles Mitchell who had been visiting

66 NCR Case 6a/1, fol. 55, 4 July 1690.
67 For a general introduction to women's work and the gendered division of labour see Capp, *When Gossips Meet*, pp. 127–84, 298–305; Patricia Crawford and Laura Gowing, eds, *Women's Worlds in Seventeenth-Century England: A Sourcebook* (Abingdon, 2008), pp. 71–104, 107–8, 123–4; Wiesner, *Women and Gender*, pp. 102–42; R. Shoemaker, *Gender in English Society, 1650–1850: The Emergence of Separate Spheres?* (Harlow, 1998), pp. 145–208.
68 Anon, *The Severall Places where you may hear News* (London, 1640). The woodcut was likely a reworking of the French image *Le Caquet des femmes*, revisited with images specific to an English urban landscape. See http://www.bpi1700.org.uk/research/printOfTheMonth/december2006.html#fn01 for more information.

Norwich from Devon and who drunkenly fell into the river after a festive night at the alehouse on the thirty-first of December 1693.[69] The one woman to die outside at night was Elizabeth Reeve, who wandered from her bed in the grip of a terrible fever and fell into the river.[70] In this respect, men and women conformed to gender expectations about when and where they moved in public space, largely dictated by their patterns of work, but perhaps also the prevailing expectation that it was less acceptable, or more dangerous, for women to remain out late at night.[71] However, the same set of expectations also constrained respectable men. Official records that note men out late at night usually concern men who were drunk and disorderly or engaged in criminal activity, not respectable men who had done nothing wrong. The clearest observation to result from the coroner's reports is that the bulk of investigated male deaths actually occurred in the semi-public space of the Common Gaol, rather than in public, or in private places.

The findings of this small survey in many ways confirm those of Barbara Hanawalt's more extensive survey of coroner's inquests for accidental deaths in England during the fourteenth century, in respect to her conclusion that men had a wider and more varied range of movement from place to place than did women.[72] Nevertheless, her discovery that only twelve per cent of men, as opposed to thirty per cent of women, died in the home is not supported by the Norwich evidence, though it is hard – given the three-hundred year gap and different geographical area – to make a meaningful comparison. Norwich's late seventeenth-century coroner's records do not prove that any particular urban place was more associated with men than with women, but the records do suggest that people's movements about the city were dictated by occupational choice and social expectations about appropriate behaviour, both of which were related to prevailing gender stereotypes.

Based on the evidence of women's presence in Norwich's streets from the locations given in court records and coroner's inquests, and supplementary evidence of the way women in the streets were addressed in defamation suits, there is clearly some negative bias towards women roaming Norwich's streets, something that was most keenly felt by men. Tacit perceptions of women's apposite place meant that the streets were gendered in such a way that women – more so than men – had to be more aware of their surroundings, not walk abroad after dark, or do anything that might reflect badly on their reputation. Nevertheless, we should avoid taking these assumptions too far. Before the

---

[69] NCR Case 6a/1, fol. 13, 23 March 1687/8; NCR Case 6a/2, fol. 12, 1 January 1693.

[70] NCR Case 6a/2, fol. 51, 6 October 1699.

[71] Paul Griffiths, for example, argues that women's presence on the streets at night was easily misconstrued and they might be mistaken for prostitutes or petty criminals: P. Griffiths, 'Meanings of Nightwalking in Early Modern England', *The Seventeenth Century* 13:2 (1998), 212–38.

[72] Hanawalt, 'Of Good and Ill Repute', pp. 76–83.

mid-century dissolution of the courts, for example, as many men as women carefully guarded their public persona for the sake of their own, and their families', reputations. It was only after 1680 that the gender composition of court clients definitively shifted toward women.[73]

If we also consider the number of women who lived in Norwich over the course of the century out of the total adult population (estimated at anywhere between 7,000 and 10,000), the number of suits where a woman was known to have been verbally assaulted in Norwich in any location (seventy-four) or insulted in a public place (only forty-two) was actually incredibly low.[74] Just over half the women slandered were in public places (including alehouses and markets). Certainly this suggests that women had to guard their reputation, and quite possibly more so than men (only fifty-three men prosecuted for libel during the seventeenth century), but to state that there was a *preoccupation* with women's reputations might be to overstate the case. The evidence from Norwich suggests that although assumptions about appropriate gendered behaviour undoubtedly affected women's identities and opportunities – especially in public life – there were no hard and fast rules governing how women might be regarded in the streets, or that the streets were unsuitable places for a woman, during the day at least. It would have been highly impractical and largely impossible for women to avoid the streets, and neither would most people have felt this to be a desirable state of affairs.

Markets

Markets were the social and economic nucleus of seventeenth-century cities and Norwich was no exception. Norwich had several markets, but the largest was in St Peter Mancroft. Norwich's corporation rented semi-permanent stalls in rows assigned to the sale of particular goods, such as Murage Row for yarns and worsteds, or Parmenter Row, so named for the skinners who had originally worked there.[75] Local historian and antiquarian Francis Blomefield described the market at Mancroft 'as the very best single market in all England'.[76] Blomefield's claim may have had some basis in truth. At Mancroft city dwellers could find glovers, mercers, spicers, needlers, ironmongers, and

---

[73] There is a marked difference in the numbers of men and women accused of making defamatory remarks before and after the church court's mid-century closure. Between 1600 and 1640 forty-nine men stood accused of making defamatory remarks, whereas after 1660 this figure falls to thirty-five. For women, on the other hand, the number increases from eleven before 1640, to twenty-nine after 1660.

[74] There are no exact figures for the number of women living in Norwich at this time, but the total population was approximately 13,000 in 1600, rising to 30,000 in 1700. We can assume that women made up just over fifty per cent of this population.

[75] John Kirkpatrick, *The Streets and Lanes of Norwich* (Norwich, 1889), pp. 3–4.

[76] Francis Blomefield, *An Essay towards a Topographical History of the County of Norfolk, Vol. IV: The History of the City and County of Norwich, Part II* (1806), p. 224.

coblers; they could buy fresh herrings, oysters, and mackerel from Yarmouth; poultry, butter, eggs and cheese from neighbouring villages; oats, wheat, rye, pease and beans from Norfolk's farmers; herbs, seeds and apples from local gardens, and all kinds of spiced breads.[77] Inhabitants could also find luxuries such as figs, currants, raisins, molasses, citrus fruits, wine, sugar and prunes imported from the continent.[78] There was even a pudding market.[79] Blomefield was not the only commentator to wax lyrical about the range of delicious goods on sale; Thomas Baskerville wrote enthusiastically about the variety of meat and dairy products, 'heaps of grain' and a 'great store of gingerbread'.[80] The city's main market comprised these stalls, but there were also separate hay, cattle, timber, and horse markets.[81] All the markets fell under the jurisdiction of the corporation; rent and fees were gathered by the Chamberlain's office; day-to-day administrative tasks were undertaken by the dedicated market clerk, and prosecutions for contravening market law – such as blowing meat or underselling measures – were enacted by the mayor's court.

Women have been little discussed in connection to this predominantly masculine world of trading and selling because historiography has traditionally viewed women's paid work as an extension of their role in the domestic economy, say making and selling butter, or buying food for the family, for example. Inequalities or differences between male and female work have been considered part of a 'dual-labour system' whereby male-dominated governments and institutions privileged and reserved high-status roles for men, and consigned women to the 'un-remunerative work of the informal economy'.[82] This view, aligned with the conceptual device of 'separate spheres' has encouraged some historians to query whether the primacy of men over women in market administration and tenure made markets a masculine domain: a claim that has been tested by several historians in recent years.[83]

There is some truth in this view but it fails to take into account the type of work ordinary urban men engaged in, and the crossover in the categories

---

[77] Kirkpatrick, *Streets and Lanes*, pp. 37, 42.

[78] John Pound, *Tudor and Stuart Norwich* (Chichester, 1988), p. 1.

[79] Blomefield, *Topographical History*, IV:II, pp. 224–5.

[80] Carole Rawcliffe, 'Introduction', *Medieval Norwich*, ed. Carole Rawcliffe and Richard Wilson (London, 2004), p. xxiii.

[81] Kirkpatrick, *Streets and Lanes*, pp. 31, 37, 42, 66.

[82] Katrina Honeyman and Jordan Goodman, 'Women's Work, Gender Conflict, and Labour Markets in Europ. 1500–1900, *Economic History Review* 44 (1991), 608–28, quoted in David Pennington, *Women in the Market-Place: Gender, Commerce, and Social Relations in Early-Modern English Towns* (Washington University Ph.D Thesis, pub., 2007), p. 3. The text that influenced many early twentieth-century views of female labour was Alice Clark's *Working Life of Women in the Seventeenth Century* (London, 1919). Critiques of Clark's capitalist approach to the division of labour include Lindsey Duffin and Lorna Charles, eds, *Women and Work in Pre-Industrial England* (London, 1985), pp. 1–23.

[83] See Pennington, *Women in the Market-Place* and Peter Stabel, 'The Market-place and Civic Identity in Late Medieval Flanders', *Shaping Urban Identity in Late Medieval Europe*, ed. Marc Boone and Peter Stabel (Leuven/Apeldoorn, 2000), pp. 43–64.

of work undertaken by both genders. For the bulk of Norwich's male inhabitants – rich and poor – weaving was the biggest employer, followed by provisioning.[84] The same was true for women. The number of men entering the professions, the church, or running specialist shops remained small and exclusive throughout the seventeenth century. This is not exactly surprising in a city whose economy was based on the textile industry. However this raises some fundamental questions about markets as predominantly male spaces of interaction, especially as a consequence of a perceived separation of work. As David Pennington suggests

> We should pause before we compare tradeswomen to the idealised and economically secure independent patriarch. To be sure, men always dominated high status trades and crafts. But these were not open to all men, nor were they closed to all women. Gender was only one factor amongst others – including ages, wealth, patronage, and marital status – which determined a town resident's opportunities.[85]

In terms of the ownership of market space, Norwich's market stalls were predominantly, though not exclusively, rented by men. However, this should not obscure the fact that many women did rent stalls in their own right, were active participants in the market's economy, and worked in the same trades as their male counterparts. Under English common law, only unmarried women or widows had the same rights to own property, or enterprises, as men.[86] A woman's ability to operate a financially independent business was thus dependent on her marital status and her husband's status as a freeman. Each trade guild also imposed their own regulations specific to every city, though few guilds prohibited widows from continuing their late husband's business. It has been suggested that the percentage of women so doing was in decline but

---

84 Penelope Corfield estimated that between 1660 and 1700 approximately forty-one to fifty-seven per cent of Norwich's freemen worked in the textile industry, followed by between ten and sixteen per cent in roles relating to food and drink. Corfield also suggests that around half of Norwich's adult male population held the freedom by the end of the seventeenth century, a statement that conflicts with Evans' approximation of thirty per cent by the 1690s. See Penelope Corfield, 'A Provincial Capital in the Late Seventeenth-Century: the Case of Norwich', *The Early Modern Town*, ed. Peter Clark (New York, 1976), pp. 241–4; J. T. Evans, *Seventeenth-Century Norwich, Politics, Religion and Government 1620–1690* (Oxford, 1979), pp. 7–12, 22–3, 32.

85 Pennington, *Women in the Market-Place*, p. 4.

86 Amy Louise Erickson, 'Coverture and Capitalism', *HWJ* 59 (2005), 1–16. Private ownership was the subject of intense philosophical debate during the early-modern period. Robert Filmer and Thomas Hobbes both argued that private property was given to Adam from God, and from thence to his heirs. Most philosophers – including the more liberal John Locke – upheld the inequalities inherent in the rights attached to private property, whether these inequalities stemmed from class, or from gender. Locke granted 'political society', that is parliament, legislature and judiciary (all exclusively male domains), the right to define and defend private property. The ownership of, and laws relating to, private property were clearly controlled by men yet the irony was that in the same patriarchal framework private homes were women's realm.

in Norwich the figures fluctuated through the century, as we shall see short-ly.[87] In Norwich, too, single women could (theoretically at least) establish a business with special permission from the authorities, though it seems that few women took this option.[88] This may have been because it was financially difficult to start their own business without a source of independent means, or help from a supportive family member.[89]

There are many accounts of women in Norwich who had claimed their right to run a stall. On 3 June 1668, for example, a 'bucheress' was fined ten shillings for opening her stall on a Friday.[90] In 1700, Ann Leasing paid one pound to rent a shop on the east row of the 'city butchery' for six months and Abigail Watts, widow of the late James Watts, paid one pound and fifteen shillings for a shop on the west row of the city butchery.[91] The butchery also reserved stalls for country butchers to sell their produce on Saturdays,[92] and it was here that women like Ann Lambe, Mary Simpson, Ann Edwards, Mary Fisher and Martha Hillyard could be found plying their wares on the busiest market day of the week.[93] The widows Mary Toake and Mary Brooke rented 'fish shoppes' alongside eight men,[94] and Mrs Ann Postle had a small com-mercial empire underway, renting five butchers' stalls 'fixed and covered with sparres' for a pound each.[95] Women with more limited financial resources might also sell dairy products and small goods directly to the retailers, thereby avoiding the cost of maintaining a permanent shop.

Female stallholders in Norwich followed the national pattern of being predominantly widows. This is clear from the city Chamberlain's records, a meticulous account of the corporation's rentals. In 1602, for example, Wid-ow Pepper rented the fifth stall in the fish market, Widow Claydon the sev-enth, Widow Thompson the eighth, and Widow Stephenson the twelfth and last, and Widow Cockett rented one of the three stalls in the ropery.[96] This group of five women should be contrasted with the number of male stall-holders, a total of forty-eight across the butchery, ropery, the 'stalls under the Leades', and the fish market.[97] Within five years the number of women renting stalls from the corporation had decreased from five to three: Widow Pepper and Widow Claydon had disappeared from the records of the fish

87 Anne Laurence, *Women in England 1500–1760* (London, 1994), pp. 127–8.
88 Evans, *Seventeenth-Century Norwich*, p. 5.
89 Crawford and Gowing, eds, *Women's Worlds*, p. 87, note supplied by Amy Froide. See also Amy M. Froide, *Never Married: Single-women in Early Modern England* (Oxford, 2005).
90 W. Rye, ed., *Depositions Taken Before the Mayor and Aldermen of Norwich 1549–1567 & Extracts from the Court Books of the City of Norwich 1666–1668* (Norwich, 1905), p. 122.
91 NCR 18b/1, fols 2v, 3v, 1700–1.
92 Kirkpatrick, *Streets and Lanes*, p. 31.
93 NCR 18b/1, fols 4v-8v, 1700–1.
94 Ibid., fol. 10r.
95 Ibid., fol. 9r.
96 Chamberlain's Accounts 1603–25, NCR Case 18a, fols 2v-3r, 25 March 1602–3.
97 Ibid., fols 1v-3v.

market.[98] Overall, the number of stalls leased out by the corporation had remained fairly steady at fifty-three in 1602 and fifty in 1607–8. By 1624, the number of women running stalls had not increased, but the diversity of their occupations had. No women were recorded at the fish stalls, but two women did have stalls at the city and county butchery, Widow Young rented two 'stalles covered with Boardes', and Widow Abel paid for a stall 'under the Leades' of the Guildhall.[99] The trend for diversity continued into the 1630s, as the numbers of women also marginally increased. In 1633, for example, six widows rented stalls from the corporation at all the locations mentioned in 1624, but also the fishery.[100] During the 1640s, there were thirteen female-run stalls, including Jane Beverley's 'Woll shoppe', however, the overall number of men leasing stalls had also increased.[101]

During the 1660s there was a decline in female stallholding. In 1661–2, for example, only one woman rented a stall in the city butchery – a Widow Lambe – and the widow Harborough rented one stall in the county butchery, as opposed to the five widows who had worked there during the 1640s. In addition, Elizabeth Barwick (it is not stated whether or not she was a widow) rented the 'seaventeenth moveable stalls right against the Inne called the wounded harte let unto her by Indenture for 40ty yeares from Lady 1640'.[102] However, as the century progressed, the number of women renting stalls gradually rose again. Only three years later this figure had increased to nine, with four widows renting stalls at the city butchery, two widows at the county butchery, and two widows and a lady named Mary Bowles renting stalls 'under the leads' of the Guildhall.[103] In 1671–2, nine women rented stalls at the butcheries and three women had stalls at the fish market; and by 1700, the Chamberlain's accounts document fourteen women who rented a market stall from the corporation.[104] All these women, with the exception of Elizabeth Barwick, Mary Bowles and Mrs Ann Postle, were recorded as widows.[105]

Women's extensive involvement in the local cloth industry also necessitated a close relationship with the marketplace. Spinsters – that is, women who spun wool or flax into yarn for domestic or commercial purposes – had to buy their raw materials from the market. In London

> ...male 'day labourers ... whilst they are employed abroad themselves ... employ their Wives and Children at home in Carding and Spinning, of which when they have 10 or 20 pounds ready for the Clothier, they go to Market with it and there

---

98 Chamberlain's Accounts 1603–25, NCR Case 18a, fols 59v-61r, 25 March 1607–8.
99 Chamberlain's Accounts 1603–25, NCR Case 18a, fols 366v-368r, 25 March 1624–5.
100 Chamberlain's Accounts 1625–48, NCR Case 18a, fols 172r-174v, 25 March 1633–4.
101 Chamberlain's Accounts 1625–48, NCR Case 18a, fols 374r-377r, 25 March 1642–3.
102 Chamberlain's Accounts 1648–63, NCR Case18a, fol. 257v, 25 March 1661–2.
103 Chamberlain's Accounts 1663–73, NCR Case18b, fols 45r-48v, 25 March 1665–6.
104 Chamberlain's Accounts 1700–1, NCR Case18b/1, 25 March 1700- 24 March 1701.
105 NCR Case18a, fol. 257v, 25 March 1661–2; NCR Case18a, fols 45r-48v, 25 March 1665–6; and NCR Case18b/1, 25 March 1700- 24 March 1701.

sell it ... there will be in Market time 3 or 400 poor People (chiefly Women) who will sell their goods in about an hour.'[106]

This was likely the case in Norwich. The 1570 census of Norwich's poor, although rather before the timeframe of this study, remains an excellent source of information on the occupations of Norwich's womenfolk because a large proportion of the city's poor comprised them. For these women (and a large proportion of poor men) spinning – especially spinning 'white warpe' – was the most common form of employment.[107] Indeed

> ...the greatest and almost the whole number of the poor inhabitants of the county of Norfolk and the city of Norwich be, and have been heretofore for a great time maintained and gotten their living, by spinning of the wool ... upon the rock [distaff] into yarn, and by all the said time have used to have their access to common markets within the said county and city, to buy their wool...[108]

One thing the Chamberlain's records do not reveal is the number of women who worked beside their husband, or ran the family business in fact, if not in name. Equally, it is hard to tell how many women took part in trading activities by selling home-produced goods directly to market retailers. They might also risk the wrath of the authorities by trading to the public as hucksters (female hawkers). Women were also regular participants in market life as the buyers, as well as the sellers, of goods. Women bought food and cooking equipment to provide meals for their families, or material to make clothes. These essential activities often go unremarked upon because of the lack of historic records that detail such everyday events. Contemporary literature, for example, often mentioned women socialising at the market, though not always in a complimentary manner. Thomas Dekker's satirical *Bachelers Banquet*, for example, portrayed a group of gossips discussing a friend who used to drink wine with them on market days but had since fallen on hard times.[109] The Yarmouth man John Wheeler, who argued that market trading and bartering came naturally to English people, including women, gave a more flattering account:

> ...nothing is so common among them as to change and rechange, buy and sell that which they bring home with them. The Prince with his subjects, the master with his servants, one friend and acquaintance with another, the captain with his soldiers, the husband with his wife, women with and among themselves, and in

---

106 Anon, *Remarks upon Mr Webber's Scheme and the Draper's Pamphlet* (London, 1741), pp. 21–2.

107 John Pound, *Norwich Census of the Poor 1570*, NRS 40 (Norwich, 1971).

108 Statute I, Edward VI quoted in John James, *The History of Worsted Manufacture in England* (1857), p. 98.

109 Thomas Dekker, *The Bachelers Banquet* (London, 1604), p. 9.

a word, all the world choppeth and changeth, runneth and raveth, after marts, markets, and merchandising.[110]

Direct evidence of women at Norwich's markets is often incidental. The mayor's court records reveal that women took part in public performances at the market, for example; a number that included a monstrous woman over seven feet tall, a woman without arms who performed tasks with her feet, and a girl 'without bones'.[111] Women did not only perform a subservient role however, but were also in charge of the entertainments. In 1677, for example, Elizabeth Sonne was given a licence to show a 'motion here called Fayre Rosamond'.[112] Women also came to the market to be entertained. Many went to see the travelling doctors who set up shop in the market next to the Guildhall. Sometimes these entailed extravagant acts of theatricality, such as that by 'Honoratus Le Begg, Chirugeon and Practioner in Phisick', who was granted special permission to erect a sixty- by thirty-foot stage to sell medicines and perform cures to Norwich's inhabitants in 1677, or Mr. Robert Bradford, 'licensed to erect a stage in the usual place' in 1678.[113] With the possible exception of the begging poor – who remained a problematic presence in the city's public spaces throughout the century – there were no restrictions on the age, gender, status, or citizenship of market voyeurs and entertainers.

Building on the argument that we should not simply consider *where* women spent their time, but how they were treated in public space, we should consider defamation cases that involved women in the marketplace.[114] Again incidental references are often our best sources of information. In 1608, for example, a witness in a church court defamation case told how John Bransby and Henry Brandon had sat in the King's Head making rude comments about the people they could see going about their work in the marketplace. Unfortunately for the pair, one of their victims – Elizabeth Blowfield – found out about their scurrilous comments and sued them for defamation.[115] In 1663, Mary Spendlove was working at her husband's fish stall and talking to Margaret Atkinson when they both witnessed Martha Moore call Henry Woolward a knave; in 1664 Mary Simonds and Judith Botewright – who both worked at the butchery – witnessed fellow butcher Alexander Wade shouting at Jane Harding, and the following May Mary Greenfield was on her way to the Saturday market when she walked past a 'great company' watching an argument near the may pole on Timberhill.[116] In 1694, a rather serious

---

[110] John Wheeler, *Treatise of Commerce* (1601), ed. G. B. Hotchkiss (New York, 1977), p. 316.
[111] Rye, *Depositions*, pp. 107–8.
[112] Ibid., pp. 137, 147.
[113] Ibid., pp. 144, 162.
[114] Gowing '"The Freedom of the Streets"', pp. 139–40.
[115] DN/DEP/32/35, fol. 485r, 19 January 1608. Elizabeth Blowfield v. John Bransby.
[116] DN/DEP/46/50, fol. 448r, 11 January 1663. Martha Moore v. Henry Woolward; DN/DEP/47/51, 8 September 1664. Harding v. Wade; DN/DEP/47/51, fol. 192r, 10 July 1665.

incident occurred when Elizabeth Boss and Anne Bush 'being at the stall of Mary Dixe who sells butchers meate' saw Anne Lockwood call Dixe's fiancé Benjamin Barber a 'theevish rogue' for stealing a guinea from her. As a result of the accusation, Dixe 'refused to entertaine [Barber] any longer as a sweetheart' adding that 'she expected to have a drunkard but not a theife' as her future husband.[117] In 1696 the spinster Cleere Adams and her friend Anne Greenwood were walking to market together when a Mr Adcock accused Greenwood of trying to cheat the butchers with her prices.[118]

These suits represent the sum total of all defamation cases entered in the Norwich Diocese involving women in the city centre markets during the seventeenth century. Of these, only three specifically targeted women. In the suit involving Elizabeth Blowfield, Blowfield simply happened to be in the wrong place at the wrong time, as were the many others who Bransby and Brandon had seen that day from their vantage point in the King's Head. In the suit between Jane Harding and Alexander Wade conflict over space, or women's encroachment into male space, was not at issue either. Wade had a belligerent temperament and had been known to argue with his fellow market workers, male and female. Eight years after the incident with Harding, for example, Wade was arrested as a 'refractory butcher' and a 'dissolute person', so 'desperate' that the constables had had to call in the sheriffs to apprehend him.[119] Finally, the suit concerning Greenwood and Adcock seemed to have little to do with Greenwood being an economically active woman, simply that she was dishonest, an accusation that was not gender specific. There seems to be little evidence that women were marginalized, or resented, for occupying market space.

Markets were important social and economic spaces for both men and women. Market days and fairs doubled as social events where everyone could enjoy the array of entertainments and refreshments on offer. The market offered women an important social space outside the home, one that they both observed and contributed to. Women had little official role in setting market rules and regulations, but arguably neither did the majority of ordinary men. Comments about the way the market was governed or the price of foodstuffs were normally expressed only when times were hard, and at these times both men and women had their say.[120] Equally, although few women rented stalls in their own right, this fact should in no way bias the onlooker into deval-

Mary Garwood v. William Roste. Evidence of Alexander Wade's trade can be found in NCR 18b, fol. 5v, 1700–1.

[117] DN/DEP/53/58a fol. xxi, 25 July 1694. Barber v. Lockwood.

[118] DN/DEP/53/58a, fol. 4r, 16 March 1696. Anne Greenwood v. Colfer.

[119] Rye, *Depositions*, p. 129.

[120] For more on this theme see A. Wood, '"Poore men woll speke one daye": Plebeian Languages of Deference and Defiance, c.1520–1640', *The Politics of the Excluded, c. 1500–1850*, ed. T. Harris (Basingstoke, 2001), pp. 67–98; R. Houlbrooke, 'Women's Social Life and Common Action in England from the Fifteenth Century to the Eve of the Civil War',

uing the role, presence and importance of women as buyers, sellers, and ne-
gotiators at seventeenth-century markets. Women were important actors in
market spaces.

Alehouses

Even more so than markets, historians have labelled alehouses as 'masculine'
places.[121] Alehouses breached the boundaries of public and private space,
offering a series of intersecting spaces: mixing private ownership with public
(civic) scrutiny, domestic accommodation (of the owner or tenant), and public and private rooms for guests. Whilst there was certainly a macho camara-
derie attached to contemporary drinking culture,[122] and occasionally particular establishments, recent studies have shown that alehouses were certainly
not exclusive to men.[123] Drinking houses provided food, work and accommodation for urban dwellers and visitors and a daily supply of cheap, drinkable
ale at a time when fresh water was hard to come by. There was often a concentration of drinking houses around market squares and it was common to
see market business extended into the alehouse as men and women bought,
sold, bartered, exchanged or pawned goods here. Indeed, this informal, un-
regulated trade may have offered women greater opportunities than did the
markets. As Garthine Walker argues, alehouses were integral sites in the fe-
male-led exchange of second-hand goods and, on occasion, stolen goods.[124]

Women also worked in, or ran, drinking houses. Large coaching inns and
taverns offered a variety of jobs for women, including brewing, cooking,
serving tables, and cleaning. These women might be apprentices, like Mary
Frohock who was apprenticed to Robert Ducher, innkeeper to the mayor of
Norwich in St Andrew, 'to be trained in houswifry', or simply paid servants.[125]
The wives of drinking-house owners often worked alongside their husbands.
For those women – like Anna Herbert who ran a house with her husband
Thomas in St John Sepulchre during the 1630s, or Mary Frogg who ran the
Golden Dog in St Saviour's parish in the 1660s with her husband Nicholas

Continuity and Change 1 (1986), 171–89; or Keith Lindley, *Fenland Riots and the English
Revolution* (London, 1982).
[121] Peter Clark, *The English Alehouse: A Social History 1200–1830* (London, 1983), p. 79.
[122] Both Alexandra Shepard and Elizabeth Foyster have discussed the significance of
male conviviality to the construction of an alternative masculine identity: A. Shepard,
Meanings of Manhood (Oxford, 2003), pp. 93–113, and Foyster, *Manhood in Early Modern
England*, pp. 39–43.
[123] A. Flather, *Gender and Space in Early Modern England* (Woodbridge, 2007), pp. 110–21.
[124] G. Walker, *Crime, Gender, and the Social Order in Early-Modern England* (Cambridge,
2003), p. 165.
[125] Package of Documents Relating to St Andrew's Parish, 1622–1773, MC 500/59,
762x2, no. 11, 21 June 1676.

– their business was as much the foundation of their status and reputation as it was for their husband.[126]

Brewing was not as common a trade for women during the seventeenth century as it had been during the medieval period,[127] but drinking-house owners were not the same as brewers, though on occasion, beer or ale was still produced in-house. To acquire an ale licence in Norwich, the applicant had to have the freedom of the city and the financial resources needed to establish their business.[128] The Frogg family (mentioned above) is a case in point. Nicholas Frogg had served his apprenticeship and gained the freedom in 1649,[129] and his inn on Golden Dog Lane was rated at six hearths in the 1666 hearth tax assessment.[130] Of course, the size and reputation of drinking houses varied greatly, not all premises were as large as the Froggs', and not all were licensed, but those that were had the foundations for longevity and success.

As we know, women could not gain the freedom of the city, but they could run a respectable and profitable business as a widow, a wife, or a *femme sole*. Far from being women in a man's world, these women were not only proud to be involved in the industry but integral to the business. This comes across very clearly in incidental evidence found in the Norwich Diocesan records. Helen Prior, for example, worked alongside her husband at an alehouse in St John Maddermarket and it was she, not her husband, who reported a customer for drunkenness at the 1633 visitation. The court clerk noted that the incident had occurred 'at her the said Helen Priors house' but her husband was certainly alive, because when Helen Prior made a second appearance at the church court seven years later, her name was entered in the record as Helen, wife of John Prior, not as a widow.[131] Likewise, Anna Herbert, whose husband Thomas owned the premises where she worked, also implied in a deposition that she was not simply on hand as Thomas' wife but that she ran the business,[132] and the married Mary Andrews of Conesford Street accused John Cullinder of stealing a quilt from *her* house. Thomas Foxe corroborated Andrews' statement, declaring that the theft had taken place at 'the [ale]

---

126 DN/DEP/44/48a, fol. 366r, 23 February 1639, and DN/DEP/47/51, fols 12r-17v, 18 December 1664. Anne Austin v. Mary Frogg.

127 Judith M. Bennett, *Ale, Beer, and Brewsters in England: Women's Work in a Changing World 1300–1600* (Oxford, 1996), p. 147.

128 In July 1668, the corporation issued a by-law to reinforce this principle, stating that 'no brewer not being a freeman is to have licenses granted to their alehouses': Rye, *Depositions*, p. 122.

129 'Nicholas Frogge apprentice Thomas Warnes, 3 September 1649, Worsted Sherman': P. Millican, ed., *The Register of the Freemen of Norwich 1548–1713* (Norwich, 1934), p. 153.

130 Seaman, *Norfolk and Norwich Hearth Tax Assessment*, p. 72.

131 DN/DEP/41/46, fol. 269r, November 1633. Moses Whitebread v. Helen Prior, and DN/DEP/45/48b, fol. 4r, 29 August 1640 and fol. 61v, 15 October 1640 respectively.

132 DN/DEP/44/48a, fol. 366r, 23 February 1639. Sara Keepis v. Frances Shelton.

howse of Mary Andrews', not Thomas Andrews, her husband.[133] Similarly, when Martha Steward sued Thomas Dunch for defamation, she had more to protect than her personal honour. Although she was married, it was she, not her husband, who defended the reputation of her alehouse against Dunch's allegations that it was 'a howse to entertain whores and rogues'. Dunch specifically referred to the premises in St Peter Mancroft as *her* house, and so did her compurgators.[134] That these married women used possessive expressions, full of pride, to convey their dominant connection to each licensed premises in question demonstrates that they considered the business to be their responsibility and a foundational building block of their personal honour, self-worth and credit in their community.

Active involvement in the trade was not only useful in establishing a woman's reputation for business, but imperative to her continued trading if her husband died. Many women made this choice. A record of the widow Catherine Northford's alehouse survives because she had offended one of her regular customers by calling him a fool in 1609.[135] Likewise, Mother Parment is remembered because her drinking house was the scene of an argument between Robert Alden and John Yarham in 1630,[136] and Hester Thorpe, who owned a drinking house at St Andrew, filed a suit against William Browne in 1672 after he 'tooke a glass of wine and said … here unto yow, yow whore' in front of her customers.[137] Similarly in 1684, Anne and Elizabeth Falconer and their widowed mother Mary, who jointly ran a house in St Peter Mancroft, filed for defamation against Mariam Paylock after she had accused them of keeping a whorehouse.[138] These hostile accusations should not be taken as evidence that women owning alehouses was not considered appropriate however. These latter two incidents represent the only defamation suits alleging that a female alehouse keeper was a whore or kept a whorehouse in Norwich that whole century.

Female alehouse owners also cropped up in secular records after they had committed a licensing offence, such as Elizabeth Gillman of St Stephen's parish who had her licence revoked in 1667 for allowing the playing of unlawful games,[139] or the brewer Judith Bowde who was fined two shillings and nine pence by the mayor's court in 1676.[140] Alice, the wife of Thomas Browne, was fined twenty shillings in 1628 for keeping an unlicensed 'Com[m]on Alehouse' and for buying twenty barrels of beer from Christ's Church at nine shillings each. When the fine remained unpaid, the court ordered her – not

133 DN/DEP/51/55, fol. 121r, 18 February 1683. Mary Andrews v. John Cullinder.
134 DN/DEP/51/55, fol. 347r, 7 March 1680. Martha Steward v. Thomas Dunch.
135 DN/DEP/35/37, fol. 157v, 17 July 1609. Catherine Northford v. Henry Justyne.
136 DN/DEP/39/44, fol. 81r, 10 May 1630. Robert Alden v. John Yarham.
137 DN/DEP/49/53, unmarked folio, 30 December 1672.
138 DN/DEP/51/55, fol. 126r, 28 July 1684. Anne Falconer v. Mariam Paylock.
139 Rye, *Depositions*, p. 121.
140 W. Hudson and J. C. Tingay, *The Records of the City of Norwich*, Vol. I (Norwich, 1906), p. 388.

her husband – to be whipped.[141] Female owners can also be found in the coroner's inquests when their drinking house had been the scene of an unusual death. In 1696, for example, a servant poisoned himself at the Rampant Horse Inn then run by the widow Ann Harman in St Stephen's parish and, only a day later, the widow Joane Ward's servant died after he was struck by a wagon at her premises, the Unicorn in St Mary's parish.[142]

Drinking houses may have provided women with many economic opportunities, but they were also essential to women's social lives. Women went to alehouses to celebrate churching, weddings, and calendar festivals, but they also refreshed themselves in alehouses on market days, purchased ale for themselves and their families to drink at home, or simply went to socialise, or spend time with their husband, like Samuel and Sarah Self who regularly drank together at the Lower Half Moon Tavern in the marketplace.[143] Women even provided the entertainment on occasion, like Mrs Marie Pease who had showed 'twoe meeremayds' and 'a devouring great eating Quaker' at the sign of the Angel in 1675.[144]

It is hard to establish the type of customers drinking at Norwich's houses, as there are no consistent records providing this information. What does exist, however, are incidental references to female customers in court records. The lists of witnesses and compurgators in church court cases, as has been demonstrated before, provide a fantastic resource for establishing who was at a certain place, when, and with whom. So, in 1639, Sara Coates and her daughter were refreshing themselves at a house in St John Sepulchre when they witnessed Francis Shelton start an argument;[145] single women Elizabeth Wring and Mary Aswich looked on as Thomas Dawson accused Henry Dodgeson of being a rogue at Dodgeson's drinking house in St Saviour's parish in 1674;[146] in November 1679 Mrs Elizabeth Yallop and the thirty-four-year-old single woman Anna Flatman were at Martha and Robert Steward's house in St Peter Mancroft; eighteen-year-old Margaret Sherwood, Mrs Jane Steward and Mrs Mary Skarfe were at the house of Mary and Thomas on Conesford Street in 1683;[147] and Goodwife Norton, Mrs Rosa Davy, and the elderly Elizabeth Mechim were all to be found at Thomas Davy's public house in St Michael in 1687.[148]

---

141   NCR 16a/16, fol. 228v, 31 January 1628.
142   NCR Case 6a/2/35 & 36, 11–12 April 1696.
143   Lawrence Stone, 'Libertine Sexuality in Post-Restoration England: Group Sex and Flagellation among the Middling Sort in Norwich in 1706–7', *Journal of the History of Sexuality* 2:4 (1992), 511–26, 514.
144   Rye, *Depositions*, p. 108.
145   DN/DEP/44/48a, fol. 366r, 23 February 1639.
146   DN/DEP/49/53, section xx, March 1674. Henry Dodgeson v. Thomas Dawson.
147   DN/DEP/51/55, fol. 347r, 7 March 1680. Martha Steward v. Thomas Dunch, and DN/DEP/51/55, fol. 121r, 18 February 1683. Mary Andrews v. Thomas Cullinder.
148   DN/DEP/52/56–7, unmarked folios, 2 January 1687. Elizabeth Grundy v. Margaret Burrell.

Female customers also entered the records when they became personally involved in disputes that took place in drinking houses, like Sara Tyler and her husband Robert who were spotted arguing with Nicholas Weston at the sign of the Castle in 1629;[149] Margaret Crewe and William Gargrave who fell out at the drinking house of Oliver Fish in 1633;[150] or Margaret Marshe who was at the signe of the Bushel in St Gregory's parish when James Reede called her a 'queene and a jade' in 1639.[151] Likewise, Dorothy Brockdale had been drinking at the Half Moon when she witnessed William Runt call Martha Read a whore in 1638;[152] in 1639 single woman Susanna Watts was at Robert Punt's drinking house in St John Maddermarket, when she witnessed John Melchior defame Christian Foster;[153] and Robena Brice acted as a witness for Elizabeth Mapes when Mapes was called a 'brazen fac[e]d whore' at the King's Head in the marketplace.[154]

Female customers might also enter the records because they had been drinking too much. In 1609, for example, Anne Swan had circulated tales that Jane Brown had been drunk at James Swan's house; a rumour that affected Brown's reputation so gravely she was compelled to prove her innocence by law.[155] In 1640, George Nelson defamed Frances Sherwood by saying she was a 'drunken whore', and in 1684 Elizabeth Fairchild called Susan Parker 'a drunken red haired bitch'.[156] Likewise, Rosa Davy – the wife of an innkeeper in St Martin's parish – overheard Elizabeth Mechim tell Martha Awbery that 'she was a long mackerill backed whore, A runagate pocky whore, if you was not yo[u]r husband would have sould you for a flagon of beare to a souldier, you goe from howse to howse and make you[r]selfe soe drunke that you fall over'; words that were spoken at the castle dikes in 1688.[157] Excess drinking was a vice whether a woman was single, married, rich or poor. If she was single, like Jane Brown or Frances Sherwood above, she had to be careful about attracting the wrong kind of reputation. If the woman in question was married, like Susan Parker or Martha Awbery, she also jeopardised her husband's masculinity, as was described in the contemporary ballad *The Gossips Meeting, Or Merry Market Wives of Taunton*. This satirical tale told the story of the

[149] DN/DEP/38/43, fol. 476r, 10 January 1629. Robert Cubitt v. Nicholas Weston.
[150] DN/DEP/41/46, fol. 5r, 10 April 1633. Margaret Crewe v. William Gargrave.
[151] DN/DEP/41/46, fol. 275r, 21 October 1633. Margaret Marshe v. James Reede.
[152] DN/EP/43/47b, fol. 228v, 18 October 1638. Martha Read v. William Runt.
[153] DN/DEP/44/48a, fol. 149v, 20 November 1639. Christian Foster v. John Melchior.
[154] DN/DEP/49/53, section xx, October 1674.
[155] DN/DEP/35/37, fol. 212v, 2 October 1609. Jane Brown v. Anne Swan. James Swan was not Anne Swan's husband.
[156] DN/DEP/45/48b, fol. 113r, 5 February 1640. Frances Sherwood v. George Nelson; DN/DEP/51/55, fol. 127r, 3 January 1684. Susan Parker v. Elizabeth Fairchild.
[157] DN/DEP/52/56&57, unmarked folios and undated case, 1688. Martha Awbery v. Elizabeth Mechim.

foolish, domesticated husband whose wife tricked him into giving her extra money for food that she spent instead on drinks with her friends.[158]

Humorous yet cautionary tales like these mocked women who placed drunken fun with their friends over their husbands and their domestic duties but, more often than not, such tales and criticisms were levelled at men, not women, probably reflecting contemporary concerns about the dangers of masculine drinking. As the head of a household, a husband or father bulwarked his family's income, reputation and order. If instead, the father or husband spent his income on drink, the whole family suffered as women had a lower earning capacity than did men. This was certainly the case in 1605 when Thomas Turner passed a whole day drinking in the White Horse Tavern. By two or three in the afternoon Turner was 'so drunken ... he ... could neither well stande or speake & was voyde of comon understanding' and did 'Blaspheme the holye name of God & swore most grevouslye by God and Gods bludd ... w[i]thout any occasion given hym by any p[er]rson'. However his female drinking companion – known only as the 'miller's wife of Cossey' – who had become 'dead drunke' and passed out in a pool of her own 'filthye sicke' was not presented at the court and was only mentioned in passing, a fact that perhaps represents the scale of responsibility attributed to each person.[159] Certainly, moralists expounded the virtues of sobriety and moderation to a masculine audience.[160]

On other occasions, the association of drinking with poor husbandly behaviour was explicitly made by men's wives. Late one winter night in 1687, for example, Goodwife Norton's husband had still not returned home. She knew she would find him getting drunk at Thomas Davy's somewhat notorious alehouse, so she stormed over to give Davy a piece of her mind. Seizing the opportunity to criticize Davy, his neighbour Margaret Burrell joined in the fray, venting her frustrations at living next door to a 'company of whores and rogues'. Both Burrell and Norton accused Norton of neglecting of his domestic duties and Davy of encouraging it.[161] On another winter's night two years later, Mary Meeke found herself in a similar situation at William Winke's alehouse in St Saviour's parish. Meeke and her friend Margery

---

158 Anon, *The Gossips Meeting, Or The Merry Market Women of Taunton* (London, 1674). See also Anon, *Five Merry Wives of Lambeth, Fowre Wittie Gossips Disposed to be Merry* (London, 1680); Anon, *The Merry Wives of Wapping* (London, 1680).

159 DN/DEP/33/36a, fol. 255r, 1605. Evidence against Thomas Turner given by Roger Styles.

160 Cautionary tales warning men about the dangers of alcohol were far more common, for example: Anon, *Jack Had-Lands Lamentation* (London, 1685); Anon, *The Bad Husbands Reformation, or, The Ale-Wives Daily Deceit* (London, 1685); R. Burton, *A Looking Glass for Drunkards: Or, The Good-Fellows Folly* (London, 1660); J. Hart, *The Dreadful Character of a Drunkard* (London, 1686); M. Killiray, *The Swearer and the Drunkard, Two Brethren in Iniquity, Arraigned at the Bar, &c.* (London, 1673).

161 DN/DEP/52/56&57, unmarked folios, 2 January 1687. Elizabeth Grundy v. Margaret Burrell.

Loades were not drinking at Winke's house, but had arrived at around midnight in search of their missing husbands. Meeke and Loades had found the men at Winke's, drinking and gambling. This was not the first time that this had happened and Meeke was at her wit's end. Only the previous evening, her husband Joseph had had to be dragged home from Winke's in a bruised and bloodied state, missing half an ear, and so inebriated that he could not stand on his own. Clearly deciding to take matters into her own hands and drag her husband away before he came to harm again, Meeke told Winke and his customers what she thought of them and was rewarded with abuse from Winke himself. Meeke and Loades' plan to humiliate the men may not have been successful that night, but they achieved a victory by reporting Winke for late-night opening and gambling. He was subsequently prosecuted at the city's sessions.[162]

Masculine drinking and, by association, troublemaking was taken seriously by the spiritual and secular courts. Between 1600 and 1700, for example, only nine of the three hundred and eighty-two suits defaming women in the entire Norwich diocese contained words that accused women of drunkenness, but there were fifty-four accusations of drunkenness from the four hundred and forty suits against men.[163] Within the city walls, suits alleging drunkenness were eight to eleven for women and men respectively. Overall the majority of defamatory comments alleging drunkenness were in the rural areas and market towns rather than in the city, but the accusations specifically targeting women, bar one, took place in Norwich itself. The remaining defamation case alleging female insobriety took place in Yarmouth: a busy, urban port. The city's secular courts told a similar story. Between June 1632 and June 1635, for example, twenty-four men were prosecuted for crimes connected to drinking, as opposed to only five women.[164]

On the surface, it is possible to claim from this that men were more involved in drinking-house culture than women, but that urban women had greater opportunities to take part in drinking-house culture than their rural counterparts. It may also be possible to argue that with this freedom came risks, as is reflected in the concentration of defamation cases in urban areas. However, only nine defamation suits over a period of one hundred years is a very low figure, considering – as the evidence above suggests – that many women socialised in, and worked at, drinking houses. We might also consider here the social background of female drinkers.

---

[162]   NCR Case 12a-b/1. The information of Mary Meeke and Margery Loades against William Winke, 9 January 1689.

[163]   This figure is taken from a survey of defamation cases from the whole diocese covering Norfolk, north Suffolk, Bury St Edmunds and Ipswich.

[164]   Figures collated from W. L. Sachse, ed., *Minutes of the Norwich Court of Mayoralty 1632–1635* (Norwich, 1967).

The women cited in this section were not the poor women or prostitutes that Peter Clark suggested frequented alehouses in his seminal study.[165] We know this because they were all witnesses or litigants in church court defamation suits where a woman's status can be deduced from the given occupation of their husband, the friends they were with, their compurgators, and the costs involved in raising a suit. Indeed, if the women of the suits above were of the middling sort, it is probable that other customers visiting the same establishments would have been drawn from the same social class. It is unlikely that a middling gentlewoman would have regularly visited a premises that had a bad reputation, was impoverished, or unlicensed. By way of example, in 1666 Mrs Reynolds of Aldeburgh made a complaint about William Locke, the rector at Forncett St Mary. Reynolds had been staying in Norwich at the very respectable Rampant Horse coaching inn when the incident with Locke took place. Reynolds had been eating in the kitchen when a drunken Locke stumbled in, demanding to know why she had refused to drink with him the previous evening. Knowing Locke had a reputation as a drunkard, Reynolds had pointedly refused. Her companions and fellow residents at the inn supported her testimony: two vintners, a silk weaver, a gentleman, a yeoman, and an armiger.[166]

A simple summary of prosecutions for drunkenness, or defamation cases aimed at men or women, is a rather simplistic way of correlating gender with place. However, if we also consider the extraneous evidence, such as social class, context (the type of record in which evidence appears), and the number of women appearing in alehouses in normal, daily circumstances, it is quite possible to conjecture that women were a significant part of seventeenth-century alehouse culture. The court records that note more men in relation to drinking offences does not necessarily reflect a fact that more men went to the alehouse; it may simply reflect a concern over men undermining behavioural ideals. Male drunkenness assaulted the roots of domestic order, undermining a man's position as a patriarch, a breadwinner and as a rational person. At the same time, excessive drinking encouraged criminal behaviour in a way that women's (supposedly) did not, especially with regard to fighting, brawling, and petty crime: all crimes that the courts took more seriously when perpetrated by men.

The evidence here has suggested that women were frequent and, more importantly, *acceptable* customers in drinking houses, and it was not expected that they always be chaperoned. As the aforementioned woodcut frontispiece of *The Severall Places where you may hear Newes* suggested, drinking houses were normal places for respectable women to work, eat, and gossip. For many

---

165 Quoted from Flather, *Gender and Space*, pp. 111, 113–14. Flather's survey of female drinking-house customers in Essex revealed a high proportion of middling sort women.
166 DN/DEP/47/51, fol. 345r, April 1666. The 1640 woodcut *The Severall Places where you may hear Newes* also supports this: the women shown were dressed in the clothes and head coverings of middling sort married women.

men and women the alehouse was – in moderation – an important part of their social lives. There is a caveat however. Men may not have laid claim to alehouse space, but female customers may have had to be more aware of their actions, words and behaviour in alehouse space than their male drinking companions. Dinner, quick refreshment, and social gatherings in alehouses were all acceptable for women,[167] but as in most areas of early-modern life, there was a double standard that women had to be aware of. Neither men nor women were expected to overindulge or spend every night at the alehouse, but more men found themselves in court because of this than did women and it seems, as the examples of William Winke and Thomas Davy's alehouses (and others like them in the secular courts) suggest, that a late-night drinking and gambling culture was exclusive to men.[168] The idea of a 'feminine drinking culture' seems rather incongruous in comparison.

A close lens on gender reveals another way to conceptualise the urban environment. Yet the distinctions between male and female 'spaces' should not be made explicit. The experience of the city may have been subtly different for some men and for some women, but these differences were as much about social standing and personal circumstances as they were about gender. Respectable men did not loiter in alehouses getting desperately drunk; neither did they hang around street corners or dark alleys after dark. This drinking culture or late-night activity only pertained to men (or women) of questionable reputation. Corporation officials (all male) set the rules dictating who could run a market stall or drinking house, and it was men, in the guise of magistrates, constables and beadles, who regulated the practice. It was also these men who patrolled the city's streets watching for inappropriate behaviour in public places. But not all men could hold these positions, especially those in the magistracy: only wealthy freemen householders. Social class governed who could make the greatest claim to the streets and public places of Norwich, for it was social class that determined who set the rules. As we saw in Chapter Two, as well as above, it was often men who were seen as a greater threat to public order on the city's streets: the same was true in the city's alehouses. In many respects this demonstrates that publically active women were not the disorderly threat to the social order that some scholars have concluded; indeed, it even raises the question of whether they had more freedoms than we might have imagined, purely by default due to their lesser standing in society. Seventeenth-century men and women were governed by a set of implicit and often unspoken guidelines relating to their gender but, as

---

[167] Amanda Vickery, *The Gentleman's Daughter: Women's Lives in Georgian England* (London, 1998), pp. 203, 214.

[168] Refer here to Shepard's discussion of alternative masculinities, whereby men, especially young men, proved themselves amongst their peers with drinking rituals and misrule: Shepard, *Manhood*, pp. 88, 93–113.

Shoemaker has argued, the further down the social scale they were, the less gender operated as a determining factor in claiming space.

When seventeenth-century women thought about their city, they probably pictured it in relation to the places that had an immediate effect on their everyday lives; perhaps the section of the river where they met their friends and washed clothes, or the alehouse where they stopped for a drink on the way to the Saturday markets. But these were likely the same places that men pictured when they thought about their city. Perhaps they fished or bathed at the river, and visited the same alehouse as their wife, sister, or daughter. There was no clear 'gendered' map of the city that equated to public or private space. Instead, men and women conceived of the spaces and places around them in relation to their own subjective experiences, of which gender was only one factor alongside status, interests, and occupation. The difference was in perception, not place.

5

Political Landscapes

The inhabitants of seventeenth-century Norwich had a healthy and proactive relationship with their city's politics. From participating in the formal mechanisms of governance through the practice of holding a local office,[1] debating (or on occasion directing) the course and outcome of a local election, negotiating terms of the corporation's charter, by expressing opinions about political events or personalities in the alehouse, or even by rioting on the streets, it seems that Norwich people all had something to say about local affairs. Norwich's 'vibrant' and 'participatory' political culture was very much a part of the city's history and landscape.[2]

Provincial politics is often thought of as the poor cousin to national affairs but it often closely emulated, and occasionally influenced, the direction of national politics. Popular politics on the other hand has been given an in-depth treatment over recent years, often by historians using case studies of provincial towns and rural areas.[3] These historians have built on Patrick Collinson's argument that ordinary people were aware of and played a role in shaping the politics of their day, and have also revealed connections between national affairs and provincial politics.[4] Since the 1990s post-revisionists have moved the study of popular politics away from the heartland of disgruntled rural la-

---

[1] See Goldie's discussion of the extensive network of office holding, especially his claim that 'governance was not something done from on high to the passive recipients of authority, but something actively engaged in by the lesser agents of government; and every citizen was in some measure a lesser agent of government': Mark Goldie, 'The Unacknowledged Republic: Officeholding in Early Modern England', *The Politics of the Excluded, c. 1500–1850*, ed. T. Harris (Basingstoke, 2001), pp. 153–94, 155.

[2] Knights' claim that Norwich's political culture was 'vibrant, exuberant, partisan and sometimes violent' refers to the period after 1660 but he acknowledges the city's 'long-standing appetite for political conflict and participatory politics'. Mark Knights, 'Politics, 1660–1835', *Norwich Since 1550*, ed. Carole Rawcliffe and Richard Wilson (London, 2004), pp. 167–92, 168.

[3] E.g. Andy Wood, *Riot, Rebellion and Popular Politics* (Basingstoke, 2002); John Walter, *Understanding Popular Violence in the English Revolution: the Colchester Plunderers* (Cambridge, 1999).

[4] P. Collinson, *Elizabethan Essays* (1994), esp. Ch. 1.

bourers, to acknowledge the variety of actors that took part in urban and rural protests, riots, and seditious speeches, recognising that there was no clear-cut polarity between elite or popular politics. David Underdown's work was critical in drawing attention to this, as too has been Tim Harris' research on later Stuart politics and crowd action, influenced in part by the pioneering work of George Rudé and Edward Thompson.[5] In the case of Norwich specifically, Andy Wood has been explicit in making the connection between the local gentry and the ordinary people in guiding and steering the course of Kett's Rebellion in the mid-sixteenth century.[6]

The connection between politics and physical place on the other hand has been well made in recent studies. Beat Kümin's pioneering collection of essays on political spaces in pre-industrial Europe demonstrated just how the social forces of politics shaped 'architectural, ceremonial, territorial' and 'cultural' spaces, intimately creating and connecting politics with places in our landscape.[7] The work of geographers such as Mike Crang and the engagement of social and urban historians, such as Steve Hindle, Bernard Capp or Peter Clark, in the 'spatial turn' of history have enriched the field still further. It is from such studies that this chapter draws, building on the argument that political spaces were not necessarily those connected to official political buildings, ritual or ceremonial places, or political elites, but that these spaces extended far more widely across social and geographical spectrums, were not fixed in time, or left uncontested. As Kümin has argued, political spaces can be envisaged as the 'dynamic product of interactions between locations, objects and human agents, that is to say as situational syntheses dependent on mental perceptions and the networks in which individuals find themselves'.[8]

In Norwich, the places in which popular politics were most frequently enacted were also those public places most commonly associated with the communication of news and information and an emerging public sphere, especially drinking houses. Indeed, the landscape of popular politics was intimately linked to passage of news through the city, connecting traditional oral and newer printed avenues of dissemination. News was spread, as it always had been, via word of mouth in the markets and the streets, but the increasing availability of cheap printed material – including newsletters and 'separates' from the 1620s and pamphlets, newspapers and political propaganda from the 1640s – particularly tied political discourse to print and the places in which print was circulated. The developments in the printed news also

5   David Underdown, *A Freeborn People: Politics and the Nation in Seventeenth-Century England* (Oxford, 1996); Tim Harris, *London Crowds in the Reign of Charles II: Propaganda and Politics from the Restoration until the Exclusion Crisis* (Cambridge, 1987); E. P. Thompson, *Customs in Common* (London, 1991); G. Rudé, *The Crowd in History, 1730–1848* (London, 1964).

6   A. Wood, *The 1549 Rebellions and the Making of Modern England* (Cambridge, 2007).

7   J. C. Scott, 'Preface', *Political Space in Pre-Industrial Europe*, ed. Beat Kümin (Aldershot, 2009), pp. 1–4, 1.

8   Beat Kümin, 'Introduction', *Political Space*, ed., Kümin, pp. 6–15, 8–9.

offered a more concrete 'sense of the integration of local and national'[9] especially by facilitating the speed at which the provinces were kept informed of national affairs. Indeed, this sense of grounding of discourse and place can be considered part of what Phil Withington described as the 'discursive public sphere'[10] in contrast to Jürgen Habermas'[11] rather socially exclusive and rigid conceptualisation and periodization of the public sphere. Indeed many historians have recently argued that a public sphere can be detected from as early as the 1580s, evidence for which can be found in the range of places in which news could be heard, read and discussed, such as markets, streets, inns, alehouses and taverns.[12]

This chapter builds from this historiographical background taking as its starting point the methodology of the recent 'spatial turn', with its emphasis on dynamic and socially constructed spaces, and connecting this with the slightly older – yet no less relevant today – field of popular politics to make a connection between non-formal political activities and the places in which these activities happened. In so doing, it seeks to uncover whether there were any patterns to political happenings in Norwich and ask whether, perhaps over time, certain places became fixed as 'political' in inhabitants' common memory of the landscape. Second, as the relationship between place and politics becomes evident, it seeks to explore the dynamics of this relationship in greater depth, asking whether the assumption that a space was 'political' added anything to engagements subsequently enacted within that place. Finally, it builds on the recent historiography of popular politics by asking questions

[9] Richard Cust, 'News and Politics in Early Seventeenth-Century England', *Past and Present* 112:1 (1986), 60–90, 69. See also Clive Holmes, 'The County Community in Stuart Historiography', *Journal of British Studies* XIX (1980), 54–73; Ann Hughes, 'Warwickshire on the Eve of the Civil War: A County Community?', *Midland History* VII (1982), 42–72; and Derek Hirst, 'Court, Country and Politics before 1629', *Faction and Parliament*, ed. Kevin Sharpe (Oxford, 1978), pp. 105–38.

[10] Philip Withington, 'Two Renaissances: Urban Political Culture in Post-Reformation England Reconsidered', *The Historical Journal* 44:1 (2001), 239–67, 248–9.

[11] Jürgen Habermas, *The Structural Transformation of the Public Sphere: An Inquiry into a Category of Bourgeois Society*, trans. Thomas Burger and Frederick Lawrence (Cambridge, MA, 1991). For critical analysis see Harold Mah, 'Phantasies of the Public Sphere: Rethinking the Habermas of Historians,' *Journal of Modern History* 72:1 (March 2000), 153–82; David Zaret, *Origins of Democratic Culture: Printing, Petitions, and the Public Sphere in Early-Modern England* (Princeton, 2000); Phil Withington, 'Public Discourse, Corporate Citizenship and State-Formation in Early Modern England', *American Historical Review* 112:4 (2007), 1016–38; Brian Cowan, 'Geoffrey Holmes and the Public Sphere: Augustan Historiography from Post-Namierite to the Post-Habermasian', *Parliamentary History* 28:1 (2009), 166–78.

[12] Peter Lake and Steven Pincus, 'Rethinking the Public Sphere in Early Modern England', *Journal of British Studies* 45:2 (April 2006), 270–92; Peter Lake and Steven Pincus, eds, *The Politics of the Public Sphere in Early Modern England* (Manchester, 2007); Peter Lake and Michael Questier, 'Puritans, Papists, and the "Public Sphere" in Early-Modern England: the Edmund Campion Affair in Context', *Journal of Modern History* 72 (2000), 586–627.

about the social composition of the people who were at the forefront of these political activities. As we have already established, seventeenth-century Norwich's culture of political activity was focussed around its drinking houses, its public places and the passage of political news. It may well also be considered part of an emerging public sphere. However it was not exclusive to either an urban elite – the governing class of aldermen, sheriffs, mayors and magistrates – or a labouring class. Critically, Norwich's political participants were, more often than not, drawn from across the whole social spectrum, from the aldermen, to middling freemen citizens, to the ordinary men and women on the street. While this claim in itself is not new, the investigation of social class in conjunction with place lends a new dimension to the study of popular politics. This becomes particularly apparent as patterns begin to emerge in the reputation, type and location of places that were time and again associated with political activities. Some drinking houses, for example, might be exclusive to a particular social group, but incidents that took place on the streets or at the market less so. Thus this chapter seeks to address how the dynamics of popular politics and place interacted with social status, viewing Norwich's political culture as dynamic, spatially focussed and socially inclusive.

Drinking Houses and Provincial Politics

Thanks to the lasting legacy of Habermasian thought on the public sphere and its links to the coffee-house culture of the eighteenth century, coffee houses have been afforded a key position in the development of the nucleus of formal and informal political discourse over the course of the seventeenth and eighteenth centuries.[13] Coffee houses were indeed important political spaces, where debating societies, clubs and political groups tended to congregate and where news, letters, post and printed literature were collected, circulated and articulated.[14] Before the mid-century and particularly outside of London, however, coffee houses had far less of a role to play in the nascent public sphere. Indeed, until relatively late in our period, coffee houses barely featured in the political landscape of regional towns and cities. Norwich's first known coffee house only opened its doors in 1676,[15] and we know from incidental references that only a few others opened around the central

---

13   Wood, *Riot, Rebellion*, p. 172.

14   On coffee-house culture see Brian Cowan, *The Social Life of Coffee: The Emergence of the British Coffeehouse* (New Haven, 2005); Markman Ellis, *The Coffee House: A Cultural History* (London, 2004); Helen Berry, 'An Early Coffee House Periodical and its Readers: the *Athenian Mercury* 1691–1697', *London Journal* 25 (2000), 14–33; or Steve Pincus, '"Coffee politicians does create": Coffee Houses and Restoration Political Culture', *Journal of Modern History* 67 (1995), 807–34.

15   Knights, 'Politics', p. 180.

marketplace in St Peter Mancroft by 1700, a number that included Frank Drake's,[16] Frome's,[17] Mr Harvey's,[18] and William Browne's at New Hall.[19] We do know from legislative records that these places operated as channels for the printed news, but there are no reports of political or seditious conversations, clubs, or political activities at any of the above-named establishments until the eighteenth century.[20] Thus it fell to alehouses, inns and taverns to provide a platform for the articulation of political discourse, political meetings, politicking and popular politics that we know took place in Norwich. Critically, drinking houses offered the room for relatively ordinary people to become part of an identifiable political and public culture.

Peter Clark has highlighted how, over the course of the seventeenth century, drinking houses became 'more respectable'; considered less 'the enemy of the political establishment' by the state but a potential 'weapon of political influence'.[21] Certainly, the post-Restoration era saw a rise in fairly elitist political clubs and debating societies operating out of alehouses, especially in the capital, but arguably drinking houses had long played this role informally in provincial towns and cities, largely due to the lack of other viable alternatives for social gatherings, political meetings, and so forth. Buchanan Sharp also recognised that 'high politics were routinely the stuff of alehouse

---

[16] Drake's coffee house is mentioned in a Diocesan Court libel suit: DN/DEP/52/56&57, fol. 6v, 4 November 1691. Anne Lulman v. John Inman.

[17] The corporation's City Committee held their meetings at Frome's Coffeehouse. We know this because the committee's expenses (which included oranges, beer, and wine) survive: NCR 18b/1, fol. 14v, 1700.

[18] A newspaper advertisement for the sale of Mr Harvey's Coffeehouse at the marketplace tells us of its existence in the early eighteenth century: Norfolk Heritage Centre (NHC), The Norwich Postman, 1706.

[19] Ursula Priestly and Alayne Fenner, *Shops and Shopkeepers in Norwich 1660–1730* (Norwich, 1985), pp. 8–9.

[20] Mayor's court order concerning the apprehension of political literature at coffee houses and booksellers, NCR 16a, 25, fol. 65r, 7 April 1680. It was under this by-law that Londoner Thomas Firman was prosecuted for circulating a seditious pamphlet and a Norwich coffee seller was prosecuted for distributing the *Address of the Corporation of London*: quoted in Mark Knights, *Politics and Opinion in Crisis, 1679–81* (Cambridge, 1994), p. 173. There is precious little known about political clubs in Norwich until the early eighteenth century when between 1715 and 1745 sixty clubs are known to have existed, see Knights, 'Politics', p. 180. Angela Dain also discusses the growth of political clubs and freemasonry in Norwich in Angela Dain, 'An Enlightened and Polite Society', *Norwich Since 1550*, ed. Rawcliffe and Wilson, pp. 193–218, 196–8.

[21] Peter Clark, *The English Alehouse: A Social History 1200–1830* (London, 1983), pp. 225, 232, 237. Also useful here is Peter Clark, 'Politics, Clubs and Social Space in Pre-Industrial Europe', *Political Space*, ed. Beat Kümin, pp. 81–94.

conversations',[22] and Beat Kümin has argued that coffee-house politics were 'built on foundations laid by traditional drinking establishments'.[23]

The study of drinking-house culture has provided an important baseline for this study of politics and place. From the pioneering work of Peter Clark and Keith Wrightson, who brought drinking houses to scholars' attention as not simply places of sociability but as windows into early-modern social, political and economic worlds, historians have delved into drinking-house culture in new and innovative ways.[24] Andy Wood, influenced by the work of anthropologist James C. Scott, has offered the view, for example, that drinking houses were a 'sequestered social site' where the poorer sorts and labouring men found vent in 'seditious mutterings' against their masters, words that occasionally fell foul of the surveillance culture of the state.[25] Adam Fox and John Walter have likewise conceptualised drinking houses as important sites for the expression of grievances, especially in relation to Scott's claim that the sites saw the expression of the 'hidden transcripts' of a plebeian subculture.[26] Nevertheless, the drinking houses of these discussions have most commonly been the alehouses frequented by the labouring sorts, the disaffected working men who had cause to complain about their employers over an ale at the end of a long, hard day. As Alan Everitt and John Chartres have so rightly pointed out, the social centre of most provincial towns were the chief inns.[27] John Brewer too has shown how provincial inns offered the middling sorts a variety of avenues – including public and private rooms – to facilitate political clubs and debating societies and has also pointed to the similarities between coffee-house culture and inn culture in the eighteenth century.[28]

Beat Kümin, Anne Tlusty and James R. Brown have more recently reassessed the view of drinking houses that couched them as sites of disorder,

[22] Buchanan Sharp, 'Popular Political Opinion in England 1660–85', *History of European Ideas* 10:1 (1989), 13–29, 13–14.

[23] Beat Kümin, *Drinking Matters: Public Houses and Social Exchange in Early Modern Central Europe* (Basingstoke, 2007), pp. 188, 195–6.

[24] Clark, *The English Alehouse*, p. x; Keith Wrightson, 'Alehouses, Order and Reformation in Rural England, 1590–1660', *Popular Culture and Class Conflict, 1590–1914: Explorations in the History of Labour and Leisure*, ed. Eileen Yeo and Stephen Yeo (Brighton, 1981), pp. 1–27.

[25] Wood, '"Poore men woll speke one daye"', pp. 67–98, 91.

[26] Adam Fox, 'Ballads, Libels and Popular Ridicule in Jacobean England', *Past and Present* 145:1 (1994), 47–83; John Walter, 'Public Transcripts, Popular Agency and the Politics of Subsistence in Early Modern England', *Negotiating Power in Early Modern Society: Order, Hierarchy and Subordination in Britain and Ireland*, ed. Michael J. Braddick and John Walter (Cambridge, 2001), pp. 149–65.

[27] Alan Everitt, 'The English Urban Inn, 1560–1760', *Perspectives in English Urban History*, ed. Alan Everitt (London, 1972), pp. 91–137; John Chartres, 'The Place of Inns in the Commercial life of London and Western England, 1660–1760' (Oxford University, D. Phil, unpub., 1973).

[28] John Brewer, *Party Ideology and Popular Politics at the Accession of George III* (Cambridge, 1976), pp. 159–60.

seeing them instead as positive sites for affirmative social action and interaction.[29] It is from this point that this chapter builds, accepting that although seventeenth-century legislation reflected anxiety about drinking houses' potential for engendering politically subversive activities, those same people who were responsible for upholding this legislation were also those who most often used them in this context. Thus we should not view these activities as fundamentally subversive, but as part of an emerging discourse of positive public, political debate and expression, one that was to play a significant role in shaping the political transformations of the seventeenth century. Equally it sets out to discover not the landscape of drink (the term coined by James Brown in his study of Southampton's drinking-house culture), but the landscape of politics in seventeenth-century Norwich.

It has been claimed that seventeenth-century drinking houses were – next to the home and the workplace – one of the most important lived spaces of contemporary urban inhabitants.[30] In Norwich this must have been especially true. The city was, and still is, known for its exceptional number of drinking houses. For a population that had reached approximately 28,881 residents in 1693,[31] there were at least two hundred and eighty-one alehouses: a ratio of one for every one hundred inhabitants.[32] There were drinking houses to suit all pockets and needs: from large, well-to-do coaching inns for the better sorts and visiting county gentry, like the Rampant Horse Inn on the street of the same name,[33] to the tiny premises like that of Widow Garneham 'in the Lazer Howse without Magdalene Gates' that attracted poor customers

---

[29] James R. Brown, *The Landscape of Drink: Inns, Taverns and Alehouses in Early Modern Southampton* (Warwick University, Ph.D Thesis, unpub. 2007), p. 3; James Brown, 'Drinking Houses and the Politics of Surveillance in Pre-Modern Southampton', *Political Space*, ed. Kümin, pp. 61–80; Kümin, *Drinking Matters*; Beat Kümin and Anne Tlusty, eds, *The World of the Tavern: Public Houses in Early Modern Europe* (Aldershot, 2002); Anne Tlusty, *Bacchus and Civic Order: The Culture of Drink in Early Modern Germany* (Charlottesville, 2001).

[30] A. Lynn Martin, 'Drinking and Alehouses in the Diary of an English Mercer's Apprentice, 1663–1674', *Alcohol: A Social and Cultural History*, ed. Mack P. Holt (Oxford, 2006), pp. 93–106, 93.

[31] Parochial List of the Number of Houses and Inhabitants within the City of Norwich, 1693 and 1752, MC 453, Loose papers. See also Penelope Corfield, 'A Provincial Capital in the Late Seventeenth Century: the Case of Norwich', *The Early Modern Town: A Reader*, ed. Peter Clark (New York, 1976), pp. 233–72, 234–6.

[32] Approximate number of drinking houses in 1702: cited in Knights, 'Politics', pp. 167–92, 180.

[33] The Rampant Horse's clientele can be reconstructed through incidental records, in this case witness statements from the Norwich Diocesan Court, see DN/DEP/47/51, fol. 345r, 16 April 1666. On this occasion, they included a cleric, an armiger, various gentlemen, a silk weaver and a vintner. The inn, originally known as the Ramping Horse, had been operating since the thirteenth century.

and was quickly shut down by the authorities.[34] There was a clear hierarchy when it came to alehouses, inns, and taverns. Coaching inns were at the top, and alehouses were at the bottom of the pecking order.[35] What they all had in common was the provision of essential services. Coaching inns served selections of wines, beers, ales, and meals, provided private rooms for meetings or for lodgings, hosted travelling players and musicians for the entertainment of their paying clientele, and allowed the sale of selections of ballads, news sheets, corantos and pamphlets which could be purchased and read privately, or read aloud.[36] On the other end of the scale, small alehouses might consist of a simple front room, brew their own ale and make or buy in a small selection of snacks, and hold games for customers' entertainment.

Some patterns can be detected in the location of these establishments. The busiest, and hence the largest and most successful houses, were generally to be found lining the city's main roads and clustered around the ancient marketplaces of Tombland and St Peter Mancroft. These encompassed a concentration of houses – all inns – that ran along each edge of the main market at St Peter Mancroft, a number that included the Half Moon, the King's Head, the Bear, the Angel, and the White Lion along the eastern edge (indeed the back lane running behind this strip passed into common memory as 'the back of the inns') in addition to the Star, the White Hart, the White Swan, Abraham's, and the Three Barrels amongst several others. The other city inns were also fairly central, most located on the main roads leading from the south and west gates like St Stephen's Street, St Giles' Street, Bethel (formally Bedlam) Street, Pottergate, Westwick Street, and around the Colegate and Gildengate intersection north of the river. This pattern was likely a practical one. These areas were the most densely populated, the most ancient, and the roads the most heavily used. There was a sprinkling of other inns, notably the Unicorn off Coslany Street to the northwest and the Elephant to the north of Fye Bridge just a few yards from Stump Cross. Some of the inns were owned and rented out by the corporation and those, like the Castle, the Blue Bell, the Black Swan, the Bear and the Angel, leave consistent records of rentals throughout the century.

Taverns and alehouses were more scattered and evidence for them is harder to come by. The Rose Tavern was situated at the northern end of London Street before the Red Well junction, another tavern of the same name could be found from at least 1688 on Rose Lane, and the Dove could be found just south of Coslany Bridge. Many of Norwich's taverns or alehouses can only be

---

34   W. L. Sachse, ed., *Minutes of the Norwich Court of Mayoralty 1632–1635* (Norwich, 1967) p. 53, 2 Feb 1632. Widow Garnham had inherited a family business, run by Thomas Garnham, freeman: P. Millican, ed., *The Register of the Freemen of Norwich 1548–1713* (Norwich, 1934), p. 20. Widow Garnham's impoverished status in 1632 is a poignant example of how difficult it could be for elderly widowed women to make ends meet.

35   Clark, *The English Alehouse*, pp. 5–15.

36   Cust, 'News and Politics', 66. Norwich's first newspaper – the *Norwich Post* – was published from 1701.

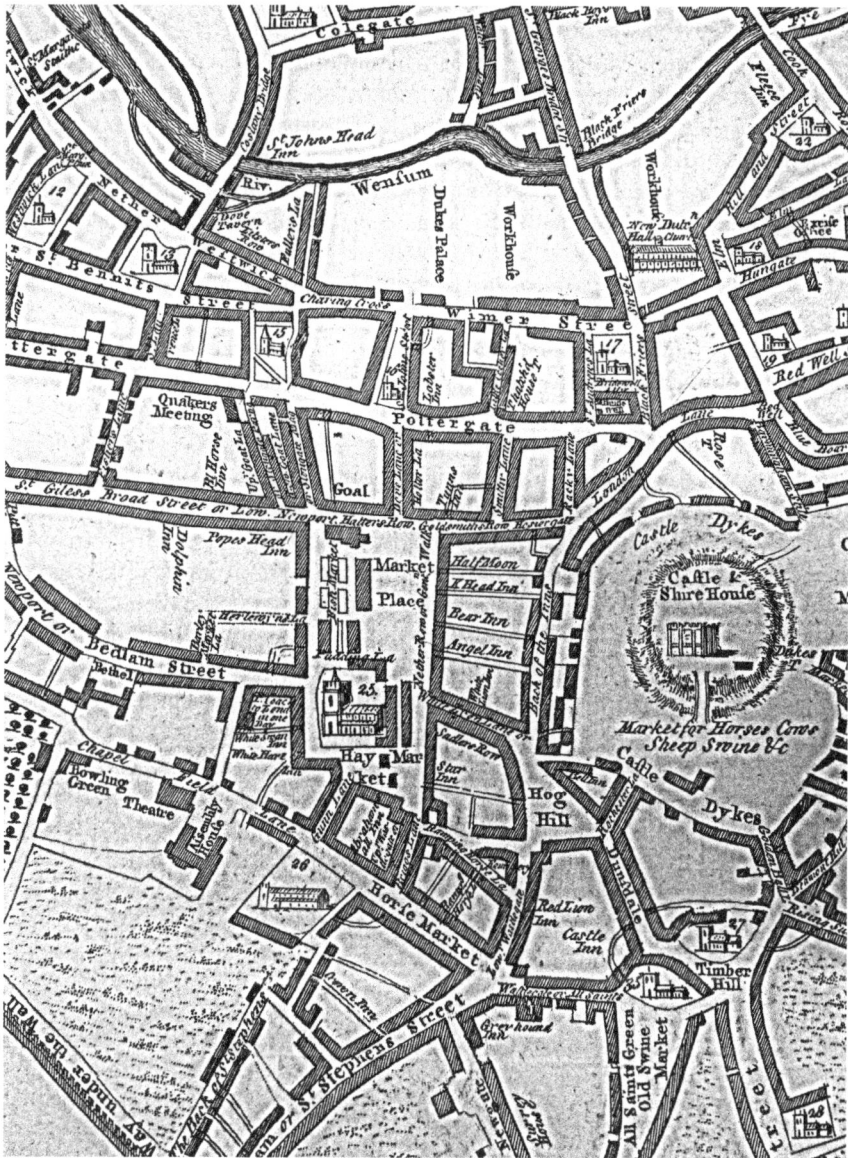

5 Detail of illustration 4 (p. 70) by Samuel King, 1766 (showing Norwich alehouses and marketplaces).

discovered from incidental records, such as when the authorities intervened to regulate one. Such was the case in 1634 when James Carter, tapster at the Three Bells in St Stephen, was found to have actually been apprenticed to a master in Newton and thus was ordered to depart the city. John Shawe, 'a drawer of wyne with John Clarke who keepeth the Sunne Taverne in St Peters of Mancroft', was likewise found to have been indentured in service to

169

Mistress Greenleafe at the Greyhound in Ipswich, and in 1674 one Mathew Wetherby and alehouse keeper of St Clement had his licence taken away because he regularly suffered 'great disorder in his house,'[37] but mostly there are no consistent records of these places during this century. Without better evidence it is not possible to make any sweeping generalisations about the location of these smaller and occasionally transient establishments. It is quite likely, from what we know of the inns, that the more established taverns and alehouses were likewise situated in the city's busiest areas. It is possible however to note some patterns in the type of establishments that had links to political activities.

During the 1620s, for example, Norwich's Maid's Head Inn had provided the backdrop for two controversial political incidents. The Maid's Head was at the top of its field. It was one of the city's largest and most reputable establishments; a record of the inn (later a hotel) has been known since at least the 1200s. By the 1600s it was popular amongst the better sorts, especially during the assizes circuits when rural landowners and their families came to Norwich for the 'seasons'.[38] The first of two political incidents known to have taken place here happened during 1624 when Sir Robert Gawdy used it as his base of operations in the lead-up to the 1624 parliamentary election. Gawdy, a notable county landowner, objected to the nomination of Sir Thomas Holland and Sir John Corbet for Norfolk's parliamentary seat.[39] According to the historian Derek Hirst, Gawdy's objection was based on the fact that that the pair had been *selected* in accordance with their rank and service, as opposed to having been *elected*.

The issue of the selection or election of candidates had been gathering momentum in Norwich since the 1590s. There was a small but powerful minority of aldermen and freemen who believed that seniority and longevity of service alone should not automatically guarantee an individual's political post. This issue had been most obviously expressed during elections for the city's mayor and between 1595 and 1619. The freemen, exercising their right

---

[37] Sachse, *Minutes, 1632–1635*, p. 158; W. Rye, ed., *Depositions Taken Before the Mayor and Aldermen of Norwich 1549–1567 & Extracts from the Court Books of the City of Norwich 1666–1668* (Norwich, 1905), p. 134.

[38] Corfield, 'A Provincial Capital', pp. 254–6. During the eighteenth century the Maid's Head was patronized by notable diarists Parson Woodforde and John Longe, and local gentry including the Townsend, Cornwallis, and Windham families: John Beresford, ed., *James Woodforde: The Diary of a Country Parson 1758–1802* (Norwich, 1999), p. 192 and M. *Du Quesne and other Essays* (1931), p. 58; Michael John Stone, ed., *The Diary of John Longe 1765–1834* (Woodbridge, 1999), p. 106.

[39] The Gawdy family were familiar faces in East Anglian politics. Robert Gawdy's relations Bassingbourne and Framlingham Gawdy had held the parliamentary seat for Thetford with regularity across the early seventeenth century, and the former held the Norfolk seat in 1601: *The History of Parliament: the House of Commons 1604–1629*, ed. Andrew Thrush and John P. Ferris, online edn, accessed 28 March 2013. In 1625 Robert Gawdy stood for the parliamentary seat for the shire, and lost: HMC, *Report on the Manuscipts of the Gawdy Family of the County of Norfolk* (London, 1885), p. 122.

of charter to elect a separate mayoral candidate to the aldermen, made a series of nominations that upset the traditional order of nominees. By 1619 James I, exasperated by the instability that this situation had engendered, ordered that the procedure for selecting mayoral candidates be locked down. Seniority and service, he declared, would prevent junior aldermen rising above their station and only the aldermen should have the ability to nominate candidates in future. The issue of selection versus election split the electorate and remained a significant topic for debate throughout the early seventeenth century.[40]

It is hard to determine whether Gawdy's stand reflected his personal political ideals or whether he simply saw it as a convenient way to muster votes in his own interest, but he had certainly tapped into an established undercurrent of dissent. He proposed instead the nomination of Sir Roger Townshend as a counter to Holland and Corbet.[41] Interestingly, Townshend had no interest in the position – having already declared in favour of his now rivals – but Gawdy persevered in making his point. Gawdy's plan was to garner support from Norwich's electorate who, for the past twenty years, had been polarised by the question of selection by seniority versus election by free choice. Arriving in Norwich, Gawdy swiftly adopted a recognised strategy of public performance more commonly associated with the assertion of civic or royal authority. Starting at the Norman Castle, symbol of Norwich's ancient heritage and power, he progressed through the streets to the Guildhall: home to the city's charter of incorporation that set out its citizen's electoral rights. Then, passing through the market square, he made his way to the Maid's Head Inn.[42] Here, at the culmination of his contrived and profoundly symbolic journey, Gawdy had the opportunity to meet with the city's freemen and citizens – the electorate – who frequented the inn. The choice of the inn was both symbolic and practical. Symbolic because of the inn's location at the ancient marketplace at Tombland and practical because it would have enabled Gawdy to make contact with the city's most influential people on the political scene. Indeed, not only was the inn the destination of the city and county's great and good, but it was at that point in time owned by Thomas Hyrne, then member of parliament for Norwich. Hyrne, a three-time former mayor, had caused a stir when he had bypassed his seniors to become a sheriff and

40 J. T. Evans, *Seventeenth Century Norwich: Politics, Religion and Government 1620–1690* (Oxford, 1979), pp. 66–73.

41 Robert Gawdy played no significant part in parliament but other members of his family did. Framlingham Gawdy and Thomas Holland were rivals for the Thetford parliamentary seat that Framlingham held during the 1620, 1623 and 1624 elections. In 1625, Holland had penned a very personal letter to Framlingham Gawdy a few days before that April's election, asking respectfully whether he might instead transfer his interests to Sir Charles Le Grosse. Clearly, Gawdy declined as he won one of the two Thetford seats again in 1625, the other held by Sir John Hobart.

42 D. Hirst, *The Representative of the People? Voters and Voting in England under the Early Stuarts* (Cambridge, 1975), pp. 121, 144.

then an alderman in 1597, only one year after he had gained his freedom.[43] Though we have little direct evidence it is very likely that Hyrne was one of the faction who had been rigorously campaigning to maintain the freemen's ancient right to select their own candidate during elections, a statement that becomes increasingly clear when looking at events three years later.

Three years on, in 1627, a freeman named John Kettle decided to hold a meeting at the Maid's Head. Since 1619, the issue of selection had not gone away. Those people who maintained their belief in the freemen's right to nominate an independent candidate had simply moved their focus to the elections for sheriff, proceedings for which had not been affected by the changes enacted in electoral rights as a result of the 1619 controversy. Kettle was the freeman's choice in the 1627 election for the position of sheriff and a more contentious candidate could not have been found. With a history of verbal abuse against the corporation, many unpaid taxes and numerous small offences against the city, Kettle was the deliberate spearhead of a grieved electorate. On the day of the election however, despite the packing of the voting hall with his supporters who filled the air with 'loude cryes [of] (Kettle Kettle)',[44] he lost by a mere ten voices to his rival, Thomas Atkin. Atkin was an unpopular choice – he was currently fulfilling the role of a collector of the Forced Loan, but we have next to no evidence as to his ideological perspective on the election versus selection principle.

Kettle let it be known that he thought that the election results had been rigged by his opponents and declared on losing that '[I]f any citizen did find himselfe grieved to the wronge to him done in the said Election That they should repayre ... to the signe of the maydes head ... And there they should be heard, or otherwise the Comons of the city should not hereafter have their freedom of choice.'[45] According to Kettle, no less a man than Sir Thomas Hyrne[46] had promised that 'Twenty of the best of them should come downe in the afternoon' to support the meeting though, sadly, there is no record of who eventually attended.[47]

Hyrne's interest in the election and involvement with Kettle might also be surmised from other evidence. Kettle was arrested after the meeting, ostensibly for trying to cause a tumult disturbing the swearing in of the new sheriffs – Thomas Atkin and Henry Lane – but it was not difficult for the magistrates to find a variety of reasons to keep him in prison and out of the way of the

[43] Evans, *Seventeenth Century Norwich*, p. 66.
For biographical information see B. Cozens-Hardy and E. A. Kent, *The Mayors of Norwich 1403–1835* (Norwich, 1938), p. 68 and www.historyofparliamentonline.org/volume/1604–1629/member/hyrne-sir-thomas-1566–16378.
[44] Mayor and Aldermen of Norwich to the Privy Council, NA, SP 16/78, fol. 53, 18 December 1627.
[45] Letter from the Mayor and Aldermen of Norwich to the Privy Council, 27 September 1627, NA, SP 16/79, fol. 38.
[46] Hyrne was Norwich's mayor in 1604 and 1609, and MP for Norfolk in 1625 and 1626.
[47] NCR 16a/16 fol. 169r–170r.

swearing in ceremony. Immediately after the election, the twenty-four had penned two missives to the Privy Council reporting Kettle's actions in the lead up to and during the election, also filling them in on his contentious history with the corporation. On both documents Hyrne's signature is noticeably absent.[48] Kettle's persistent non-payment of local taxes and fines for the same had left a trail of unpaid debts to the corporation for which Kettle served a one-month sentence at Fleet Prison in London. When Kettle was returned to Norwich he was ordered to appear before the mayor and magistrates to make his humble submission, apologising for his actions and paying his debts. The piece of public theatre did not go quite as well as perhaps the magistrates had hoped however. Kettle had not been cowed by his time in the Fleet and appeared before the corporation as cantankerous and abusive as ever. Only apologising after some persuasion, it was later reported that Kettle had been heard to tell his friends of Hyrne's support, the latter having apparently declared that if 'the commons did not assist [Kettle] ... they should never have any free election'.[49] This bold statement is perhaps the clearest indication yet of Hyrne's involvement and political preferences, but coming from Kettle and not Hyrne himself it is hard to be absolutely sure that the statement represented the truth. Nevertheless, that fact that Hyrne's name keeps appearing in connection to these events is intriguing. The Maid's Head Inn was later sold to the Edgbastion family, but the connection between the inn and politics continued throughout the century and beyond.[50]

The Maid's Head was not the only reputable drinking house to attract a political crowd in the early seventeenth century. The Unicorn Inn, for example, tucked away in an industrialised but lightly populated northwest corner of the city by the New Mills in the parish of St Mary Coslany, was a regular watering hole for many of Norwich's mayors, aldermen, and officials and the setting for many of the corporation's official meetings.[51] It was also here in 1635 that the journeymen Augustine Thurton and Thomas Evered had

---

[48] Mayor and Aldermen of Norwich to the Privy Council, NA, SP 16/79, fol. 38, 27 September 1627; Mayor and Aldermen of Norwich to the Privy Council, NA, SP 16/78, fol. 53, 18 December 1627.

[49] NRO, NCR, 16a/16 fols 169r-170r.

[50] Thomas Edgbastion, freeman innholder: Millican, *Register of the Freemen*, p. 89. The inn was closely connected with Whig politics across the late seventeenth and eighteenth centuries; in 1724 the inn became one of Norwich's first Masonic Lodges: Dain, 'An Enlightened and Polite Society', p. 196; in 1788 Norfolk's Protestant political elite, including Thomas Coke of Holkham, met here to celebrate the centenary of William and Mary's landing in England: Susanna Wade Martins, *Coke of Norfolk, 1754–1842: A Biography* (Woodbridge, 2010), pp. 77–8; and on 28 January 1798 William Windham delivered his first public speech speaking out against the American War of Independence here: Thomas Amyot, ed., *Some Account of the Life of William Windham* (London, 1812), p. 141; Earl of Rosebery, ed., *The Windham Papers*, Vol. I (London, 1913), p. 20.

[51] The records of the corporation's committees reveal how they used private rooms at the larger inns as meeting spaces. The Unicorn was only one of many that the corporation preferred: NCR 18b/1–20.

planned 'to gather a multitude of people together ... to doe unlawfull Act' as the authorities insisted. Troubled by their low pay and inability to join their respective trade guilds, with all the social and economic benefits that membership would have entailed, the two men proposed to set up their own independent equivalent. They would 'elect 4 feastmakers ... to have yearly a feast amongst themselves ... [and] to consent howe they might drawe their sevrall masters to give greater wages ... [by] ... no lesse than vi d a weeke more then noe ... [i]f they could get [i]t'.[52] Taking place as it did during a moment of particular financial crisis in the city, their demand for better wages could not have been more badly timed.[53] When questioned Evered had claimed that 'the intent of this meetinge was onely to know howe the journeymen would holde all together concerninge the mendinge of their wages' but the investigative constables deduced that they were intending to riot to get their way, peppering their report with loaded terms such as 'multitudes' and 'unlawful'.[54]

During the 1640s, drinking houses were more and more often mired into the politics of the day. Cases of seditious speech, at this time judged to be that which was pro-royalist in tone, abounded. In 1642 for example, John Baldwin had, with his drinking companions William Symonds and Robert Riches, argued that 'If the king should go to parliament they would take away his prerogative and commit him to prison and take off his head' before the company drank to Charles I's good health at the Turkey Cock Tavern on Elm Hill. Riches was the same man who had also called the brothers Robert and Henry Rich, Earls of Warwick and Holland respectively, 'bastards' whose 'mother was a whore' for which he had been indicted at the quarter sessions.[55] Riches' interrogatories noted him in the records as a gentleman and we can assume from this that his companions were of a similar social status. It is possible that Symonds was alderman William Symonds, though the evidence is rather tenuous and likewise evidence of his political affiliations is contradictory.[56] The

[52] Quarter Sessions Book of Depositions and Orders, NCR 20a/10, fol. 60r, 11 July 1635. An important part of every guild's ceremonial year was the annual feast, which conferred honour on the guild and cemented its social network.

[53] The summer of 1635 saw two demands on the city's taxpayers for the unpopular ship money. The corporation petitioned the Crown for exemption on grounds of poverty, but they were only able to negotiate a thirty per cent decrease in the sum levied. Evans, *Seventeenth-Century Norwich*, p. 82.

[54] NCR 20a/10, fol. 60r, 11 July 1635.

[55] Quarter Sessions Interrogations and Recognisances, 1642–1643, NCR Case 11a 46 & 47, July 1643.

[56] J. T. Evans identified alderman William Symonds as a parliament man; he was certainly appointed by the House of Lords to the Eastern Association in 1643: Evans, *Seventeenth-Century Norwich*, pp. 126n, 135n; *Journals of the House of Lords* Vol. 6, 6–10 August 1643, p. 176. Nevertheless, Symonds notably did not contribute to parliament's Subscription for the Regaining of Newcastle when it was levied in Norwich in 1643, though whether this was for financial or ideological reasons is impossible to ascertain – indeed, not all those who refused to pay were royalists: Evans, *Seventeenth-Century Norwich*, pp. 135n, 133. More significantly perhaps, Blomefield noted how Symonds was suspected

same year, one Robert Holmes, a brewer, freeman, and future sheriff in 1646, was presented for abusing the watch having confronted them with the statement that he and his companion William Hardingham were of the 'king's watch'.[57] These examples may well be evidence of a 'tavern based' royalist sub-culture alluded to by Clive Holmes of which the Maid's Head may have been a part, although there is no conclusive evidence to prove the latter.[58] That the network of royalists in Norwich certainly did use drinking houses as nodes of operation however becomes clearer as the 1640s progressed.

The events of 1646–8 make the connection between certain drinking houses, the middling sort, politics and even a possible underground royalist movement, ever more apparent. What is even more significant is that these events provide evidence of a co-ordinated and planned network of associates who not only operated out of the drinking houses but actively used the venues as avenues to manage information and direct popular opinion. Between 1646 and 1647 there were a series of riots that took place across East Anglia (which will be discussed at greater length in the next section) as a result of a new excise tax intended to finance the parliamentarian war effort. There is evidence that much of the planning for the Norwich part of the uprising was arranged from the Castle Inn on White Lion Street which ran between the market and Norwich Castle.[59] Andrew Hopper has described these riots

of supporting the royalist cause when on March 18 1642/3 Symonds, along with sheriffs Samuel Puckle and Matthew Linsey, and aldermen John Greenwood and Thomas Toft, were 'placed in their rooms' as five aldermen were put out of office for supporting the King. However Symonds, Puckle and Linsey kept their offices and remained in key roles in the parliamentarian war effort: BHO, 'The city of Norwich, chapter 29: Of the city in Charles I's time', *An Essay towards a Topographical History of the County of Norfolk, Vol. III: The History of the City and County of Norwich, Part I* (1806), pp. 371–398. URL: http://www.british-history.ac.uk/report.aspx?compid=77999&strquery=william symonds. Date accessed: 03 June 2013. The Symonds family were grocers by trade and Symonds' son, and grandson, shared both his name and occupation. In 1689, one William Symonds – probably alderman Symonds' grandson – was involved in an incident of seditious speech at a drinking house, see fn. 125.

[57] Collection of original papers, with a few copies, relating to Norwich, 1633–1730, etc., BL, Add. MSS 22619, fol. 40, 3 December 1642; Norwich City Quarter Sessions Minute Book 1639–1654, NCR 20a/11, fol. 38r cited in Andrew Hopper, 'The Civil Wars', *Norwich Since 1550*, ed. Rawcliffe and Wilson, pp. 96–7. Holmes' freeman status is registered in Millican, *Register of the Freemen*, p. 21, 28 December 1624. Interestingly, in an echo of previous elections where the sheriff's post was the focus of local politicking, Holmes was the freemens' choice for sheriff in 1646. Evans, *Seventeenth Century Norwich*, pp. 163, 166.

[58] Clive Holmes, *The Eastern Association in the English Civil War* (Cambridge, 1974), p. 56. There are several mentions of royalist meetings at the Maid's Head in popular histories of the city, see for example, P. H. Ditchfield, *Vanishing England* (Teddington, 2007), p. 119, but there is limited scholarly or archival evidence to support such claims.

[59] Drinkers at the Castle Inn were arrested for their part in the riot: Walter Rye, *The History of the Bethel at Norwich* (Norwich, 1906), p. 114. This was not the only occasion that the Castle Inn's customers entered the criminal records for violence or violent speeches against the corporation and its representatives. A constable had been verbally abused here

as anti-parliamentarian and, although it is just as likely that their root cause was resentment to the extra tax and poverty, anti-parliament feeling cannot be ruled out.[60] In Norwich, free butchers and brewers led the riots and, armed with clubs, they violently rescued a butcher who had been imprisoned for refusing to pay the tax.

At the same time as the riots were taking place, hostilities were mounting between several factions in the city who disagreed over the style and expression of religious worship, ranging from Puritans and Laudians who both favoured a national church, albeit in a very different style, to those sectarians who favoured the establishment of individual congregations.[61] The issues were not new, indeed corporation affairs had been mired in religious controversy for more than twenty years, but the ongoing civil war served to heighten extant tensions. By the 1640s, religious grievances had erupted into violent outbursts of iconoclasm during which time few of the city's churches or cathedral escaped. All the different religious proclivities seen in the populace found representation amongst the corporation and the twenty-four were facing intensifying pressure from these often disparate groups and, beset by their own internal divisions, had failed to resolve fundamental religious questions – the issue of church decoration or the censure of traditional popular festivities for example – to the satisfaction of any party. The attack on popular custom attracted particular disapproval from many quarters, with the exception of the most godly reformers. Religious festivals and even guild day ceremonies were scaled back at a time when a little light-hearted exuberance might have been most welcome. Resentment began to converge from several avenues, from royalists most obviously but also from traders, retailers, and apprentices still reeling from the excise tax and on whom the suppression of guild day ceremonies must have seemed a double blow.[62] Thus it was that on 1 December 1647 a group of apprentices presented mayor John Utting with a petition defending the celebration of Christmas.

The Christmas controversy had begun in earnest on 25 December 1643 when many of London's Puritan traders opened their shops contrary to parliamentary orders. Over the next few years, the celebration was attacked by a series of parliamentary directives including the *Directory for the Public Worship of God throughout the Three Kingdomes* in 1645/6. Finally, on 10 June 1647, an ordinance had been passed declaring celebrating Christmas to be a punishable offence. Christmas that year saw apprentices run riot in Bury St Edmunds,

---

in 1603; Adam Dobleday had called the ex-mayor Thomas Pye a knave for carting an honest woman in 1605, and a constable had been violently assaulted here in 1612: NCR 16a/14, fol. 63r, 28 November 1603 and fol. 155r, 6 December 1605; NCR 16a/14, fol. 385v, 27 February 1612. The Castle's clientele were also implicated in the riot of 1648, known as the Great Blow. The Castle was a common inn owned and rented out by the corporation: NCR 18a, Chamberlain's Account Book, 1648.

60 Hopper, 'Civil Wars', p. 99.
61 Ibid., p. 105.
62 Hopper, 'Civil Wars', p. 107–8.

Ipswich and Norwich, supported by traders who closed their stalls and shops as normal.

Their petition was received by the mayor and inspired criticism by the strong godly faction in the corporation. This group, led by Sheriff Ashwell (a parliamentary army sergeant major) and Thomas Baret, accused the mayor and his supporters of allowing many popular festivities to continue (especially those on Charles I's accession day), of allowing known royalist clergy to preach in the city's churches, and of holding back further Puritan reforms. Utting, a moderate Presbyterian and conservative politician, had walked a tightrope between the religious extremists in his city, favouring balance over nepotism but by so doing he had managed to alienate the corporation's powerful Puritans: a mistake he was soon to regret.

Fear of a royalist uprising in this Parliamentary city had recently reached new heights. There had been a series of anti-army riots across East Anglia and rumours that the royalist faction in Norwich might be gaining in strength.[63] Taking full advantage of Utting's rumoured royalist sympathies – hearsay that had gained ground after he had permitted the election of an ineligible royalist, Roger Mingay, to Mancroft ward's aldermanic seat contrary to two ordinances of 1620 and 1648 – Ashwell and Baret drafted a petition to the Commons reporting all of Utting's supposed royalist acts and asking that Utting be replaced by the Puritan Christopher Baret, Thomas Baret's ageing father.[64] The Commons responded just as Ashwell and Baret had hoped, immediately sending a messenger to bring Utting to London for questioning and agreeing to the installation of Christopher Baret as a temporary deputy mayor.[65]

The Commons' messenger arrived in Norwich on Saturday 22 April where he spent the weekend with Utting at the King's Head deep in talks. The King's Head was a popular inn with overnight rooms. It was a respectable marketside establishment offering large-scale plays and entertainments for its guests and was a favoured place for the corporation's many committees and specially convened meetings over the course of the century.[66] The mayor and aldermen had officially confirmed it with the status of 'an ancient inn'

[63] Ibid., p. 94.

[64] Ibid., pp. 100, 108; Evans, *Seventeenth Century Norwich*, p. 174; The humble Petition of divers of the Justices, Sheriffs, Aldermen, and Citizens, of the City of Norwich, 18 April 1648, *House of Commons Journal* Vol. 5, 1646–1648 (HMSO, 1802), p. 534.

[65] Order concerning the mayor of Norwich, 18 April 1648, *House of Commons Journal*, 5, p. 535. Christopher Baret was an experienced, if elderly, civic officer. He had held the position of sheriff in 1615 and mayor in 1634. Cozens-Hardy and Kent, *Mayors of Norwich*, p. 79.

[66] See NCR 18b/1–20 for records of regular committee meetings. See also: Letter of Sir Phillip Wodehouse to Francis Parlett asking him to notify the mayor of Lynn of a special meeting to be convened at the King's Head, Bradfer-Lawrence Collection (BL)/F 4/23 October 1618; Letter of John Holland, John Potts and others of a special council to be held at the King's Head regarding Norfolk's coastal defences, BL/F 3/11, 3 December 1642.

in 1619.[67] It was also very close to Utting's own home in St Peter Mancroft.[68] The King's Head was the obvious choice for an official messenger to take rooms but it also meant that news of his arrival could not be kept a secret. The news spread like wildfire. Richard Haddon the barber, for example, had been drinking in the White Lion (three doors down from the King's Head) on the Saturday evening when he heard the news. When he told his customer Robert Cooke in his shop the next day, Cooke responded that he already knew about the 'care' to be 'taken for the Malignant Maior' from the 'printed nuse'.[69]

The mayor and his supporters had until the Monday morning before Utting was expected to leave with the messenger for London. Worried about what might await him, Utting and six aldermen asked Thomas Balleston, the town clerk, to draft a petition that Utting might take with him, highlighting his 'good government and behaviour' in office.[70] With less than thirty-six hours to garner signatures, the document's existence was announced during Sunday morning services, and it was passed around the city's busiest inns and taverns to reach the widest audience in the shortest possible time. As darkness fell across the city on the Sunday evening, however, it seems the petition had stirred more than just quills to parchment.

> The commons ... began to assemble ... calling out that [they] might thank Tom Baret, but before they had done, they would make him a poor Tom Baret indeed, and as for the pursuivant and sheriff, they would hang them upon the Castle-hill, upon Gardiner's mare, (meaning the gallows) and ham-string any body that should offer to carry Mr. Mayor away; and it being reported that the Mayor was to be carried off in the night, they went in a body to all the gates, locked them up, and carried away the keys ... about midnight they grew into a large body in the marketplace, being armed, and gave out a watch-word to be known by, viz. For God and King Charles.[71]

By the time the sun rose on Monday 24 April, anywhere between five hundred and a thousand people had gathered in the market square outside the King's Head.[72] Many waited peacefully, hoping to intercept Utting's departure. Oth-

---

67 Certificate from the Mayor and Aldermen of Norwich that the King's Head in St Peter Mancroft, Norwich, is an ancient inn, MS 10961, 36F8, 16 April 1619. This term gave the inn some status, legally defining it as an established, licensed premises.

68 Cozens-Hardy and Kent, *Mayors of Norwich*, p. 83.

69 NCR 12c/1, no. 94, 6 May 1648. Cooke was a Norfolk gentleman from Forncett who had been having his hair cut at Haddon's shop in Norwich that weekend.

70 Hopper, 'Civil Wars', pp. 89–116, 108; Rye, *Bethel*, p. 85 and Francis Blomefield, *An Essay towards a Topographical History of the County of Norfolk: The History of the City and County of Norwich*, Vol. III, Part I (1806), p. 394.

71 Blomefield, *Topographical History* III:I, p. 394. 'Poor Tom' referred to alderman Thomas Baret.

72 Estimates differ. J. T. Evans claims that the Mayor's Court Books recorded 500–600 people, but the book in question (NCR 16a/22) is missing from the collection, so I am

ers did not. Fuelled by a night of heavy drinking and violent outbursts often punctuated with pro-royalist sentiment,[73] a mob ran riot through the streets in pursuit of the messenger who was then rumoured to be leaving. Failing in that plan – the messenger had been forewarned and escaped earlier – the mob turned their attention instead to Sheriff Ashwell. Not only was Ashwell one of the ringleaders of the anti-Utting faction but as sheriff and a sergeant major he was also responsible for the city's armoury. The mob plundered the weapons stores at Ashwell's house. From there the mob ransacked the excise office at Alderman Parmenter's before capturing the Committee House where gunpowder had been stockpiled for the war effort. Here, the rioters also set to throwing sequestration and tax records out of the windows.[74]

Fearing the worst, Thomas Baret sent an urgent message to the nearest Eastern Association regiment under the command of Colonel Charles Fleetwood at East Dereham. Fleetwood mobilised his troops immediately and they arrived in Norwich that very afternoon. Chasing the rebels through the streets and lanes of St Stephen, St Peter Mancroft and the marketplace they cornered them at the Committee House. In the mess that had been left from their earlier pilfering, all it took was a few stray sparks from a pistol to ignite the gunpowder lying underfoot and the gunpowder barrels exploded.

> … behold here armes and there legges of dead men scattered: every where some tokens of Gods Justice on these wretches and mercy to his poore people. Thus these blody men that but now threatened to make the ensuing night the most blody night *Norwich* ever saw, were before night sent into the land of darknesse…[75]

Colonel Fleetwood later recalled how the explosion 'did shake the whole City [and] threw down part of some Churches, wounded and killed a great many of the Inhabitants',[76] the exact number of whom remains unknown. The antiquarian Walter Rye confirmed eleven deaths in a survey of parish

---

unable to confirm this. However, Evans writes that over one thousand people gathered in the market square, a figure also claimed by Andrew Hopper: Evans, *Seventeenth Century Norwich*, p. 175 and Hopper, 'Civil Wars', p. 108. Walter Rye suggests even more people may have been involved, writing that 'nigh on two thousand people' went to Sheriff Ashwell's house that morning: Rye, *Bethel*, p. 90.

[73] Richard Buddery had, for example, apparently told George Whiting he was a 'Roundheaded rouge' and said 'he hoped to see a hundred such roundheaded rouges as he was hanged'; George Woolbright was set upon by men who called him a 'roundheaded rogue & cryed out knocke him downe'; and Samuel Wilkinson witnessed James Sheringham shouting 'take them alive … theise roundheadly rouges & whores': NCR 12c/1, deposition 108, 29 April 1648; NCR 12c/1, deposition 46, 29 April 1648; NCR 12c/1, deposition 83, 9 May 1648.

[74] Hopper, 'Civil Wars', p. 108.

[75] BL, TT E438(6), Anon, *A true Relation Of the late great Mutinie Which was in the City of Norwich* (London, 1648), p. 3.

[76] John Rushworth, *Historical Collections of Private Passages of State, 1647–8*, Vol. VII (London, 1721), pp. 1071–2.

registers, a letter from Christopher Baret written on May 4 that year confirmed forty dead and many more injured, but a contemporary pamphlet, the *True Relation of the Late Great Mutinie*, suggests nearer two hundred people perished.[77] As people fled the scene in terror, in fear for their lives, or in fear of arrest, the nearby White Lion in Bethel Street (not the White Lion next to the King's Head at the centre of the affair), the Black Swan, and the Borrow's Head on Upper St Giles' Street were common ports of call, as evidenced in later depositions recalling the event, for the weary, frightened inhabitants. These drinking houses also followed a direct path from the scene of the explosion to the nearest gate out of the city.

John Utting and his fellow petitioner, the alderman and former mayor John Toly,[78] were arrested on suspicion of instigating the riot, their actions in creating the petition argued to have led directly to the gathering of a 'great concourse of people' which Utting 'knowing of was negligent to appease', referring to the fact that he purportedly blocked early efforts to raise the city's troops.[79] Christopher Baret duly took over as deputy mayor.[80] Utting was charged with permitting to 'elect unduly some persons in the place of aldermen ... countenancing malignant and sequestered ministers publickly to preach in the city' (referring back to Ashwell and Baret's original complaints), and creating a rabble-rousing petition.[81] For this Utting was fined the sum of five hundred pounds and committed to London's Fleet Prison for six months. Toly, as a co-conspirator, was fined one thousand pounds and spent three months in the Fleet. Nonetheless, the corporation officials escaped lightly in comparison to the rioters, eight of whom were hanged.[82]

The riot of 1648 was not a royalist riot. The history leading up to the events is too complex – the inability to reach a satisfactory religious compromise, economic unrest and resistance to taxation to name but two factors – and there were too many actors who sat on both sides (or neither) of the political fence. Toly and Alderman Matthew Lindsey, for example, were parliament-men, yet Toly was implicated in creating the petition that stirred so many inhabitants to arms and Lindsey in bribing men out with rounds of drinks. Utting himself of course was a mayor serving a city declared for parliament and there is little evidence to demonstrate that he was a secret

[77] Rye, *Bethel*, p. 96; Henry Cary, ed., *Memorials of the Great Civil War in England from 1646–52*, Vol. I (London, 1842), pp. 399–403; BL, TT E438(6), Anon, *A true Relation*, frontispiece.

[78] John Toly had been mayor in 1638 and 1644: Cozens-Hardy and Kent, *Mayors of Norwich*, p. 80.

[79] Rye, *Bethel*, p. 102; Evans, *Seventeenth-Century Norwich*, p. 175.

[80] Baret replaced Utting temporarily by order of the Commons on 18 April 1648 and led an investigation into the riot. Baret died the following year at the age of eighty-seven: T. Hawes, *An Index to Norwich City Officers 1453–1835* (Norwich, 1989), p. 13; Cozens-Hardy and Kent, *Mayors of Norwich*, p. 79.

[81] Rye, *Bethel*, p. 102.

[82] Ibid., p. 104; Cozens-Hardy and Kent, *Mayors of Norwich*, p. 80.

royalist. The petition was created to support Mayor Utting as the rightful, elected head of the corporation and to defend Norwich's ancient rights as an incorporated city from central interference, something that inhabitants from all areas of the political and religious spectrum could empathise with. However, once created, it was seen as a rallying point for the royalist cause and, given the tension that the city was then under from religious and political avenues, it is no wonder that the petition was tinder to the flame. Certainly, it is even possible that the King's Head, the Angel, and the White Lion may have been part of the royalist tavern-based network alluded to by Clive Holmes. Likewise the subsequent investigation into the riot was led by acting mayor Christopher Baret who, supported by parliament, his son Thomas and sheriff Thomas Ashwell, undertook to purge the corporation of anyone suspected of royalist sympathies. Nevertheless, the purge could also be read as the culmination of the efforts by the city's godly, of whom the three men above were key figures, to attain a majority within the twenty-four, thus enabling them to further their agenda of religious reforms.[83]

The events of that fateful weekend in April 1648 hung on the network of city centre drinking houses, their middling sort clientele and possible links to royalism. The White Lion, the King's Head and the Angel of St Peter Mancroft were at the centre of the intrigue and the Black Bull at the Tombland end of Magdalen Street and the Popinjay in Tombland were rallying points for the mob. It has been suggested by the scholars who have researched Norwich's social topography in some depth that St Peter Mancroft was at the geographical heart of royalism in the city. This assumption is based largely on evidence from the voluntary contributions for the Newcastle subscription of 1643, where it is fairly clear that the largest number of refusals to pay came from that parish. Given that this was one of the wealthiest parishes with the highest concentration of mayors and aldermen, for that period the fact that only seven people contributed is perhaps surprising.[84] Interestingly St Giles – the destination of many of the fleeing rioters, as mentioned above – has, by the same marker, been judged to have been an anti-parliamentarian area as well. How far subscription to the Newcastle rate can be considered conclusive evidence of royalism however is debatable.

Nevertheless, there is other evidence in the depositions that might link the riot to a royalist agenda (though it should not be considered a royalist riot) as well as middling support for the same. The aforementioned barber Richard Haddon, for example, told how he had heard 'certain gentlemen' in the White Lion Inn discussing publically how 'they wo[u]ld stand by' Utting.

---

[83] For more on this see Evans, *Seventeenth-Century Norwich*, Ch. 4–5; M. Reynolds, *Godly Reformers and their Opponents in Early Modern England: Religion in Norwich c. 1560–1643* (Woodbridge, 2005), esp. Ch. 11.

[84] F. R. Beecheno, 'The Norwich Subscription for the Regaining of Newcastle', NA, xviii (1914), pp. 149–60, cited in Hopper, 'Civil Wars', p. 100; Evans, *Seventeenth-Century Norwich*, pp. 132–4; Jones, *Social Geography*, pp. 198–9 and Fig. 11.7.

Cooke had refused to believe the men 'that dare speake such words' could have been gentlemen, but Haddon insisted that 'they wer[e] men of quality who said they had lost nere two parts of their estate & wo[u]ld now win the horse or loose the sadle'.[85] Presumably the unnamed gentlemen in question had been victims of Norwich's sequestration committee, of which body Thomas Baret was the treasurer for Norfolk.[86] The speakers were not the 'rude' people Cooke had first imagined for 'Mr Toly and Watts were with them, and ... Sheringham had collected funds for them'.[87] Nicholas Dawes' testimony also suggested that the men behind the riot had either had their estates threatened by sequestration, or feared the possibility of such, stating 'ther[e] wer[e] Comittee men who had sayde to the people doe you the work as for us we have estates to loose you have none & we will assist you'.[88] George Woolbright informed that Thomas Barker had been heard to say at the King's Head that among the mutinous company were freemen who were bound 'by the[i]r oathes to keep the mayor within the Citty duringe his year' and when questioned on his assertation by the said Woolbright 'fell into a rage' and called him 'roundheaded rogue'.[89]

Other well-to-do men were also involved. Thomas Palgrave, a merchant and friend of the Norfolk landowner Sir John Potts, for example had been seen buying drinks to encourage people to support Utting's cause,[90] and the watch reported how several 'gentlemen' had bought rounds at the Angel on the understanding that the recipients would obstruct the mayor's departure from Norwich. One of the men linked to the purchase of beer bribes at

85 NCR 12c/1, deposition 94.

86 Loose pages from the minute book of the [? county] sequestration committee, NCR 10h 21/2, 19 February–12 August 1648.

87 NCR 12c/1, deposition 94a, 6 May 1648. Henry Watts had been sheriff in 1639 and mayor in 1646: Cozens-Hardy and Kent, *Mayors of Norwich*, p. 83. Sheringham was James Sheringham, butcher, who had previously been arrested (and later rescued) for his leading role in Norwich's Excise Riots in 1646. He had also been heard crying out against roundheads during the riots. Sheringham was a freeman (he served his apprenticeship under his father between 1628 and 1635) and rented the first stall on the east row of the city butchery for three pounds per annum. See Millican, *Register of the Freemen*, p. 240; Chamberlain's Accounts, 1648–1663, NCR Case 18a, fol. 257v, 25 March 1661–1662. Andrew Hopper suggests that Sheringham was instrumental in collecting signatures for Utting's petition and Walter Rye noted his involvement as well: Hopper, 'Civil Wars', p. 109; Rye, *Bethel*, p. 86. Sheringham was convicted after the Great Blow but escaped with only a fine: NCR 18d, 1646–1733, fol. 4r, 18 December 1648. Evans places Toly firmly into the parliamentarian bracket: Evans, *Norwich*, p. 159.

88 NCR 12c/1, deposition 36.

89 NCR 12c/1, deposition 46.

90 Hopper, 'Civil Wars', p. 111. According to Clive Holmes, Sir John Potts worked extensively with Sir John Holland during the 1640s to prevent Norfolk from being torn apart by factionalism in the wake of the Commission of the Array and the Militia Ordinance and Propositions. It is because of this connection that Potts was mistakenly assumed to have been a royalist by the antiquarian Walter Rye: Holmes, *Eastern Association*, pp. 56–60.

the Angel had been Leonard Spurgeon, a mercer. Spurgeon had apparently charged his pistol to inspire the twenty or so men then at the inn and had stayed with them until all the rounds had been finished at around midnight, informing them that there would be a call to arms at eight the following morning.[91] Doctor Brooke and Christopher Bransby – the latter described as alderman Matthew Lindsey's man – had also met at the Angel.[92] Bransby then left for the White Lion where he argued to all who would listen 'that if they suffered the mayor to be carried away, they would have a governour put in (as was done at Lyn) and then all would be tried by martial law; and ... freemen would have no freedom at all in any choice'.[93] Bransby's fellow drinking companions would have recalled with fear King's Lynn's three-week siege when, after declaring for the royalists in 1643, they were beset by forces commanded by Edward Montagu, Earl of Manchester. To avoid bloodshed Lynn's mayor had capitulated and the town effectively became a military garrison under the command of Colonel Valentine Walton.[94]

The White Lion, only a few yards away from the Angel, commanded a view of the market square and the comings and goings from the other nearby inns. It was here that 'men of quality'[95] had also conspired to rouse Norwich's inhabitants with alcohol and provocative speeches and to lock the city's gates against troops. Some inn employees were also complicit. William Blackamoore, the White Lion's tapster, for example was heard using 'any motive or speech to stir up the people against the Tro[o]pe that wer[e] come into Norwich to stand upon the[i]r g[u]ard & shew them selves men'.[96] Certainly, it is very likely that the events of that weekend could not have been so successful without support from the innkeepers themselves. Late-night drinking, rounds of drinks being purchased, and overtly political meetings could not have gone unnoticed or unsanctioned by the owners, or at least the tapsters working that night.

Evidence, erroneous or otherwise, was also presented about Utting's part in steering events but Utting, as we know, had been based at the King's Head for most of the weekend with the messenger from London. Mary Fordham however deposed that she had seen Utting at Gooch's shop asking a man to find some muskets, and when he could not Utting 'bade him go and re-solve the people'.[97] James Sheringham likewise told his interrogators that the

---

91 NCR 12c/1, deposition 274.

92 Rye, *Bethel*, p. 87. Evans describes Lindsey as a parliamentarian: Evans, *Norwich*, p. 139.

93 Perhaps a nod to Norwich's deep seated and unresolved relationship with the selection versus election principle: Blomefield, *Topographical History*, III:I, p. 394.

94 For more on King's Lynn during the civil wars, see Susan Yaxley, ed., *The Siege of King's Lynn, 1643* (Dereham, 1993) and BL, TT E67, 28, *A briefe and true Relation of the Seige and Surrendering of King's Lyn*, 20 September 1643.

95 NCR 12c/1, deposition 93 & 94, 6 May 1648.

96 NCR 12c/1, deposition 98, 6 May 1648.

97 NCR 12c/1, deposition 95, 6 May 1648.

petition had come straight from the hand of Mayor Utting.[98] Others were more inclined to defend the mayor. John Graye testified, for example, that 'ther[e] beinge a great company of people before the Maiors dore a mayde of his came out & told them that her maister gave them many thancks for the[i]r care & love & desired them to goe whome'.[99]

The White Lion, the Angel and the King's Head were at the heart of the events of Great Blow, but the episode also shows that many other drinking houses operated as part of a wide social network, fulfilling an important role as nodal points through which information was filtered. John Cornelius, for example, a trooper in Colonel Fleetwood's company, swore that he had seen Robert Clarke, a barber, coming out of the White Horse near Tombland market, shouting 'downe w[i]th this rounde headed rogue he will have no kinge'.[100] Upset by his words Cornelius, who had been on horseback, 'did violently rise upon [Clarke] & made a thrust att him' before being overpowered by two of Clarke's companions, who, rushing out of the inn, violently forced Cornelius to the ground.[101] It seems that this incident was not to be the end of Cornelius' troubles that day: he also described how he had been chased by a butcher armed with a large club, who 'fell on him and beat him very much, and would have killed him had not relief came to him'.[102] Likewise, the foot soldier John Allen told the investigating officials how, being off duty on the Sunday evening, he had visited the Three Fishes and the Popinjay and watched the trouble brewing at first hand.[103] Christopher Bransby had also been seen at the Popinjay, from where he had collected a pistol before heading over to the White Lion and the Angel.[104]

An overwhelming feature of all these depositions was the prominence of drinking houses in inhabitants' conceptualisation of their city and in the construction of their spatial memory. For example, witness Christopher Hill had spent two pence at Edward Lodse's drinking house before then 'hearinge of the Company att Mr Ashewells ... [Hill] did not goe home but went to Mr Ashwells where he mett with Thomas Lee att St Michaells at plea churchyard stile wher he continued untill the Arms were cast out of Mr Ashewells window, & then he went from there ... to Edward Eades [drinking house] ...

---

98 NCR 12c/1, deposition 90, 5 May 1648.
99 NCR 12c/1, deposition 66, 4 May 1648.
100 In 1624 the White Horse at Tombland had been at the centre of a controversy concerning the Princess Elizabeth's stage players and the Puritan mayor Robert Craske. The case centred on the suitability of the establishment as a playhouse as well as the players' assumption that they could circumvent the corporation's authority in gaining a licence to perform: NCR 16a/15, fol. 525v, 26 April 1624 and NCR 16a/16, fol. 12v, 25 September 1624. This case is considered in some detail in Glynne Wickam, William Ingram and Herbert Berry, eds, *English Professional Theatre 1530–1660* (Cambridge, 2000), pp. 255–6.
101 NCR 16a/47/1, 25 April 1648. The Information of John Cornelius.
102 NCR 12c/1, deposition 114, 4 May 1648.
103 NCR 12c/1, deposition 1, 27 April 1648.
104 Rye, *Bethel*, p. 89. Bransby had spent the night in lodgings at the Angel.

wher[e] he tarryed untill ne[a]re fower of the clocke'.[105] Likewise, Edward
Marshall described how on leaving 'Mr Whinotts [drinking house] … he
came through the markett [and] did se[e] a great company ther … & after
goeing from Whinott to Sunderlands he did se[e] a great company before
Parmenters wher[e] he stood by the shomaker beyond the blew bell & stayed
ther[e] … after the company was gone … he came home from Sunderlands by
the white hart'.[106] Similarly, Mary Burman noted that she was by the Maid's
Head when William Racker asked her whether the 'Roundheads wheel
should turne round this day',[107] and Edward Damme was at the back gate
of the Black Swan when he heard the explosion at the Committee House.[108]
Drinkers at the Castle, on the southern side of the marketplace near the
swine market, were also arrested for their part in the riot.[109] The witnesses'
words vividly detail the mental map that inhabitants used to describe, navigate and think about their city.

The events of the first half of the seventeenth century and the civil war period point to the centrality of drinking houses in the city's political landscape.
However it is clear that a simple equation between drinking houses and political activity does not suffice to explain the link or the relationship. The inns
of the St Peter Mancroft and Tombland area feature far more prominently in
Norwich's political history than drinking haunts in other areas. So, how can
we better understand the situation in Norwich? There are several general
connections that can be made, as well as some specific to the city's own set of
political circumstances and actors.

First must be the connection between drinking houses and civic life. The
places most linked to political activities were some of the busiest and in some
of the areas most likely visited by travellers. They were also mainly inns,
as opposed to taverns or alehouses, visited by the better sorts and freemen,
many of whom had links to the corporation, perhaps as officers themselves.
The Castle and the King's Head, for example, were patronised by mayors,
aldermen and chief inhabitants, and were the location for the meetings of
Norwich's Workhouse Committee, City Committee, Town Close Committee, Hellesdon Bridge Committee, and numerous other bodies set up to look
into particular aspects of civic business.[110] In 1668, for example, 'The dinner
upon Monday senight being the day for perambulatinge the bounds of [th]e
city shall be at [th]e kings Heade in [th]e markett'; a meal that would have

---

[105] NCR 12c/1, deposition 118, 3 May 1648.

[106] NCR 12c/1, deposition 4, 27 April 1648.

[107] Rye, *Bethel*, p. 125.

[108] NCR 12c/1, deposition 146, 26 April 1648. The Black Swan was located in the parish
of St Peter Mancroft. It was mentioned in the city chamberlain's accounts for 1631: NCR
18b/1, 1700–1.

[109] Rye, *Bethel*, p. 114.

[110] Many of the committees meticulous accounts survive: NCR 18b/1–20 for the late
seventeenth and early eighteenth century.

only included the city's great and good.[111] This is not to denigrate the political awareness or involvement of non-citizens, indeed the Excise Riots or the Great Blow could never have happened without their tacit involvement, but it does suggest that, in Norwich at least, some of the larger political happenings required the involvement of a wide variety of social actors to escalate. During the 1627 election controversy for example, the city's freemen voters were very specifically involved, though Kettle had a wide social support base who aided him during his campaign and mustered support on election day.[112]

The inns may also stand out because they were more likely to have operated as staging posts for the city's post and printed news. Norwich's postal service had been set up in 1568,[113] rather ironically financed by a tax levied on unlicensed alehouse keepers and tipplers.[114] At a time before house numbers, the best way to receive post was via a locally recognised landmark; inns were perfect for this because they had the capacity to receive and hold a communication until the rightful recipient could spare the time to collect it. Likewise, the trade in pamphlets, news sheets, and ballads operated via the same network – on some occasions a bookseller and a drinking establishment were even one and the same. In Norwich, the Half Moon Inn, next door to the King's Head at the marketplace in St Peter Mancroft, fulfilled this dual function. The inn had a tradition of renting space to booksellers; during the seventeenth century records reveal that Edward Martin, bookseller and printer, lived here with his journeyman Robert Bartlett until their deaths in 1653 and 1654 respectively. Martin's many publications included *An Hue-and-Cry after Vox Populi, or an Answer to Vox Diaboli*, the polemical response to the anonymous 'publick remonstrance', *Vox Populi, or the Voice of the People* in 1646. *Vox Populi*, described as 'a libellous pamphlet … reviling the Magistrates and Ministry of Norwich', had been published after an announcement on 25 December 1646 had advertised the cancellation of the following day's religious services and the public holiday. After Martin died, William Franklin purchased the shop for £300 and carried on the trade until his own death in 1664. Interestingly, before he moved to the Half Moon, Franklin had also been involved in the 1640s pamphlet 'war', publishing *Vox Norwici* in 1646 from his newly established shop in the marketplace not far from the Half Moon. Franklin also served on a corporation committee to

---

111   NCR, 16a/24, fol. 70v, 13 May 1668.

112   As well as some of the county's elite, including Sir Charles Cornwallis, Kettle's supporters counted in their number men described by the corporation and Privy Council as 'forrainers and strangers' and 'mechanicall men' of the 'meanest quality'. These helped promote Kettle during a short campaign and also flocked to the hall on election day: NA, SP 16/79, fol. 38, 27 September 1627; NA, SP 16/78, fol. 53, 18 December 1627.

113   Blomefield, *Topographical History*, III:I, p. 294; Anon, *A compleat history of the famous city of Norwich: From the Earliest Account, to this Present Year 1728* (1728), p. 38. The latter lists the city's post collection points.

114   Blomefield, *Topographical History*, III:I, p. 294.

enquire into the state of the city's postal service.[115] Other booksellers who operated from inns included Edmund Casson at the sign of the Bible from 1613 until 1635, Christopher Ponder at the Angel from 1615 to 1624, and William Pinder at the Crown from 1665 to 1689, all of whom were located in the marketplace of St Peter Mancroft. Close by in the parish of St Andrew were Samuel Oliver at the Bible, Cockey Lane, which led into the marketplace, from 1695 and Samuel Selfe from the Bible and Crown, also on Cockey Lane, from 1700.[116]

The significance of this was not only that the inns were some of the first points in the city to receive communications about political affairs and current events, but that they were also places from where news and printed publications were being distributed, as well as recognised social spaces where this news was being read and discussed. Thus, although news would be discussed in most alehouses and taverns (and later coffee houses), some of the city's inns were more intimately connected with the rapid dissemination of news than their counterparts. Indeed, given the prominence of certain inns in the examples used in this chapter so far, it is noteworthy that the Maid's Head, the King's Head, and the Unicorn were all beneficiaries of the post and there is a definite concentration of booksellers in and around the marketplace (both within or near the inns) and adjacent streets in St Peter Mancroft, St Andrew and St John Maddermarket.[117]

A second reason to connect drinking houses with political activities more generally is a simple one: alcohol loosened the tongue and might help fire people to a cause, something that can be clearly witnessed taking place on Sunday 23 April 1648. Over the course of the century there were many other instances where drinking establishments came under scrutiny from the authorities and where we can see good reason for the official preoccupation with intemperance, seditious speech, and the regulation of drinking houses.[118] John Assand, for example, discovered this to his cost after witnesses reported how he had drunk 'A helth to the divell and damnacon & all that wold pledge him' at the Castle Inn in 1612.[119] Worse still was the example of Thomas and John Woodhouse, the sons of Sir Henry Woodhouse, who

---

[115] David Stoker, 'The Norwich Book Trades Before 1800', *Transactions of the Cambridge Bibliographical Society*, VIII (1981), 79–125; Blomefield, *Topographical History*, III:I, p. 392; John Chambers, ed., *A General History of the County of Norfolk* (1829), p. 1286.

[116] Stoker, 'Norwich Book Trades', 79–125.

[117] For the complete list of known booksellers and their addresses, see Stoker, 'Norwich Book Trades', 79–125.

[118] Much scholarly attention has been devoted to exploring alehouses as 'sequestered social sites' in which the 'hidden transcripts' of disgruntled labouring men were enacted, quoted in J. C. Scott, *Domination and the Arts of Resistance: Hidden Transcripts* (New Haven, 1990), pp. 15–22. Works influenced by Scott's interpretation include Wood, '"Poore men woll speke one daye"', esp. p. 91; Walter, 'Public Transcripts', 128, 139–40; Fox, 'Ballads, Libels and Popular Ridicule'.

[119] NCR 16a/14, fol. 385v, 27 February 1612.

were arrested in Norwich after a night's heavy drinking had turned into a violent street brawl in 1621. Apparently the pair had, amongst other drunken speeches, threatened to kill the King. They were imprisoned and news of the affair was sent to Thomas Howard, Earl Marshall Arundel. Luckily for the Woodhouse family, John and Thomas were released on the grounds that 'they were so overcome with drink as hardly to be able to stand, and remembered little of what passed', following a line of reasoning that drunkenness was akin to temporary insanity.[120] Instances of seditious speech punctuated the court records over the entire century, especially at times of political change. In 1689 for example, after drinking for six hours at Barnard Skinner's alehouse in St. Stephen, John Scrimpson had announced that the King 'was the sone of a whore' during a toast,[121] and at Fowler's alehouse the landlord 'drank a health to James the third, wishing the Crowne well settled on his head' in 1704.[122]

The connection between alcohol and intemperate behaviour was recognised by moralists as well as by the government.[123] Richard Allstree, for example, fretted as to why on the Sabbath people were more often to be found in the pub than in church. 'But this Rest' he argued 'was commanded … to give us time to attend the service of God and the need of our souls'.[124] Through the cautionary tales of characters like Poor Jack Had-Lands, who whittled away his income and estate on alcohol,[125] or the drunkard who 'casts his mony into a deluge of drink, both drowning it and himself with it', moralists and satirists proclaimed the evils of excessive drinking and hoped to educate the populace.[126] As Thomas Adams warned, the Devil found men though drink:

> In a moderate, temperate *dry* braine, he findes no footing: but in the soule of the swilling drunkard, as a foggy and fenny ground, hee obtaines some residence. Abstemious moderation, and temperate satisfaction of nature is too dry a place, for so

---

120   Mayor and Aldermen of Norwich to Earl Marshall Arundel, 26 September 1621, NA, SP, Dom., James I, 122, no. 145-145i.

121   NCR 12b/1, 4 November 1689. The information of Zachariah Mulyew (loose papers).

122   Cited in Knights, 'Politics', pp. 171–2.

123   The contemporary connection between drinking cultures and political sedition is noted in: Anon, *A curse against Parliament-ale. With a blessing to the juncto; A thanksgiving to the councel of state; and psalm to Oliver* (London, 1649); Anon, *Oxford in mourning, for the loss of the Parliament* (London, 1681); and Anon, *The pot companions: Or, Drinking and smoaking preferr'd before caballing and plotting* (London, 1682).

124   Richard Allestree, *The whole duty of man* (London, 1659), p. 48.

125   Anon, *Jack Had-Lands lamentation* (London, 1685–1688).

126   Richard Younge, *The prevention of poverty, together with the cure of melancholy, alias discontent* (London, 1655), p. 15. See also: Anon, *The Drunkards Character* (London, 1646); R. Burton, *A Looking Glass for Drunkards: Or, The Good-Fellows Folly* (London, 1660); J. Hart, *The Dreadful Character of a Drunkard* (London, 1686); or M. Killiray, *The swearer and the drunkard, two brethren in iniquity, arraigned at the bar, or, A charge drawn up against those two great sins of these nations, swearing and drunkenness* (London, 1673).

hot a *spirit* as hell fire hath made him, to quench his malicious thirst: but in those that are *filled with wine, & strong drinkes, suauiter, molliter acquiescit.*[127]

Alcohol was of course a motivating factor for many seemingly spontaneous outbursts that were treated as seditious speech but this does not explain the preponderance of organised meetings at drinking spots, especially inns. A third reason then for this correlation is largely a practical one. Inns were one of the few public places large enough to have rooms available for private or semi-private meetings at that time. Drinking houses of all forms were liminal spaces, neither entirely public, nor entirely private, a paradox that patrons could bend to their needs, disguising potentially subversive conversations under the cover of drink and conviviality. Indeed, although drinking houses were open to legislation and surveillance, a private booth or a sympathetic landlord might go some way to abrogating these constraints.[128] The larger inns however, could host more private political meetings, and the better off patrons could afford the hire.

Policing drinking houses ostensibly relied on staff or customers reporting private conversations. In 1689, for example, Edmond Nockalls had called Phillip Stebbing 'a pitiful rogue' at the sign of the Fleur De Lys in St Julian's parish. Stebbing was a former city sheriff and mayor who had been a leading Tory integrally embroiled in the anti-Whig politicking that had been a key feature of the 1680s. On the day he was slandered he had been riding in support of Robert Davy's election for city recorder. Nockall's opprobrious words might have gone unpunished were it not for the civic-minded John Mard and Phillip Barthe, who reported Nockalls to the watch.[129] Likewise, in the September of that same year, Robert Poynter fell foul of his drinking companions at Mr Crome's drinking house in St Gregory's parish. As William Symonds and Joseph Smith had raised a toast to King William's health, Poynter countered with his opinion that 'King William was none of the kings of England but a Deputy and fitt for no better and that he did nott question but once in a moneths time to see a hundred such rogues as [Smith] should be hanged for speaking against King James'.[130] Later, when the conversation had turned to a relieved discussion of how 'Ireland was in a great measure reduced', referring to the ongoing Jacobite insurgency, Poynter had added 'that eare long there would goe a great many men over to Ireland as was there before, And that the

---

[127] Thomas Adams, *The blacke devil or the apostate Together with the wolfe worrying the lambes* (London, 1615), p. 30.

[128] For more on the legislative framework see Judith Hunter, 'English Inns, Taverns, Alehouses and Brandy Shops: The Legislative Framework, 1495–1797', *World of the Tavern*, ed. Kümin and Tlusty, pp. 65–82.

[129] NCR 12a-b, 5 March 1689. The information of John Mard and Phillip Barthe against Edmond Nockalls. Evans, *Seventeenth-Century Norwich*, pp. 287, 297; Hawes, *Norwich City Officers*, pp. xxxvii, 145.

[130] NCR 12a-b, 7 September 1689. The information of Joseph Smith of St Julian's parish in the city, labourer, taken upon oath.

late King James would come againe in halfe a years time or less & cause many to suffer here for what is already done … King William was but an elective King and not hereditary'.[131]

Relying on inhabitants to present their friends and colleagues had many drawbacks, however, not least the inability to know how many seditious conversations or activities were going on unreported. The combination of public access and private conversations presented numerous difficulties that were reflected in the authorities' style and direction of drinking house legislation. The first step on this path was to make the comings and goings of customers more obvious. For example, keepers were expected to 'deliver the Names of all unknown Passengers that lodge in their Houses; and if they stay suspiciously at any Time, to present them to the Governour: whereby dangerous Persons seeing these strict Courses, will be more wary of their Actions, and thereby mischievous Attempts will be prevented', a piece of legislation specifically engineered with strangers and travellers in mind.[132] Another solution was to discourage customers from using a back door by enforcing the hanging of a sign at the front door, highlighting the entrance.[133] It had been the law for all drinking houses to use a sign, with the purpose of distinguishing such places from domestic property, since at least the fourteenth century, but it was hoped that a front-facing sign would discourage people from stealing in and out, an act associated with criminal intent.[134]

The corporation were active in enforcing state policy on drinking establishments and also added to existing legislation with additional by-laws to help monitor what took place within a drinking house's four walls. In 1633, for example, the corporation ordered all ward constables to visit inns and alehouses during the time of morning and evening prayers, to take down the names of all brewers supplying beer during these hours and all customers found partaking in it.[135] During the heightened anxieties of the civil wars, ward constables were authorised to make 'searches for such Apprentices or other Servants in Taverns, Ale-houses, or Gaming-houses, and such Apprentices or other Servants as shall be found in any such place after eight of the

---

[131] NCR 12a-b, 12 September 1689. The information of William Symonds of St Gyles, grocer, taken upon oath. This is not the same William Symonds who had been alderman during the civil war period, see fn. 57. Alderman Symonds had died in 1654: NA, PROB 11/239/629.

[132] John Rushworth, *Historical Collections of Private Passages of State, 1618–29*, I (London, 1721), pp. 17–21.

[133] For more on this topic see Catherine Dent, 'The Function of Inn Signs and their Place in Early Modern British History', *Reinvention: a Journal of Undergraduate Research* 4:1 (2011); Eric Delderfield, *Introduction to Inn Signs* (Newton Abbot, 1969).

[134] In 1690 for example, Richard Smith was considered a man of ill-repute because he allowed the back door of his drinking house to be used by beggars and 'such sort of people who make it their business to goe up & downe all day and goe their againe att night': DN/ DEP/52/56 & 57, 1687–1691, fol. 1r. Thomas Browne v. Mary Tarnell, 2 April 1690.

[135] Sachse, *Minutes 1632–1635*, p. 93. Order passed by the court Monday 12 August 1633.

clock in the evening, or being drunk, or otherwise disorderly, or shall there remain after eight of the clock in the evening on such day of Recreation' and to bring them to justice.[136]

The idea that drinking houses might be associated with subversive intentions continued throughout the century.[137] Even after the Restoration, when political clubs gradually became normalised within drinking-house culture, they were still viewed with great suspicion. In 1662, for example, Charles II decreed that 'No one not well affected to government is to be allowed to keep an alehouse or victualling house',[138] and in 1680 Norwich's magistrates agreed to 'send to anie publique house or coffee house or book seller for such news as they have lately and doe for [th]e future receive from London & upon p[er]usal of such as they have already and shall have ... to c[o]llect therof w[hi]ch they apprehend to be false or dangerous to [th]e disturbance of ye peace of the Kingdome'.[139]

In practice, monitoring what took place in semi-private space was a difficult task. In 1628, for example, when servant William Jary was caught sampling the pleasures of an alehouse in Pockthorpe rather than turning up for work, he 'utterly refused to goe w[i]th the constable' sent to fetch him away. Clement Atwood, the constable in question, appealed to the staff to help him remove Jary, but had the door shut in his face by a maidservant.[140] The problem was even more acute when the numbers of revellers outweighed the numbers of the watchmen. This was the case in 1633, when William Steward of the night watch had discovered 'p[er]sons ... drinkeinge and disordering themselves' long after midnight in the Green Dragon on Bishopgate. Steward had ordered the drinkers 'to goe to bedd' so they would be fit for work on the following morning but the merrymakers ignored him. One of their number, Robert Sheringham, told the watch that they 'were fooles' to tell them what to do. The landlord was no more sympathetic, probably because he knew that although he was contravening the law, the watch lacked the power to enforce it at that particular moment in time.[141] The following year, Steward encountered a similar stumbling block. He had caught John Tillersley entertaining five friends with beer purchased from an unlicensed brewer: Tillersley's brother James. When Steward tried to tell John Tillersley that he could be arrested, Tillersley insolently replied 'that he cared not [i]

---

136 An *Ordinance concerning days of Recreation allowed unto Scholars, Apprentizes and other Servants*, June 1647: C. H. Firth, *Acts and Ordinances of the Interregnum, 1642–1660* (1911), pp. 985–6.

137 Clark, 'Politics, Clubs and Social Spaces', pp. 81- 94, 82.

138 M. A. Everett Green, ed., *CSPD*, Charles II, 1661–2 (London, 1861), no. 25, 6 June 1662. The order was motivated by Quaker and Fifth-Monarchist meetings in London but applied nationally.

139 NCR 16a/24, fol. 65r, 7 April 1680.

140 NCR 16a/16, fol. 229r, 4 February 1628.

141 NCR 20a/10, fol. 36v, 25 July 1633.

f [Steward] fetched all the maiors warrants in the towne', he would not send his friends home.[142]

The reasons mentioned above make a compelling case for the association of drinking houses, especially inns, with Norwich's provincial politics. Nevertheless, the question of why some houses and not others were more often the setting for political meetings, or other such activities, remains to be fully addressed. The answer lies in unique factors, including location, clientele, and reputation. The King's Head, the White Lion, the Angel and the Maid's Head are good examples here. At the Maid's Head, for example, men like Robert Gawdy or John Kettle might expect a receptive crowd because of their local knowledge of the type of people who drank there: their social class and, possibly, political leanings. In the early part of the century a network clearly existed that was sympathetic to the principle of freemen's electoral privileges in city and county elections, over pre-determined selections. Although we do not have concrete evidence, we can assume that many from this network drank at this establishment, given its proximity to the major thoroughfares, centrality to the city centre, proximity to the cathedral, and incidental references to likeminded corporation officials drinking at this establishment. These men included Sir Thomas Hyrne (who had provided support for Kettle), Richard Rosse and Lionel Claxton, who had all stood opposed to changes to the freemen's electoral privileges. That these men formed part of a network or faction is evident from those who stood in opposition, including Thomas Atkin (John Kettle's rival in the 1627 election) and other corporation officials including Robert Craske, Thomas Shipdham, Christopher Baret (the ex-mayor who took over from John Utting in 1648), George Birch, Thomas Cory[143] and Augustine Scottowe.

We also find factionalism in Norwich polarising under religious banners during the 1640s as the radical Puritans, under the leadership of Thomas Ashwell and Thomas and Christopher Baret, manoeuvred to remove corporation opponents to radical religious reform under the guise of attacking royalism. In this latter instance it was networks operating from the Angel, the White Lion and the King's Head at the marketplace that provided the geographical focus for that decade's politicking, showing how certain drinking houses remained popular for certain groups.

In the early part of the seventeenth century, the inns that were associated with politics were those frequented by the better sorts generally, often corporation men and freemen, although it is hard to pinpoint any formal clubs or associations. In the latter part of the century this began to change however, as politics became dominated by rivalries between Tories and Whigs. As Mark Knights explains, the White Horse at Tombland became the regular

---

[142] NCR 20a/10, fol. 53v, 8 December 1634.
[143] Cory had his estate sequestered by parliament's sequestrations committee for Norfolk. He later applied his case for compounding in December 1644: M. A. Everett, *Calendar, Committee for Compounding: Part 2* (1890), p. 874.

haunt of the Society of True Protestant Britons, the anti-Gallican Association, and the Brethren of True Blues.[144] The White Horse was also the customary meeting place for current and ex-members of parliament including Horatio Townshend and Sir John Holland, especially during the period of the Exclusion Crisis.[145] Other places that had barely featured in the early seventeenth century's political landscape became far more prominent as the century progressed. The Blue Bell (later the Bell), situated south of Norwich Castle in St John Timberhill, and a regular meeting place for the City Committee, was taken over by a Tory landlord sympathetic to the Jacobite cause. In the eighteenth century, the Bell became synonymous with the Hell Fire Club.[146] There is much in the picture outlined above to make a generalised connection with St Peter Mancroft, St Andrew, and St John Timberhill with a royalist and, later, Tory agenda. In contrast, some scholars have argued that the area known as 'over the water', especially the southernmost parishes of Coslany, Colegate, and Fye Bridge wards, was aligned with a more sectarian, puritanical and Whiggish politics, though we should take care not to overlook the complex realities of allegiance and ideologies and creating a picture of a divided city.[147]

To summarise, the drinking houses most associated with political activities and events, certainly those that most often occurred in the records, can thus be located in and around the marketplaces of St Peter Mancroft, Tombland in St Andrew and St John Timberhill. They were places more often associated with a Presbyterian and conservative political agenda, the classification of an established inn (as opposed to tavern or alehouse), a middling sort clientele with links to the corporation, and proximity to printers and booksellers, some of which had been known to print political pamphlets. The main places were the Maid's Head Inn and, to a lesser extent, the Popinjay and the White Horse Inn at Tombland, and the King's Head, the Angel and the White Lion on the eastern side of the main market, the Castle Inn and the Blue Bell moving toward Timberhill. The best answer then to the question of why some drinking establishments became part of the political landscape when others

---

144   Knights, 'Politics', p. 181.

145   Townshend Family Papers, Letters to Sir Horatio, 1st Viscount Townshend, Sir John Holland, Quidenham, MC 1601/26, 7 July 1682. Sir John Holland of Quidenham writes to Horatio Townshend suggesting that if there is the customary meeting at the White Horse, Townshend could vindicate himself against aspersions that he does not support the opposition.

146   Knights, 'Politics', p. 181. For further reading on eighteenth-century political clubs in Norwich see N. Rogers, 'Popular Jacobitism in Provincial Context: Eighteenth Century Bristol and Norwich', *The Jacobite Challenge*, ed. E. Cruickshanks and J. Black (Edinburgh, 1988), pp. 123–41 and K. Wilson, *The Sense of the People: Politics, Culture and Imperialism in England 1715–1785* (Oxford, 1995).

147   Mark Knights, 'London Petitions and Parliamentary Politics in 1679', *Parliamentary History* 12:1 (1993), 29–46, 41–2; Mark Knights, 'London's "Monster" Petition of 1680', *Historical Journal* 36:1 (1993), 39–67, 61–3; Knights, Politics, p. 170.

did not, is that it was the social networks and interests of the patrons that inspired politicking within their walls.

That the connection of drinking houses and politics was conceived of as a problem was, somewhat ironically, also addressed by the corporation officials. Despite the best efforts of the moralists, magistrates, and constables to suppress this culture of politics and drink, Norwich's drinking houses flourished.[148] Indeed, the magistrates complained that although there had 'bene greate paynes ... to reduce the Alehowses in this City to a small number' they were unable to cope with the 'multitudes' of new houses opening without licence, whose owners 'convert dwellinge howses to Innes and take liberty to erect & hange out signes'.[149] By 1702 some two hundred and eighty-one alehouses probably existed in Norwich: a ratio of one for every one hundred inhabitants.[150] Arguably, attempts at suppression – or at the very least control – could be seen as a failure, as by the end of the century the connection between drinking houses and politics was even more deeply entrenched than it ever had been. The formalisation of loose political groupings into established clubs and societies that operated from urban drinking houses had become a normalised, if not always sanctioned, part of contemporary political culture, crucial to the emerging party politics of the later seventeenth and early eighteenth centuries.

Market Politics

The parishes where some of Norwich's most notoriously political drinking houses were situated were also connected with another important place hitherto only mentioned in passing: the market. Yet its connection with the landscape of drink and its own place in Norwich's political landscape should not be underestimated. Norwich had several specialist markets but the largest concentration could be found at the ancient market plain of Tombland (where also could be found the Maid's Head, the Popinjay and the White Horse inns) and the central market of St Peter Mancroft (home to the King's Head, the White Lion and the Angel inns). Tombland marked the confluence of two major roads that linked the northern and southernmost parts of the city across the river at Fye Bridge. The cathedral walls formed the market's easternmost boundary; thus the ancient building formed a magnificent

---

148 During the seventeenth-century new statutes in 1609, 1625, and 1627 largely built on, or reconfirmed, the principles as set out in the 1551 Licensing Act. The 1627 statute, for example, specifically referred to the 1551 Act, giving 'Reasons why the said Statute has not wrought the Reformation intended'. The continual review and reissue of drinking-house licensing and regulatory acts certainly points towards their ineffectiveness.
149 NCR 16a/20, fol. 11v, 1634.
150 Cited in Knights, 'Politics', p. 180.

and awe-inspiring backdrop for the city's traders. Here could be found the city's fish market and every Maundy Thursday before Easter a special fair drew people from across the city and the county.[151] The marketplace in St Peter Mancroft was dominated by its namesake church on its southern edge and the Guildhall and courthouse to the north, and commanded a view of the castle that loomed over a row of inns and alehouses from the east. Here discerning customers could find anything from meat and dairy, herbs and seeds, or books and patterns and, on Saturdays, county traders were allowed to ply their wares. Both markets also had a market cross. The cross was the ancient symbol of the city's right to hold a market and thus it operated as a symbol of economic privilege and secular authority. Here people would gather to hear official proclamations or news, such as the announcement of Charles II's death in 1685 by 'the Mayor and Justices in scarlet with their cloaks, the sheriffs in Voylett' and 'the Aldermen in scarlet' at the cross in St Peter.[152]

Marketplaces were a convenient – and symbolic – place to accommodate civic events and popular entertainments. Every midsummer inhabitants would come to see the newly elected mayor arrive for his inauguration ceremony at the Guildhall and witness the grand procession of city officers, councilmen, and musicians wend their way to a feast at the New Hall.[153] The corporation also licensed a wide variety of musicians, puppeteers, players and performers across the seventeenth century, from the sublime to the ridiculous. The city's official troop of musicians, the Norwich Waits, could regularly be heard at the market cross.[154] The Red Bull Company and the King's Revels Company played in the marketplace during the early 1630s and exotic animals such as lions, camels and dancing bears were common sights over the entire course of the century. Norwich's inhabitants also had the pleasure of witnessing a monstrous root-eating man from the hills of Carinthia, hairy children, and people with an unusual number of fingers and toes.[155] These acts were staged at either the market cross or inside one of the numerous marketside drinking houses, especially the Angel Inn. It was here that inhabitants saw Peter Dolman's 'motion called his Majesty's Puntionella' in 1683, an exceptionally tall man called Edmund Mellon in 1684,[156] and an array of exotic foreign entertainments such as a German who 'showeth tricks with his feet', the German

---

[151] Penelope Corfield, 'From Second City to Regional Capital', *Norwich Since 1550*, ed. Rawcliffe and Wilson (London, 2004), pp. 139–66, 152.

[152] Rye, *Depositions*, p. 176, 6 and 11 February 1685.
A special tax on the city's inhabitants had paid for the cross at St Peter Mancroft to be repaired and 'new paved' in 1646: Francis Blomefield, *An Essay towards a Topographical History of the County of Norfolk, Vol. IV: The History of the City and County of Norwich, Part II* (1806), p. 234–5.

[153] Notice of the Procession on Guild-Day: printed at Norwich, MS 453, 1732.

[154] Rye, *Depositions*, p. 130.

[155] W. L. Sachse, ed., *Minutes of the Norwich Court of Mayoralty 1630–1631* (Norwich, 1942), pp. 81, 85, 86; Rye, *Depositions*, p. 107.

[156] Rye, *Depositions*, pp. 173–4, 22 December 1683 and 3 November 1684 respectively.

'motion ... called Slight of Hand', or the famous 'dancing mare' of 'Switzer' Daniel Smith.[157]

Whilst the markets were often associated with entertainments and festivities they also had a darker history, one punctuated by popular unrest. This history helped shape inhabitants' shared perceptual landscape and lend a different set of associations to the impression of market spaces. Many people would have heard the stories of the 1549 rebellion, for example, when the market had been overtaken first by forces of rebels and latterly by soldiers. Fighting had broken out when rebels, camped out at Mousehold Heath, ostensibly led by William and Robert Kett of Wymondham, decided to take advantage of the better defensive capabilities that the city could offer over the open countryside and to replenish dwindling supplies. A series of street fights developed, first between the rebels and a small military force under William Parr, Marquis of Northampton, and then a much larger force under the command of the Earl of Warwick. According to the local antiquarian Francis Blomefield, Northampton had made St Peter Mancroft's market his base and it was from here that his plans for 'the defence of the city' and to restrain 'the assault of the enemy' were discussed with Norwich's citizens. It was also here that Norwich's mayor negotiated the issue of rebel pardons with a royal herald in the event that the rebels could be persuaded to lay down their arms.[158] The Earl of Warwick likewise found 'the marketplace very spacious [and] made it his head quarters', lighting huge bonfires 'least by darkness and ignorance of the place they should be enclosed in the night by their enemies'.[159] When fighting did break out between rebel and royal forces, much of the fighting was concentrated in the market. The chamberlain's accounts for 1549 detail repairs caused by the insurrection and show quite clearly how the violence affected Tombland and the main market square.[160] After the rebellion had been put down the market space was put to use again, this time for executions. Around two hundred and twenty men were sentenced to death, and of these, forty-nine men were sentenced to hang at a specially erected gallows at the marketplace. The rebellion damaged the city's landscape just as it left a lasting impression on the lives of individual inhabitants who had known the executed rebels or who had been in some way involved. For many the memories of local men sent to their deaths in the marketplace were not easily forgotten.

During the seventeenth century the city's markets continued to stand out as hubs in the topography of disorder. In 1634, for example, several angry men threatened 'some stirre in the m[ar]kett' if their long-standing complaints

---

157 Rye, *Depositions*, pp. 174, 180, 5 December 1684, 25 September, 9 October and 11 December 1686 respectively. The Norwich Waits had their instruments confiscated for playing at the Angel without permission on 18 August 1683: Rye, *Depositions*, p. 172.

158 Blomefield, *Topographical History*, III:1, pp. 240.

159 Ibid.

160 Wood, *1549*, p. 70.

were not dealt with.[161] Nine years earlier, copper farthing tokens had been issued to resolve a shortage of small coins in the local economy.[162] Meant only as a temporary measure, the farthings were still being paid out in 1634 by unscrupulous employers in place of actual currency. Worse still, their real value had plummeted because of the ready availability of counterfeits and many suppliers of basic provisions now refused to accept the tokens as payment for goods. George Fowler was one of many workers whose wages had been paid using the worthless tokens. Fowler had warned the corporation that '[i]tt would be a hott m[ar]kett' if they continued to ignore the problem.[163] Threatening a commotion at the market was significant for many reasons. It would strike at the city's social and economic heart, guaranteeing maximum visibility for the perpetrators, disrupting trade, and attacking the corporation's authority at this ancient, symbolic site of civic identity. In plain view of the Guildhall and courthouse, it would be the regional equivalent of holding a demonstration outside parliament. Thus it was that George Fowler was arrested on the rather pre-emptive charge of disturbing the peace, but the corporation did accept that he had a point and ordered constables to investigate further. A large haul of tokens was seized and several employers were arrested and prosecuted for receiving and paying the counterfeit coins.

Although the relationship between the corporation and the inhabitants of Norwich was not always easy, there were no serious riots during the seventeenth century until the Excise Riots of 1646. Like many of the city's major political confrontations, the main action took place in and around the markets. The Excise Riots, mentioned briefly in the previous section, were a reaction to an extraordinary tax levied on everyday goods such as ale and meat in 1643. For most people, a tax on such basic, everyday foodstuffs was tough but for the poor and the brewers and butchers especially it presented even more of a challenge. Nevertheless, riots did not break out immediately. The situation only deteriorated in 1646 because 'the plague was at Norwich ... and on the 15th of November was a very great flood, so that boats were rowed in St. Edmund's, Magdalen, and many other streets in the city'.[164] Indeed, it can be no coincidence that urban rioting began shortly after the floods had caused significant damage to the low-lying lands abutting the river, home to a goodly proportion of the city's poorest inhabitants who had already suffered from disease.

The disorder was started by a group of butchers led by James Sheringham, the freeman butcher who, two years later, was involved in the Great Blow. He rented a stall on the market at St Peter Mancroft, and was vocal in his criticism of the tax, inspiring disturbances to take place in the market on

---

161 NCR 20a/10, fol. 44v, 3 May 1634.
162 Sachse, *Minutes 1632–1635*, pp. 138–41.
163 NCR 20a/10, fol. 44v, 3 May 1634; Sachse, *Minutes, 1632–1635*, pp. 138–41.
164 Blomefield, *Topographical History*, III:I, p. 392.

Saturday 10 December 1646.[165] Despite the best efforts of the constables to apprehend Sheringham in a 'private' manner, it was a Saturday market day, the one day of the week that the marketplace was crowded and both city and county butchers were present.[166] The city gaol was situated at the eastern side of the marketplace towards the castle (and the Castle Inn), so once the rumours of Sheringham's arrest had been made public, it would not have taken long to mobilise the butchers into action. Indeed, it is highly likely that Sheringham would have been escorted through, or past, the market by the constables to reach the gaol. A number of them 'furiously & tumultuously And violently rescued him although he was in the hands of the Sheriffe'.[167] The following Monday morning, the butchers (and others) went armed with clubs and staves to the market to threaten the aldermen who were then in session at the Guildhall discussing the disturbances. Several attempts were made to appease the mob, but it seems that the corporation, unable to raise any trained bands to stop them with force, simply waited out the violence until the mob dispersed of their own accord.[168]

Unable to collect the tariff and now in fear of the mob, the corporation appeared paralysed as the situation spiralled out of control, the rioting spreading across Norfolk and lasting through the winter, into spring, and then into summer. Parliament accused the corporation of failing to execute effectively their governmental responsibilities and it was only when the Commons agreed to make some tax concessions that outright resistance finally died out.[169] Nonetheless, the tax continued to be a serious sticking point in the corporation's relationship with the people of Norwich and did little for their reputation in the eyes of their inhabitants, or the Crown. In many respects, the affair demonstrated the city government's problematic position as an intermediary between parliament and region: responsible for the effective administration of parliamentary taxation, yet aware of the reality of trying to collect taxes from an obstinate population, and understanding first hand the grim financial circumstances of the people upon whom the burden of tax fell the hardest.

The marketplace continued to be a locus for popular discontent. Much of the crowd action during the Great Blow of 1648, for example, took place not only in the alehouses surrounding the market, but also in the marketplace itself. There were several practical reasons why this was so: its proximity to the network of actors and inns involved and its convenience as the nearest open space where people could congregate. From this vantage point the crowd could also command an unobstructed view of the main places involved: the

---

165   See Millican, *Register of the Freemen*, p. 240; Chamberlain's Accounts, 1648–1663, NCR Case 18a, fol. 257v. 25 March 1661–1662.

166   J. Kirkpatrick, *The Streets and Lanes of Norwich* (Norwich, 1889), p. 31.

167   Letter of Alderman Adrian Parmenter and others to the commissioners of the excise describing violence in Norwich, BL, Tanner MS, 59b, fol. 610.

168   Ibid. The letter describes the events as they took shape.

169   Thomas Atkin to the Mayor of Norwich, 25 January 1646/7 and fol. 56, Atkin to the Mayor, 4 March 1646/7, BL, Add. MSS 22620, fol. 45.

King's Head where the messenger waited to escort the mayor to London, the mayor's house, and the Guildhall where any official meetings would have been held. The symbolism of a gathering in the market would also not have been lost on its people. The location reinforced the crowd's ancient rights and traditions as citizens, freemen and inhabitants and, by taking up this position, the crowd appropriated the ghosts of popular heroes in a place redolent with the memories of common solidarity.

Likewise in 1682 local weavers chose the market as the place to best express their concerns regarding immigrant workers. The market's significance in this dispute was its role and symbolism as the ancient heart of the cloth trade, as evoked by the market cross, Guildhall and cloth hall. The place evoked inhabitants' economic independence and civic identity. The French weavers in question had been hired the year before by Onias Philipo, himself a third generation stranger, in Ipswich and brought to Norwich where they resided in one of Philipo's properties. Bringing in foreign labour had always been a risky strategy for employers who, although benefitting from better labour costs and new skills, risked resentment from established workers in the same trade. For the most part locals and new arrivals coexisted peaceably but the 1680s witnessed greater numbers of strangers and foreigners than normal arriving in England because of an influx of refugees – mainly French Huguenots – fleeing religious persecution in Europe.[170] In Norwich there were periodic outbursts of violence against the French weavers including an incident where a French female worker was mortally injured. Despite this, the corporation was reluctant to discipline the perpetrators who, although initially arrested and imprisoned, were not punished. As one contemporary commentator later recalled, their unwillingness was a grave mistake as it only made 'the people more insolent' and led them to assume 'that they may finish entirely what has been only half begun'.[171] This was realised when, taking advantage of a large crowd gathered to witness the execution of Elizabeth Brooks on Castle Hill, the local weavers 'still discontented at the French which were left in the city … coming in a large body into the marketplace, declared that the French came to underwork them, and that they would then quit the city of them'. From there 'they pulled them and their goods out of their houses, [and] abused their persons … till the trained bands were raised to appease them'.[172]

The connection between the market and protest was so explicit that in years of crisis the corporation knew to prepare for trouble before it had even

---

[170] The persecution of Huguenots intensified after 1681 with the introduction of forced conversions to Catholicism and the revocation of the Edict of Nantes in 1685 outlawing the practice of the Protestant faith.

[171] Letter from P. Chauvin to Sir John Chardin, 4 September 1683: F. H. Blackburne Daniel, ed., CSPD: Charles II, 1683–4 (London, 1938), p. 363.

[172] Blomefield, Topographical History, III:I, p. 418; John Miller, 'The Fortunes of the Strangers in Norwich and Canterbury, 1565–1700', Memory and Identity: The Huguenots in France and the Atlantic Diaspora, ed. Bertrand Van Ruymbeke and Randy J. Sparks (Carolina, 2003), pp. 110–27, 118.

started. In the previous year, for example, heightened gossip, rumours, and news about the forthcoming Oxford Parliament election, stimulated by a surfeit of propaganda literature that circulated around the city's drinking houses, inspired Norwich's government to fear that riots might break out during the electoral proceedings held at the Guildhall. To deal with the impending crisis the mayor ordered that on the morning of the election every constable in the city turn out for service by 'eight in the morning at the Market Cross with their staffs' to help prevent the crowds of people expected there from becoming a mob.[173]

Mark Knights, who has explored the disunion created by Tory-Whig enmity during this period in some depth, suggests that from the 1680s to the 1720s Norwich was a deeply divided city.[174] Between 1679 and 1682, for example, Norwich was deeply affected by the national events often labelled the Exclusion Crisis. However, although the question of James, Duke of York's succession to the throne has received much scholarly attention, in Norwich, as elsewhere, the 'crisis' was created by much wider religious and political debates that had polarised under the single parliamentary issue of succession. During these years, animosity between Tory and Whig factions shaped national and regional politics.[175] Each election was a playground for local rivalries and in Norfolk these were focussed behind the successive Earls of Yarmouth, Robert and William Paston for the Tories, and the Townshend family, particularly Horatio Townshend and his son Charles of Raynham, with Sir John Hobart of Blickling for the Whigs. Norwich and Norfolk politics were closely linked and the county magnates openly courted their corporation supporters. The Whig contingent identified with the leadership of alderman John Man and the Tory sympathisers went directly to Yarmouth, who extended a great deal of influence in the city's politics.[176] His involvement pushed many citizens to support Whig interests because they resented the peer's interference in civic affairs.

One of the issues that affected Norwich directly during the crisis was the renegotiation of the city's charter. Traditionally a bone of contention between Crown and corporation, in 1682 the King's order to surrender the charter became mired in the politics of the day. Relinquishing the charter would have allowed Charles II to remodel the corporation into a body more compliant with his wishes, placing Tory sympathisers into key positions of power and lessening Whig influence. As a result, those people opposing the surrender of the charter became identified with Whig interests. Precipitating

---

[173] Rye, *Depositions*, p. 161. 12 February 1680.

[174] Knights, 'Politics', pp. 167–8.

[175] Though it is easy to discuss later seventeenth century politics as a dichotomy between Whigs and Tories, Jonathan Scott warns that to speak of a cohesive and organised two-party system at this time would be to fundamentally misrepresent the politics of the day: Jonathan Scott, *Algernon Sidney and the Restoration Crisis 1677–1683* (Cambridge, 1991), pp. 21–4.

[176] Evans, *Seventeenth-Century Norwich*, p. 269.

a political stand off over the charter, Tory sympathisers organised a ceremonial effigy burning of Jack Presbyter, Henry Care and Francis Smith, a copy
of the Nineteen Propositions and the Exclusion Bill at the market square
on 29 May 1682.[177] Just north of the river, a rival effigy of the pope was
burned: an attack on the supposed religious sympathies of the Tories.[178] Over
the next month, everyday city business was neglected as the charter negotiations dragged on. The Tory Earl of Yarmouth lost patience and issued an
ultimatum to Norwich's Assembly urging them to make haste in finalising
their negotiations. Yarmouth's letter was received by the corporation on 17
June 1682 and was met by 'heates' so great that 'no businesse of the daie
proceeded, but the assemblie was dissolved'.[179] The corporation Whigs engineered a petition in response, signed by around nine hundred freemen and
citizens. The petition argued that to surrender the charter was the equivalent
of relinquishing the city's ancient rights and liberties, and singled out the
'endeavours of some of their fellow citizens to destroy them'.[180] The petitioners also claimed that if their entreaties were not given consideration they
would bring at least a thousand of their supporters to the marketplace. The
threat was a step too far. The mayor, Hugh Bokenham, had no choice but to
reject the petition, although he refused to prosecute its authors.[181] The affair
dragged on and in August 1682, Yarmouth was forced to travel to Norwich in
person, where he remained until a new mayor – the Whig John Lowe – and
several new Tory aldermen had been elected. Despite the political inclinations of the new mayor, the corporation's political balance had been tipped
in favour of the Tories. Mayor Lowe had no option but to promise an Assembly vote on the charter on the 21 September 1682. Sensing their imminent
demise, the Whigs organised a protest near the castle (interestingly avoiding
the marketplace) on 18 September but were dispersed by force.[182] The vote
proceeded unopposed and the Tories won forty votes to twenty-two.[183] The
new charter was formally presented to the city the following year amidst celebrations of 'arms and instruments', the ringing of church bells, and a bonfire
in the marketplace.[184]

That the Tory faction appropriated the marketplace for their symbolic protest and their celebrations (and that the Whigs were seen to avoid it) should

---

[177] Tim Harris, 'The Parties and the People: the Press, the Crowd and Politics "Out-of-
Doors" in Restoration England', *The Reigns of Charles II & James II*, ed. Lionel K. J. Glassey
(Macmillan, 1997), pp. 125–51, 143.
[178] Cited in Harris, 'The Parties and the People', pp. 138, 147.
[179] Robert Hill, ed., *The Correspondence of Thomas Corie* (Norwich, 1956), p. 41.
[180] Letter from the Mayor &c to Lord Yarmouth 25 June 1682, with copy of the petition,
NA, SP/419, fol. 117, 28 June 1682.
[181] Evans, *Seventeenth-Century Norwich*, p. 285. Evans suggests that Bokenham was behind the petition.
[182] Lord Yarmouth to his wife, BL Add. MSS 27448, fol. 127, 18 September 1682.
[183] Evans, *Seventeenth-Century Norwich*, p. 289.
[184] Rye, *Depositions*, p. 170. 21 March 1683.

perhaps come as no surprise. As the previous section alluded, there was a correlation between St Peter Mancroft and a large proportion of Tory voters; likewise Whig support tended to come from the cloth-working and finishing areas north of the river. Mark Knights first highlighted this during his extensive research into the petition signatories during the 1679–82 crisis but other scholars have also noted the topographical difference.[185] This research suggests that social geography – that is geographical location, religion, political allegiance, and occupation – was tightly bound. Certainly, three years later the predominantly Tory twenty-four ordered 'bells to be rung and a load of wood bought for a bonfire in the market place' on hearing the news of Monmouth's 'rebels' defeat.[186]

Norwich's marketplace was as much a political space as it was a social and economic space. It was not simply a 'passive backdrop' to political action because it was a convenient space for large gatherings. If the correlation were this simple, then more of Norwich's open urban spaces would have seen their fair share of collective action. Norwich's central market was special because of its geographic centrality and its proximity to the seat of corporation power. A demonstration here would be guaranteed an audience and would most seriously threaten the corporation's authority. The appropriation of a place more usually associated with civic ceremonies and the conspicuous display of governance through the practice of public punishment was a very powerful and symbolic message that inverted the proper order of things. There were other reasons too. Proximity to the city's most political drinking houses could not have hurt matters either, indeed in 1648 people had spilled directly from the drinking houses in the marketplace, or used the inns as platforms from which to observe the goings on as they developed. It is also interesting that there was a concentration of booksellers, binders and printers in St Peter Mancroft. Though it is unlikely that this coincidence would have inspired individual events, the connection of the parish with the printed news should not be overlooked. There were at least twenty-three booksellers known to have traded from in and around the marketplace and Guildhall between 1600 and 1700 and it is likely that much of their stock would have found their way into the nearby drinking houses to be read and discussed.[187]

---

[185] Knights, 'London Petitions', 41–2; Knights, 'London's "Monster" Petition', 61–3; Knights, Politics, p. 170. J. T. Evans also noted the tradition of dissent amongst the freemen 'Over-The-Water', the collective term for Coslany, Colegate and Fye Bridge: Evans, Norwich, p. 309. D. T. Jones found the same correlation in his analysis of the 1710 election votes: St Peter Mancroft and St Andrew had the highest percentage (proportional to population) of Tory voters and St George Colegate and St Michael Coslany north of the river had the highest number of Whig supporters: Jones, Social Geography, Figs 10.13, 10.15.
[186] Rye, Depositions, 176. 9 July 1685.
[187] See Stoker, 'The Norwich Book Trades', 79–125 for information on the individual sellers.

It is therefore possible to conclude that the central market at St Peter Mancroft was identified with a spatial presence that was significantly different from that of other urban open spaces. The market's spatial identity evolved through the multilateral input of all of Norwich's inhabitants, rich and poor; their shared traditions, cultural heritage, and collective memories about that place. In this way the marketplace was, perhaps uniquely, a chimera, a place of shifting, unstable identities, claimed exclusively by none, yet appropriated by many.

In Norwich, as in other cities, an alternative urban landscape can be constructed through the memory of collective action and popular politics. This landscape crossed the boundaries of occupation and class, to leave its own unique imprint on the city's collective memory. Of course political action was not exclusive to drinking houses or market squares, but the frequency of political activities in certain places over and above others suggests that contemporaries made both considered and subconscious choices about where political action, or politicking, should best be performed. At the end of this chapter, the parish of St Peter Mancroft stands out as a centre of unofficial political activities and, to a lesser extent, the adjacent parishes of St Andrew and St John Timberhill. This is not to say that no political activities or discussion would have been heard elsewhere. St Stephen, for example, had a share of drinking houses that crept into the criminal records over the course of the century and, after the Restoration, was also identified with Tory inclinations. Nevertheless, it was adjacent to St Peter Mancroft and far from the *ultra aquam* Whiggish weaving parishes. Certain drinking houses, especially the inns that crowded the marketplace at St Peter Mancroft, also stand out in the political landscape. Their concentration here does, to some extent, reflect the density of drinking houses around the main roads, the market and the most heavily populated areas[188] – a correlation that likely grew from practical reasons – but this only partially explains why only a few of the drinking houses there, or the marketplace, as opposed to other open spaces, were at the centre of the political landscape. This association can best be explained by the social backgrounds and networks of customers; routes of oral and written communication through the city; and the shared traditions and associations of inhabitants. Inhabitants' perceptions of the places they visited were created by their shared social memories and they saw the city through this lens. Markets and drinking houses were not simply places in which social and political life unfolded, 'but rather ... a medium through which social relations

---

[188] An interesting contrast here is James R. Brown's study of drinking house geography in Southampton. From the known location of establishments in 1620, there is a clear, linear concentration along the main road that bisected the town from east to west: Brown, *Landscape of Drink*, p. 31. In Norwich, drinking houses tended to be more widely distributed across the city in clusters.

[were] produced and reproduced'.[189] In this way then, inhabitants created their own landscape and, thus located, the landscape worked to determine those same inhabitants' future exchanges.

[189] Derek Gregory and John Urry, eds, *Social Relations and Spatial Structures* (London, 1985), p. 3.

Conclusion

A City of Many Faces

Telling the story of a city entails more than a retelling of chronological events. This book has attempted to reveal a different side to seventeenth-century Norwich by re-reading its records with a close lens on the words and actions of its inhabitants in the context of the place in which they lived. It has explored perceptions of space and place from different perspectives and considered some of the conceptual landscapes available to, and created by, inhabitants and their networks. It has endeavoured to show that people negotiated their city in ways that reflected their specific socio-cultural perspectives and that the city was not simply a blank canvas about which people moved, but the spaces and places of the urban environment played an active part in shaping people's experiences. This was possible because every space and place had meaning; as ideas from dominant discourses became inscribed into memory as common knowledge, they also became inscribed onto spaces, lending them significance that then coloured the subsequent human actions that took place within them. The process was mutual and reciprocal as spaces and places – shaped by human needs and ideas – then radiated those influences outwards.

Just as seventeenth-century people's lives were specific to their time, created through a process of culture, shared sets of assumptions and memories, customs and conventions, so too were the spatial meanings imbued in the landscape a product of these processes. Thus it is possible to recover spatial meanings through reading people's interactions with, thoughts about, and actions in, those spaces, just as we decipher seventeenth-century culture through the words, actions and deeds of its people. In particular this book has explored the record of where events took place, how spaces were used and by whom, and the adoption of common linguistic tropes used when referring to those spaces and places. It has considered the possibility of separate spaces, whereby inhabitants occupied different conceptual frames of geographic reference created by pervasive socio-cultural assumptions about people and place. Spatial meanings often reflected the dominant values of (or beliefs about) a particular social group, and this book has considered the impact of this practice on the lives of the city's poor, women, and immigrant communities and, although spatial understanding was in many ways unique to each individual, shown how there were shared commonalities in perceptions of place.

The cognitive maps and spatial understandings familiar to seventeenth-century inhabitants are hard, though not impossible, to recover but no reconstruction can ever be complete; in any story there are frustrating omissions, gaps in the chronology, and missing links in the evidence. These limitations are part of the frustrations of the historian's job. Nevertheless, at the end of this book, three things seem very clear. First, seventeenth-century Norwich was a city of many different perceptual landscapes. These landscapes subverted the imagery available in early cartographic projects, revealing the reality of the cityscape as a polycentric lived organism thriving around multiple centres based on neighbourhoods, parishes and occupational networks, but also abstract cognitive maps that overlaid the corporeal landscape. Elements of these maps were highly personal, specific to an individual's status, circumstances and networks, or formed during the acquisition of local knowledge. They also incorporated the imagery, symbolism and ideals that were specific to seventeenth-century cultures more generally. Thus there were points of crossover at which we can detect the presence of shared cognitive landscapes, perhaps related to memory and local history, gender, or community identity. Although this book has treated five different landscapes as largely separate entities, it should be remembered that none of them were exclusive and by no means were they the only landscapes available. People entered into, and exited, different landscapes as they traversed the city, perhaps as unwitting outsiders in a landscape they could not claim as their own, at other times as deliberate intruders on other's spaces, and on many occasions simply unaware or unknowing of all the ephemeral landscapes that lay at their feet. We are left with a strong sense of the interconnectivity and reciprocity of the many overlapping mental and physical landscapes that existed in the historic city, as many and as varied as the city's inhabitants themselves. Seventeenth-century Norwich was a lived space best understood as a communocentric city.[1]

Second, although this book has relied heavily on cartographic sources for recovering the seventeenth-century built landscape, and the record of the location of events, the most significant information about urban spaces has been contained in sources about the lives of the city dwellers, especially that evidenced in their own voices and speeches. Norwich's surviving records capture the essence of what it was to live in a seventeenth-century city. The extensive administrative, judicial and church records, laws, minutes, accounts, and proceedings are revealing, but without the responses and opinions of the ordinary people at which they were aimed they will always be lacking. The records used during this study contain many voices and, if we bear in mind the constraints elicited by the mediation of those same voices through the pens of court officials, they enable an improved understanding of how

---

[1] Term cited in Tom Conley, 'Introduction' in Graham Ward, ed., *The Certeau Reader* (Oxford, 2000), pp. 55–60, 56.

seventeenth-century culture was negotiated in practice – the contradictory treatment of the poor as deserving recipients of help or as criminals, or welcoming and marginalising outsiders, for example.

Even more significantly, the study of inhabitants' voices with an eye to the scholarship of spatial methodology sheds new light on known evidence. In those voices we hear what people thought about their city, how they navigated it, and how they conceptualised or perceived each place. We witness at first hand, for example, how women were treated in public spaces, or how the poor destabilised the efforts of the authorities to keep them, literally, in their place. Others subverted spatial meanings to achieve their own ends. Rioters, for example, appropriated spaces associated with corporation authority to deliver their message best. Inhabitants' words are a compelling narrative of spatial imagery, conveying a sense of people's relationship with place. By exploring Norwich using these tools we are able to recreate a little more of inhabitants' mentalities and identities as well as understand more of humans' interrelationship with their urban environment.

Finally, changing social, cultural and political ideas have worked in tandem with the evolving landscape. Thus, much of the city that the inhabitants of seventeenth-century Norwich knew has been lost. Changing architectural trends, building projects, environmental degradation and economic development have fundamentally altered many features of the built landscape. Take the marketplace at St Peter Mancroft for example. It still operates as a regional market and is a focal point of the city centre but it is highly unlikely that anyone, bar a historian, archivist, or someone with a keen interest in local history, would connect Norwich's market with past political uprisings, and even less likely that anyone today would consider market retail a masculine occupation, reflecting changed cultural assumptions about women's roles. The market has survived because it is a symbol of Norwich; as other regional cities have lost their permanent markets, Norwich's inhabitants have strived to retain this unique aspect of their city's identity. The vibrant social culture that was so firmly entrenched in the marketside drinking houses however has found a modern focus along the recently regenerated southwest portion of the river, in what was an industrial dockside in the seventeenth century. Of the original string of marketside inns – the Half Moon, the King's Head, the Angel and the White Lion – few survive. The Half Moon was closed in 1923 and demolished shortly after. The King's Head continued to be a favourite with the city's political elite into the eighteenth century, hosting amongst other events a reception for Sir John Woodhouse and Sir Edward Astley on the event of the parliamentary election of 1784, but is now incorporated into a row of shops. The Angel became a coffee house and tavern, home to one of the city's masonic lodges before becoming the Royal Hotel in the nineteenth century. The White Lion also became a hotel in the 1800s, but by the early 1900s had evolved into the Haymarket Stores. The Stores closed in the 1970s and the building now homes one of a well-known chain of coffee shops. The Guildhall still lies at the geographic heart of the city but, rather than looming over the market as an expression of civic authority, its symbolism to be appropriated and subverted, it is now a quaint tearoom serving tourists and retirees. The functions of local government were dispersed over the course of the twentieth century and, as the city grew, the connection between the city centre and governmental authority has declined. The city council moved to adjacent premises built during the 1930s but many responsibilities went to the county council at a twentieth-century build in Lakenham; in the seventeenth century Lakenham was a small village outside the city walls.

The ways of marking and conceptualising space that were once so significant to seventeenth-century inhabitants are now largely forgotten. Most of the medieval churches and parishes that so dominated the cognitive maps of the 1600s survive but few people would recognise them or use them to navigate the city now. In the churches that have not been closed or refurbished for a variety of modern uses, rogation ceremonies are still known to take place, but people's sense of parish space is very limited. Parish churches might feature in inhabitants' dialogues but the sense of where a parish begins or ends is indistinct or entirely unknown. Yet, modern city dwellers share experiences with past inhabitants in many ways. Buildings like the castle or the Guildhall are still important landmarks used to describe location, despite the modern reliance on Ordnance Survey maps, postal addresses and GPS. Indeed, there remains a distinct difference between inhabitants' sense of what they see on the ground and the bird's eye view of a paper or digital map. Likewise, modern city dwellers still base the ideas of the city on their own social networks and places that matter to their lives. In this sense then, although our modern mental maps of the city share few similarities with those of our seventeenth-century forebears, we should not forget that most inhabitants, then and now, experience the city as a lived space which they see not from the perspective of a map, but from walking the streets and living from day-to-day.

Bibliography

Primary Sources

British Library

A briefe and true Relation of the Seige and Surrendering of Kings Lyn (1643), TT E67, 28

Anon, *A true Relation Of the late great Mutinie Which was in the City of Norwich* (London, 1648), TT E438, 6

Collection of original papers, with a few copies, relating to Norwich, 1633–1730, consisting chiefly of letters and accounts relative to Norwich, as a member of the Associated Eastern Counties, in 1641–1650, etc., Add. MSS 22619–22620

Letter of Alderman Adrian Parmenter and others to the commissioners of the excise describing violence in Norwich, BL, Tanner MS, 59b, fol. 610

Lord Yarmouth to his wife, BL Add. MSS, 27448, fol. 127, 18 September 1682

Historic Manuscripts Commission (HMC)

Report on the Manuscripts of the Gawdy Family of the County of Norfolk (London, 1885)

Sixth Report of the Historical Manuscripts Commission (London, 1877)

National Archives (Kew)

Articles from the Mayor and Aldermen of Norwich to the Privy Council, SP 79/38, 1627

Deputy Lieutenant of Norfolk to the Privy Council: SP 16/24, fol. 44, 6 Ap. 1626, 1 Sep. 1626; SP 16/52, fol. 3, 30 Jan 1626–7

Forced Loan returns for Norwich and Norfolk, E401/1913, 1914 and 2443, 1627

Hearth Tax Assessment for the city of Norwich, Michaelmas, E179/154/701, 1662

Hearth Tax Assessment for the city of Norwich, Michaelmas, E179/154/697, 1672

Letter from the Mayor &c to Lord Yarmouth 25 June 1682, with copy of the petition, SP/419, fol. 117, 28 June 1682

Mayor and Aldermen of Norwich to Earl Marshall Arundel, 26 September 1621, NA, SP, Dom., James I, 122, no. 145-145i

Mayor and Aldermen of Norwich to the Privy Council, SP 16/79, fol. 38, 27 September 1627; SP 16/78, fol. 53, 18 December 1627

Petition written to the Privy Council by the Norwich Corporation, SP, 16/535/158, c. 1635

Society of Friends, Norwich: Monthly Meeting Minute Book 1671–90: www.nation-alarchives.gov.uk/a2a/records.aspx?cat=153-sf_1&cid=0#0
State Papers of the Reign of Charles I, SP 16a/470/92, c. October 1640
Will of Alderman William Symonds, PROB 11/239/629

Norfolk Heritage Centre (NHC)

A new mapp of the ancient and famous city of Norwich by Tho. Cleer, 1696
Map 5, Norwich prior to the dissolution of the monasteries
Map 10, Parts 1 & 2 The Liberties of City of Norwich, 1589
Map 16, Francis Blomefield Parts 1& 2, Norwich 1746
Map 17, Norwich 1783 (T. Smith)
Mapp of the city of Norwich by J. Corbridge, 1747
The city and county of Norwich by Samuel King, 1766
The Norwich Postman, 1706

Norfolk Museums and Archaeology Service, Shirehall Study Centre

S. & N. Buck, South East Prospect of the City of Norwich, 1741
Francis Blomefield, A Plan of the City of Norwich, 1746, NWHCM: 1999.71.35 M
George Braun and Franz Hogenburg, Nordovicum Angliae Civitas, 1581, NWHCM: 1997.550.75 M
William Cuningham, Nordovicum Angliae Civitas, 1558, NWHCM: 1899.4.21 M

Norfolk Record Office (NRO)

Assembly Book of Proceedings, NCR 16d/4 – 16d/8 1585–1707
Assembly Minute Books, NCR 16c/5–7, 1585–1714
Book of Orders for the Dutch and Walloon Strangers in Norwich, NCR 17d, 1564–1643
Books of Proceedings of City Committees: Bridewell, 1585–1686, NCR 19c
Boy's and Girl's Hospital Accounts, NCR 25f, 1620–52
Certificate from the Mayor and Aldermen of Norwich that the King's Head in St Peter Mancroft, Norwich, is an ancient inn, MS 10961, 36F8, 16 April 1619
Chamberlain's Accounts, NCR 18a, 1600–1700
Chamberlain's Accounts, NCR 18b/1–20, 1700–1720
Clavors' Accounts, NCR 18d, 1550–1601, 1555–1646, 1625–1717, 1647–1733
Company of Strangers in Parliament's Army, NCR 16a/20, fol. 417r, 26 March 1644
Copies of Letters Patent allowing Norwich Corporation to admit thirty Dutch families, etc., FC 29/2, 1565
Coroner's Reports NCR 6a 1–2, 1669–99
Depositions relating to the Great Blow, NCR 12c/1, 1648
Diocese of Norwich (DN), Depositions: DN/DEP/31/34 – DN/DEP/53/58A, 1600–1703
Diocese of Norwich Probate Inventories, DN/INV/3-68b, 1587–1700
Dutch Congregation Numbers, NCR 10h/11
Extract from the will of Elisha Phillipo, FC 29/26, 1678

Family and Estate Papers of the Ketton-Cremer Family of Felbrigg Hall, WKC 7/6/17

Guardians of the Poor, Minute Book, NCR 20e, 1712–14

Letter of John Holland, John Potts and others of a special council to be held at the King's Head regarding Norfolk's coastal defenses, BL/F 3/113, December 1642

Letter of Sir Phillip Wodehouse to Francis Parlett asking him to notify the mayor of Lynn of a special meeting to be convened at the King's Head, Bradfer-Lawrence Collection (BL)/F 4/2, 3 October 1618

Letters patent granting permission of settlement, NCR 17d, 1564

Loose pages from the minute book of the [? county] sequestration committee, NCR 10h 21/2, 19 February-12 August 1648

Manuscripts of the Antiquary John Kirkpatrick: River, NCR Case 21f/76

Mayor's Court Books, NCR 16a/13–26, 1595–1709

Mayor's Court Papers, depositions, petitions and evidences, NCR 16a/47/1, 1521–1700

Muster list of Dutch soldiers of Norwich NCR 13a/17–20

Norfolk County Quarter Sessions (NCQS) C/S3/13-C/S3/58, 1600–1700

Norfolk and Norwich Archaeological Society references to Anthony Solempne, MC 2577/2/7

Norwich City Quarter Sessions Interrogations and Depositions, NCR 12a-b

Norwich City Quarter Sessions Minute Book, NCR 20a/11, 1639–54

Notice of the Procession on Guild-Day: printed at Norwich, MS 453, 1732

Package of Documents Relating to St Andrew's Parish, 1622–1773, MC 500/59, 762x2, no. 11, 21 June 1676

Parochial List of the Number of Houses and Inhabitants within the City of Norwich, 1693 and 1752, MC 453, Loose papers

Quarter Sessions Book of Depositions and Orders, NCR 20a/10, 1630–8

Quarter Sessions Interrogations and Depositions, NCR 12a-b/1, 1648, 1684–9

Quarter Sessions Interrogations and Recognisances, NCR Case 11a, 1642–3

Register of Swan Marks, MC2712/1, 1649-c.1900

Rolle of the Wallons Companie, COL 5/5/3, 18 September 1620

Saint Andrew Overseer's Accounts, MC 992/1, fol. 1r, 1623–1713

Saint Augustine Overseer's Accounts, PD 185/41, 1689–1713

Saint Peter Mancroft Overseer's Accounts, PD 26, 1600

Series of Antiquarian Notes, MS 453

Suckling Jay Legacy Book, PD 165/114, 1691–1856

Survey of Strangers in Norwich, NCR 17d, fols 69–70

Three vagrant passes for Norfolk, PD 100/129, 1649

Townshend Family Papers, Letters to Sir Horatio, 1st Viscount Townshend, Sir John Holland, Quidenham, MC 1601/26, 7 July 1682

Warnes Charity Accounts, PD 162/80, 1712–1804

Will of John De Hague, ANW, will register, 1687–8, fol. 97, 1687

Primary Printed Sources

J. Beresford, ed., *James Woodforde: The Diary of a Country Parson 1758–1802*, reprinted and introduced by R. Blythe (Norwich, 1999)

J. Beresford, ed., *M. Du Quesne and other Essays* (1931)

F. H. Blackburne Daniel, ed., *CSPD: Charles II, 1677–8* (London, 1911)

F. H. Blackburne Daniel, ed., *CSPD: Charles II, 1683–4* (London, 1938)

F. Blomefield, *An Essay towards a Topographical History of the County of Norfolk, Vols III & IV: The History of the City and County of Norwich*, Parts I and II (1806)

H. Cary, ed., *Memorials of the Great Civil War in England from 1646–52*, Vol. I (London, 1842)

T. Cooper, ed., *The Journal of William Dowsing: Iconoclasm in East Anglia during the English Civil War* (Woodbridge, 2001)

B. Cozens-Hardy, ed., *Norfolk Lieutenancy Journal 1676–1701* (Norwich, 1961)

B. Cozens-Hardy and E. A. Kent, *The Mayors of Norwich 1403–1835* (Norwich, 1938)

E. S. De Beer, *The Diary of John Evelyn* (Oxford, 1959)

D. Defoe, *A Tour through the Whole Island of Great Britain* (London, 1971)

M. A. Everett, *Calendar, Committee for Compounding: Part 2* (1890)

M. A. Everett Green, ed., *CSPD: James I, 1623–25* (London, 1859)

M. A. Everett Green, ed., *CSPD: Charles II, 1660–1* (London, 1860)

M. A. Everett Green, ed., *CSPD: Charles II, 1661–2* (London, 1861)

M. A. Everett Green, ed., *The Diary of John Rouse 1625–42* (London, 1856)

M. A. Farrow and T. F. Barton, eds, *Index of Wills proved at the Consistory Court of Norwich, 1604–1686* (Norwich, 1958)

K. Fincham, *Visitation Articles and Injunctions of the Early Stuart Church, 1625–42*, Vol. II (Woodbridge, 1998)

C. H. Firth, *Acts and Ordinances of the Interregnum, 1642–1660* (1911)

W. Harrison, *Description of England* (1577)

T. Hawes, *An Index to Norwich City Officers 1453–1835* (Norwich, 1989)

R. Hill, ed., *The Correspondence of Thomas Corie* (Norwich, 1956)

History of Parliament Trust, *Journal of the House of Commons*, Vol. 5, 1646–8 (1802), British History Online edn.

History of Parliament Trust, *Journal of the House of Lords*, Vol. 6, 1642–3 (1767–1830), British History Online edn.

D. E. Howell James, ed., *Norfolk Quarter Sessions Order Book 1650–1657* (Norwich, 1955)

W. Hudson and J. C. Tingay, *The Records of the City of Norwich*, Vols I and II (Norwich, 1906–10)

J. Kirkpatrick, *The Streets and Lanes of Norwich* (Norwich, 1889)

J. V. Lyle, ed., *Acts of the Privy Council 1621–3*, Vol. 38 (1932)

P. Millican, ed., *The Register of the Freemen of Norwich 1548–1713* (Norwich, 1934)

C. Morris, ed., *The Illustrated Journeys of Celia Fiennes, 1685-c.1712* (London, 1995)

W. Page, ed., *A History of the County of Norfolk*, II (London, 1906)

P. A. Penfold, ed., *Acts of the Privy Council 1630–1*, Vol. 46 (1964)

J. Pound, ed., *The Norwich Census of the Poor, 1570*, NRS 40 (Norwich, 1971)

J. Raithby, ed., *Statutes of the Realm, 1628–80*, Vol. 5 (1819)

F. de La Rochefoucauld, *A Frenchman's Year in Suffolk: French Impressions of Suffolk Life in 1784*, ed. N. Scarfe (Woodbridge, 1988)

Earl of Rosebery, ed., *The Windham Papers*, I (London, 1913)

J. Rushworth, *Historical Collections of Private Passages of State*, Vols I and VII (1721)

W. Rye, ed., *Depositions Taken Before the Mayor and Aldermen of Norwich, 1549–1567 & Extracts from the Court Books of the City of Norwich 1666–1668* (Norwich, 1905)

W. Rye, *The History of the Bethel at Norwich* (Norwich, 1906)

W. Rye, ed., *The Norwich Rate Book, 1633–1634* (Norwich, 1903)

W. L. Sachse, ed., *Minutes of the Norwich Court of Mayoralty 1630–1631* (Norwich, 1942)

W. L. Sachse, ed., *Minutes of the Norwich Court of Mayoralty 1632–1635* (Norwich, 1967)

P. Seaman, ed., *Norfolk and Norwich Hearth Tax Assessment: Lady Day 1666*, NG XX (Norwich, 1988)

P. Seaman, ed., *Norfolk and Norwich Hearth Tax Assessment: Michaelmas 1664*, NG XV (Norwich, 1983)

P. Seaman, J. Pound and R. Smith, eds, *Norfolk Hearth Tax Exemption Certificates 1670–1674* (Norwich, 2001)

M. J. Stone, ed., *The Diary of John Longe, 1765–1834* (Woodbridge, 1999)

R. H. Tawney and E. Power, eds, *Tudor Economic Documents*, Vol. I (London, 1924)

E. M. Thompson, ed., *Letters of Humphrey Prideaux to John Ellis, 1674–1722*, NRS XV (1875)

A. Thrush and J. P. Ferris, ed., *The History of Parliament: the House of Commons 1604–1629*, Online edn.

D. Turner, ed., *Narrative of the Visit of His Majesty King Charles II to Norwich in the September of the Year 1671* (Yarmouth, 1846)

A. Whiteman, ed., *The Compton Census of 1696: A Critical Edition* (Oxford, 1986)

Primary Printed Texts

R. Abbot, *The Young-Mans Warning Peece, or, A sermon preached at the Buriall of William Rogers, Apothecary with an History of his Sinful life and Woefull death* (London, 1639)

T. Adams, *The Blacke Devil or the Apostate, Together with the Wolfe Worrying the Lambes* (London, 1615)

R. Allestree, *The Whole Duty of Man* (London, 1659)

Anon, *A curse against Parliament-ale. With a blessing to the juncto; a thanksgiving to the councel of state; and psalm to Oliver* (London, 1649)

Anon, *A health to all vintners, beer-brewers and ale-tonners, &c.* (London, 1642)

Anon, *A true relation of the late great Mutinie* (London, 1648)

Anon, *An Hue-and-Cry after Vox Populi, or an Answer to Vox Diaboli* (London, 1646)

Anon, *Bloody Newes from Norwich: or a True Relation of a Bloody Attempt of the Papists in Norwich to consume the Whole City by Fire* (London, 1641)

Anon, *Five Merry Wives of Lambeth, Fowre Wittie Gossips Disposed to be Merry* (London, 1680)

Anon, *Jack Had-Lands Lamentation* (London, 1685)

Anon, *Oxford in mourning, for the loss of the Parliament* (London, 1681)

Anon, *Remarks upon Mr Webber's Scheme and the Draper's Pamphlet* (London, 1741)

Anon, *The Bad Husbands Reformation, or, The Ale-Wives Daily Deceit* (London, 1685)

Anon, *The Drunkards Character* (London, 1646)

Anon, *The Gossips Meeting, Or The Merry Market Women of Taunton* (London, 1674)

Anon, *The Merry Wives of Wapping* (London, 1680)

Anon, *The Pot Companions: or, Drinking and Smoking Preferr'd Before Caballing and Plotting* (London, 1682)

Anon, *The Severall Places where you may hear News* (London, 1640)

Anon, *Vox Norwici* (London, 1646)

Anon, *Vox Populi, or the Voice of the People* (London, 1646)

R. Burton, *A Looking Glass for Drunkards: Or, The Good-Fellows Folly* (London, 1660)

G. Chapman, *Monsieur D'Oliue, A comedie* (London, 1606)

M. Dalton, *The Countrey Justice Conteyning the Practice of the Justice of the Peace Out of their Session* (London, 1618)

T. Dekker, *Lanthorne and Candle- Light. Or, The bell-mans second nights-walke* (1608)

T. Dekker, *O per se O. Or A new cryer of Lanthorne and Candle-light Being an Addition, or Lengthening, of the Bell-Mans Second Night-Walke* (London, 1616)

T. Dekker, *The Bachelers Banquet* (London, 1604)

T. Dekker, *The Belman of London Bringing to light the Most Notorious Villanies that are now Practised in the Kingdome* (London, 1608)

T. Dekker, *The Seven deadly Sinnes of London* (1606)

T. D' Urfey, *Madam Fickle, or, The witty false one* (London, 1677)

T. Elyot, *The Book Named the Governour* (1531), ed. A. T. Eliot (London, 1834)

R. Filmer, *Patriarcha* (London, 1680)

R. Gardiner, *The History of Pudica: A Lady of Norfolk* (1754)

W. Gouge, *Of Domesticall Duties* (1622), ed. Greg Fox (2006)

R. Greene, *A Notable Discovery of Cozenage* (1591)

R. Greene, *The Black Book's Messenger* (1592)

J. Hall, *Hard Measure* (London, 1680)

T. Harman, 'A Caueat or Warning for Common Cursetors 1573', *Nash's Lenten Stuff*, ed. C. Hindley (London, 1871)

J. Hart, *The Dreadful Character of a Drunkard* (London, 1686)

T. Hobbes, *Leviathan* (1651), ed. J. Plamenatz (London, 1969)

T. Jackson, *A Collection of the Works of that Holy Man and Profound Divine, Thomas Jackson &c* (London, 1653)

M. Killiray, *The Swearer and the Drunkard, Two Brethren in Iniquity, Arraigned at the Bar* (London, 1673)

M. Laroon, *The Cryes of the City of London* (c.1710)

A. Le Grand, *An entire body of philosophy according to the principles of the famous Renate Des Cartes in three books* (London, 1694)

T. Nabbes, *The Muse of New-market, or, Mirth and drollery being Three Farces Acted before the King and Court at New-market* (London, 1680)

A. Neville, *Norfolke Furies, and their foyle under Kett* (London, 1623)

B. Rich, *The Excellency of Good Women* (London, 1613)

F. Rojas, *The Spanish bavvd, represented in Celestina: or, The tragicke-comedy of Calisto and Melibea* (London, 1631)

T. Smith, *De Republica Anglorum* (1583)

J. Taylor, *A Late Weary, Merry Voyage and Journey* (London, 1650)

T. Tusser, *Five Hundreth Points of Good Husbandry* (London, 1573)

J. Wheeler, *Treatise of Commerce* (1601), ed. G. B. Hotchkiss (New York, 1977)

R. Younge, *The prevention of poverty, together with the cure of melancholy, alias discontent* (London, 1655)

BIBLIOGRAPHY

Articles and Reports

S. Bendall, 'Draft Town Maps for John Speed's "Theatre of the Empire of Great Britaine"', *Imago Mundi* 54 (2002), 30–45

M. Berlin, 'Civic Ceremony in Early-Modern London', *Urban History* 13 (1986), 15–27

H. Berry, 'An Early Coffee House Periodical and its Readers: the *Athenian Mercury* 1691–1697', *London Journal* 25 (2000), 14–33

M. Biggs, 'Putting the State on the Map: Cartography, Territory, and State Formation', *Comparative Studies in Society and History* 41:2 (1999), 374–405

L. G. Bolingbroke, 'St John Maddermarket, Norwich: Its Streets, Lanes, and Ancient Houses, and their Old-time Associations', *Norfolk Archaeology* 20 (1921), 215–39

L. Bondi, 'Gender and Geography: Crossing Boundaries', *Progress in Human Geography* 17:2 (1993), 241–6

F. E. Brown, 'Continuity and Change in the Urban House: Developments in Domestic Space Organisation in Seventeenth Century London', *Comparative Studies in Society and History* 28 (1986), 558–90

B. Capp, 'The Double Standard Revisited: Plebeian Women and Male Sexual Reputation in Early Modern England', *Past and Present* 162 (1999), 70–100

P. Carroll, 'Articulating Theories of States and State Formation', *Journal of Historical Sociology* 22:4 (2009), 553–603

A. Carter, ed., *East Anglian Archaeology Report No. 15 – Excavations in Norwich, 1971-1978 Part I* (Norwich, 1982)

T. Cogswell, 'The Politics of Propaganda: Charles I and the People in the 1620s', *JBS* 29:3 (1990), 187–215

B. S. Cohn and N. B. Dirks, 'Beyond the Fringe: The Nation State, Colonialism, and the Technologies of Power', *Journal of Historical Sociology* 1:2 (1988), 224–9

M. R. G. Conzen, 'Alnwick, Northumberland: A Study in Town-Plan Analysis', *Transactions and Papers (Institute of British Geographers)* 27 (1962, reprinted 1969), iii-121

J. T. Coppock, 'Maps as Sources for the Study of Land Use in the Past', *Imago Mundi* 22 (1968), 37–49

B. Cowan, 'Geoffrey Holmes and the Public Sphere: Augustan Historiography from Post-Namierite to the Post-Habermasian', *Parliamentary History* 28:1 (2009), 166–78

A. Cowen, 'Gossip and Street Culture in Early Modern Venice', *Journal of Early Modern History* 12 (2008), 313–33

B. Cowen, 'What was Masculine about the Public Sphere? Gender and the Coffee House Milieu in Post Restoration England', *History Workshop Journal* 51 (2001), 127–57

B. Cozens-Hardy, 'The Norwich Chapelfield House Estate since 1545 and some of its Owners and Occupiers', *Norfolk Archaeology* 27 (1941), 351–84

D. Cressy, 'Describing the Social Order of Elizabethan and Stuart England', *Literature and History* 3 (1976), 29–44

R. Cust, 'News and Politics in Seventeenth Century England', *Past and Present* 112 (1986), 60–90

F. Dabhoiwala, 'The Construction of Honour, Reputation, and Status in Late Seventeenth- and Early Eighteenth-Century England', *TRHS* 6 (1996), 201–13

C. Delano Smith, 'Cartographic Signs on European Maps and Their Explanation Before 1700', *Imago Mundi* 37 (1985), 9–29

R. Dennis, 'Urban Modernity, Networks and Places', *History in Focus* 13 (2008)

C. Dent, 'The Function of Inn Signs and their Place in Early Modern British History', *Reinvention: a Journal of Undergraduate Research* 4:1 (2011)

P. Eden, 'Land Surveyors in Norfolk 1550–1850', *Norfolk Archaeology* 35 (1970), 474–81

B. Englisch, 'Erhard Etzlaub's Projection and Methods of Mapping', *Imago Mundi* 48 (1996), 103–23

J. Epstein, 'Spatial Practices/Democratic Vistas', *Social History* 24 (1999), 294–309

A. L. Erickson, 'Coverture and Capitalism', *History Workshop Journal* 59 (2005), 1–16

W. E. Everett and A. Goodbody, eds, *Revisiting Space: Space And Place in European Cinema* (Bern, 2005)

J. Ferguson and A. Gupta, 'Spatializing States: Toward an Ethnography of Neoliberal Governmentality', *American Ethnologist* 29:4 (2002), 981–1002

J. Fisher and B. C. Mennel, eds, *Spatial Turns: Space, Place, and Mobility in German Literary and Visual Culture* (Amsterdam and New York, 2010)

A. Fletcher, 'Manhood, the Male Body, Courtship and the Household in Early Modern England', *History* 84 (1999), 419–36

A. Fox, 'Ballads, Libels and Popular Ridicule in Jacobean England', *Past and Present* 145:1 (1994), 47–83

T. Frangenberg, 'Chorographies of Florence: The Use of City Views and City Plans in the Sixteenth Century', *Imago Mundi* 46 (1994), 41–64

D. Garrioch, 'Sounds of the City: the Soundscape of Early-Modern Towns', *Urban History* 30:1 (2003), 5–25

M. Goldie and J. Spurr, 'Politics and the Restoration Parish: Edward Fowler and the Struggle for St Giles Cripplegate', *English Historical Review* 109 (1994), 572–96

L. Gowing, 'Women, Status and the Popular Culture of Dishonour', *TRHS* 6 (1996), 225–34

P. Graves, 'Social Space in the English Medieval Parish Church', *Economy and Society* 18:3 (1989), 297–322

P. Griffiths, 'Meanings of Nightwalking in Early Modern England,' *The Seventeenth Century* 13:2 (1998), 212–38

V. Harding, 'Space, Property and Propriety in Urban England', *Journal of Interdisciplinary History* 32:4 (2002), 549–69

J. B. Harley, 'Silences and Secrecy: The Hidden Agenda of Cartography in Early-Modern Europe', *Imago Mundi* 40 (1988), 57–76

R. Helgerson, 'The Land Speaks: Cartography, Chorography, and Subversion in Renaissance England', *Representations* 16 (1986), 50–85

B. Hindess, 'Politics as Government: Michel Foucault's Analysis of Political Reason', *Alternatives* 30 (2005), 389–413

S. Hindle, 'Dependency, Shame and Belonging: Badging the Deserving Poor, c.1550–1750', *Cultural and Social History* 1:1 (2004), 6–35

S. Hindle, 'Hierarchy and Community in the Elizabethan Parish: The Swallowfield Articles of 1596', *Historical Journal* 42:3 (1999), 835–51

C. Holmes, 'The County Community in Stuart Historiography', *Journal of British Studies* 29 (1980), 54–73

K. Hotblack, 'The Dutch and Walloons at Norwich', *History* 6:24 (1922), 234–9

R. Houlbrooke, 'Women's Social Life and Common Action in England from the Fifteenth Century to the Eve of the Civil War', *Continuity and Change* 1 (1986), 171–89

A. Hughes, 'Warwickshire on the Eve of the Civil War: A County Community?', *Midland History* VII (1982), 42–72

M. Ingram, 'Ridings, Rough Music and the "Reform of Popular Culture" in Early Modern England', *Past and Present* 105 (1984), 79–113

T. J. Jackson-Lears, 'The Concept of Cultural Hegemony: Problems and Possibilities', *American Historical Review* 90:3 (1985), 567–94

J. Kelly-Godal, 'The Social Relation of the Sexes: Methodological Implications of Women's History', *Signs: Journal of Women in Culture and Society* 1 (1976), 809–33

E. A. Kent, 'The Gildencroft in Norwich', *Norfolk Archaeology* 29 (1946), 222–7

L. Kerber, 'Separate Spheres, Female Worlds, Women's Place: The Rhetoric of Women's History', *Journal of American History* 75 (1988), 9–39

P. King, 'Bishop Wren and the Suppression of the Norwich Lecturers', *Historical Journal* 6:2 (1968), 237–8

P. King, 'Edward Thompson's Contribution to Eighteenth-Century Studies: The Patrician-Plebeian Model Re-Examined', *Social History* 21:2 (1996), 215–28

R. Kingston, 'Mind Over Matter? History and the Spatial Turn', *Cultural and Social History* 7:1 (2010), 111–21

M. Knights, 'London Petitions and Parliamentary Politics in 1679', *Parliamentary History* 12:1 (1993), 29–46

M. Knights, 'London's "Monster" Petition of 1680', *Historical Journal* 36:1 (1993), 39–67

R. Laitinen and T. Cohen, 'Cultural History of Early-Modern Streets – An Introduction', *Journal of Early-Modern History* 12 (2008), 195–204

P. Lake and S. Pincus, 'Rethinking the Public Sphere in Early Modern England', *Journal of British Studies* 45:2 (2006), 270–92

P. Lake and M. Questier, 'Puritans, Papists, and the "Public Sphere" in Early-Modern England: the Edmund Campion Affair in Context', *Journal of Modern History* 72 (2000), 586–627

E. Lewinnek, 'Mapping Chicago, Imagining Metropolises: Reconsidering the Zonal Model of Urban Growth', *Journal of Urban History* 36:2 (2010), 197–225

K. D. Lilley, 'Mapping the Medieval City: Plan analysis and Urban History', *Urban History* 27:1 (2000), 5–30

M. D. Lobel, 'The Value of Early Maps as Evidence for the Topography of English Towns', *Imago Mundi* 22 (1968), 50–61

H. Mah, 'Phantasies of the Public Sphere: Rethinking the Habermas of Historians,' *Journal of Modern History* 72:1 (2000), 153–82

C. Marsh, 'Order and Place in England, 1580–1640: The View from the Pew', *Journal of British Studies* 44 (2005), 3–26

C. Marsh, 'Sacred Space in England, 1560–1640: The View from the Pew', *Journal of Ecclesiastical History* 53:2 (2002), 286–311

L. McDowell, 'Space, Place and Gender Relations', *Progress in Human Geography* 17:2 (1993), 157–79

S. Pincus, '"Coffee politicians does Create": Coffee Houses and Restoration Political Culture', *Journal of Modern History* 67 (1995), 807–34

D. Postles, 'The Politics of Diffuse Authority in an Early-Modern Small Town', *Canadian Journal of History* 45:1 (2010), 1–20

M. J. Power, 'London and the Control of the Crisis of the 1590s', *History* 70 (1985), 371–85

U. Priestly, 'Marketing of Norwich Stuffs, c. 1660–1730', *Textile History* 22:2 (1991), 193–209

U. Priestly and P. J. Corfield, 'Rooms and Room Use in Norwich Housing 1580–1730', *Post Medieval Archaeology* 16 (1982), 93–123

C. Richmond, 'Ruling Classes and Agents of the State: Formal and Informal Networks of Power', *Journal of Historical Sociology* 10:1 (1997), 1–26

D. Rickwood, 'The Norwich Strangers, 1565–1643: a Problem of Control', *Proceedings of the Huguenot Society* 24 (1984), 119–28

D. Rollison, 'Exploding England: the dialectics of mobility and settlement in early modern England', *Social History* 24:1 (1999), 1–16

D. Romano, 'Gender and the Urban Geography of Renaissance Venice', *Journal of Social History* 23: 2 (1989), 339–53

W. Rye, 'The Dutch Congregation in Norwich', *Norfolk Archaeology* 16 (1907), 320–7

C. Shammas, 'The Domestic Environment in Early Modern England and America', *Journal of Social History* 14 (1980), 3–24

B. Sharp, 'Popular Political Opinion in England 1660–85', *History of European Ideas* 10:1 (1989), 13–29

J. A. Sharpe, *Defamation and Sexual Slander in Early-Modern England: the Church Courts at York*, Borthwick Papers, 58 (York, 1980)

A. Shelley, ed., 'Dragon Hall, King Street, Norwich: Excavation and Survey of a Late Medieval Merchant's Trading Complex', *East Anglian Archaeology* 112 (Norwich, 2005), 29–88

A. Shepard, 'Manhood, Credit and Patriarchy in Early Modern England, c.1580–1640', *Past and Present* 167 (2000), 75–106

Q. Skinner, 'Meaning and Understanding in the History of Ideas', *History and Theory* 8 (1969), 3–53

T. R. Slater, 'Ideal and Reality in English Episcopal Medieval Town Planning', *Transactions of the Institute of British Geographers: New Series* 12:2 (1987), 191–203

D. Stoker, 'Blomefield's History of Norfolk', *Factotum: Newsletter of the XVIII Century STC* XXVI (1988), 17–22

D. Stoker, 'Prosperity and Success in the Eighteenth-Century Book Trade: The Firm of William Chase & Co.', *Publishing History* 30 (1991), 1–58

D. Stoker, 'The Norwich Book Trades Before 1800', *Transactions of the Cambridge Bibliographical Society* VIII (1981), 79–125

L. Stone, 'Libertine Sexuality in Post-Restoration England: Group Sex and Flagellation among the Middling Sort in Norwich in 1706–7', *Journal of the History of Sexuality* 2:4 (1992), 511–26

R. Tittler, 'Civic portraiture and Political Culture: English Provincial Towns, c.1560–1640', *Journal of British Studies* 37 (1998), 306–29

R. Tittler, 'Seats of Honour, Seats of Power: The Symbolism of Public Seating in the English Urban Community, c. 1560–1620', *Albion* 24:2 (2002), 205–23

D. Turnbull, 'Cartography and Science in Early-Modern Europe: Mapping the Construction of Knowledge Spaces', *Imago Mundi* 48 (1996), 5–24

J. Vance, 'Land Assignment in Pre-Capitalist, Capitalist and Post-Capitalist Cities', *Economic Geography* 47 (1971), 101–20

C. Vane, 'The Walloon Community in Norwich: the First One Hundred Years', *Proceedings of the Huguenot Society* 24 (1984), 129–37

A. Vickery, 'Golden Age to Separate Spheres? A Review of the Categories and Chronology of English Women's History', *Historical Journal* 36 (1993), 383–414

G. Walker, 'Expanding the Boundaries of Female Honour in Early Modern England', *TRHS* 6:6 (1996), 235–45

J. Wallach-Scott, 'Gender: A Useful Category of Historical Analysis', *American Historical Review* 91:5 (1986), 1053–75

J. Walter, 'Confessional Politics in Pre-Civil War Essex: Prayer Books, Profanations and Petitions', *The Historical Journal* 44:3 (2001), 677–701

J. Walter, 'Popular Iconoclasm and the Politics of the Parish in Eastern England, 1640–42', *The Historical Journal* 47:2 (2004), 261–90

J. Walter and K. Wrightson, 'Dearth and the Social Order in Early Modern England', *Past and Present* 71 (1976), 22–42

F. Williamson, 'Space and the City: Gender Identities in the Seventeenth Century', *Cultural and Social History Journal* 9:2 (2012), 169–85

P. Withington, 'Public Discourse, Corporate Citizenship and State-Formation in Early Modern England', *American Historical Review* 112:4 (2007), 1016–38

P. Withington, 'Two Renaissances: Urban Political Culture in Post-Reformation England Reconsidered', *Historical Journal* 44:1 (2001), 239–67

Monographs and Edited Collections

S. Amussen, *An Ordered Society: Gender and Class in Early Modern England* (Oxford, 1988)

T. Amyot, ed., *Some Account of the Life of William Windham* (London, 1812)

Anon, *A Compleat History of the Famous City of Norwich: From the Earliest Account, to this Present Year 1728* (1728)

I. Archer, *The Pursuit of Stability: Social Relations in Elizabethan London* (Cambridge, 1991)

S. Ardener, ed., *Women and Space: Ground Rules and Social Maps* (Oxford, 1981)

M. Aston and J. Bond, *The landscape of Towns* (London, 1976)

B. Ayers, *Norwich: A Fine City* (Stroud, 1994)

M. Backhouse, *The Flemish and Walloon Communities at Sandwich During the Reign of Elizabeth I, 1561–1603* (Brussels, 1995)

P. Barber, *The Map Book* (London, 2005)

J. M. Bennett, *Ale, Beer, and Brewsters in England: Women's Work in a Changing World 1300–1600* (Oxford, 1996)

J. Bold and E. Chaney, eds, *English Architecture Public and Private* (London, 1993)

M. Boone and P. Stabel, eds., *Shaping Urban Identity in Late Medieval Europe* (Leuven/Apeldoorn, 2000)

P. Borsay, *The English Urban Renaissance: Culture and Society in the English Provincial Town 1660–1770* (Oxford, 1989)

P. Bourdieu, *Outline of a Theory of Practice* (Cambridge, 1977)

M. J. Braddick, *State Formation in Early Modern England c.1550–1700* (Cambridge, 2000)

M. J. Braddick and J. Walter, eds, *Negotiating Power in Early Modern Society: Order, Hierarchy and Subordination in Britain and Ireland* (Cambridge, 2001)

C. Brant and S. Whyman, eds, *Walking the Streets of Eighteenth Century London: John Gay's Trivia* (Oxford, 2007)

J. Brewer, *Party Ideology and Popular Politics at the Accession of George III* (Cambridge, 1976)

S. Brigden, *London and the Reformation* (Oxford, 1989)

J. R. Brown, *The Landscape of Drink: Inns, Taverns and Alehouses in Early Modern Southampton* (Warwick University, Ph.D Thesis, unpub. 2007)

D. Buisseret, ed., *Envisioning the City: Six Studies in Urban Cartography* (Chicago, 1998)

D. Buisseret, ed., *Monarchs, Ministers and Maps: The Emergence of Cartography as a Tool of Government in Early-Modern Europe* (Chicago, 1992)

P. Burke, *Popular Culture in Early-Modern Europe* (Farnham, 1978)

B. Capp, *When Gossips Meet: Women, Family and Neighbourhood in Early Modern England* (Oxford, 2003)

M. Carmona, T. Heath, T. Oc, S. Tiesdell, eds, *Public Places-Urban Spaces: The Dimensions of Urban Design* (Oxford and Burlington, MA, 2012)

J. Chambers, ed., *A General History of the County of Norfolk* (London, 1829)

M. Champion, *The Doctor, the Printer and the Queen's Favourite: William Cuningham and the First Printed Plan of Norwich*, Online edn.

J. Chartres, 'The Place of Inns in the Commercial life of London and Western England, 1660–1760' (Oxford University, D. Phil, unpub., 1973)

A. Clark, *Working Life of Women in the Seventeenth Century* (London, 1919)

G. Clark, J. Owens and G. T. Smith, eds, *City Limits: Perspectives on the Historical European City* (Montreal, 2010)

P. Clark, *European Cities and Towns, 400–2000* (Oxford, 2009)

P. Clark, *The Early Modern Town* (London, 1976)

P. Clark, *The English Alehouse: A Social History 1200–1830* (London, 1983)

P. Clark and P. Slack, eds, *English Towns in Transition 1500–1700* (Oxford, 1976)

P. Collinson, *Elizabethan Essays* (1994)

P. Collinson, *Godly People: Essays on English Protestantism and Puritanism* (London, 1983)

P. Collinson, *The Elizabethan Puritan Movement* (London, 1967)

M. R. G. Conzen, 'The Plan Analysis of an English City Centre', *Proceedings of the IGU Symposium in Urban Geography*, ed. K. Norborg (Lund, 1960), pp. 383–414

A. Cowen and J. Steward, eds, *The City and the Senses: Urban Culture Since 1500* (Aldershot, 2007)

B. Cowan, *The Social Life of Coffee: The Emergence of the British Coffeehouse* (New Haven, 2005)

L. Cowen Orlin, *Locating Privacy in Tudor London* (Oxford, 2008)

P. Crawford and L. Gowing, eds, *Women's Worlds in Seventeenth-Century England: A Sourcebook* (Abingdon, 2008)

D. Cressy and L. A. Ferrell, eds, *Religion and Society in Early Modern England* (Abingdon and New York, 2005)

W. Cunningham, *Alien Immigrants to England* (London, 1897)

R. Cust, *The Forced Loan and English Politics 1626–1628* (Oxford, 1987)

L. Davidoff and C. Hall, eds, *Family Fortunes: Men and Women of the English Middle Classes, 1780–1850* (London, 1987)

W. K. D. Davies and D. T. Herbert, eds, *Communities within Cities: An Urban Social Geography* (London, 1993)

R. C. Davis, 'The Geography of Gender in the Renaissance', *Gender and Society in Renaissance Italy*, ed. J. Brown and R. C. Davis (London, 1995), pp. 19–38

M. De Certeau, *The Practice of Everyday Life*, trans. S. Randall (Berkeley, 1984)

E. Delderfield, *Introduction to Inn Signs* (Newton Abbot, 1969)

S. Devereaux and P. Griffiths, eds, *Penal Practice and Culture, 1500–1900: Punishing the English* (Basingstoke, 2004)

P. H. Ditchfield, *Vanishing England* (Teddington, 2007)

M. Douglas, *How Institutions Think* (Syracuse, 1986)

Z. Dovey, *An Elizabethan Progress* (New Jersey, 1996)

L. Duffin and L. Charles, eds, *Women and Work in Pre-Industrial England* (London, 1985)

D. Eastwood, *Government and Community in the English Provinces 1700–1870* (Basingstoke, 1997)

J. Edwards, *Writing, Geometry and Space in Seventeenth Century England and America: Circles in the Sand* (Abingdon, 2006)

M. Ellis, *The Coffee House: A Cultural History* (London, 2004)

C. Estabrook, *Urbane and Rustic England: Cultural Ties and Social Spheres in the Provinces, 1660–1780* (Manchester, 1998)

J. Evans and J. Britton, *The Beauties of England and Wales: or Delineations Topographical, Historical and Descriptive of each County* (1810)

J. T. Evans, *Seventeenth Century Norwich: Politics, Religion and Government 1620–1690* (Oxford, 1979)

J. T. Evans, *The Political Elite of Norwich, 1620–1690: Patterns of Recruitment and the Impact of National Affairs* (Stanford University, Ph.D Thesis, unpub., 1971)

A. Everitt, 'The English Urban Inn, 1560–1760', *Perspectives in English Urban History*, ed. A. Everitt (London, 1972), pp. 91–137

I. Fay, *Health and Disease in Medieval and Tudor Norwich* (University of East Anglia, Ph.D Thesis, unpub., 2007)

A. Flather, *Gender and Space in Early Modern England* (Woodbridge, 2007)

A. Fletcher, *Gender, Sex and Subordination in England, 1500–1800* (London, 1995)

A. Fletcher, *The Outbreak of the English Civil War* (London, 1981)

A. Fletcher and J. Stevenson, eds, *Order and Disorder in Early Modern England* (Cambridge, 1985)

M. Foucault, *Discipline and Punish: The Birth of the Prison* (London, 1977)

A. Fox, *Oral and Literate Culture in England, 1500–1700* (Oxford, 2000)

L. Foxhall and G. Neher, eds, *Gender and the City before Modernity* (London, 2012)

E. Foyster, *Manhood in Early Modern England: Honour, Sex and Marriage* (London, 1999)

D. Freist, *Governed by Opinion: Politics, Religion and the Dynamics of Communication in Stuart London, 1637–1645* (London, 1997)

H. French and J. Barry, *Identity and Agency in England, 1500–1800* (Basingstoke, 2004)

H. R. French, *The Middle Sort of People in Provincial England, 1600–1750* (Oxford, 2007)

C. R. Friedrichs, *The Early-Modern City, 1450–1750* (Harlow, 1995)

A. M. Froide, *Never Married: Single-women in Early Modern England* (Oxford, 2005)

R. Frostick, *The Printed Plans of Norwich, 1558–1840* (Norwich, 2002)

C. Frugoni, *A Distant City: Images of Urban Experience in the Medieval World* (Princeton, 1991)

P. Fumerton, *Unsettled: The Culture of Mobility and the Working Poor in Early Modern England* (Chicago, 2006)

M. Gaudoin, *The Green Spaces and Culture of Late Medieval Norwich: Municipal, Ecclesiastical and Medical* (University of East Anglia, MA Thesis, unpub., 2007)

C. Geertz, *Local Knowledge: Further Essays In Interpretive Anthropology* (New York, 2000)

L. K. J. Glassey, ed., *The Reigns of Charles II and James VII and II* (Basingstoke, 1997)

A. Goldgar and R. I. Frost, eds, *Institutional Culture in Early Modern Society* (Leiden, 2004)

C. Goodson, A. E. Lester and C. Symes, eds, *Cities, Texts and Social Networks 400–1500* (Farnham, 2010)

N. Goose and L. Luu, eds, *Immigrants in Tudor and Early Stuart England* (Brighton, 2005)

P. Gould and R. White, eds, *Mental Maps*, 2nd edn (London, 1986)

L. Gowing, *Common Bodies: Women, Touch and Power in Seventeenth Century England* (Cambridge, 2003)

L. Gowing, *Domestic Dangers: Women, Words and Sex in Early Modern London* (Oxford, 1998)

L. Gowing, M. Hunter and M. Rubin, eds, *Love, Friendship and Faith in Europe, 1300–1800* (Basingstoke, 2005)

D. Gregory and J. Urry, eds, *Social Relations and Spatial Structures* (London, 1985)

P. Griffiths, *Lost Londons: Change, Crime and Control in the Capital City 1550–1660* (Cambridge, 2008)

P. Griffiths, *Youth and Authority: Formative Experiences in England, 1560–1640* (Oxford, 1996)

P. Griffiths, A. Fox, and S. Hindle, eds, *The Experience of Authority in Early Modern England* (Basingstoke, 1996)

P. Griffiths and M. Jenner, eds, *Londinopolis: Essays in the Cultural and Social History of Early Modern London* (Manchester, 2000)

P. Griffiths, J. Landers, M. Pelling and R. Tyson, 'Population and Disease, Estrangement and Belonging, 1540–1700', *The Cambridge Urban History of Britain*, Vol. 2, ed. P. Clark (Cambridge, 2000), pp. 195–234

R. D. Gwynn, *Huguenot Heritage: the History and Contribution of the Huguenots in Britain* (Brighton, 2001)

J. Habermas, *The Structural Transformation of the Public Sphere: An Inquiry into a Category of Bourgeois Society*, trans. T. Burger and F. Lawrence (Cambridge, MA, 1991)

C. Hall, *White, Male and Middle Class: Explorations in Feminism and History* (Cambridge, 1992)

B. A. Hanawalt, *'Of Good and Ill Repute': Gender and Social Control in Medieval England* (Oxford, 1998)

B. A. Hanawalt and M. Kobialka, eds, *Medieval Practices of Space* (Minnesota, 2000)

O. Handlin and J. Burchard, eds, *The Historian and the City* (Cambridge, MA, 1963)

J. B. Harley, ed., *The New Nature of Maps: Essay in the History of Cartography* (Baltimore and London, 2002)

T. Harris, *London Crowds in the Reign of Charles II: Propaganda and Politics from the Restoration until the Exclusion Crisis* (Cambridge, 1987)

T. Harris, ed., *The Politics of the Excluded, c.1500–1850* (Basingstoke, 2001)

E. Higgs, *The Information State in England: The Central Collection of Information on Citizens Since 1500* (Basingstoke and New York, 2004)

C. Hill, *Economic Problems of the Church from Archbishop Whitgift to the Long Parliament* (Oxford, 1956)

C. Hill, *Society and Puritanism in Pre-Revolutionary England* (London, 1964)

B. Hindess, *Discourses of Power: From Hobbes to Foucault* (Oxford, 1996)

S. Hindle, 'Destitution, Liminality and Belonging: The Church Porch and the Politics of Settlement in English Rural Communities, c.1590–1660', *The Self-contained Village? The Social History of Rural Communities, 1250–1900*, ed. C. Dyer (Hertfordshire, 2006), pp. 46–71

S. Hindle, *On the Parish? The Micro-politics of Poor Relief, c. 1550–1750* (Oxford, 2004)

S. Hindle, *The State and Social Change in Early Modern England, 1550–1640* (Basingstoke, 2002)

D. Hirst, 'Court, Country and Politics before 1629', *Faction and Parliament*, ed. K. Sharpe (Oxford, 1978), pp. 105–38

D. Hirst, *The Representative of the People? Voters and Voting in England under the Early Stuarts* (Cambridge, 1975)

T. Hitchcock and R. Shoemaker, *Tales from the Hanging Court* (London, 2007)

L. Holloway and P. Hubbard, eds, *People and Place: The Extraordinary Geographies of Everyday Life* (Harlow, 2001)

C. Holmes, *The Eastern Association in the English Civil War* (Cambridge, 1974)

M. P. Holt, ed., *Alcohol: A Social and Cultural History* (Oxford, 2006)

R. Holt and N. Baker, eds, 'Indecent Exposure – Sexuality, Society and the Archaeological Record', *Towards a Geography of Sexual Encounter: Prostitution in English Medieval Towns*, ed. L. Bevan (Glasgow, 2001), pp. 201–2

W. G. Hoskins, *The Making of the English Landscape* (London, 1955)

R. Houlbrooke, *Church Courts and the People during the English Reformation 1520–1570* (Oxford, 1979)

W. Hudson, *How the City of Norwich Grew into Shape: Being an Attempt to Trace Out the Topographical History of the City* (Norwich, 1896)

M. Ingram, *Church Courts, Sex and Marriage in England 1570–1640* (Cambridge, 1987)

P. Jackson, *Maps of Meaning* (London, 1989)

C. Jacob, *The Sovereign Map: Theoretical Approaches in Cartography throughout History*, trans. T. Conley and E. H. Dahl (Chicago, 2006)

J. James, *The History of Worsted Manufacture in England* (1857)

M. James, *Society, Politics and Culture* (Cambridge, 1986)

M. Johnson, *An Archaeology of Capitalism* (Oxford, 1996)

M. Johnson, *Housing Culture: Traditional Architecture in an English Landscape* (London, 1993)

D. T. Jones, *Aspects of the Social Geography of Early-Modern Norwich: Applications of Computer Techniques I* (University of East Anglia, Ph.D Thesis, unpub., 2003)

R. Jütte, *Poverty and Deviance in Early Modern Europe* (Cambridge, 1994)

J. Kamensky, *Governing the Tongue: The Politics of Speech in Early Modern New England* (Oxford, 1997)

J. R. Kent, *The English Village Constable, 1580–1642: A Social and Administrative Study* (Oxford, 1986)

K. J. Kesselring, *Mercy and Authority in the Tudor State* (Cambridge, 2003)

T. Kilian, 'Public and Private, Power and Space', *The Production of Public Space*, ed. A. Light and J. Smith (Lanham, 1998)

C. King and D. Sayer, eds, *The Archaeology of Post-Medieval Religion* (Woodbridge, 2011)

M. Kishlansky, *A Monarchy Transformed: Britain 1603–1714* (London, 1996)

M. Kishlansky, *Parliamentary Selection: Social and Political Choice in Early Modern England* (Cambridge, 1986)

M. Knights, *Politics and Opinion in Crisis, 1678–81* (Cambridge, 2006)

M. Knights, *Representation and Misrepresentation in Britain: Partisanship and Political Culture* (Oxford, 2006)

J. Knowles, 'The spectacle of the Realm: Civic Consciousness, Rhetoric and Ritual in Early Modern London', *Theatre and Government Under the Early Stuarts*, ed. J. R. Mulryne and M. Shewring (1993)

B. Kümin, *Drinking Matters: Public Houses and Social Exchange in Early Modern Central Europe* (Basingstoke, 2007)

B. Kümin, ed., *Political Space in Pre-Industrial Europe* (Aldershot, 2009)

B. Kümin and B. A. Tlusty, eds., *The World of the Tavern: Public Houses in Early-Modern Europe* (Aldershot, 2002)

R. Laitinen and T. Cohen, eds, *Cultural History of Early-Modern European Streets* (Leiden, 2009)

P. Lake and S. Pincus, eds, *The Politics of the Public Sphere in Early Modern England* (Manchester, 2007)

A. Laurence, *Women in England 1500–1760* (London, 1994)

H. Lefebvre, *The Production of Space*, trans. D. Nicholson-Smith (Oxford, 1991)

A. Leftwich, *Redefining Politics: People, Resources and Power* (London, 1983)

R. T. Le Gates and F. Stout, *The City Reader*, 3rd edn (London, 2003)

L. Levy Peck, *Court Patronage and Corruption in Early Stuart England*, 3rd edn (New York, 1990)

S. Lindenbaum, 'Ceremony and Oligarchy: the London Midsummer Watch', *City and Spectacle in Medieval Europe*, ed. B. A. Hanawalt and K. Reyerson (Minneapolis, 1994)

V. D. Lipman, *The Jews of Medieval Norwich* (London, 1967)

M. D. Lobel, ed., *Historic Towns*, Vol. II (London, 1975)

D. Lord Smail, *Imaginary Cartographies: Possession and Identity in Medieval Marseille* (New York, 1999)

S. M. Low and D. Lawrence-Zúñiga, eds, *The Anthropology of Space and Place: Locating Culture* (Oxford, 2003)

W. D. Macray, ed., *The History of the Rebellion and Civil Wars in England begun in the year 1641 by Edward, Earl of Clarendon*, Vol. I (Oxford, 1888)

A. Mandanipour, G. Cars and J. Allen, eds, *Social Exclusion in European Cities: Processes, Experiences and Responses* (London, 1998)

A. L. Martin, *Alcohol, Sex and Gender in Late Medieval and Early Modern Europe* (Basingstoke, 2001)

D. Massey, *Space, Place and Gender* (Cambridge, 1994)

M. McKeon, *The Secret History of Domesticity: Public, Private and the Division of Knowledge* (Baltimore, 2005)

S. Mendelson and P. Crawford, eds, *Women in Early Modern England* (Oxford, 1998)

J. F. Merritt, ed., *Imagining Early Modern London: Perceptions and Portrayals of the City from Stow to Strype, 1598–1720* (Cambridge, 2001)

J. Miller, 'The Fortunes of the Strangers in Norwich and Canterbury, 1565–1700', *Memory and Identity: The Huguenots in France and the Atlantic Diaspora*, ed. B. Van Ruymbeke and R. J. Sparks (Carolina, 2003)

W. J. C. Moens, *The Walloons and their Church at Norwich* (London, 1887)

L. Montrose, *The Subject of Elizabeth: Authority, Gender, and Representation* (Chicago, 2006)

L. Nead, 'Gender, Space and Modernity in London', *Rewriting the Self: Histories from the Renaissance to the Present*, ed. R. Porter (London, 1997)

J. Nichols, ed., *Thomas Fuller: The History of the Worthies of England* (1811)

M. Pelling, *The Common Lot: Sickness, Medical Occupations and the Urban Poor in Early Modern England* (Harlow, 1998)

D. Pellow, ed., *Setting Boundaries: the Anthropology of Spatial and Social Organization* (London, 1996)

D. Pennington, *Women in the Market-Place: Gender, Commerce, and Social Relations in Early-Modern English Towns* (Washington University, Ph.D Thesis, pub., 2007)

D. Pennington and K. Thomas, eds, *Puritans and Revolutionaries: Essays in Seventeenth-Century History Presented to Christopher Hill* (Oxford, 1978)

S. Pincus, *1688: The First Modern Revolution* (Yale, 2009)

R. Porter, ed., *Rewriting the Self: Histories from the Renaissance to the Present* (London, 1997)

D. A. Postles, *Social Geographies in England, 1200–1640* (Washington, 2007)

J. Pound, *Tudor and Stuart Norwich* (Chichester, 1988)

U. Priestly, ed., *Men of Property: An Analysis of the Norwich Enrolled Deeds, 1285–1311* (Norwich, 1983)

U. Priestly and A. Fenner, *Shops and Shopkeepers in Norwich 1660–1730* (Norwich, 1985)

S. Rappaport, *Worlds within Worlds: Structures of Life in Sixteenth Century London* (Cambridge, 1989)

C. Rawcliffe, *Leprosy in Medieval England* (Woodbridge, 2006)

C. Rawcliffe, *The Hospitals of Medieval Norwich* (Norwich, 1995)

C. Rawcliffe, R. Virgoe and R. Wilson, eds, *Counties and Communities: Essays on East Anglian History presented to Hassell-Smith* (Norwich, 1996)

C. Rawcliffe and R. Wilson, eds, *Medieval Norwich* (London, 2004)

C. Rawcliffe and R. Wilson, eds, *Norwich since 1550* (London, 2004)

J. Raymond, *Pamphlets and Pamphleteering in Early-Modern Britain* (Cambridge, 2006)

B. Reay, ed., *Popular Culture in Seventeenth Century England* (Worcester, 1985)

J. Rendell, *The Pursuit of Pleasure: Gender, Space and Architecture in Regency London* (London, 2002)

J. Rendell, B. Penner and I. Borden, eds, *Gender Space Architecture: An Interdisciplinary Introduction* (London, 2000)

M. Reynolds, *Godly Reformers and their Opponents in Early Modern England: Religion in Norwich c. 1560–1643* (Woodbridge, 2005)

N. Rogers, 'Popular Jacobitism in Provincial Context: Eighteenth Century Bristol and Norwich' *The Jacobite Challenge*, ed. E. Cruickshanks and J. Black (Edinburgh, 1988)

D. Rollison, *A Commonwealth of the People: Popular Politics and England's Long Social Revolution 1066–1649* (Cambridge, 2010)

G. Rudé, *The Crowd in History, 1730–1848* (London, 1964)

J. R. Ruff, *Violence in Early-Modern Europe, 1500–1800* (Cambridge, 2001)

D. W. Sabean and M. Stefanovska, eds, *Space and Self in Early Modern European Cultures* (Toronto, 2012)

J. Scott, *Algernon Sidney and the Restoration Crisis, 1677–1683* (Cambridge, 1991)

J. C. Scott, *Domination and the Arts of Resistance: Hidden Transcripts* (New Haven, 1990)

J. C. Scott, *Seeing Like A State: How Certain Schemes to Improve the Human Condition Have Failed* (New Haven, 1998)

J. C. Scott, *Weapons of the Weak: Everyday Forms of Peasant Resistance* (New Haven, 1985)

K. Sharpe, *Selling the Tudor Monarchy: Authority and Image in Sixteenth Century England* (Yale, 2009)

A. Shepard, *Meanings of Manhood* (Oxford, 2003)

A. Shepard, 'The Worth of Married Women in the English Church Courts, c. 1550–1730', *Married Women and the Law in Premodern Northwest Europe*, ed. C. Beattie and M. F. Stevens (Woodbridge, 2013), pp. 191–211

A. Shepard and P. Withington, eds, *Communities in Early Modern England* (Manchester, 2000)

S. Shesgreen, ed., *The Criers and Hawkers of London: Engravings and Drawings by Marcellus Laroon* (Aldershot, 1990)

R. Shoemaker, *Gender in English Society, 1650–1850: The Emergence of Separate Spheres?* (London, 1998)

R. Shoemaker, 'Reforming Male Manners: Public Insult and the Decline of Violence in London, 1660–1740', *English Masculinities, 1660–1800*, ed. T. Hitchcock and M. Cohen (London, 1999), pp.133–50

R. Shoemaker, *The London Mob: Violence and Disorder in Eighteenth Century England* (London, 2004)

T. A. Sinclair, ed., *Aristotle: The Politics* (London, 1969)

G. Sjoberg, *The Pre-Industrial City: Past and Present* (New York, 1960)

P. Slack, *Poverty and Policy in Tudor and Stuart England* (Harlow, 1998)

P. Slack, *The Impact of Plague in Tudor and Stuart England* (London, 1985)

A. Smyth, ed., *A Pleasing Sinne: Drink and Conviviality in Seventeenth Century England* (Woodbridge, 2004)

K. Snell, *Parish and Belonging: Community, Identity, and Welfare in England and Wales, 1700–1950* (Cambridge, 2006)

J. Southerden Burn, ed., *The History of the French, Walloon, Dutch, and other foreign refugees settled in England, etc.* (1846)

D. Spaeth, *The Church in an Age of Danger: Parsons and Parishioners, 1660–1740* (Cambridge, 2000)

M. Spufford, *Figures in the Landscape: Rural Society in England 1500–1700* (Farnham, 2000)

M. Spufford, ed., *The World of Rural Dissenters, 1520–1725* (Cambridge, 1995)

J. Spurr, *The Post Reformation: Religion, Politics and Society in Britain, 1603–1714* (London, 2006)

T. Stretton, *Women Waging Law in Elizabethan England* (Cambridge, 1998)

R. Strong, *The Cult of Elizabeth: Elizabethan Portraiture and Pageantry* (Berkeley, 1977)

A. Tarver, *Church Court Records: An Introduction for Family and Local Historians* (Chichester, 1995)

E. P. Thompson, *Customs in Common* (London, 1991)

R. Tittler, *Architecture and Power: the Town Hall and the English Urban Community, c. 1500–1640* (Oxford, 1991)

R. Tittler, *The Face of the City: Civic Portraiture and Civic Identity in Early Modern England* (Manchester, 2007)

R. Tittler, *Townspeople and Nation: English Urban Experiences, 1540–1640* (Stanford, 2001)

A. Tlusty, *Bacchus and Civic Order: The Culture of Drink in Early Modern Germany* (Charlottesville, 2001)

J. D. Tracy, *City Walls: The Urban Enceinte in Global Perspective* (Cambridge, 2000)

D. Underdown, *A Freeborn People: Politics and the Nation in Seventeenth Century England* (Oxford, 1996)

G. Valentine, *Social Geographies: Space and Society* (Harlow, 2001)

J. A. Van Houtte, *An Economic History of the Low Countries, 800–1800* (London, 1977)

J. Venn, ed., *Biographical History of Gonville and Caius College*, Vol. I (Cambridge, 1897)

A. Vickery, *The Gentleman's Daughter: Women's Lives in Georgian England* (London, 1998)

R. Vigne and C. Littleton, eds, *From Strangers to Citizens: The Integration of Stranger Communities in Britain* (Brighton, 2001)

N. Virgoe and T. Williamson, eds, *Religious Dissent in East Anglia: Historical Perspectives* (Norwich, 1993)

S. Wade Martins, *Coke of Norfolk, 1754–1842: A Biography* (Woodbridge, 2010)

G. Walker, *Crime, Gender and Social Order in Early-Modern England* (Cambridge, 2003)

J. Walter, *Understanding Popular Violence during the English Civil Wars: The Colchester Plunderers* (Cambridge, 1999)

G. Ward, ed., *The Certeau Reader* (Oxford, 2000)

R. Weil, *Political Passions: Gender, the Family and Political Argument in England, 1680–1714* (Manchester, 1999)

G. Wickam, W. Ingram and H. Berry, eds, *English Professional Theatre, 1530–1660* (Cambridge, 2000)

M. Wiesner, *Women and Gender in Early Modern Europe* (Cambridge, 2000)

M. Wiesner-Hanks, *Early Modern Europe, 1450–1789* (Cambridge, 2006)

T. S. Wilan, *River Navigation in England, 1600–1750* (London, 1936)

F. Williamson, ed., *Locating Agency: Space, Power and Popular Politics* (Newcastle, 2010)

E. Wilson, *The Sphinx in the City: Urban Life, the Control of Disorder and Women* (London, 1991)

K. Wilson, *The Sense of the People: Politics, Culture and Imperialism in England, 1715–1785* (Oxford, 1995)

P. Withington, *The Politics of Commonwealth* (Cambridge, 2005)

A. Wood, *Riot, Rebellion and Popular Politics in Early Modern England* (Basingstoke, 2002)

A. Wood, *The 1549 Rebellions and the Making of Modern England* (Cambridge, 2007)

S. J. Wright, ed., *Parish, Church and People: Local Studies in Lay Religion 1350–1750* (London, 1998)

K. Wrightson, 'Alehouses, Order and Reformation in Rural England, 1590–1660', *Popular Culture and Class Conflict, 1590–1914: Explorations in the History of Labour and Leisure*, ed. E. Yeo and S. Yeo (Brighton, 1981), pp. 1–27

S. Yaxley, ed., *The Siege of King's Lynn, 1643* (Dereham, 1993)

L. Yungblut, *Strangers Settled Here Among Us: Policies, Perceptions and the Presence of Aliens in Elizabethan England* (London, 1996)

D. Zaret, *Origins of Democratic Culture: Printing, Petitions, and the Public Sphere in Early-Modern England* (Princeton, 2000)

Index

CPSIA information can be obtained at www.ICGtesting.com
Printed in the USA
BVOW09*1153101014

370094BV00002B/5/P